ELECTRONIC THESES AND DISSERTATIONS

BOOKS IN LIBRARY AND INFORMATION SCIENCE

A Series of Monographs and Textbooks

FOUNDING EDITOR

Allen Kent

School of Library and Information Science
University of Pittsburgh
Pittsburgh, Pennsylvania

1. Classified Library of Congress Subject Headings: Volume 1, Classified List, *edited by James G. Williams, Martha L. Manheimer, and Jay E. Daily*
2. Classified Library of Congress Subject Headings: Volume 2, Alphabetic List, *edited by James G. Williams, Martha L. Manheimer, and Jay E. Daily*
3. Organizing Nonprint Materials, *Jay E. Daily*
4. Computer-Based Chemical Information, *edited by Edward McC. Arnett and Allen Kent*
5. Style Manual: A Guide for the Preparation of Reports and Dissertations, *Martha L. Manheimer*
6. The Anatomy of Censorship, *Jay E. Daily*
7. Information Science: Search for Identity, *edited by Anthony Debons*
8. Resource Sharing in Libraries: Why · How · When · Next Action Steps, *edited by Allen Kent*
9. Reading the Russian Language: A Guide for Librarians and Other Professionals, *Rosalind Kent*
10. Statewide Computing Systems: Coordinating Academic Computer Planning, *edited by Charles Mosmann*
11. Using the Chemical Literature: A Practical Guide, *Henry M. Woodburn*
12. Cataloging and Classification: A Workbook, *Martha L. Manheimer*
13. Multi-media Indexes, Lists, and Review Sources: A Bibliographic Guide, *Thomas L. Hart, Mary Alice Hunt, and Blanche Woolls*
14. Document Retrieval Systems: Factors Affecting Search Time, *K. Leon Montgomery*
15. Library Automation Systems, *Stephen R. Salmon*
16. Black Literature Resources: Analysis and Organization, *Doris H. Clack*
17. Copyright–Information Technology–Public Policy: Part I–Copyright–Public Policies; Part II–Public Policies–Information Technology, *Nicholas Henry*
18. Crisis in Copyright, *William Z. Nasri*
19. Mental Health Information Systems: Design and Implementation, *David J. Kupfer, Michael S. Levine, and John A. Nelson*

ELECTRONIC THESES AND DISSERTATIONS
A Sourcebook for Educators, Students, and Librarians

EDITED BY

EDWARD A. FOX
SHAHROOZ FEIZABADI
Virginia Polytechnic Institute and State University
Blacksburg, Virginia, U.S.A.

JOSEPH M. MOXLEY
University of South Florida
Tampa, Florida, U.S.A.

CHRISTIAN R. WEISSER
Florida Atlantic University
Jupiter, Florida, U.S.A.

MARCEL DEKKER, INC.   NEW YORK · BASEL

Although great care has been taken to provide accurate and current information, neither the author(s) nor the publisher, nor anyone else associated with this publication, shall be liable for any loss, damage, or liability directly or indirectly caused or alleged to be caused by this book. The material contained herein is not intended to provide specific advice or recommendations for any specific situation.

Trademark notice: Product or corporate names may be trademarks or registered trademarks and are used only for identification and explanation without intent to infringe.

Library of Congress Cataloging-in-Publication Data
A catalog record for this book is available from the Library of Congress.

ISBN: 0-8247-0973-X

This book is printed on acid-free paper.

Headquarters
Marcel Dekker, Inc., 270 Madison Avenue, New York, NY 10016, U.S.A.
tel: 212-696-9000; fax: 212-685-4540

Distribution and Customer Service
Marcel Dekker, Inc., Cimarron Road, Monticello, New York 12701, U.S.A.
tel: 800-228-1160; fax: 845-796-1772

Eastern Hemisphere Distribution
Marcel Dekker AG, Hutgasse 4, Postfach 812, CH-4001 Basel, Switzerland
tel: 41-61-260-6300; fax: 41-61-260-6333

World Wide Web
http://www.dekker.com

The publisher offers discounts on this book when ordered in bulk quantities. For more information, write to Special Sales/Professional Marketing at the headquarters address above.

Current printing (last digit):

10 9 8 7 6 5 4 3 2 1

PRINTED IN THE UNITED STATES OF AMERICA

Preface

WHY YOU SHOULD READ THIS BOOK, AND WHAT IT COVERS

This book has something for almost everyone. In seven parts and 28 chapters you will find discussions on ETDs, NDLTD, PDF, XML, ETD-ms, and OpenURLs, information on training and on training the trainers, and reports from the U.S. and Australia, Germany, Portugal, and Brazil. A number of chapters should fit *your* needs, whether you are a student, faculty member, researcher, librarian, lawyer, administrator, or technologist. The contributors come from all walks of life, and are quite authoritative in their respective areas.

Please forgive me for two unpronounceable acronyms: ETD (electronic thesis or dissertation) and NDLTD (Networked Digital Library of Theses and Dissertations). But the idea behind them is simple, and easy to remember: make available graduate research, in the form of electronic versions of theses or dissertations (ETDs), at the same time that colleges, universities, and other supporting institutions band together to develop a worldwide digital library (NDLTD).

This simple idea is a bit like Post-It® notes. Many of us have said "Why didn't I think of that?" It is obvious, and has many benefits and wide influence. We can consider ETD efforts from this perspective. This book goes into detail on this, so a quick roadmap to help orient you to the book and to the issues follows.

A first question is "Why?" This is addressed in Part I, Motivation. One reason is to help graduate education (see Chapter 1, written by the graduate dean who has been most vocal on this matter, and who won the first award for service in this area at ETD 2002). Another reason, discussed (in Chapters 2 and 3) by two persistent and innovative students who were among the first to put these ideas into practice through their own ETDs, is to promote understanding and use by students of more expressive and flexible modes of expression made possible by means of electronic publishing methods. Chapter 2 looks at this in terms of hypermedia, in the humanities, where the matter is a real challenge. Pushing further in this direction, Chapter 3 provides examples of heroic students whose innovations have paved the way for others, in some cases winning acclaim for their ETDs.

A second question is "How?" This is addressed in Part II, NDLTD. This section of the book also further answers the question of why, but adds a treatment of mechanisms; that leads us to the Networked Digital Library of Theses and Dissertations and some of its projects. Chapter 4, written in the fall of 1996, paints an initial vision of how ETD efforts could be connected and lead to a rich collection that would be in demand for students, researchers, and teachers. Chapter 5, written five years later, reaffirms that vision, and demonstrates both the breadth of support (e.g., having authors from three institutions) and the progress achieved. Chapter 6 gives a specific realization of how digital libraries (which can also be thought of as super-information systems, or as well-supported and organized collections of content and services) can support ETD efforts, by developing a worldwide comprehensive catalog. We urge all who have collections of ETDs to help us quickly reach critical mass in this effort, and to help turn this into a very significant scholarly service.

A third question, addressed in Part III (Guidelines for Writing and Designing ETDs), is "What do I do?," which is of particular concern to students, who in very large numbers will prepare their own ETDs. Chapter 7 summarizes the process, including discussion of student–advisor relations/ mentoring, and opens up the possibility of sharing of the raw data of scholarship more widely through ETDs. Chapter 8, written by the most articulate professor of writing/English interested in ETD activities, gives clear guidance, addressing seven key questions that students often face when considering an ETD. Chapter 9, written by experts in the multimedia field who were among the very first in that field to support ETD activities, explains how multimedia authoring can support students preparing rich ETDs.

A fourth question, "Using what?," addressed in Part IV (Technologies), is of special interest to those involved in, wanting to learn about, or concerned with technology. Although relatively long, this part is easy to follow, and provides a comprehensive treatment of the main technical concerns related to ETDs in particular, as well as to scholarly communication in general. Chapter 10 is a gentle introduction to eXtensible Markup Language (XML), which has

achieved considerable prominence in recent years for information interchange and representation. Chapter 11 steps back, providing justification
for the use of XML in ETDs, giving an evolutionary perspective based on
ongoing work in this direction. Chapter 12 helps us address the challenges of
using XML when there is a great deal of mathematics, or many equations, in
an ETD. After chapter 12, we shift to cover a variety of important technology
concerns related to ETDs. Chapter 13 explains the popular free software
system developed at Virginia Tech, widely adopted by universities interested
in ETD initiatives, to help automate submission and handling of ETDs,
allowing efficient workflow management. Chapter 14, written by a retired
digital library expert at IBM, explores in depth the key concerns raised by
many regarding ETDs, namely their durability and how automated preservation techniques should be integrated with ETD programs. Chapter 15
further connects the discussion with the WWW and with the rest of the
publishing world, solving the problem of "link rot" and indicating how links
from ETDs to other content on the Internet—even when that content is
secured inside for-profit publisher digital libraries—can be conveniently
referred to, using one of the newest standards in the field: OpenURLs.
Chapter 16 rounds out this part of the book by explaining metadata concerns
for describing ETDs, reporting on the results of roughly three years of effort
led by the NDLTD's Standards Committee.

Part IV, of particular interest to those in a college or university, gives
multiple campus perspectives on ETDs, addressing the question "How can
this work here?" Chapter 17 is an excellent lead-in, providing a conceptual
framework for moving into an ETD program. Chapter 18 addresses the fear
and concern that many have had regarding how preparing ETDs might help
or hurt one's publishing career and provides clear data to dispel most of the
fears and concerns. Chapter 19, written by the experienced and knowledgeable lead person at UMI/ProQuest who has been involved in the dissertation
area, provides counterpoint from the business world. Chapter 20 explains
copyright and helps clarify legal issues. Finally, Chapter 21 reports on the first
of many studies that will explore social and political aspects of moving
toward an ETD initiative, as an illustration of innovation development and
adoption.

Although this entire book should be of interest to librarians, Part V,
Library Perspective, focuses on "How does this relate to libraries?" Chapter
22, written by the leading library-world figure in the ETD community,
provides answers, numbers, details, and methods that have proven effective
in the longest-running library-group support effort for campus ETDs.
Chapter 23 adds a library perspective to ensure that citations in ETDs
promote scholarship while simultaneously encouraging use of popular timely
resources. Chapter 24 argues for careful indexing to ensure that ETDs can be

discovered by those interested, many of whom will have access only to something like the union catalog discussed in Chapter 6.

To round out the book, Part VI, International Perspectives, addressing the question "What is the world view?," provides insight from a small number of the active sites around the globe, demonstrating the extraordinary spread of ETD initiatives. Chapter 25, explaining efforts in Australia, demonstrates how a nation can build on a pilot effort to develop a national program. This is an excellent model that we hope will be widely adopted. Chapter 26, documenting the evolution of ETD efforts in Germany, the real home for dissertations, demonstrates how professional societies and publishers can band together to promote scholarship and electronic publishing by supporting ETD efforts. This is another excellent model that we hope other associations will follow. Chapter 27 provides yet another model, illustrating how a national library (in Portugal) can exercise leadership and collaboration by working closely with interested universities to develop a valuable national resource, at the same time working through needed changes in laws and policies. Chapter 28, from Brazil, written by the foremost trainer of trainers in the ETD world, explains how teams can learn about ETD activities and help diffuse this innovation and practice even more widely.

HISTORY

Now that it is clear what this book covers, it is important to provide some background and perspective. While the story is told well in the many chapters mentioned above, a quick summary is in order, as well as a brief update to explain the latest developments.

The technological push behind this idea was first discussed at a workshop in the fall of 1987 in Ann Arbor, Michigan, when Nick Altair, Vice President for UMI, who was engaged in the Electronic Manuscript Project, posed the question of how SGML might be used with dissertations. Taking up this challenge, I convinced Gary Hooper to invest $5000 of Virginia Tech funds, and began working with a graduate student as well as Yuri Rubinsky of SoftQuad. By 1988 we had the first Document Type Definition for ETDs, and a few dissertations were "marked up" using SGML and the new DTD (a process analagous to putting a thesis into HTML, or into a more suitable form using XML).

But this was 7 years before HTML appeared on the center stage of the Internet, and tools were expensive, so ETD efforts shifted to building community interest and support. In the early 1990s the first of a long series of small workshops convened in Washington, D.C., led by a team involving the Coalition for Networked Information, the Council of Graduate Schools,

UMI, and Virginia Tech. Soon Adobe's Portable Document Format (PDF) was available for beta testing; today it is moving forward as Version 6. This has been a key to enabling technology for ETDs.

Efforts moved forward rapidly from there. Meeting have been held annually, and sometimes more often. Hundreds are expected for ETD 2003, in Berlin, Germany, and plans have been set for ETD 2004 at the University of Kentucky. From a small number of interested universities, there now are over 175 members of NDLTD, representing over 25 countries, and incorporation is in process. If one counts all the scanned works available worldwide, including through corporate channels (e.g., Proquest), there are over 300,000 ETDs. We are aware of at least 30,000 ETDs prepared by the student authors. In the future there will be millions.

SIGNIFICANCE AND FUTURE PROSPECTS

One might ask what the significance is of all this, and wonder whether all the work has been done. Is this book a recap that will put the subject to rest? My guess is that we are just at the beginning of what will continue for many many years. Having worked in this area for over 15 years, perhaps it is appropriate to assess, reflect, and predict.

Clearly students can prepare their own ETDs. Universities can organize, often through efforts of the library and other partners (e.g., graduate school, research division, registrar, provost), a support program to help students prepare for the world of electronic publishing and learn by doing. There are tools and technologies to help in this process, and we can apply these to construct union catalogs and digital libraries, so that works can be discovered and accessed. All of this will change as technologies evolve, but everything involved should grow along with these changes.

We can probably continue to work together harmoniously in this regard. Since NDLTD is a "lightweight" organization, with minimal administrative overhead and a clear focus on standards, services, and collaboration, it appears to be a proper vehicle for change. It still faces many challenges, for example, how can membership grow by a factor of 10 or more?

In the future, we see that an ETD union catalog will have millions of entries. At that point, theses and dissertations, a unique and valuable but rather different type of work, will become much more widely used. As this genre emerges, it will change. We hope that it will promote scholarly communication. We hope that it will help empower students. We hope that students will more rapidly gain recognition. We hope that worldwide collaboration will expand, even across boundaries of language. We hope that new discoveries will more quickly be built upon, by researchers located anywhere on the globe, leading to new scholarship and useful technology transfer. We hope that world understanding will increase!

Most of all, we hope that you will benefit from this book. It may convince you to prepare an innovative ETD, or to launch an ETD program in your university or nation. You may find it useful as a reference work. You may use it to plan other scholarly communication efforts. You may use it to learn about new technologies and how they can be applied in an integrated fashion. You may meet some of the authors at ETD events, and share your views, as well as find new friends.

Do let us know your thoughts and views so that ETD efforts in general, and NDTLD in particular, can provide even greater benefit.

Edward A. Fox

Contents

Contents

Contributors

Suzie Allard University of Tennessee, Knoxville, Tennessee

Emilio Arce Virginia Polytechnic and State University, Blacksburg, Virginia

Anthony Atkins Virginia Polytechnic Institute and State University, Blacksburg, Virginia

Thorsten Bahne Universität Duisberg-Essen, Duisberg, Germany

José Luis Borbinha National Library of Portugal, Lisbon, Portugal

Martin J. Bunch[*] University of Waterloo, Waterloo, Canada

Tony Cargnelutti University of New South Wales, Sydney, Australia

Vinod Chachra VTLS Inc., Blacksburg, Virginia

Betsy Coles California Institute of Technology, Pasadena, California

Murray Crowder VTLS Inc., Blacksburg, Virginia

---

[*]*Current affiliation*: York University, Toronto, Canada.

Joan T. Dalton   University of Windsor, Windsor, Canada

Peter Diepold   University of Berlin–Humboldt, Humboldt, Germany

Robert N. Diotalevi   Florida Gulf Coast University, Fort Myers, Florida

John L. Eaton[*]   Virginia Polytechnic Institute and State University, Blacksburg, Virginia

Shahrooz Feizabadi   Virginia Polytechnic Institute and State University, Blacksburg, Virginia

Stephan Fischer   Technische Universität Darmstadt, Darmstadt, Germany

Edward A. Fox   Virginia Polytechnic Institute and State University, Blacksburg, Virginia

Robert K. France   Virginia Polytechnic Institute and State University, Blacksburg, Virginia

Ilene Frank   University of South Florida, Tampa, Florida

Nuno Freire   Engineering Institute for Systems and Computers, Coimbra, Portugal

H. M. Gladney   HMG Consulting, Saratoga, California, U.S.A.

Marcos A. Gonçalves   Virginia Polytechnic Institute and State University, Blacksburg, Virginia

Scott Guyer   Virginia Polytechnic Institute and State University, Blacksburg, Virginia

Christine Jewell   University of Waterloo, Waterloo, Canada

Seth Katz   Bradley University, Peoria, Illinois

Neil A. Kipp   KIPP Software, Denver, Colorado

---

[*]Retired.

Matthew G. Kirschenbaum   University of Maryland, College Park, Maryland

Marie-France Lebouc   Laval University, Quebec, Canada

Gail McMillan   Virginia Polytechnic Institute and State University, Blacksburg, Virginia

Joe Moxley   University of South Florida, Tampa, Florida

Ana M. B. Pavani   Pontifical University of Rio de Janeiro, Rio de Janeiro, Brazil

Frédéric Potok   Laval University, Quebec, Canada

Walter C. Rowe   University of South Florida, Tampa, Florida

William E. Savage   ProQuest Information and Learning, Ann Arbor, Michigan

Nancy H. Seamans   Virginia Polytechnic Institute and State University, Blacksburg, Virginia

Ralf Steinmetz   Technische Universität Darmstadt, Darmstadt, Germany

Hussein Suleman*   Virginia Polytechnic Institute and State University, Blacksburg, Virginia

Günter Törner   Universität Duisberg-Essen, Duisberg, Germany

Eric F. Van de Velde   California Institute of Technology, Pasadena, California

Janice R. Walker   Georgia Southern University, Statesboro, Georgia

Laura Weiss   Virginia Polytechnic and State University, Blacksburg, Virginia

Jeff Young   OCLC Online Computer Library Center, Dublin, Ohio

---

**Current affiliation*: University of Capetown, Capetown, South Africa.

Electronic Theses and Dissertations

1

Enhancing Graduate Education Through Electronic Theses and Dissertations

John L. Eaton*
Virginia Polytechnic Institute and State University
Blacksburg, Virginia

INTRODUCTION

The move by graduate schools to allow or even require students to submit theses and dissertations as electronic or digital documents (ETDs) has created much excitement, both positive and negative, among the students and faculty who will be affected by this initiative to digitize these important documents. These positive and negative views have been tempered through increased knowledge of the ETD process and increased experience in creating and archiving ETDs. At this time in the development of the ETD process, I believe the importance of an open-minded approach to this new way of expressing the outcomes of masters and doctoral research is captured very well in the following statement by Jean-Claude Guédon of the University of Montreal:

> When print emerged, universities failed to recognize its importance and almost managed to marginalize themselves into oblivion. With a new major transition upon us, such benign neglect simply will not

---

*Retired.

do. Yet the challenges universities face in responding to an increasingly digitized and networked world are staggering. Universities need a vision allowing them to express their dearest values in new forms, rather than protect their present form at the expense of their most fundamental values.

The ETD initiatives now under way in universities around the world are about bringing fundamental change to the concept that we now have of what constitutes a thesis or a dissertation. In the United States this concept of the thesis or dissertation had not changed significantly since students first began to submit paper theses and dissertations in our first research universities over 120 years ago. By moving from a paper presentation of research results to a digital presentation, we make available to the ETD author a powerful array of presentation and distribution tools. These tools allow the author to reveal to masters and doctoral committees, to other scholars, and to the world the results of their research endeavors in ways and with a level of access never before possible.

CHANGES IN PRESENTATION

I believe graduate schools and faculty, in the name of maintaining quality, have all too often inhibited the creativity of graduate students by forcing them into a mold to which they must all conform. This is nowhere more evident than in the thesis or dissertation where format restrictions abound. Some graduate schools have special paper with printed margins within which all written material must be contained. Some graduate schools still read and edit the entire text of every thesis or dissertation. Many have thesis or dissertation editors whose reputation for using fine rulers and other editorial devices for enforcing graduate school format are legendary.

I believe that the student must submit a high-quality document that is legible, readable, and that conveys the results of the research or scholarship in a manner that is clear and informative to other scholars. The document does not, however, need to be narrowly confined to a specific format if it meets the above criteria. To create a high-quality ETD, students must be information literate. That is, they must, at a minimum, have a level of knowledge of office software that will allow them to create a document that, if printed, would result in a high-quality paper document. This kind of properly formatted digital document thus becomes the primary construct of the author, rather than a paper document. In conducting training workshops for Virginia Tech students, a number of which are older, nontraditional students, we have found that this lack of office software skills is the single greatest impediment to their being able to produce a good "vanilla" ETD—that is, an ETD that has the appearance of a paper ETD, but is submitted as a digital document. In 2001 about 80% of Virginia Tech's 3500 ETDs were vanilla ETDs. Accordingly, we have emphasized the development of these skills, which number fewer than 10 and can be taught in an hour, in our student ETD workshops. Once the students have the fundamental skills to produce an ETD, they are ready, if they desire, to move on to more advanced topics for producing a visually and audibly enhanced ETD. Advanced topics include landscape pages, multimedia objects like graphs, pictures, sound, movies, and simulations, and reader aids like internal and external links, thumbnail pages, and text notes. Students are not required to use these enhancement tools, but by giving them access to the tools, we open creative opportunities for students to express more clearly the outcomes of their masters or doctoral research. To maintain quality, the student's thesis or dissertation committee must actively participate as reviewers in this process and must be prepared to exercise judgment concerning the suitability of material for inclusion in the ETD. The resulting "chocolate ripple"—or in some cases "macadamia nut fudge"—ETDs are the forerunners of a new genre of theses and dissertations that will become commonplace in the future.

Whether tomorrow's graduate students are employed inside or outside the university environment, the ubiquitous presence and use of digital information will certainly be a major part of their future careers. For this reason, efforts to increase information literacy are certain to benefit graduate students long after they have used these skills to produce a thesis or dissertation.

VALUABLE CONTENT

The traditional view is that the doctoral dissertation, and less so the masters thesis, provides a one-time opportunity for the student to do an in-depth study of an area of research or scholarship and to write at length about the topic, free of the restrictions on length imposed by book and journal editors. Such writings may contain extensive literature reviews and lengthy bibliographies. They also may contain results of preliminary studies or discussions of future research directions that would be very valuable to the researchers and scholars who follow. Primarily because of restrictions on the length of journal articles, such information exists only in theses and dissertations. I believe this view is correct and should be maintained in the digital thesis or dissertation.

ACCESS AND ATTITUDES

The attitudes of students and faculty toward the value of theses and dissertations vary greatly. For the reasons given above, some value them highly.

Others, particularly some faculty, see them as requirements of graduate schools that have little value. For these individuals, the journal publication is considered to be the primary outcome of graduate student research. I do not dispute the value added of the peer review process for journal articles and for books. Yet, I do firmly believe that as long as the scholar or researcher using ETDs as information sources recognizes theses and dissertations for what they are, these documents are valuable sources of information. Indeed, these information sources have been grossly underutilized because of the difficulty in obtaining widely available, free access to them either through university libraries or through organizations like University Microfilms (now called Proquest). If a comprehensive worldwide networked digital library of theses and dissertations existed, I believe the impact and utilization of these sources of information would rise in proportion to the increased access. This view is supported by experience at Virginia Tech in our ETD project. Research done in 1996 by the Virginia Tech library showed that the average thesis circulated about twice a year and the average dissertation about three times a year during the first 4 years they were in the library. These usage statistics do not include the use of copies housed in the home departments of the students or the usage of dissertations in the University Microfilms collection. Even so, the usage of the 5000 ETDs in our digital library far outpaces the use of paper documents. Growth in usage has been steady and remarkable. For the calendar year 2000 there were over 700,000 downloads of the PDF files of the 3000+ ETDs that were in the VT library. This averages to over 650 downloads for each ETD in the collection. The distribution of the interest in the ETDs is equally remarkable. The majority of the interest comes from the United States, with inquiries in 1998 coming from the following domains: 250,000 from .edu, 88,000 from .com, 27,000 from .net, 6800 from .gov, and 3400 from .mil. Inquiries also come from countries around the world, including the United Kingdom, 8100; Australia, 4200; Germany, 7300; Canada, 3900; and South Korea, 2200. The most accessed ETDs have been accessed tens of thousands of time, with a large number yielding over 1000 accesses. To learn more about accesses, see http://scholar.lib.vt.edu/theses/data/somefacts.html.

PUBLICATION AND PLAGIARISM

When the ETD project began at Virginia Tech, some students and faculty expressed great concern that publishers would not accept derivative manuscripts or book manuscripts from ETDs. For some publishers this concern is legitimate, and the ETD project has put into place a system for students and advisors to restrict access to ETDs until after journal articles appear. This system seems to satisfy faculty, students, and publishers. Publishers that have discussed this matter with us usually have not expressed concern about the release of the ETD after the journal article is published. One exception may be small scholarly presses that publish books derived from ETDs. These presses view the book as having a sales life of several years after the initial date of publication. In these cases it may be necessary to extend the period of restricted access well beyond the publication date of the book. For the longer term, however, it is important that researchers and scholars regain control of their work by becoming more knowledgeable about their rights as original creators and as holders of the copyrights to the work. This requires universities to have active programs to educate their faculty and students about copyright. Publishers also need to be educated to be less concerned about ETDs interfering with the marketabilty of their journals. This can be done, in part, by an effort on the part of researchers and scholars to educate publishers of professional journals. They need to help persuade journal editors that ETDs most often are not the same as the journal articles derived from them and that there is a serious difference because they have not been subject to the stamp of approval that is the result of peer review. As such, they should not be considered as a threat to the news value or to the sales potential of the journal. It is interesting to note that a Virginia Tech survey of students who had released their ETDs worldwide showed that 20 students had published derivative manuscripts from the ETDs with no publisher resistance to accepting the manuscripts.

It is also noteworthy that the American Physical Society has a practice of sharing electronic copies of preprints of manuscripts undergoing peer review http://xxx.lanl.gov/). Those that successfully pass peer review are published in the society's journals. This practice is essentially the same as the practice being proposed for ETDs above.

After concerns about publication, the risk of plagiarism is next on the list of concerns of students and faculty. We do not yet have enough experience with ETDs to speak authoritatively about this issue. If one thinks a bit about it, it seems that the risks of exposure of plagiarism will deter such activity. Most researchers and scholars still work in fields where a fairly small group of workers have detailed knowledge of their work. It follows that because of the size of the field and because of the ease of detecting plagiarized passages in electronic documents, the risks of detection will make widespread plagiarism unlikely.

More disconcerting to me is the closely related concern of researchers and scholars that by reading their students' ETDs, other researchers and scholars will achieve a competitive edge in the contest for grants and contracts. Most research at U.S. universities is done in the name of supporting the well-being of the nation and is being sponsored directly or indirectly with public tax dollars. There is something wrong with a view that research and scholarship should not be shared among other researchers and scholars for the above reasons. Yet the concern is understandable in today's financially stretched research universities where the competition for promotion and tenure among young faculty is fierce. Similarly, faculty are encouraged to develop intellectual property in which the university claims a share. I'm not sure if we have gone too far down this road, but I am concerned that our obligation as scholars to make our work known to other scholars is being compromised. A result of this compromise is that the goal of scholars to advance knowledge through sharing of scholarship may also be slowed.

HOW VIRGINIA TECH IMPLEMENTED THE ETD REQUIREMENT

ETD discussions with the graduate dean, the library, and Ed Fox, a faculty member conducting research on digital libraries, began in 1991. At that time we were exploring the possibilities of optional submission. Shortly thereafter, Adobe Acrobat® software for creating and editing portable document format (PDF) files came on the market. This software for the first time provided a tool that was easy to use and allowed documents to be moved between computer operating systems and platforms while retaining the original document formatting. This was a great step forward in increasing worldwide access to information while retaining the original author's formatting style. At this time we began a pilot study to determine if Acrobat met our needs. We determined rather quickly that it was the most suitable product for our needs at that time. In my opinion that conclusion holds true today. We continued discussions with the graduate school and the library, and in the fall of 1995 we decided to seek to make the submission of ETDs a requirement of the graduate school. We took a proposal to the Commission on Graduate Studies and Policies for discussion. There it was discussed by a degree standards subcommittee, which discussed the proposal with ETD team members: Ed Fox from Computer Science, Gail McMillan from the library, and John Eaton from the graduate school. In these discussions the concerns expressed were about archiving and preservation, the burden to the students, and the burden to the faculty and departments. After full discussion, the subcommittee recommended approval of the proposal in spring 1996. The commission discussed and approved the proposal, subject to the following provisions:

> That a student-training process be conducted to show students how to produce an ETD
> That necessary software (Adobe Acrobat) be made available to students in campus computer labs
> That the faculty not be burdened by this process

That a faculty/graduate student advisory committee be established to advise the Commission on Graduate Studies and Policies on the ETD project

With these provisions agreed to, the Commission approved a one-year voluntary submission period to be used for beginning the student ETD workshops, informing the university community, and developing the infrastructure needed to move to requiring ETDs, after which ETDs would become a requirement in the spring semester of 1997. All went very smoothly while the process was voluntary. Workshops were started, software was placed in campus computer labs, visits were made to departments, articles were published in the campus newspaper, and the advisory committee was formed. Late in the spring semester of 1997, after the mandatory requirement began, a small but vocal group of faculty, mostly from the life sciences and chemistry, expressed serious concerns about compromising the publication of derivative manuscripts from ETDs made available worldwide. While we had a provision for withholding release of ETDs pending publication of manuscripts, the time period of 6 months was thought to be too short. The ETD team responded to this concern by giving the student and the advisor greater control over access to the ETD through an approval form (available at http://etd.vt.edu/). The modifications made to the ETD approval form seem to have satisfied faculty concerns about publication. Since that date the ETD project has operated very smoothly at Virginia Tech, and, it is now an integral part of graduate education.

CONCLUSION

The ETD project has provided the opportunity for fundamental change in the expression of and access to the results of scholarship done by students in research universities around the world. These tools can also be easily extended to the research done by faculty. As scholars, we should not let this opportunity slip by. As Jean-Claude Guédon said, "Benign neglect simply will not do."

2

Innovative Hypermedia ETDs and Employment in the Humanities

Seth Katz
Bradley University
Peoria, Illinois

INTRODUCTION

There are three general types of electronic theses and dissertations (ETD): (1) those that use little or no electronic enhancement and are, effectively, print texts stored electronically; (2) those that incorporate links to material on the World-Wide Web or multimedia elements as illustrations, footnotes, or appendices; and (3) those that are full-blown innovative hypermedia documents including text integrated with sounds, movies, or simulations (Young, 1998). Innovative hypermedia ETDs are the most different from conventional print theses and dissertations. These innovative documents receive different degrees of acceptance in different professions and academic disciplines. At one end of the spectrum are high-tech industries and academic fields that are immersed in computer technology (e.g., computer science, engineering, multimedia production, etc.). Employers in these fields will have a greater interest in hiring and retaining new Ph.D.s who can show their proficiency with computer technology by producing innovative hypermedia ETDs. At the other end of the spectrum, however, are the core disciplines of the humanities (e.g., English, philosophy, history, etc.), whose members largely remain resistant to the new technologies. Students who produce ETDs are likely still to find their work undervalued by established members of these latter disciplines, even if their work is little more than a plain vanilla text with a few multimedia add-ons, and especially if they attempt something so bold as an innovative hypermedia ETD.

As yet, there is no empirical evidence to support my claims about the reception of ETDs in the humanities. In talking about academic humanists' attitudes towards ETDs and electronic publication more generally, I am largely speaking on the basis of anecdotal evidence—my own experience, conversations at conferences, postings to online discussion groups, scuttle among my colleagues—as well as reasonable supposition. It is true that a few major institutions have embraced ETDs, even in the humanities. However, those institutions are a handful among the less than 10% of universities that grant Ph.D.s. Much of the other >90% of the academy (second- and third-tier state campuses, small to mid-sized private schools, and community colleges) (Neel, 1987) is far more conservative in its approach to the new technologies: many at those schools—especially in the humanities—may not yet even know what ETDs are. In an anthology such as this *ETD Sourcebook*, it is easy for authors to forget that we are, after all, each preaching from the comfort of a group pulpit shared by the converted.

For the author of an innovative hypermedia ETD who is looking for employment or advancement in the humanities, there is clearly bad news and good news. The most obvious *bad* news is that, for the near future, at *best*, innovative hypermedia ETDs will, in most cases, have little or no positive value for job candidates in the humanities. And, at *worst*, innovative hypermedia ETDs will prove a liability for those candidates. Nonetheless, it is reasonable to predict that, in the near future, the news will improve. The *good* news will be that, even in the most technology-resistant areas of the humanities, changes in the structure of universities, and a shift towards more online course delivery, will increase the value of students who show that they can work deftly with hypermedia by producing innovative hypermedia ETDs. Not too long from now, the most successful candidates for jobs, tenure, and promotion will likely be those who create innovative hypermedia ETDs who are comfortable producing, revising, and using highly flexible electronic publications in their teaching and research.

REASONS FOR THE BAD NEWS

Within the humanities, innovative hypermedia ETDs are commonly under-valued largely because traditional criteria for evaluating academic work are inadequate for evaluating research presented in the new medium. At most institutions, innovative hypermedia ETDs are evaluated in the same terms as print publications. "As the chair of English at a major research university put it: ' ... generally we evaluate the new in the same terms and by the same standards as the old' " (Cronin and Overfelt, 1995). This simple equation creates several problems, not only for adequately evaluating innovative hypermedia ETDs, but for evaluating other types of ETDs and electronic publications as well. One would think that, even in the humanities, there would be little trouble with evaluating a simple ETD—one that is no more than a print text stored electronically—in the same terms as print text. Nonetheless, there are several problems with applying traditional evaluative criteria even to print texts published electronically. When a document includes linked text and multimedia, it becomes more difficult to evaluate the work in traditional terms.

Evaluating Print Texts Published in Electronic Form

In theory, for decisions on hiring, tenure, and promotion, a peer-reviewed electronic journal on the Web ought to carry the same value as a comparable print journal. No value should be lost by simply taking a print article, saving it as electronic text, and having it published in a Web-based journal with a strong peer-review process, a recognized editorial staff, and regular contributions from noted scholars. Unfortunately, within the humanities, in many cases, no matter how good the electronic journal, the electronic text is commonly regarded as having less value than the print version. The largest problem is simply the bias for print, which causes many academics to remain suspicious of electronic publication. Seminoff and Wepner (1997) note that print "journal articles and textbooks continue to be the convincing forms of evidence of an education professor's scholarly contribution to a discipline for tenure and promotion." Cronin and Overfelt (1995) have made note of the "implicit bias toward print" in the academic reward system. Perhaps the underlying problem is that in electronic publishing there is no substantive, tangible, material product by which the author may show that he or she has *done* something. Perhaps the problem is that a great deal of the electronic text published on the Web is available free of charge: after all, what is the value of something that is *free*? Some academics may simply be resisting what they perceive as an overly hyped, trendy technology: how can a substantial, enduring work of scholarship be produced in a medium that is constantly changing? If my institution cannot keep up with the replacement-and-upgrade cycle on computers, so that the machine in my office can't run a Java-compatible

Web-browser (or VRML-compatible, or whatever comes next), so that I can't even access a particular online publication, then that publication, no matter how good, is worthless to me. If a student composes an innovative hypermedia ETD in a particular proprietary format and I don't have the software to read it, then, again, what is it worth to me? Fear of and frustration with the technology are easy sources of biases for print and against the electronic medium.

Related to the print bias against electronic text is the more substantial issue of archiving. How long will the text of an electronic publication be available? And in what form? Will accessing it be as simple as going to the library or placing an interlibrary loan request? Or will the archiving process be more obscure? Print is solid and, at the least, durable for centuries. How do we know that the digital archive is reliable for periods of 50 years or more? What if online text-representation formats change and your electronic thesis or article text becomes unreadable? And, for the present, how reliable is the Web as a means of publication and resource storage? After all, the technology is of uneven quality; many servers run slowly, or they may go down unexpectedly. Files can be easily lost. And there is the omnipresent problem of "link rot": Web sites are regularly moved or directory structures rearranged without adequate notice to users. Other chapters in this volume address these problems. But in the heart of the humanities, there is a strong conviction that print text is clearly stable; electronic text is clearly ephemeral.

Furthermore, print publications are commonly evaluated by the range of their distribution, that is, whether the journal in which an article is printed has a local, regional, national, or international readership. The broader the distribution, the greater the value. Print dissertations commonly receive no distribution and are laborious to access; their value as a "publication" is clearly low. But an ETD or other electronic text in a public site on the Web is accessible to almost anyone, anywhere: it doesn't matter whether it is published on your personal Web site, in the electronic version of the Bradley University English Department newsletter, the online *PIPA: Publication of the Illinois Philological Association*, or the online version of a Johns Hopkins print journal, made available through Project Muse. All freely accessible publications on the Web have, potentially and effectively, an international circulation. And, once research is published on the Web, the conventional ways of measuring its circulation (number of copies per issue and range of distribution) are no longer available. Moreover, anyone can set up a Web site or an electronic journal and publish their own or others' work, with or without a peer review process. The site owner can then index the site or the electronic journal's content on the burgeoning number of Web indexes (e.g., Yahoo, Lycos, Hotbot, etc.) and thereby make the entirety of those published texts highly accessible and searchable for anyone on the Internet. Given the proliferation of computers and Internet access, Web-based electronic publications are more available and more easily searched for useful information than *any* print text, even if that print text is right on the shelf in one's home or office. As Burbules and Bruce (1995) note, whether it passes through a peer review process or not, a thoroughly researched and carefully constructed Web-based work of scholarship may well have broad and enduring scholarly value, and its accessibility may serve only to increase that value.

Evaluating Innovative Hypermedia ETDs

Innovative hypermedia ETDs and other innovative hypermedia publications further complicate the evaluation process in the context of traditional print-based evaluative criteria. Innovative hypermedia documents thwart the expectations of traditional hiring committees who are trying to determine a job candidate's "scholarly potential"—by which they mean "potential for publication." How does one judge the publication potential of a "chunk" of an innovative hypermedia ETD as an article? Or of the whole ETD as a "book"? Tenure and promotion criteria at most institutions still fail to even mention electronic publication (Katz, 1997). A job candidate whose ETD cannot be made to mesh with institutional expectations about publication may not make it past the first cut.

The bias in much of the humanities against innovative hypermedia publication forms the basis for further prejudice. It is sometimes difficult within traditional criteria to judge whether an innovative hypermedia document is a publication or not. For example, if I produce an innovative hypermedia CD-ROM that is then published commercially and used by some as a teaching tool and by others for research, some of my peers might still not regard it as a publication. Rather, they might see it as work that supports others' teaching and research—and so as a "service" project! This, despite the fact that, if I were to produce a print article that was used in the same way, there would be no question that it was a publication. If I used the CD-ROM in my own teaching, I might receive credit for it as part of faculty development— promoting "innovative teaching." I have heard many stories about junior faculty in the humanities being warned by senior colleagues to avoid innovative hypermedia projects because such projects will work against their bids for tenure and promotion. Humanities faculty remain widely suspicious of innovative hypermedia publications.

A further source of suspicion arises from the structure and flexibility of hypermedia documents. Conventional print texts typically follow a strict Aristotelian rhetorical structure, with a branching, tree-like arrangement of thesis, supporting claims, and evidence. Innovative hypermedia typically incorporates varieties of webbed structure, in which support for an initial thesis may be conceived of as radiating out from a common center. Supporting claims may themselves become the centers of new webs of discussion. And any individual node within the web may be linked directly to any other, so that the same node may be used to support any number of different points or arguments within the document. Rather than a tree structure that is intended to be traversed by a single path, the structure of an innovative hypermedia document will incorporate repetition, circles, return loops, tangents, dead-ends, and even entire documents authored by others. All of these structures are unusual in or even antithetical to the structure of traditional print argument. Such unconventional rhetorical structures may lead readers who are unfamiliar or uncomfortable with innovative hypermedia to condemn the author as sloppy or ignorant of convention.

Furthermore, Burbules and Bruce (1995) note that, unlike static print texts, even after publication, electronic texts can be readily and repeatedly revised and extended. The whole work can even be easily recast in light of the author's new research, teaching needs, or interests. Clearly, ETDs and electronic publication can break down the line between research and publication, since the "final" published text can easily and repeatedly be made over. Is such a publicly revisable text a single publication or a series of publications? And what if the author places his or her work on the Web, receives feedback on it in the form of e-mail, cuts and pastes some of that e-mail into the text, solicits more comments, and repeats this collaborative revision process several times? Who then is the author? And what version of the text is definitive, if any? The student who produces and files an ETD on the Web might well continue to revise and extend that ETD, using it as the basis for their research and publication for years after graduation. Forget the well-worn print practice of revising the dissertation into the typically different format of a book for publication: an ETD filed in a public Web archive is already "published." The shift from "dissertation" to "book" could be nearly seamless: the distinction between an innovative hypermedia ETD and an innovative hypermedia "publication" could be a moot point.

Because it is so easily revised, and because new material can so easily be inserted in or linked to old text, an electronic publication especially lends itself to collaborative authorship, which is still viewed with suspicion and is still undervalued throughout much of the academy. But collaborative authorship appears to be emerging as a natural form in the composition of electronic scholarship (Burbules and Bruce, 1995; see also Harnad, 1998). Clearly, traditional criteria for evaluating print publications offer no means for measuring the value of an evolving or dynamic electronic text.

REASONS FOR THE GOOD NEWS

Changes in traditional criteria for evaluating scholarly work will be driven by changes in the nature of the academy—changes that will make innovative hypermedia ETDs and electronic publishing commonplace and so give them greater value in the job, tenure, and promotion markets. At least three major changes already are occurring.

First, more and more course content is being delivered online. A simple search on the Web for online and distance-education courses and degree programs shows that a huge number of institutions make a vast number and range of courses available over the Internet. This change in teaching practice is fueled by several factors. The technology for online course delivery is ever more widely available, continually improving, and continually dropping in price. The technology allows regional institutions to reach rural and other remote populations—and even to matriculate students from abroad who cannot afford to come to the United States. Add to this an increasingly competitive education market: colleges and universities are competing feverishly for a shrinking pool of students. Under the influence of this competition, institutions of higher education think of themselves more and more as competing businesses within a service industry. This competition will be won, so the argument goes, by institutions that can best serve their customers by tailoring courses to deliver the broadest variety of content in the most convenient manner to the largest number of students and at the lowest cost.

Students who produce innovative hypermedia ETDs will show themselves well prepared to produce innovative online course materials and deliver exciting new online courses. Online courses so far offer the strongest tool in the competition for new student markets. As a complement to face-to-face instruction both on and off campus, colleges, departments, and continuing education programs can produce, package, and market courses to target populations including "nontraditional" students and businesses. They also can offer the service of creating courses to meet the particular needs of a business or other group or organization.

The authors of innovative hypermedia ETDs will be well positioned to take positions in the new online course industry. The success of efforts to market tailored courses and curricula depends on the flexibility of the instructors, their course designs, and their course materials. As curricula and disciplinary boundaries become more fluid, jobs and professional advancement will increasingly go to candidates who show strong facility with producing and revising innovative hypermedia, with using such text in their teaching, and with flexibly augmenting and revising the content of electronic documents to meet changes in their student audience (Meyer, 1997). Authors of innovative hypermedia ETDs will come out of their graduate programs with just the experience demanded by this new job market.

Two other changes in the academy that will work to raise the value of innovative hypermedia ETDs and electronic scholarship are closely related. As publishing costs rise, libraries are cutting journal subscriptions and, at the same time, are working to develop online text and information management resources. Simultaneously, many publishers are working to establish Web-based ventures to support, complement, and even replace a growing number of established print journals. Libraries and publishers are thus playing a pivotal role in legitimizing electronic texts as having scholarly (and so academic-professional) value.

Meyer argues that, with the increasing fluidity of disciplinary boundaries and curricula, there will be an increased demand for flexible library holdings and access to information resources. The model of the large, stable library collection "will give way in importance to collections that can be restructured to help with faculty retooling and can support new curricula more quickly" (Shreeves, 1992). Libraries are experimenting with a growing range of ways of managing and cataloguing electronic resources so as to make them most effectively accessible to and searchable by library patrons (see Association of Research Libraries, 1998; Feldman, 1997; Smith, 1997). Again, if electronic scholarship becomes a prominent feature, or even the predominant feature of university library collections, then institutional guidelines for evaluating scholarly work will, of necessity, change to reflect the increased value of innovative hypermedia ETDs and publications.

Just as libraries are shifting their collections to include a growing volume of electronic resources, so, too, are publishers looking to gain a share of any available market for producing and selling electronic publications. Already in such "high-cost arenas" as the scientific, medical, and technical disciplines, subscription electronic journals have proliferated and electronic publication is becoming common and accepted. The humanities and social sciences are following more slowly for at least two reasons: journal costs are not rising as fast in those fields, and scholars in these fields have largely resisted the new technology. Of course, as libraries cut subscriptions to print journals and purchase access to more electronic resources, they are actively fueling the shift from print to electronic scholarship, since that shift will help them to maintain collection quality while cutting maintenance costs (Shreeves, 1992; Soete, 1997; see also Bailey, 1998). As publishing costs rise and libraries cut journal subscriptions, more publishers, journals, disciplines, and scholars will turn to the Web as the preferred venue for publishing new scholarship. This shift in academic publishing will only serve to increase the value of innovative hypermedia ETDs for the job search, tenure, and promotion, even in the most technology-resistant sectors of the humanities. Innovative hypermedia ETDs will serve as valuable markers of a candidate's facility with the new medium. And innovative hypermedia ETDs will, even more essentially than print theses and dissertations, become the direct basis of the new academics' initial publishing and teaching careers.

CONCLUSION

In a mailing from Prentice Hall (1998) describing their 1999 textbooks in Western Civilization, in a section titled "Distance and Distributed Learning," the brochure asserts the publisher's commitment "to being the leader in developing Web-based content to help students learn." The brochure goes on to state that "Prentice Hall is dedicated to continuing its role in 'publishing'— in whatever form appropriate—the best content from the most eminent authors and experts in the field." As the publishing industry embraces innovative hypermedia, and as the use of technology in teaching continues to grow, academic institutions will be forced by the market to recognize the value of electronic publishing. And the graduate student who, early on in his or her career, starts to develop proficiency in electronic publishing by composing an innovative hypermedia dissertation project and publishing and promoting it on the Web will be the student who succeeds in the job, tenure, and promotion markets.

Some departments, institutions, and field-specific professional organizations are making the first, tentative steps towards changing traditional evaluative criteria so as to provide more adequate measures of the worth of innovative hypermedia ETDs and publications. And, certainly, the growing movement towards required ETDs will serve to hasten the process of acceptance and understanding of electronic scholarship, as both dissertation committees and students become more familiar with the medium and its capacities. However, in the meantime, students in the humanities who produce innovative hypermedia ETDs as a first step in their scholarly careers need to know that they will encounter resistance and skepticism from many in the academy. Students producing innovative hypermedia ETDs must be ready to explain what an ETD is, what their particular electronic thesis or dissertation does, and why they have used the new electronic medium. They may also have to be ready to make a case for the value and rigor of their electronic scholarship—in job applications, in interviews, and to colleagues in the years leading up to tenure. For the near future, arguing for the value of innovative hypermedia ETDs will, in the humanities, be a losing battle, but those who persist in the battle will, eventually, reap the rewards of foresight.

REFERENCES

Association of Research Libraries (ARL) Digital Initiatives Database. Web site. [cited November 28, 1998]. Available. ⟨http://www.arl.org/did/⟩.

Bailey, C. W. Jr. (1998). Scholarly Electronic Publishing Bibliography. Version 22. Web site. [cited November 28, 1998]. Available. ⟨http://info.lib.uh.edu/sepb/sepb.html⟩.

Burbules, N. C., Bertram, B. C. (November 1995). This is not a paper. *Educational Researcher* 24:12–18.

Cronin, B., Overfelt, K. (1995). E-journals and tenure. *Journal of the American Society for Information and Science* 46:700–703.

Feldman, S. E. (October 1997). It was here a minute ago!': archiving the net. *Searcher: The Magazine for Database Professional* 5:52–64.

Harnad, S. "E-prints on interactive publication." Web site. [cited 28 November, 1998]. Available. ⟨http://www.princeton.edu/~harnad/intpub.html⟩.

Katz, S. (1997). One Department's Guidelines for Evaluating Computer-Related Work. In: Kairos 2:1. [electronic journal]. [cited November 24, 1998] Available. ⟨http://english.ttu.edu/kairos/2.1/⟩.

Meyer, R. W. (July 1997). Surviving the change: the economic paradigm of higher education in transformation. *Journal of Academic Librarianship* 23:291–301.

Neel, J. (1987). On job seeking in 1987. *ADE Bulletin* 87:33–39.

Prentice Hall Western Civilization, 1999. (Fall 1998). Advertising brochure. Upper Saddle River, NJ: Prentice Hall Higher Education.

Seminoff, N. E., Wepner, S. B. (Fall 1997). What should we know about technology-based projects for tenure and promotion? *Journal of Research on Computing in Education* 30:67–82.

Shreeves, E. (Spring 1992). Between the visionaries and the luddites: collection development and electronic resources in the humanities. *Library Trends* 40:579–595.

Smith, L. (March/June, 1997). Monash university library electronic resources directory: extending the library catalogue to access electronic resources. *Cataloguing Australia* 23:28–34.

Soete G. J. (June 1997). Transforming Libraries: Issues and Innovations in Electronic Publishing. Transforming Libraries Series #3. SPEC Kit 223.Washington, DC: Association of Research Libraries. ERIC ED409904.

Young, J. R. (February 1998). Requiring theses in digital form: the first year at virginia tech. *Chronicle of Higher Education* A 29. Web site. [cited September 23, 1999] Available. ⟨http://chronicle.com/colloquy/98/thesis/background.htm⟩.

3

From Monograph to Multigraph: Next Generation Electronic Theses and Dissertations

Matthew G. Kirschenbaum
University of Maryland
College Park, Maryland

Our writing materials contribute their part to our thinking.

Friedrich Nietzche

BREVIS VITA, ARS LONGA

According to the primary publisher of graduate research in the United States, Bell and Howell Information and Learning (formerly UMI):

> The first American Ph.D. program was initiated at Yale University in 1860, with requirements that included at least one year of study on campus, an examination, and a dissertation based on original research. The first recipient was James Morris Whiton, whose dissertation in Latin on the proverb 'Brevis vita, ars longa' was accepted in 1861. Handwritten, it was six pages long.[1]

This bit of academic lore reminds us that conventions of scholarly work appropriate for a doctoral thesis have evolved and changed over time. Moreover, we see that the standards and practices of dissertation writing as we now know them must *prima facie* bear the mark of at least one major technological rupture, that of the mechanical typewriter, which entered into common usage not very long after Whiton penned his longhand opus. The severe strictures governing margins, spacing, page numbering, and so forth engrained in every doctoral candidate are a direct outgrowth of the new—and as Friedrich Kittler and others have observed, *industrial*—control over writing space that the typewriter enabled. As Scott Bukatman (1993) puts it, "The typewriter ... makes potential cyborgs of us all in our attempt to match its machine-tooled perfection." Thus, the typewriter, one could argue, has shaped the form and even the substance of scholarly work for much of the twentieth century.

More recently, of course, the norm has been for theses and dissertations to be composed electronically with word processing software. In the current day and age, theses and dissertations exist first as electronic data files and only secondarily as bound and printed documents. Given this state of affairs, it seems reasonable to consider the implications of submitting, archiving, and disseminating graduate theses and dissertations *exclusively* in electronic form. This idea was first discussed well over a decade ago at a 1987 meeting in Ann Arbor arranged by UMI and attended by representatives of the Virginia Polytechnic Institute and State University (Virginia Tech), the University of Michigan, and two software developers (SoftQuad and ArborText).

That particular history—and its fruition today in the pioneering ETD projects at Virginia Tech and a growing number of other universities, as well as the federally funded Networked Digital Library of Theses and Dissertations (NDLTD)—is recounted elsewhere in this volume. In what follows, I will devote my attention to those electronic theses and dissertations that are undertaken at the behest of individual graduate students rather than from institutional mandate. These students have chosen to pursue ETDs of their own initiative, in departments and programs that often have no local precedent to support the writing of the ETD, no formal guidelines for its evaluation, and no tested solutions for its storage, preservation, or distribution. Yet these ETD projects are nearly always driven by their authors' desire to conduct research and present results of a kind that cannot be accommodated by the printed page. Many of these ETD authors also share the conviction that electronic environments offer the potential to radically redefine scholarship as it has traditionally been practiced in their disciplines. I will argue here that the efforts of these ETD authors (who often expose themselves to considerable professional risk due to the skepticism that often surrounds their projects) are as important in shaping the future of graduate scholarship in the digital age as the electronic theses and dissertations that are being generated at institutions with a formal ETD initiative.

Moreover, I would argue that independent ETD authors are working with an intellectual urgency of a kind often lacking in degree candidates producing ETDs solely to fulfill an institutional requirement. Independent ETD authors know that electronic theses and dissertations can teach important lessons about disciplinary methodologies since the shift to the new medium foregrounds conventions and practices that have been normalized and rendered transparent by years of monographic output. Consider a discipline such as film studies, where, as Robert Kolker (1999) has pointed out, scholars or critics writing printed books and articles have never had access to the most of basic critical tools: the means to "quote" the material under discussion (except of course as still images, which convey neither motion nor sound). But now film scholars can quote quite effectively by embedding digital video clips in electronic documents and annotating them to reveal camera angles, lighting effects, and so forth. Graduate students working in film studies, if they choose to adopt an electronic format, will be able to present and explicate content in ways their faculty mentors never could.

WHAT ARE MULTIGRAPHIC THESES AND DISSERTATIONS?

Before I discuss such matters in more detail, however, I want to introduce a basic distinction between two very different uses of the term "electronic thesis or dissertation." Though the distinction ought to be self-evident, the fact is that these two different kinds of ETDs are often conflated. Most broadly then, the term "electronic thesis or dissertation" should apply to any thesis or dissertation that is submitted, archived, and distributed *solely or at least primarily* in an electronic format. Such a dissertation might be written on any conceivable subject, and need avail itself of no method of presentation or organization that could not be duplicated on paper. (Thus, Adobe PDF is often the electronic data format of choice.) The important contexts for discussion of ETDs of this "plain vanilla" sort are library science, document encoding, and information retrieval.

Now, in addition to this plain vanilla model, electronic thesis or dissertation can also mean something like a hypertext or multimedia dissertation—that is, a dissertation which is not only submitted, archived, and accessible solely in an electronic format, but which is also *self-conscious of its medium* and which uses the electronic environment to support scholarship that could not be undertaken in print. Examples of this might include a dissertation written as a set of nonlinear hypertext documents, or a dissertation consisting not only of static media forms such as text and image, but also sound, video, animation, data visualizations, and computational models. I will call ETDs of this sort "next generation" ETDs, or *multigraphs*, since they are native to electronic environments and incorporate the perspectives of multiple media formats. These ETDs must be discussed not only in terms of library science and related fields, but also in relation to much broader questions about the nature of the scholarly work dissertations have traditionally been expected to perform.

Graduate students undertaking ETDs of their own initiative—without local precedent—can expect to encounter resistance at various points in the process. Clearly for some, ETDs raise questions of academic decorum. Of course, if one cannot put together a willing committee, an ETD will be all but impossible from the outset. But even with the support of their supervisor and committee, candidates should be prepared to resolve any number of nontrivial obstacles. Indeed, candidates may find themselves called upon to find solutions for procedural problems in the library or administration engendered by the need to accommodate electronic objects rather than printed documents. Deena Larsen,[2] completing one of the very first multigraphic ETDs for a Master of Arts at the University of Colorado in 1992, recounts her experience (which is not without humor) as follows:

> The [Graduate School Committee] refused to accept any part of my thesis whatsoever that was not written on paper. I asked why. They replied that the library could not store, catalogue, or lend disks. So I donated several hypertexts [on disk] to the library, got a friend of mine in cataloging to fix up a system to loan them out, and went back to the committee. They acknowledged that the library could indeed handle disks and could therefore accept a thesis on a disk. I got a pat on the back and was told to come back tomorrow.
>
> When I went back, they refused to accept my thesis on a disk. I asked why. They said that it did not meet the format requirements, which had not been broken in the last century. I asked for specifics. They said, well it doesn't have one inch margins. I carefully held out a disk, measured it and said, look, if I use one inch margins then I won't have any space at all to write. They looked at this and it actually took them about three minutes to realize that you don't write your thesis on the *outside* of a disk.

Larsen's diskette *was* eventually accepted by the Graduate School, but with a printed introduction that constituted (in their eyes) the "official" thesis document. Since these early skirmishes, anecdotal evidence suggests that prospects have gradually begun to improve. But to understand multigraphic ETDs in their proper context, we should start by surveying the general impact of new media technologies on scholarly communication and academic production. Since my own background is in English, I will speak to the academic culture I know best, the humanities.

It is a coincidence that the Ann Arbor ETD meeting I noted above was held in 1987, the same year as the founding of the first electronic discussion list in the humanities, called simply "Humanist" (and still active today). Though computers have long been valuable research aids in the hard sciences and social sciences, it is only comparatively recently—in the years since the Humanist list's inception—that computers have begun to play a significant role in humanities teaching and research (with the real watershed coming only since the mid-1990s, with the widespread advent of networked electronic publishing via the World-Wide Web). Today there are *hundreds* of humanities-related discussion lists covering every major field and specialization; humanists have access to ever-expanding electronic research archives and digital text collections, representing tremendous investments of time, research funding, and professional expertise; humanities teaching and instruction is regularly conducted with the aid of virtual chat-spaces and online environments; electronic journals publish scholarship on topics from early modern literary studies to postmodern culture; and, measured (conservatively) by Alan Liu's *Voice of the Shuttle* index, one can bookmark some 15,000 Web sites given over to humanities-related content.[3] With an estimated 3,000 humanities doctorates conferred last year by American universities alone, it should not be surprising that a growing number of graduate students are finding it appealing—often irresistible—to begin engaging in new media scholarship at the masters or doctoral level.[4] And though it is certainly true that not all humanists have embraced the new technologies—a small but vocal minority have rejected them outright, and a silent majority may still be indifferent—it is correct to say that there is now a critical mass of scholars (many of them senior faculty) from various fields devoting significant portions of their time to high-profile ventures in digital scholarship. This is a key point: a candidate's proposal for an electronic thesis or dissertation should be regarded not as an isolated curiosity but rather as part of a continuum of intellectual activity encompassing academics of all ranks working in the full range of scholarly genres—from the journal article to the textbook to the critical edition or archive.

A DIRECTORY OF ELECTRONIC THESES AND DISSERTATIONS IN THE HUMANITIES

Rather than generalize from current conditions in the humanities to the hard sciences and social sciences (areas I know relatively little about), let me instead recount the circumstances that led to my own decision to pursue an electronic dissertation. After developing a broad-based interest in the relationship between new media technologies and literary theory encouraged by the example of faculty mentors involved in humanities computing initiatives at the University of Virginia, I put together a proposal for a then vaguely defined "hypertext" dissertation, which was approved by the Department of English in late 1995. There was, I had noticed, a fair amount of hypertext criticism and theory already on the shelves, but that's precisely where most of it was—on bookshelves, and not, by and large, in the medium it claimed to explicate. An important component of my own project, I decided, would be to use an electronic environment in a performative mode in order to embody and respond to the ideas developing in my writing.

Not long after I began that work, I attended the 1996 ACM Hypertext conference in Washington, D.C., where I spoke with graduate students from other universities who had independently hit upon the idea of an electronic dissertation, but who had been refused the necessary permission by their departments or advisors. I decided that it would be useful to have a centralized repository or clearinghouse of ETD-related materials to which prospective ETD authors could direct administrators as well as dubious (or simply uninformed) faculty for examples of similar projects already underway. Since early 1996 I have maintained a Web site devoted to online references and resources for ETD writers in the humanities (the site's audience also includes faculty, librarians, administrators, and publishers).[5] At the heart of the site is a directory of electronic theses and dissertations currently in progress, providing affiliation and contact information for their authors, documentation of the project's history, information as to choice of electronic formats, project descriptions, and (whenever the work is Web-based) a link to its homepage. The site also archives and indexes listserv threads, online articles and reports, and other items pertaining to the subject. The ETD directory, which listed just a handful of theses and dissertations when the site first went online, has now grown to include some three dozen entries representing every major humanities discipline. Additions are made on a regular basis, and the site has received notice in the *Chronicle of Higher Education* and in the *MLA Style Manual and Guide to Scholarly Publishing*, 2nd ed.

It is important to understand that the projects documented at this site are not electronic postprints of paper-based theses and dissertations (itself an increasingly commonplace practice); rather, they are research projects that have been designed and executed *exclusively* for presentation in digital form. Those students who are most attracted to working with new technologies will generally already possess at least some facility and experience with the tools of the medium, and they will not be satisfied with creating an electronic document that could just as easily have been presented in print. Allen Partridge, a doctoral candidate in an interdisciplinary fine arts program at Texas Tech University, at work on a dissertation evaluating the impact of digital media on contemporary theater, is representative:

> My topic is so deeply entrenched in hypermedia that it would be impossible to document the research in any other form. . . . The plan

as of November 1996, is to create the piece for Internet enhanced CD-ROM. The finished work will incorporate multimedia technology, HTML, and VRML in a custom designed interface, which I hope will be generated with Microsoft's Visual Basic Five or Macromedia Director, or some combination of these.[6]

A more sedate but no less substantive example is provided by Frank Grizzard, from the history department at the University of Virginia, who defended in 1997 an electronic dissertation entitled "The Construction of the Buildings at the University of Virginia, 1817–1828." The dissertation is a documentary editing project consisting of, in addition to a 400-page monograph, "approximately 1,700 primary documents, transcribed and annotated [and] 2,800 images from microfilm." Electronic presentation and encoding of these items makes the full texts and images available to the reader as a searchable archive of primary sources, a key dimension of functionality that would have been absent in a printed compilation of the same materials.

Likewise, Craig Branham at Saint Louis University is completing an electronic master's thesis on a set of Old English manuscript materials known to scholars as "Con^2." But in addition to his editorial work on the manu-

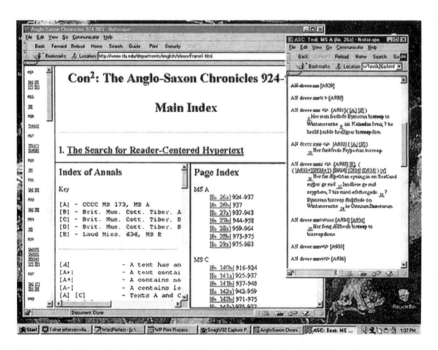

FIGURE 1   Master's thesis by Craig Branham, Saint Louis University.

scripts, Branham has also developed an elaborate frames-based layout to accommodate the complex documents that he is explicating (Fig. 1).

Branham's efforts in developing this customized interface should, I believe, be recognized as an integral aspect of the project, with the potential to make a professional contribution in its own right. As Branham notes:

> The Con^2 archive illustrates a number of inherent problems in the design of hypertext authoring environments that complicate editing and reading electronic editions of Old English texts. Current web browsers are poorly equipped to handle many of the tasks that Old English scholars are required to perform because they rely on design metaphors which afford connective, rather than comparative, linking schemes. . . . Wider recognition of the central role of the user interface in shaping the reader's experience of literary texts would improve the design and effectiveness of hypertext applications.[7]

Though interface design is not the primary subject of the thesis, the project nonetheless suggests important avenues for future exploration in that field.

Multigraphic ETDs are especially appealing for their ability to combine text with images and other nonverbal kinds of presentation. Constanze Witt, for example, defended an electronic dissertation at the University of Virginia in art history and archeology; her research focused on artifacts found within Celtic tombs. What attracted Witt to an electronic format was her "need to present high-quality images of works of art that are not represented in U.S. museums, together with a large amount of (also unfamiliar [or] not readily available in United States) information." Witt's work (Fig. 2) is a good example of what is essentially a text-based dissertation enhanced by the presentational capabilities of multimedia—not least because the monetary cost of reproducing the necessary illustrations in print would have drastically curtailed the scope of the project.

Several of the projects listed in the ETD directory depart much more dramatically from conventional writing practices. Michele Shauf's *Memory Media* (authored in Macromedia Director) is a montage of text, still and moving images, and sound. In the screenshot shown here (Fig. 3), a figure in a video clip, presumably Shauf, offers a response to the question "What are CD-ROMs?" (Note the importance of visual rhetoric and design: here, a self-reflexive gesture toward the digital medium—the pixilated backdrop—contrasts with the gilt Victorian aesthetic of the frame that surrounds the Shauf's moving, speaking image.)

Likewise, my own work in the medium attempts various experiments with the rhetorical and narrative forms inherent in monographic prose. Though parts of my dissertation, entitled "Lines for a Virtual T[y/o]pography," simply use the digital environment as a platform for incorporating

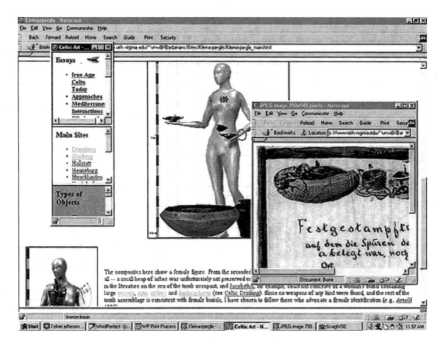

FIGURE 2   Ph.D. dissertation by Constanze Witt, University of Virginia.

images, video, and computer-generated animations (akin to Witt), other parts of the work are interactive explorations of language and textuality in new media environments. For example, the dissertation includes a three-dimensional annex (authored in the Virtual Reality Modeling Language, VRML) that experiments with rhetorical conventions when text is freed from the flatland constraints of the two-dimensional page (Fig. 4).

While about half of the projects listed in the ETD directory focus explicitly on the social and cultural implications of new media technologies, it is important to recognize that the electronic format is capable of enriching—indeed, in many cases of transforming—the way scholarship is performed even in more traditional areas. This is a broad assertion, but by using the word "transform" I want to maintain that there is more at stake than simply adding some new tools to the scholar's desktop. Charles Bernstein has argued that the split between the (often radical) critiques of knowledge and representation now commonplace in the humanities and the conventional, prose stylistics of the monographs in which these critiques are typically articulated reveals "an often repressed epistemological positivism about the representation of ideas."[8] In other words, Bernstein is suggesting that the same division

FIGURE 3   Ph.D. dissertation by Michele Shauf, University of Delaware.

between form and content that inspired a number of the electronic projects cataloged on my site is pervasive throughout much of the academy. The most salient point here is not, I think, that every ETD must harbor a subversive gesture, but rather that a shift to new technologies of writing and new modes of academic production necessarily entails a critical examination of the dominant, normalized, and therefore often transparent codes of mainstream academic discourse. Theses and dissertations are particularly significant in this regard as they are by definition the first major academic project a scholar will undertake. Surely some professional self-scrutiny at this stage of a career is both healthy and desirable.

I also want to be clear that in characterizing all of the preceding projects—from Branham and Grizzard's to Shauf's and my own—as "next generation" ETDs, I am not adopting the rhetoric of technological determinism. Though it is arguable that all theses and dissertations will eventually be electronic (other chapters in this volume detail that scenario), I have no illusions about an accompanying widespread shift from monographic to multigraphic writing. Not all electronic theses and dissertations will be *multigraphic* electronic theses and dissertations, even though sounds, images, video, and

FIGURE 4   Ph.D. dissertation by Matthew Kirschenbaum, University of Virginia.

other multimedia elements will almost certainly begin to infiltrate mono-graphic discourse. Clearly not every graduate student will be interested in interrogating the "repressed epistemological positivism" of the monograph form, and the plain vanilla ETD may continue to occupy the ranks and files of large-scale ETD collections like the NDLTD. Nor is this a bad thing: print, after all, has been a remarkably resilient medium that has proven adequate to any number of important and inventive research projects. So, too, will the plain vanilla ETD.

ETDs AND PREPROFESSIONALISM

No discussion of electronic theses and dissertations would be complete without some consideration of the extreme professional circumstances confronting many graduate students today—most obviously, but by no means exclusively, the all-but-collapsed academic job system in many areas of the humanities and social sciences. A generation ago, a doctoral dissertation was the occasion for a young scholar to spend a year or two immersed in his or her subject matter; the doctorate is still that, of course, but increasingly dissertations have also come to be seen as the draft of a book-length manuscript which will be the first of several major publications before an untenured professor receives a promotion (or indeed, before a graduate student or adjunct instructor will have an opportunity to get onto the tenure track). In today's academy, at the same time that a candidate is supposedly "immersed" in researching and writing the dissertation, he or she is also likely to be delivering conference papers, publishing articles, editing collections, and generally struggling to establish a professional presence and profile—a phenomenon that the critic John Guillory has dubbed "preprofessionalism." And that's to say nothing of the teaching load that many doctoral candidates and ABDs carry or other part-time jobs they work to make ends meet.

It is too soon to tell what, if any, impact completing a dissertation in an electronic format will have on a beginning scholar's prospects; there have simply not been enough cases to judge. But anecdotal evidence (including my own experiences) suggests that *multigraphic* electronic dissertations tend to provoke one of two extreme reactions, either working very much to a candidate's advantage—distinguishing him or her from the rest of the field—or else quickly sealing the candidate's fate as someone whose work is simply too "experimental" to be taken seriously. These reactions vary widely from one department and hiring committee to the next.

With this in mind, I'd like to close with a short bit of verse that is printed after the title and signatures page of a dissertation at the University of Virginia. If you are ever in Charlottesville you can read it for yourself, assuming you're willing to make the descent to the basement floor of Alderman Library, where dissertations and theses are shelved. The poem's lines are addressed "To the Reader in the Stacks":

> Thief? Voyeur? Which one you are
>   Is no concern of mine. But know
> How those who labored years to get
> Their prose into these binders black
>   As body-bags regard the type
> Who rifle them: Go home and work.
>   Or don't. But put my pages back.[9]

The puritanical work ethic grafted to the sharp anger of this wicked little booby-trap of a text is surely the product of the long periods of grueling personal isolation that completing a dissertation entails, coupled with the frank recognition that the lack of jobs (and the consequent lack of entrée into the distribution channels of university presses) will very likely ensure the work's consignment to the bleak binders that encase it. Had the dissertation been electronic, it might not have found its author a job, but it would at least have ensured that the work was accessible to a scholarly community beyond chance wanderers in the basement stacks (the occasional order from DAI notwithstanding). Electronic theses and dissertations in general, and multigraphic ETDs in particular, are no panacea for hard times in academe, but they do provide graduate students with a powerful instrument for taking control of their work and the means of its production and dissemination.

WORKS CITED

Bernstein, C. (June 6, 1997). "Frame Lock." ⟨http://wings.buffalo.edu/epc/authors/ bernstein/frame.lock.html⟩.

Bukatman, S. (Fall 1993). "Gibson's typewriter." *South Atlantic Quarterly* 92.4:627–645.

Guillory, J. (1996). "Preprofessionalism: What graduate students want." *Profession* 91–99.

Kolker, R. (July 23, 1999). "Digital tools to parse the language of film." *Chronicle of Higher Education* B9.

NOTES

1. See ⟨http://www.umi.com/hp/Support/DExplorer/shortcut/lore.htm⟩.
2. Larsen's remarks here are from a longer commentary available online at ⟨http:// etext.lib.virginia.edu/ETD/about/larsen.html⟩.
3. The H-Net consortium alone sponsors more than 50 electronic discussion lists in the humanities ⟨http://h-net2.msu.edu/⟩; see the research archives and digital text collections at the University of Virginia's Institute for Advanced Technology in the Humanities ⟨http://www.iath.virginia.edu/⟩ and Electronic Text Center ⟨http://etext.lib. virginia.edu/⟩; Diversity University and Lingua MOO both offer a virtual MOO-based campus to students and educators from all over the world ⟨http://www.academic.marist.edu/1/duwww.htm⟩ and ⟨http://lingua.utdallas. edu/⟩; *Early Modern Literary Studies* ⟨http://unixg. ubc.ca:7001/0/e-sources/emls/ emlshome.html⟩, founded by R.G. Siemens, published its first issue in 1995; *Postmodern Culture* ⟨http://jefferson.village.virginia.edu/pmc/contents.all.html⟩, founded by Eyal Amiran and John Unsworth has been publishing since 1990 and is generally recognized as the oldest peer-reviewed electronic journal in the humanities; The Voice of the Shuttle, maintained by Alan Liu, may be accessed at ⟨http:// humanitas.ucsb.edu/⟩.
4. Statistic is from data available at The National Center for Education Statistics ⟨http://www.ed.gov/NCES/index.html⟩.

5. *Electronic Theses and Dissertations in the Humanities: A Directory of Online References and Resources* can be found at ⟨http://etext.lib.virginia. edu/ETD/⟩.

6. Partridge's remarks are from his project description available online at ⟨http://etext.lib.virginia.edu/ETD/directory/browse.html⟩; unless otherwise noted, all of the quotations in the following paragraphs are likewise drawn from individual project descriptions available at this URL.

7. See ⟨http://www.slu.edu/departments/english/chron/digest.html⟩.

8. See Bernstein's essay "Frame Lock," available at ⟨http://wings.buffalo. edu/epc/authors/bernstein/frame.lock.html⟩.

9. The dissertation was completed in 1994 on a subject in twentieth-century poetry. I have elected to not include the title and author's name here.

4

National Digital Library of Theses and Dissertations: A Scalable and Sustainable Approach to Unlock University Resources*

Edward A. Fox, John L. Eaton,† Gail McMillan,
Laura Weiss, Emilio Arce, and Scott Guyer
Virginia Polytechnic Institute and State University
Blacksburg, Virginia

Neill A. Kipp
Kipp Software
Denver, Colorado

INTRODUCTION

As of September 1, 1996, the U.S. Department of Education provided grant support for a 3-year, Virginia Tech–led project to improve graduate education with a National Digital Library of Theses and Dissertations (NDLTD),

---

Note: NDLTD was changed to mean "Networked" instead of "National" in 1997 to reflect international interest.

* D-Lib Magazine, September 1996 ISSN 1082-9873.

† Retired.

adding to 1996 funding from the Southeastern Universities Research Association (SURA) for development and beta testing of the Monticello Electronic Library thesis and dissertation program. True success in these projects will potentially mean a permanent change in graduate education and scholarly publishing, with digital libraries playing a more dominant role in supporting and disseminating research.

This chapter serves as an overview of the project, indicating what benefits are likely, what roles various partners (including, we hope, you, the reader) may play, and what related work has occurred in the past. It is also an invitation to universities to unlock their resources in connection with this collaborative project.

If many in the international community join in, the project could lead to a multilingual corpus of vast proportion and significance. Our collection focus is on doctoral dissertations and masters theses, so we will repeatedly refer to TDs (theses and dissertations) or ETDs (electronic theses and dissertations). However, we also welcome special reports (especially those prepared by graduate students) and bachelor theses. Since there are over 40,000 doctoral and 360,000 masters degrees awarded in the United States alone each year, and since our aim is for all graduate students to learn how to publish electronically, the annual growth rate of the collection could exceed 100,000 new works per year by the turn of the century. If there is a fair amount of multimedia content included, as we expect will be the case, the collection might increase in size at the rate of about a terabyte each year.

EXPECTED BENEFITS

The NDLTD should help almost everyone, and so, through broad cooperation and participation, should be a sustainable effort. Let's take a moment to consider its likely effects on the key parties involved: students, universities, the research community, and the publishing world.

Students

Our project is primarily an effort to improve graduate education. We will work so that graduate students become information literate, learning how to become electronic publishers and knowing how to use digital libraries in their research. The overall process is shown in Figure 1: the life cycle of an ETD. Toward this end we continue to develop written documents, extensive WWW materials, and a distributed education and evaluation program in which universities accept responsibility for local support.

With access to the NDLTD, graduate students will be able to find the full texts of related works easily, to read literature reviews prepared by their

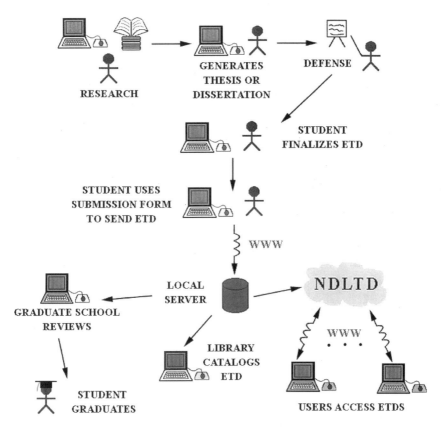

FIGURE 1   The life cycle of an ETD.

peers, and to follow hypertext links to relevant data and findings. Their professors will be able to point to the best examples of research in their area, even
to the level of an interesting table, an illustrative figure, or an enlightening
visualization. Also, students can benefit by learning how to become electronic
publishers, preparing them for their future work. Since this educational initiative targets all graduate students, it is unique in its potential to train future
generations of scholars, researchers, and professors. If they can publish electronically and add to digital libraries, future works they write will not have
to be scanned or rekeyed. Graduate students also may be empowered to be
more expressive as they prepare their submissions for the NDLTD, if such is
allowed by their committee, department, and university. Some students have
already prepared hypertexts as literature, included color images or graphics,
illustrated concepts with animations, explained processes with video, or used

audio when dealing with musical studies. One masters project about training students to use Authorware included an Authorware tutorial in the appendix. This has already helped people in South America learn more about multimedia technology.

Access begets access, so having more graduate works in the NDLTD is likely to simulate greater interest in TDs. Studies at Virginia Tech of the average number of times a paper TD circulates per year indicate a steady growth from 0.55 to 0.85 circulations between years 2 and 4 for dissertations, with a roughly parallel line for theses reflecting an increase from 0.4 to 0.68 circulations over the same period. Based on the increases we have seen in numbers of accesses to electronic journals as they became available on WWW, we expect that there will be a dramatic increase in the average number of accesses to TDs when they shift from paper to NDLTD availability. Most students are eager for their works to be cited, and we plan for our monitoring and evaluation system to record such accesses. With bibliographies online too, a citation index among NDLTD entries will be possible as well, helping students keep track of new studies related to their investigations.

Finally, students are likely to benefit financially from the NDLTD. Publishing electronically should save them the costs of preparing at least some of the paper copies now required. There also may be lower fees from their university and other parties for filing their final copy.

Universities

Few universities have a university press, and many of those are not profitable. Yet, through the NDLTD, every university can publish the works of its graduate students with a minimal investment. This should increase university prestige and interest outsiders in the research work undertaken.

University libraries can save shelf space that would otherwise be taken up by TDs, and the costly handling of paper TDs by personnel in the graduate school and library can be reduced or eliminated. At Virginia Tech, for example, the catalogers decided to have students assist with cataloging by adding keywords to the cover page, thus reducing processing in the library. It seems likely that at least one person in each large university can be freed to work on other tasks if proper automation takes place, resulting in simplification of the workflow related to TDs. In addition, library online catalogs can provide fuller information by including the abstract from the electronic text.

Research and Publishing

Student research should be aided by the NDLTD since graduate students will have a single repository for the work of their peers, supported by full-text search. Other researchers, including people in companies interested in opportunities for technology transfer, can look to the NDLTD as a way to quickly learn of new findings.

Suppliers of electronic publishing software have already found it valuable to participate in the NDLTD. Adobe is making generous donations of their Acrobat software, in part because they realize that having all graduate students exposed to the Acrobat line of tools will ensure a large base of future users. Associations like ACM (the First Society in Computing) are supportive, in part, because having their members learn to publish electronically in graduate school can help reduce the anticipated cost of shifting to electronic publishing, when authors will be expected to submit final copies of acceptable articles in proper forms (e.g., using SGML) for publication and electronic archiving. Indeed, it is likely that future shifts in publication practices will be facilitated by the effort to build the NDLTD. This is of particular interest to universities, which now cannot control what happens to the research publications they support and later spend large sums to buy back research publications from commercial publishers. Through the NDLTD, universities can control one important class of the intellectual property they produce and can share it freely with other universities to reduce overall costs.

HOW YOU CAN HELP

Since almost everyone stands to benefit from the development of the NDLTD, we encourage you to help in this process in a way that fits the mission of your institution. For example, if you are engaged in the development of software or systems for digital libraries or helping with standards efforts, you can help directly with building the NDLTD. If you are at a university, you can help build local consensus and devise a supporting infrastructure so the NDLTD is a key part of graduate education.

Software, Standards, Systems

The NDLTD presents unique challenges on many fronts, and help is needed in various technical areas. On the one hand, it is desirable for graduate students to be expressive, using multimedia representations, but this can lead to very large works, even when compression is required. While we observe that many ETDs only require on the order of a megabyte, we expect that with images and other media forms the average size will approach 5–10 megabytes. A single video file can consume one or two orders of magnitude more space; it is fortunate that a computer system with 2 terabytes of hierarchical storage is available at Virginia Tech to support this project! But even more important will be good software to undertake content analysis of multimedia information. Other software is needed to help with electronic publishing and other aspects of digital library operations.

Standards also are essential for the success of the NDLTD. If the archive will last for decades, hopefully centuries, its content must be usable many years after publication. If authors work with standard representations, those are more likely to be understood than are representations that are unpublished and proprietary in nature. If the number of standards supported is kept to a minimum, there will be less work in refreshing the archive as technologies and standards change, calling for conversion to more modern storage and representation schemes.

The NDLTD must operate as a production service if it is to replace current library approaches to handling TDs. Thus, reliable, commercially supported digital library systems are needed for long-term success. Companies like University Microfilms International (UMI), IBM, and Online Computer Library Center (OCLC) are participating in the unfolding of the NDLTD. Thus, IBM donated a large SMP computer that will serve as the central host for this effort and that can run IBM digital library software. Various IBM products for handling databases, image collections, searching on image content, and rights management have great potential for helping with the NDLTD.

Building Local Consensus

At universities, while moving toward the NDLTD is clearly advantageous, such a shift requires many changes in policies and practices. The best way to accomplish this seems to be to develop a local plan, with guidance from key staff in the graduate school(s), the library, and the computing or information technology operations, as seen in Figure 2, ETD site implementation. Then workflow changes and automation opportunities are likely to be grasped and become practice. With leadership from these three groups, students and faculty can be consulted and involved in detailed planning. It appears likely that a transition period of about a year is required to effect the change from introduction of concept to widespread acceptance and participation in the NDLTD. Note that real benefits of workflow improvement and universal access to online graduate research require a nearly complete shift to electronic submissions of all TDs.

Supporting Infrastructure

If *every* graduate student is to submit an ETD, enhancement to the campus infrastructure is required in most institutions. Usually, this is more a matter of will and coordination than large expense, and most would agree that the end result is highly desirable. Let us consider several possible scenarios.

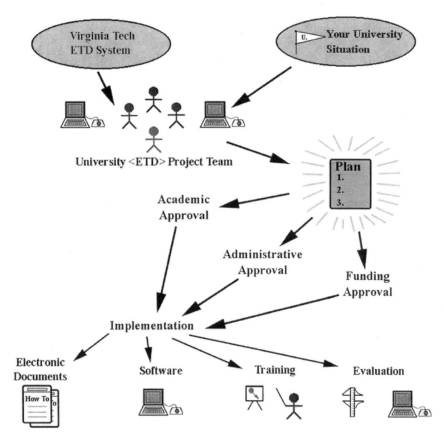

FIGURE 2   ETD site implementation.

First, if Adobe's Portable Document Format (PDF) is the target representation, most PC, Mac, and Unix systems can run the software required to prepare PDF files. Though there are minor complexities related to fonts and special formatters like LaTeX, these can be worked out, and the investment by students or labs in Adobe software is not high (e.g., about $40 per copy of *Exchange*).

Second, if SGML (herein used to refer as well to related standards such as XML) is the target representation, there are various solutions. One is to use a standard editor, inserting tags, much like what is done by many HTML authors. While possible, the number of tags needed makes this cumbersome. Thus, it is better to use an SGML editor, but those are expensive. Microsoft is assisting with the investigation of the SGML Author extension to Word as an appropriate tool, which could be made available in small numbers in campus labs. Virginia Tech is working on conversion software and templates to enable students to use preferred environments like LaTeX and to automatically make a 100% accurate conversion to SGML.

Third, there is the question of images. Since many TDs have some type of artwork, color scanners with high-quality capture capability at 600 dpi must be available, along with computers, adequate RAM and disk storage, software (e.g., Adobe Photoshop), technical assistance, and network transfer capabilities to move the results to locations students can more easily access.

Finally, there is the higher end requirement of supporting special multimedia forms. Special systems for audio and video capture and compression are required for these media types. Note, however, that if no special multimedia laboratories are available on campus, students can pay for such services themselves.

SINCE 1987

Though the NDLTD is new to many readers, work on it actually began late in 1987! A brief history is in order.

UMI and Electronic Manuscripts

Nick Altair, then at UMI, who had recently worked on the Electronic Manuscript Project, convened a meeting in 1987 in Ann Arbor, Michigan. Representatives from University of Michigan, ArborText, SoftQuad, and Virginia Tech participated. Soon after, Yuri Rubinsky of SoftQuad worked with Virginia Tech to develop the first SGML Document Type Definition (DTD) for TDs. (This was revised in 1996 in connection with efforts supported by SURA—see below.) Virginia Tech continued work in 1989 and 1990, experimenting with conversion of TDs that were obtained on diskette from student volunteers.

CNI and Project Discovery

In 1992 the Coalition for Networked Information sponsored a project discovery workshop with 11 invited universities, each of which had documented the interest of their graduate school, library, and computing/information technology groups. This meeting was planned by representatives of UMI, Council of Graduate Schools, and Virginia Tech. Subsequently, a number of further discussions were held at CNI meetings. In connection with one of these, representatives from UMI and Virginia Tech visited Adobe to learn about plans for the Adobe Acrobat family of tools.

SURA/SOLINET and Unlocking University Resources

In 1993, SURA and SOLINET (Southeastern Libraries Network) joined forces to work toward the Monticello Electronic Library. At the first open meeting, Edward Fox of Virginia Tech was invited to give a presentation, reintroduced the idea of the ETDs, and subsequently became co-chair of the working group on theses, dissertations, and technical reports. There was widespread interest in this and subsequent meetings, and university presidents saw the potential benefits as well at various SURA discussions. Consequently, a group of interested universities sent representatives to a workshop at Virginia Tech in August 1994, hoping to develop specific plans for ETDs. One key decision from that meeting was to work toward a dual representation scheme. Thus, two copies of each TD would be archived, one using Adobe PDF and the other using SGML. Virginia Tech and UMI agreed to explore the SGML conversion problem in more detail. Virginia Tech began to convert some of the TDs it received to PDF.

SURA and Beta Testing

Late in 1995, Virginia Tech prepared a preproposal to the U.S. Department of Education regarding a 3-year effort to build the NDLTD and also requested that SURA fund initial work on establishing a part of the Monticello Electronic Library for ETDs for the Southeast. The first of these led to funding September 1, 1996, and the latter covered calendar year 1996 pilot efforts in the Southeast. North Carolina State University was the first institution seeking to join the initiative. The first regional workshop for southeastern universities was held August 1–2, 1996, hosted by University of North Carolina, Charlotte. Many discussions have been held, and presentations given, in the region, nation, and even internationally. There appears to be interest at such institutions as Auburn, Clemson, Georgia Tech, Michigan State, Mississippi State, MIT, Oklahoma State, University of Georgia, University of Utah, University of Virginia, and Vanderbilt.

PILOT EFFORTS AT VIRGINIA TECH

Interest in ETDs has continued and spread since 1987.

DTD Development

While SGML has always seemed the logical choice for an archive of TDs, serious technical and economic problems have delayed its usage. First, few graduate students had heard about SGML, and it seemed unlikely that we could educate them about it. However, with the growth in interest in HTML, this problem has been largely eliminated. Second, there are few freely available editors for SGML. While this continues to be the case, discussions are underway with a number of vendors to work out economically feasible solutions in the context of the NDLTD. Third, there has been the problem of how to find an acceptable DTD that would be suitable for authors, technically sound, and could be adopted nationwide. We believe we have solved this problem—see the DTD and related documentation at our WWW site (http://www.ndltd.org/). While it may evolve as comments are received, we hope some version of it will be universally adopted so that TDs are tagged to facilitate searching and formatting. In particular, we have developed software to convert from documents prepared according to the DTD to HTML (for WWW delivery, see Figure 3, ETD hypertext structure) or LaTeX (for rendering to paper or page images).

Finally, there is the outstanding problem of conversion from word processors and formatters to SGML. We are developing a set of LaTeX macros to ensure reliable conversion from LaTeX to SGML. Similar efforts

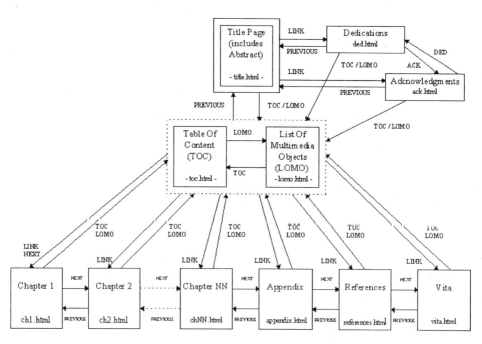

FIGURE 3 ETD hypertext structure.

are planned for Microsoft Word, but these may be simplified if SGML Author for Word will fit into the plans.

Capture with PDF

In the last several years, PDF has matured and been more widely supported, with freeware tools like xpdf aiming to round out the ability to read such documents on UNIX systems. Any computer with Adobe Acrobat can write to the PDFwriter instead of a laser printer and create a PDF file. PostScript files can be converted to PDF using Adobe Distiller. Since almost every tool used in document creation can either work with the PDFwriter or yield a PostScript file, electronic publishing to PDF is relatively straightforward and can be taught during a 1- to 2-hour training session.

One technical problem with PDF that troubled our early efforts was solved in 1996. There are now publicly available outline fonts that allow authors who work with LaTeX to prepare PDF files without including bitmap fonts (which increase file size, make display and reading on screen impossible, and restrict text searching options). We are developing automated services on Sun systems to allow authors to prepare PDF files with the proper outline fonts included.

Workflow Automation

Automation is the key to increasing efficiency in handling TDs. The library and graduate school have completely redone the flow of work at Virginia Tech to eliminate steps and carryovers from the world of paper. For example, authors now are encouraged to submit single-spaced documents, which are easier to read on the screen than double-spaced documents. Authors assign keywords to their documents, since catalogers have trouble assigning categories to new works like TDs. Authors directly upload their submissions to a library server, where the graduate school can check for proper form; there is no longer a need to deliver to the graduate school and have them move completed works to the library.

Central to our automation is a WWW submission page, which is filled in by the author and leads to uploading and archiving of the TD. This operation includes students authorizing the university to handle access (nonexclusively) to their works, classifying the work (e.g., thesis or dissertation), and providing email information about them and their chair (so that completion of processing can lead to automatic notification).

When SGML submissions are easily accomplished, they will be the basis for a variety of derivatives. One is the HTML version already mentioned. Another is the MARC record needed for cataloging. Third is the entry for

Dissertation Abstracts. Once these can be produced, the submission process will be simplified even further.

Workshops

Since spring 1996, there have been a variety of workshops to train students regarding electronic publishing (using PDF, tools like Word and Exchange, LaTeX) and the automated submission effort. By holding events every few months, handling email questions, making special visits to interested groups, and providing online FAQ files, the needs of graduate students are being addressed.

The Faculty Development Initiative at Virginia Tech involves training the entire faculty over a 4-year period about electronic publishing, work-stations, networked computing, and educational technologies. A regular part of the FDI is for faculty to learn about Adobe Acrobat and the handling of ETDs—thus over 600 have been trained in this initiative. Others have been exposed in college meetings, through newspaper explanations, or through open workshops.

Requirement

In spring 1996, the Commission on Graduate Affairs agreed to require ETDs at the start of 1997. Thus, all students must prepare an electronic submission, and the Library and Graduate school will not accept or receive paper sub-missions. This is a serious plan! We hope that after months or perhaps a year of working with the NDLTD, other universities will follow this scheme so that students will learn how to publish electronically and use digital libraries.

RELATED WORK

Development of the NDLTD fits in with other digital library and other electronic publishing efforts. Some of the most closely related ones are as follows.

NCSTRL

Beginning in 1992, with the Wide Area Technical Report Service (WATERS), Virginia Tech has been involved in digital library efforts related to computer science technical reports. In 1995 the WATERS group joined the CSTR group to form the Networked Computer Science Technical Report Library (NCSTRL). Virginia Tech is a regular member. Fox is a member of the NCSTRL Working Group, and the NCSTRL backup server runs in the Virginia Tech Computing Center.

The software used with NCSTRL is available for use with NDLTD and can support a distributed system, including situations in which UMI and Virginia Tech, for example, serve sites that do not wish to maintain their own servers.

NCSTRL is one of the early adopters of the CNRI handle system. Virginia Tech has obtained permission for a top-level naming authority for theses and will run a local handle server for TDs so that persistent names can be guaranteed.

Envision

Since 1991 Virginia Tech has worked with ACM and others to develop a prototype digital library for computer science and to apply it to improve related educational efforts. Some of the software developed may be of use for NDLTD. The methods and tools used for monitoring WWW use and analyzing the data will be a part of the evaluation component for NDLTD.

IBM Digital Libraries

IBM has collaborated with Virginia Tech in several ways regarding digital libraries. The central server for the NDLTD will run IBM digital libraries software. Where possible, local development will be reduced when commercially available solutions apply.

SUSTAINABILITY

For digital libraries to be successful, they must be sustainable, scalable, and usable. With a world-class Center for Human–Computer Interaction at Virginia Tech, and with a Department of Computer Science the main focus of which is HCI, working toward a usable system will be an ongoing and central concern for our efforts. Usability labs and research in remote usability evaluation should help our efforts, as will related projects for WWW monitoring and analysis. So, we turn our attention to the other two legs of successful digital libraries, starting with sustainability.

Mission

Every university with a graduate program is obliged to deal with TDs and to ensure that graduate students are properly educated. As argued above, the NDLTD is in the best interest of students and universities. Thus, to carry out the mission of educating graduate students and handling their TDs, universities should ensure that they know how to publish electronically and how to use digital libraries, which can be accomplished most efficiently by joining the NDLTD effort.

Similarly, many university libraries and/or archives have assumed the responsibility of having copies of works written by local faculty, staff, and students. This has been a particularly strong tradition in the arena of theses and dissertations. On many campuses the library is committed to maintaining such works indefinitely, which fits into the long-term goals of the NDLTD.

Infrastructure

Universities support students in their roles of publishers and researchers. Having the right infrastructure to support local involvement in the NDLTD fits in with the general type of support that universities need to provide.

Economics

Because of the cost-saving aspects of copying and submitting paper versions of their TD, we believe students have an economic incentive to participate in the NDLTD. Similar savings are expected for universities, in particular the graduate school and library. Since students still will provide some payment to the university when submitting the TD, there is an economic foundation for continuing the effort as a self-sustaining enterprise.

SCALABILITY

The NDLTD effort is scalable by its very nature. First, it builds upon a system of higher education (in the United States) that demonstrated its ability to scale to meet needs throughout the twentieth century. Second, it makes use of technology that is modular and distributed, and which is addressing needs of a growing number of computer science departments. Further, this effort piggybacks upon other normal activities of universities, relating to education, scholarly communication, and libraries—each of which demonstrates a fair degree of scalability.

University

Each university has responsibility for its own TD collection but can handle that locally or assign it to others. At the level of a university, the problems are not terribly large—even if 1000 ETDs are submitted in a year, the disk space required to store them probably would cost less than $3,000.

State

In some cases there are statewide consortia for library information sharing. Thus, the VIVA (VIrtual library of VirginiA) initiative could allow for a statewide coordination of part of the NDLTD, supporting the needs of small universities where running suitable servers is not warranted.

Region

As in the case of the Monticello Electronic Library, having a regional consortium for NDLTD is quite sensible and feasible. There are parallel groups to SURA, SOLINET, and the Conference of Southern Graduate Schools in other regions of the United States.

Nation

In the United States, the NDLTD represents the national effort. Researchers in other countries like Korea are looking into similar efforts that would connect with NDLTD.

Repositories

For NDLTD to be successful, there must be long-term support. UMI already has an archive of 1.3 million TDs in microform and is willing and able to provide long-term electronic archive services. Other groups are also interested in this opportunity. Negotiations between universities and UMI are needed to work out the proper arrangement for all parties in the context of the growth of NDLTD.

PLANS

Future work on the NDLTD is laid out in the proposal to the U.S. Department of Education, which is included in PDF form on the WWW pages for the project. Collaboration with UMI is expected on all fronts. Some of the other highlights are as follows.

Technical Development

The NDLTD effort will involve collaboration with the Cornell Digital Library Research Group, which has developed the software used with NCSTRL, and with CNRI, which has developed the handle system and other digital library services. There also is collaboration with IBM regarding their digital library systems and software. OCLC has promised support from its Office of Research, especially regarding useful tools. Other collaboration will take place in the context of electronic publishing work, such as with Adobe.

Administrative Collaboration

The NDLTD has support from many groups interested in universities, graduate education, libraries, and networked information. There will be close coordination with the national and regional graduate school groups, presentations supported by CNI, and of course ongoing work with SURA and SOLINET, as well as similar associations in other regions.

Education and Evaluation

Since we aim to improve graduate education, we must afford equal access and undertake a careful evaluation. A detailed evaluation plan is given in the proposal to include surveys, logging, focus groups, and other efforts. Usability studies will help with detailed analysis and improvements of interfaces. It is expected that about one third of the project will relate to evaluation issues, both formative and summative. Thus, we hope not only to develop a large and valuable digital library to support graduate education and research, but also to show that it has proved to be of benefit and that graduate students indeed know how to publish electronically and how to use digital libraries.

ACKNOWLEDGMENTS

The U.S. Department of Education's Fund for the Improvement of Post Secondary Education supports NDLTD. Authorized funding for the first year is in the amount $69,762. Anticipated future funding for years 2 and 3 are: $69,337 and $68,941. If all federal funding is received as planned, the total would be $208,040. Virginia Tech will provide institutional support, which gives federal/nongovernmental percentages 53.3/46.7. Additional in-kind support for the FIPSE proposal has been promised by ACM, Adobe, Council of Graduate Schools, Coalition for Networked Information, Cornell Digital Library Research Group, Council of Southern Graduate Schools, IBM, OCLC, State Council of Higher Education for Virginia, SOLINET, SURA, UMI, and University of Utah Graduate School.

5

Networked Digital Library of Theses and Dissertations*

Hussein Suleman,[†] **Anthony Atkins,**
Marcos A. Gonçalves, Robert K. France,
and Edward A. Fox
Virginia Polytechnic Institute and State University
Blacksburg, Virginia

Vinod Chachra and Murray Crowder
VTLS Inc.
Blacksburg, Virginia

Jeff Young
OCLC Online Computer Library Center
Dublin, Ohio

INTRODUCTION

The Networked Digital Library of Theses and Dissertations (NDLTD), (see http://www.ndltd.org/) has emerged as a result of the efforts of thousands of

---

*Based on article by same title in D-Lib Magazine, September 2001.

[†]*Current affiliation*: University of Capetown, Capetown, South Africa.

49

students, faculty, and staff at hundreds of universities around the world, as well as the assistance of interested parties at scores of companies, government agencies, and other organizations. This federation has multiple objectives, including:

To improve graduate education by allowing students to produce electronic documents, use digital libraries, and understand issues in publishing

To increase the availability of student research for scholars and to preserve it electronically

To lower the cost of submitting and handling theses and dissertations

To empower students to convey a richer message through the use of multimedia and hypermedia technologies

To empower universities to unlock their information resources and

To advance digital library technology

Work toward those objectives has proceeded since November 1987, the date of the first meeting devoted to exploring how advanced electronic publishing technologies could be applied to the preparation of electronic theses and dissertations (ETDs). Early efforts are summarized in two D-Lib articles (Fox et al., 1996, 1997). A third article summarizes the first attempts to support, through federated search, access to the collection (see also http://www.theses.org/) of ETDs that is emerging in distributed fashion (Powell and Fox, 1998).

NDLTD activities are coordinated by an international steering committee that meets each spring and fall. Its members include those who lead the diverse regional and national efforts that promote efforts regarding ETDs. Committees help with strategic planning, standards (see http://www.ndltd.org/standards), training, and meetings. A good deal of effort by steering committee members has gone into fund-raising, so that single and groups of institutions could implement ETD initiatives. There have been national projects in the United States (Kipp et al., 1999) South Africa, Germany, Australia, and other countries. Supporting research work has been funded by NSF [in projects IIS-9986089 (Fox 2000), IIS-0086227 (Fox et al., 2000), IIS-0080748 (Fox et al., 2001)], as well as DFG (in Germany) and CONACyT (in Mexico).

At the grass roots level, one line of support for NDLTD emerged from efforts at Virginia Tech, which has developed training materials and workflow management software that have been adapted by diverse groups. Many other projects and programs interested in ETDs have arisen around the world— some independently—but all are welcome to collaborate through the growing federation that is NDLTD. This is important since open sharing of methods helps others know how to address problems as well as ongoing changes in technology. The NDLTD steering committee has its spring meetings in conjunction with the ETD conferences.

These efforts should have a strong positive effect on expanding awareness at universities around the globe. One important agent promoting learning in this arena is the UNESCO International Guide for the Creation of ETDs (see < http://etdguide.org/ >). Available in a number of different languages, this book/web site should help students, faculty, and administrators participate in NDLTD. This should extend the considerable progress already made, as discussed in the next section.

NDLTD PROGRESS

NDLTD has experienced constant progress since its formation. We have registered growth in all major facets, including membership (with an increasing international participation), collection size, access, multimedia use, and worldwide availability.

Membership

Table 1 shows NDLTD membership as of August 2001. In less than 2 1/2 years, NDLTD more than doubled the number of registered members (from 59 members in May 1999). There are currently 120 members; 52 U.S. universities, 52 non-U.S. universities, and 16 institutions, regional centers and organizations (such as UNESCO). These various partners represent 23 countries: Australia, Brazil, Canada, China, Colombia, Germany, Greece, Hong Kong, India, Italy, Mexico, Netherlands, Norway, Russia, Singapore, South Africa, South Korea, Spain, Sudan, Sweden, Taiwan, the United States, and the United Kingdom. These numbers also emphasize the growth of global interest in NDLTD as international participation grew from less than one third in 1998 to half of the total membership in 2001. Also, by early 2002 at least 11 of the registered NDLTD members required mandatory submission of electronic theses and dissertations.

Collection Size

The number of ETDs across the NDLTD universities/institutions has grown at an even faster pace. From a few dozen at Virginia Tech in 1996, to 4328 ETDs at 21 institutions in March 2000, we accounted for a total of 7268 ETDs at 25 member institutions in July 2001. Table 2 shows a breakdown of the numbers of ETDs as of July 2001 organized by member institutions. These data largely the result of an on-line survey conducted by Gail McMillan and represents only those institutions that responded to the survey. These

TABLE 1 NDLTD Membership

U.S. universities	International universities	Institutions
Air University (Alabama)	Alicante University (Spain)	Cinemedia
Alicante University	Australian National University (Australia)	Coalition for Networked Information
Baylor University	Biblioteca de Catalunya (Spain)	Committee on Institutional Cooperation
Brigham Young University	Chinese University of Hong Kong (Hong Kong)	Consorci de Biblioteques Univers. Catalunya
California Institute of Technology	Chungnam National U., Dept of CS (S. Korea)	Diplomica.com
Clemson University	City University, London (UK)	Dissertationene Online
College of William and Mary	Curtin University of Technology (Australia)	Dissertation.com
Concordia University (Illinois)	Darmstadt University of Technology (Germany)	ETDweb
East Carolina University	Freie Universitat Berlin (Germany)	Ibero-American Sci. & Tech. Ed. Cons. (ISTEC)
East Tennessee State University[a]	Gerhard Mercator Universitat Duisburg (Germany)	National Documentation Centre (NDC, Greece)
Florida Institute of Technology	Griffith University (Australia)	National Library of Portugal
Florida International University	Gyeongsang National University, Chinju (Korea)	OhioLINK
Georgetown University	Humboldt-Universität zu Berlin (Germany)	OCLC
George Washington University	Indian Institute of Technology, Bombay (India)	Organization of American States (OAS)
Marshal University	Lund University (Sweden)	SOLINET
Massachusetts Institute of Technology	McGill University (Canada)	Sudanese National Electronic Library (Sudan)
Miami University of Ohio	National Sun Yat-Sen University (Taiwan)	UNESCO
Michigan Tech	Nanyang Technological University (Singapore)	
Mississippi State University		
Montana State University		
Naval Postgraduate School		
New Jersey Institute of Technology		
New Mexico Tech		
North Carolina State University[a]		

Northwestern University
Pennsylvania State University
Regis University
Rochester Institute of Technology
Texas A&M University
University of Colorado
University of Florida
University of Georgia
University of Hawaii at Manoa
University of Iowa
University of Kentucky
University of Maine[a]
University of North Texas[a]
University of Oklahoma
University of Pittsburgh
University of Rochester
University of South Florida
University of Tennessee, Knoxville
University of Tennessee, Memphis
University of Texas at Austin[a]
University of Utrecht
University of Virginia
University of West Florida
University of Wisconsin, Madison
Vanderbilt University

National University of Singapore (Singapore)
Rand Afrikaans University (South Africa)
Rhodes University (South Africa)[a]
Shanghai Jiao Tong University (China)
St. Petersburg State Technical U. (Russia)
State University of Campinas (Brazil)
Sudanese National Electronic Library (Sudan)
Universidad de las Amèricas Puebla (Mexico)
Universitat Autonoma de Barcelona (Spain)[a]
Universitat d'Alacant (Spain)
Universitat de Barcelona (Spain)
Universitat de Girona (Spain)
Universitat de Lleida (Spain)
Universitat Oberta de Catalunya (Spain)
Universitat Politecnica de Catalunya (Spain)
Universitat Politecnica de Valencia (Spain)
Universitat Pompeu Fabra (Spain)
Universitat Rovira i Virgili (Spain)
Universitè Laval (Quèbec, Canada)
University of Bergen (Norway)

TABLE 1 Continued

U.S. universities	International universities	Institutions
Virginia Commonwealth University	University of Antioquia (Medellin, Colombia)	
Virginia Tech[a]	University of British Columbia (Canada)	
West Virginia University[a]	University of Guelph (Ontario, Canada)	
Western Michigan University	University of Hong Kong[a]	
Worcester Polytechnic Institute	University of Melbourne (Australia)	
	University of Mysore (India)	
	University of New South Wales (Australia)	
	University of Pisa (Italy)	
	University of Queensland (Australia)	
	University of Sao Paulo (Brazil)	
	University of Sydney (Australia)	
	University of Utrecht (Netherlands)	
	University of Waterloo (Canada)	
	Uppsala University (Sweden)	
	Wilfrid Laurier University (Canada)	

[a] Electronic submission mandatory.

TABLE 2   NDLTD Collection Size

University/Institution	ETD collection size
ADT: Australian Digital Thesis Program (Australia)	238
University of Bergen (Norway)	45
California Institute of Technology	2
Consorci de Biblioteques Universitaries de Catalunya (Spain)	151
East Tennessee State University	106
Humboldt-University (Germany)	430
Louisiana State University	3
Mississippi State University	33
MIT	62
North Carolina State University	301
Pennsylvania State University	83
Pontifical Catholic University (PUC) (Brazil)	90
Gerhard Mercator Universität Duisburg (Germany)	126
Universitat Politecnica de Valencia (Spain)	189
University of Florida	174
University of Georgia	121
University of Iowa	6
University of Kentucky	19
University of Maine	27
University of North Texas	337
University of South Florida	25
University of Tennessee	12
University of Tennessee, Knoxville	28
Uppsala University (Sweden)	178
Virginia Tech	3393
West Virginia University	1006
Worcester Polytechnic Institute	83
Total	7268

statistics do not take into account scanned theses and dissertations, which make up a substantial portion of the total NDLTD collection. There are 26 scanned documents at the New Jersey Institute of Technology, 150 at the University of South Florida, 5581 at MIT, and 12,000 at the National Documentation Center in Greece. These result in a total of 17,763 scanned theses and dissertations at these institutions and quite conceivably thousands of unreported ones at other institutions.

Access Statistics

To demonstrate the potential of NDLTD for global access and sharing of the knowledge produced by universities worldwide, we have periodically analyzed the access logs of the Virginia Tech ETD (VT-ETD) collections. The results for the period 1997–2000 are shown in Table 3. We can see that the number of accesses tends to increase each year. As the collection grows and gains popularity, the number of accesses will most likely continue to increase.

More specifically, Table 4 indicates that each of the seven countries with the most accesses has an increasing number of accesses each year (with the exception of Germany in the 97/98–98/99 period). The United Kingdom, and surprisingly Malaysia, dominated accesses from outside the United States. The other accessing countries are all European, a fact that is probably related to advances in network infrastructure in those countries.

Multimedia Use in ETDs

One of the main objectives of NDLTD is to promote student creativity through the use of diverse types of multimedia content in ETDs, while making

TABLE 3 Access Log Statistics from the VT-ETD Collection

	1997/98	1998/99	Increase 1997/98–1998/99 (%)	1999/2000	Increase 1998/99–1999/2000 (%)
Requests for PDF files (mostly full ETDs)	221,679	481,038	117.0	578,152	20.2
Requests for HTML files (mostly tables of contents and abstracts)	165,710	215,539	30.1	260,699	21.0
Requests for multimedia	1,714	4,468	160.7	12,633	182.7
Distinct files requested	6,419	21,451	234.2	10,409	−23.5
Distinct hosts served	29,816	57,901	94.2	87,804	51.6
Average data transferred daily	156,089 KMbB	219,132 KMbB	40.4	382 MbMB	74.4
Data transferred	55,637 GB	78,107 GB	40.4	137 GbGB	75.6

TABLE 4 Access by Non-U.S. Sites

International domain	1997/98	1997/98 rank	1998/99	1998/99 rank	Increase 1997/98–1998/99(%)	1999/2000	1999/2000 rank	Increase 1998/99–1999/2000(%)
United Kingdom	6,735	1	11,347	1	68.5	25,583	1	125.5
Malaysia	876	16	4,190	6	378.3	16,147	2	285.4
France	2,138	7	4,797	5	124.4	14,960	3	211.9
Germany	6,727	2	3,374	9	−49.8	14,384	4	326.3
Canada	3,413	4	9,632	3	182.2	13,543	5	40.6
Spain	590	18	3,647	8	518.1	9,918	6	171.9
Italy	1,430	12	3,095	10	116.4	9,300	7	200.5

TABLE 5   Multimedia Use in VT-ETD Collection

File type	Examples	Count
Still image	BMP, DXF, GIF, JPG, TIFF	328
Video	AVI, MOV, MPG, QT	58
Audio	AIFF, WAV	18
Text	PDF, HTML, TXT, DOC, XLS	7601
Other	Macromedia, SGML, XML	51

students comfortable with the use of this technology to exploit richer modes of self-expression. Table 5 indicates how much of this objective has been achieved in the VT-ETD collection, with a breakdown of the 8056 multimedia files contained in a selection of 2180 available ETDs. This illustrates both that authors are beginning to shift towards nontextual media and that some are moving away from the early single-file paradigm of digitization.

Worldwide Release

In terms of copyright, a significant issue is whether to allow the electronic document to be viewed worldwide, on campus only, or not at all. The "mixed" case, which is a unique capability of electronic documents, occurs when some portions (e.g., particular chapters or multimedia files) have restricted access while others are more widely available. The majority of Virginia Tech students allow their documents to be viewable worldwide (see Fig. 1), but some initially choose not to grant worldwide access in order to protect their publication rights. To address this concern, there are ongoing discussions with publishers to help them understand the goals and benefits of

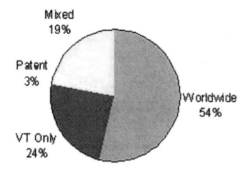

FIGURE 1   Student and committee choice for ETD availability from Virginia Tech (2668 ETDs as of July 17, 2000).

NDLTD (NDLTD, 1999). We are pleased to see a change in attitude by some publishers over the course of the project. The American Chemical Society developed a policy more favorable to NDLTD as a result of lengthy discussions, and the American Physics Society has been receptive to issues concerning the Open Archives Initiative and NDLTD.

STANDARDS ACTIVITY

In order to support many of the current and future research and service-related activities, work has begun to define standards that will enable more consistent exchange of information in an interoperable environment. Among the first of these projects is ETDMS, the Electronic Thesis and Dissertation Metadata Standard, and a related project for name authority control.

Electronic Thesis and Dissertation Metadata Standard

ETDMS was developed in conjunction with the NDLTD and has been refined over the course of the last year. The initial goal was to develop a single standard XML DTD for encoding the full text of an ETD. Among other things, an ETD encoded in XML could include rich metadata about the author and work that could easily be extracted for use in union databases and the like. During initial discussions it became clear that the methods used by different institutions to prepare and deal with theses and dissertations would make it all but impossible to agree on a single DTD for encoding the full text of an ETD. Many institutions were unwilling or unprepared to use XML to encode ETDs at all. Thus, instead of an XML DTD for encoding the full text of an ETD, ETDMS emerged as a flexible set of guidelines for encoding and sharing very basic metadata regarding ETDs among institutions. Separate work continues in parallel on a suite of DTDs or schemas, building on a common framework, for full ETDs.

ETDMS is based on the Dublin Core Element Set (DCMI, 1999), but includes an additional element specific to metadata regarding theses and dissertations. Despite its name, ETDMS is designed to deal with metadata associated with both paper and electronic theses and dissertations. It also is designed to handle metadata in many languages, including metadata regarding a single work that has been recorded in different languages. The ETDMS standard (Atkins et al., 2001) provides detailed guidelines on mapping information about an ETD to metadata elements.

ETDMS already is supported as an output format for the Open Archives interface to the Virginia Tech ETD collection. ETDMS will be accepted as an input format for the union catalog currently being developed in conjunction with VTLS (VTLS, 2001b). NDLTD strongly encourages use of ETDMS.

Authority Linking

Each reference to an individual or institution in an ETDMS field should contain a string representing the name of the individual or institution as it appears in the work. In addition, these references also may contain a URI that points to an authoritative record for that individual or institution. Associating authority control with NDLTD seems particularly appropriate since universities know a great deal about those to whom they award degrees and since a thesis or dissertation often is the first significant publication of a student.

The "NDLTD: Authority Linking Proposal" (Young, 2001) identifies several goals for a Linked Authority File (LAF) system to support this requirement:

> LAF records should be freely created and shared among participants. While a central authority database is an option, the LAF design expects the database to be distributed to share cost. Individual participants or groups should be able to host a copy of the LAF database and share changes they make to local copies of LAF records with other hosts using the Open Archives Initiative (OAI) protocol (Lagoze and Van de Sompel, 2001). The mechanism for keeping records in sync is described in the proposal.

> The URIs should be meaningful and useful to anyone outside NDLTD's domain. A benefit of using the OAI protocol is that individual LAF records will be accessible via an OAI GetRecord request (see below).

> The URIs should be persistent and current. This raises a number of challenges, such as duplicate resolution. By using PURLs (OCLC, 2001b) in ETDMS records, the underlying OAI GetRecord URLs can be rearranged without affecting the ETDMS records that rely on them.

> The model should be scalable and applicable beyond NDLTD. The LAF model was designed to work entirely with open standards and open-source software.

The LAF design has other advantages over alternatives such as the Library of Congress Name Authority Database (Library of Congress, 2001). Only the level of participation among decentralized participants limits the coverage of the collection. Because the records are based on XML, the content of LAF records can be as broad or narrow as needed. Finally, because they are distributed using the OAI protocol, multiple metadata formats can be supported.

FUTURE OF NDLTD

The statistics presented illustrate that the production and archiving of electronic theses and dissertations is fast becoming an accepted part of the normal operation of universities in the new electronic age. NDLTD is dedicated to supporting this trend with tools, standards, and services that empower individual institutions to set up and maintain their own collections of ETDs. At the same time, NDLTD promotes the use of these ETDs through institutional websites as well as portal-type websites that aggregate the individual sites and create seamless views of the NDLTD collection. Ongoing research and service-provision projects are addressing the problems of how to merge together the currently distributed and somewhat isolated collections hosted at each member institution.

THE UNION CATALOG PROJECT

Simply by virtue of being called the "Networked" Digital Library of Theses and Dissertations, NDLTD immediately conjures up images of an interconnected system of digital archives. With this aim in mind, many recent efforts have attempted to supplement increasing membership with more advanced services, such as searching and browsing that span multiple collections of ETDs. At Virginia Tech, the first of such projects was the Federated Search system (Powell and Fox, 1998). This system distributes a query to multiple sites and then gathers the result pages into a cache for browsing. The results are not merged largely due to the complexity of merging search results without knowledge of the underlying ranking algorithms. The system also suffers from high network latency and uncertain availability of servers. An alternative solution is typified by the OCLC WorldCat project (OLCL, 2001a), which that collects bibliographic data from libraries all over the world into the OCLC Online Union Catalog. Libraries may then acquire extracts from this catalog corresponding to theses and dissertations. This solution has the advantage of a single database upon which many services may be based but requires subscription to OCLC's services and obscures the differences between ETDs and their traditional paper counterparts. In response to this need for a focused and accessible catalog with a low barrier to participation, NDLTD has adopted a solution that uses the Open Archives Initiative's Metadata Harvesting Protocol (Lagoze and Van de Sompel, 2001) to gather metadata in the ETDMS format and then to make it accessible at a central portal. This central portal is maintained by VTLS, using their Virtua system (VTLS, 2001a) to provide a web interface to the ETD Union Catalog.

THE VIRTUA NDLTD PORTAL

VTLS Inc. (VTLS, 2001b) is an established developer of software to manage library collections, both digital and nondigital. Virtua ILS, their flagship product, is an integrated library automation system specifically designed to cater to the differing needs of librarians in different contexts. Virtua is especially suited to the needs of NDLTD because it is inherently a distributed system and adheres to emerging standards for encoding of metadata. All metadata are stored in Unicode, and this makes it much easier to deal with the non-ASCII character sets used by a growing number of NDLTD member sites in non–English-speaking countries. This extends Virtua's search capabilities to every language that can be represented in Unicode, thus providing users with multilingual search and retrieval services.

An instance of Virtua has been developed by VTLS to serve as the central portal for the NDLTD Union Catalog (see Fig. 2). This portal provides users with a simple and intuitive interface to search and browse through the merged collection of theses and dissertations. After potentially relevant items are discovered, a user can follow the links provided to go directly to the items in their source archives.

Part of Virtua's appeal is the high degree of customization of its Chameleon Web Gateway, appropriately named for its ability to superimpose multiple "skins" on a user portal for different communities. Besides being thus tailored to the typical information-seeking behavior of researchers, the interface also has multilingual capabilities. There are currently versions of the user interface in English, Korean, and Spanish, with planned support for all languages used by NDLTD members. The coupling of multilingual information retrieval with multilingual interfaces has the desirable effect of providing a complete and consistent digital library for users who speak languages other than English.

Virtua supports multiple modes of data entry, converting all input data into the standard USMARC format that is familiar to many librarians and archivists. Some of the data currently loaded into Virtua was acquired in batches from source archives in different countries (including Greece, Korea, Portugal, and the United States) to ensure demonstrable multilingual support at the initial launch of the portal. In parallel with the development of this portal, mechanisms have been put into place to support fully automated importing of metadata using protocols such as that developed by the Open Archives Initiative (OAI).

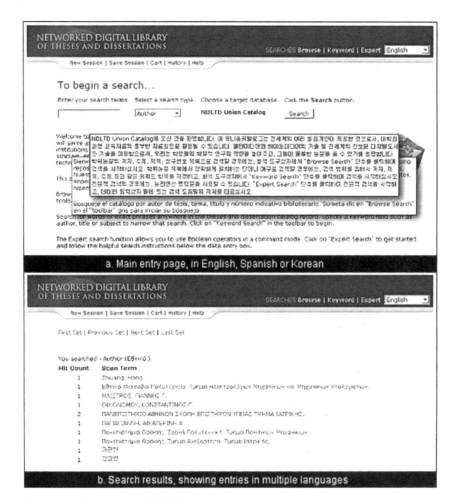

a. Main entry page, in English, Spanish or Korean

b. Search results, showing entries in multiple languages

FIGURE 2   Virtua-based NDLTD portal.

OPEN ARCHIVES AS AN INTEROPERABILITY FRAMEWORK

In order to gather metadata into the central Union Catalog, NDLTD has adopted the OAI interoperability framework. This includes using the protocol for metadata harvesting as well as defining a metadata format targeted at the community of ETD archives.

The OAI protocol is a request-response protocol layered over HTTP that allows one computer to collect metadata incrementally over time from another computer—commonly known as harvesting. The requests have a minimal number of parameters and correspond to HTTP GET or POST operations.

The responses are XML documents, whose structures are defined precisely using the XML Schema Description (Fallside, 2001) language, with protocol tags designed to support the operation of the protocol and container tags that encapsulate individual record or archive-level metadata. Multiple metadata formats can be supported for each item in an archive's collection, with Dublin Core (DC) (DCMI, 1999) being mandatory. For NDLTD, ETDMS is recommended as a community standard. The HTTP request and XML response shown in Figure 3 are a typical use of the protocol to retrieve the "oai_etdms" metadata corresponding to a single record identified by "oai:VTETD:etd-520112859651791."

Since the OAI protocol is simple and flexible, there is much leeway in designing distributed systems like the NDLTD Union Catalog. In exploiting this ability, the Union Catalog uses a two-tier approach to separate the

Request

```
http://scholar.lib.vt.edu/theses/OAI/cgi-bin/index.pl?
verb=GetRecord&metadataPrefix=oai_etdms&identifier=oai:VTETD:etd-5201128.59651791
```

Response

```
<?xml version="1.0" encoding="UTF-8" ?>
- <GetRecord xmlns="http://www.openarchives.org/OAI/1.1/OAI_GetRecord"
    xmlns:xsi="http://www.w3.org/2001/XMLSchema-instance"
    xsi:schemaLocation="http://www.openarchives.org/OAI/1.1/OAI_GetRecord
    http://www.openarchives.org/OAI/1.1/OAI_GetRecord.xsd">
    <responseDate>2001-08-18T18:03:28-05:00</responseDate>
    <requestURL>http://scholar.lib.vt.edu:80/theses/OAI/cgi-bin/index.pl?
      verb=GetRecord&metadataPrefix=oai_etdms&identifier=oai:VTETD:etd-
      520112859651791</requestURL>
  - <record>
    - <header>
        <identifier>oai:VTETD:etd-520112859651791</identifier>
        <datestamp>1996-06-05</datestamp>
      </header>
    - <metadata>
      - <thesis xmlns="http://www.ndltd.org/standards/metadata/etdms/1.0/"
          xsi:schemaLocation="http://www.ndltd.org/standards/metadata/etdms/1.0/
          http://www.ndltd.org/standards/metadata/etdms/1.0/etdms.xsd">
          <title>Analysis of Tow-Placed, Variable-Stiffness Laminates</title>
          <creator>Waldhart, Chris</creator>
          <subject>variable-stiffness laminates</subject>
          <subject>curvilinear fibers</subject>
          <subject>tow placement machine</subject>
          <subject>buckling</subject>
          <description>It is possible to create laminae that have spatially varying fiber
          orientation with a tow placement machine. A laminate which is composed of
          such plies will have stiffness properties which vary as a function of position.
          Previous work had modelled such variable-stiffness laminae by taking a
```

FIGURE 3   HTTP request and XML response for GetRecord.

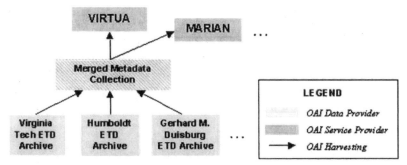

FIGURE 4 Architecture of OAI-based union collection.

merging of collections from the provision of high-level user services through the Virtua interface. This is illustrated in Figure 4.

Each of the participating member archives exports data using the OAI protocol. These data are then harvested from each site into a central merged collection and republished as a single collection through an open archives interface. The Virtua system in turn harvests data from this merged collection to provide higher-level user services. This separation between merging of collections and provision of services has the advantage that the merged collection can act as a local cache for use by production services like Virtua as well as research projects like MARIAN (Gonçalves et al., 2000). Such a local cache reduces the network load on ETD archives and also simplifies the problem of data management for service providers like Virtua. In addition, this tiered architecture supports more natural integration and serves as a proof-of-concept for NDLTD members who are inherently federations rather than single institutions, e.g., OhioLINK.

CURRENT NDLTD RESEARCH EFFORTS

NDLTD has a strong commitment to advance the state of the art in electronic publishing and digital library technologies and services, in connection with its core activities supporting graduate education and sharing of knowledge. Much of the current research into providing global services for NDLTD is taking place in the context of the MARIAN digital library system (Gonçalves et al., 2000, 2001), developed at the Virginia Tech Digital Library Research Laboratory, and its interoperability with a number of other digital library systems. MARIAN supports flexible and extensible search over networks of digital information objects, which may include documents, metadata records, or digital surrogates for people and organizations. Digital information objects and connecting links are organized into object-oriented classes, each supporting indexing, retrieval, and presentation methods. New classes of information objects can be added to a MARIAN digital library by producing new or modified code implementing these functions for the new class manager.

SEMANTIC INTEROPERABILITY

Adoption of the OAI framework as a primary harvesting mechanism for ETD metadata can help overcome interoperability problems at the system, syntactic, and structural levels (Ouksel and Sheth, 1999). However, several ETD members use underlying technologies like Z39.50 (Lynch, 1997), which are difficult to adapt for conformance to the OAI standards. Moreover, the OAI framework itself opens up the possibility of a single community utilizing several heterogeneous metadata standards. While the adoption of ETDMS as an official NDLTD standard is encouraged, with the hope that someday all NDLTD members will use it, it is realistic to assume that it will take considerable time and effort to achieve widespread adoption. Therefore, in the interim, semantic heterogeneity is a problem that has to be dealt with.

Semantic heterogeneity is solved in NDLTD by exploiting two MAR-IAN mechanisms: (1) semantically "tuned" but functionally equivalent searchers, and (2) a collection view ontology. Nodes in the MARIAN information network can be simple atomic or scalar objects, as in the semi-structured model (Abiteboul et al., 2000), but they can also be complex information objects. Information objects support methods proper to their classes, and all information objects in MARIAN support the method of approximate match to a query. For instance, MARIAN treats title text as a special sort of natural language sequence, with various rules for capitalization, punctuation, and sentence formation, but treats names of persons as sequences of atomic strings. Matching methods vary from class to class, but all have the same functional profile: given an object description of the appropriate type, they calculate how closely they match the description and return that value as a weight. Class managers draw on these methods to provide class-level search functions that, given an object description, return a weighted set of objects in the class that matches the description. MARIAN already has a library of matching functions and searchers for a number of common information object classes, a sample of which are shown in Figure 5.

Thus, the first step in bringing a new document collection into semantic interoperability is to choose appropriate matching functions and searchers for the different objects in the collection. Since class managers and searchers are object-oriented, specialized versions often can be created easily through inheritance. For truly different information objects, new matching functions sometimes need to be defined, but even in this case stock searcher algorithms often can be reused. All that is necessary is to provide methods that follow the

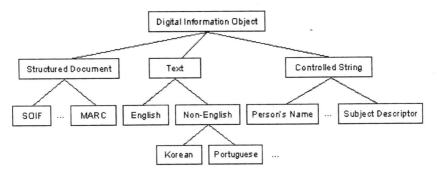

FIGURE 5   Part of the hierarchy of classes used in MARIAN.

API of generating a weight from an object description and, thence, a weighted set of objects.

We have mapped the ETDMS standard into a MARIAN information network model, thus providing a stable common view of the union collection to the outside world. A subset of the ETDMS model is presented in Figure 6; to keep things simple we show only the attributes title, creator, subject, and

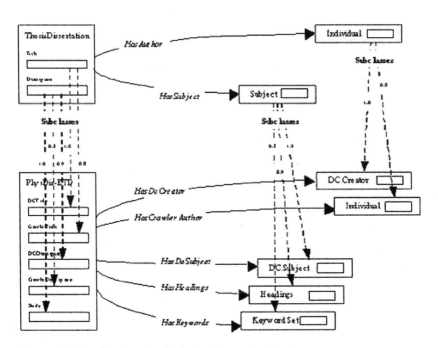

FIGURE 6   A collection view is derived from the PhysDis data to increase retrieval and usability.

description. The model consists of three classes of objects—ThesisDissertation, Individual, and Subject—together with HasAuthor and HasSubject links. The Individual class subsumes both persons and corporate individuals, while the Subject class covers diverse treatments. Mappings between this model and the underlying structures can be modified seamlessly.

In the particular case of the German PhysDis collection (Severiens et al., 2000), whose treatment is shown in Figure 6, all mappings make use of the weighted superclass construction. This construction asserts that all members of some specific class are also members of some ETDMS class, but that the extent to which they count as class members is different for different subclasses. In the case of PhysDis subject descriptions, subclass relationships are weighted to reflect the authority of the description. Weights also can be used to address data quality issues. These uses interact; while the simple construct of synthetic superclasses with weighted subclasses cannot handle every situation, we have found it strikingly effective.

MULTILINGUAL AND CROSS-LINGUAL SEARCHING

Supporting a global community means supporting multiple languages. This leads to two research topics: (1) supporting documents and queries in several natural languages simultaneously (multilingual retrieval) and (2) making it possible for queries in one language to retrieve related documents in other languages (cross-lingual retrieval) (Oard, 1997). In the MARIAN NDLTD union collection, both topics are being investigated in the context of the MARIAN class hierarchy.

Any document (part) made up of natural language can be considered to be an object of the class Text. The MARIAN Text class manager is responsible for all types of text; individual texts are stored by the manager for one or another subclass. These include class managers for text in different natural languages (including English, Spanish, German, and Korean) as well as managers for sublanguages and for personal names, which are presumed to have no linguistic structure. Each natural language class manager can recognize words in the language, generally removing inflectional and morphological affixes. Treatment of sentence structure and layout conventions may also vary among different languages. Text class managers generate indexing structures from the stream of terms discovered in text. They also make use of weight-valued matching functions to calculate how well any given text matches a free-text query.

Most ETDs are made up of (structures of) text in a particular language. During document analysis, component pieces of text are extracted from the ETD or its metadata and passed to the appropriate class manager in the union collection. Structural information describing the place and function of the text component in the document is also stored in the form of patterns of links.

These two sorts of information are used together during retrieval to calculate the overall similarity of a document to a structured query. If the language of a query component is known, it can be relayed to the class manager for that language. On the other hand, in the common case where the language of the query is not known, query components are sent to the Text (super)class manager, which broadcasts the query to all its subclasses. Matches in any language are then returned to the superclass, where they are ranked by closeness to the query, and the combined set becomes the result set for the query component.

Cross-lingual retrieval works within the same class hierarchy. Cross-lingual queries are sent to the Text class manager, which again queries its various subclasses. In this case, however, the Text class manager first translates the query into each subclass language before it passes it on. Thus the (sub)sets returned and combined are composed of matches to the concepts in the query rather than the strings. Current research on translation is based on the work of Akira Maeda and the NAIST Multilingual group (Maeda et al., 1998), using co-occurrence statistics to scale and combine different translations.

OTHER RESEARCH EFFORTS

The NDLTD community has explored several other research trends. Experimental software has been developed to add annotation capabilities to ETDs; this service was selected as the most important to add, based on focus groups, to determine the most popular use scenarios (Miller, 1999). There also is experimental software extending the SIFT package (Yan and Garcia-Molina, 1999) from Stanford University and a prototype in the MARIAN system, to provide filtering and routing services based on stored user profiles, for those who wish to be notified whenever an interesting ETD arrives. As time goes on, our work in interoperability with other digital library software like Greenstone (Witten et al., 2001), Phronesis (Garza-Salazar, 2001), and Emerge (Futrelle et al., 2001) may allow us to support other universities that choose to use those packages to provide access services for their local ETDs. Another major research trend of NDLTD deals with user interfaces and information visualization. There are multiple graphical user interfaces that relate to our various software components, including the ENVISION interface (Heath et al., 1995). In addition, ongoing experimentation is investigating how the library metaphor can be extended to virtual reality environments, specifically the CAVE (CAVE Automatic Virtual Environment) (Das Neves and Fox, 2000).

REFERENCES

Abiteboul, S., Buneman, P., Suciu, D. (2000). *Data on the Web—From Relations to Semistructured Data and XML.* San Francisco, CA: Morgan Kaufmann Publishers.

Atkins, A., Fox, E. A., France, R., Suleman, H. eds. (2001). *ETD-ms: An Interoperability Metadata Standard for Electronic Theses and Dissertations—version 1.00.* Available from ⟨http://www.ndltd.org/standards/metadata/ETD-ms-v1.00.html⟩.

Das Neves, F. A., Fox, E. A. (2000). A study of user behavior in an immersive virtual environment for digital libraries. In: Proceedings of the ACM Digital Libraries Conference. San Antonio, TX, pp. 103–111.

DCMI. (1999). Dublin Core Metadata Element Set, Version 1.1: Reference Description. Available from ⟨http://www.dublincore.org/documents/dces/⟩.

Fallside, D. (2001). XML Schema Parts 0,1 and 2. Available from ⟨http://www.w3.org/XML/Schema#dev⟩.

Fox, E. A. (2000). Core Research for the Networked University Digital Library (NUDL), NSF IIS-9986089 (SGER), 5/15/2000–3/1/2002. Project director, E. Fox.

Fox, E. A., Eaton, J. L., McMillan, G., Kipp, N. A., Weiss, L., Arce, E., Guyer, S. (1996). National Digital Library of Theses and Dissertations: A Scalable and Sustainable Approach to Unlock University Resources. D-Lib Magazine. September 1996. Available at ⟨http://www.dlib.org/dlib/september96/theses/09fox.html⟩.

Fox, E. A., DeVane, B., Eaton, J. L., Kipp, N. A., Mather, P., McGonigle, T., McMillan, G., Schweiker, W. (1997). Networked Digital Library of Theses and Dissertations: An International Effort Unlocking University Resources, D-Lib Magazine, September 1997. Available at ⟨http://www.dlib.org/dlib/september97/theses/09fox.html⟩.

Fox, E. A., Zia, R., Hilf, E. (2000). Open Archives: Distributed services for physicists and graduate students (OAD), NSF IIS-0086227, 9/1/2000–8/31/2003. Project director, E. Fox (with Royce Zia, Physics, VT, and E. Hilf, U. Oldenburg, PI on matching German DFG project).

Fox, E. A., Sánchez, J. A., Garza-Salazar, D. (2001). High Performance Interoperable Digital Libraries in the Open Archives Initiative, NSF IIS-0080748, 3/1/2001–2/28/2003. Project director, E. Fox (with co-PIs J. Alfredo Snchez, Universidad de las Amricas-Puebla—UDLA, and David Garza-Salazar, Monterrey Technology Institute—ITESM, both funded by CONACyT in Mexico).

Futrelle, J., Chen, S., Chang, K. C. (June 24–28, 2001). NBDL: A CIS Framework for NSDL. In: Proceedings of the First ACM/IEEE-CS Joint Conference on Digital Libraries (JCDL '2001). Roanoke, Virginia, pp. 124–125.

Garza-Salazar, D. A. (2001). Phronesis. Available from ⟨http://copernico.mty.itesm.mx/~tempo/Proyectos/⟩.

Gonçalves, M. A., France, R. K., Fox, E. A., Doszkocs, T. E. (2000). MARIAN Searching and Querying of Heterogeneous Federated Digital Libraries. In: Proceedings of First DELOS workshop on Information Seeking, Searching and Querying in Digital Libraries. Zurich, Switzerland, December 11–12, 2000. ⟨http://www.ercim.org/publication/ws-proceedings/DelNoe01/11_Fox.pdf⟩.

Gonçalves M. A., France, R. K., Fox, E. A. (September 4–9, 2001). MARIAN: Flexible Interoperability for Federated Digital Libraries. In: Proceedings of the Fifth European Conference on Research and Advanced Technology for Digital Libraries (ECDL2001). Darmstadt, Germany, pp. 173–186.

Heath, L. S., Hix, D., Nowell, L. T., Wake, W. C., Averboch, G. A., Labow, E., Guyer, S. A., Brueni, D. J., France, R. K., Dalal, K., Fox, E. A. (1995). Envision: A User-Centered Database of Computer Science Literature. *Communications of the ACM* 38(4):52–53.

Kipp, N., Fox, E. A., McMillan, G., Eaton, J. L. (1999). FIPSE Final Report, 11/30/99. Available from ⟨http://www.ndltd.org/pubs/FIPSEfr.pdf⟩ (PDF version) and ⟨http://www.ndltd.org/pubs/FIPSEfr.doc⟩ (MS-Word version).

Lagoze, C., Van de Sompel, H. (January 2001). The Open Archives Initiative Protocol for Metadata Harvesting. Open Archives Initiative. Available from ⟨http://www.openarchives.org/OAI/openarchivesprotocol.html⟩.

Library of Congress. (2001). Program for Cooperative Cataloguing Name Authority Component Home Page. Available from ⟨http://www.loc.gov/catdir/pcc/naco.html⟩.

Lynch, C. (1997). The Z39.50 Information Retrieval Standard—Part I: A Strategic View of Its Past, Present and Future. *D-Lib Magazine*, April 1997. Available at ⟨http://www.dlib.org/dlib/april97/04lynch.html⟩.

Maeda, A., Dartois, M., Fujita, T., Sakaguchi, T., Sugimoto, S., Tabata, K. (April 1998). Viewing Multilingual Documents on Your Local Web browser. *Communications of the ACM* 41(4):64–65.

Miller, T. (1999). Annotation System for a Collection of ETDs. Available from ⟨http://www.ndltd.org/ndltd-sc/990416/annsystem.pdf⟩.

NDLTD. (1999). Publishers and the NDLTD. NDLTD, July 1999. Available from ⟨http://www.ndltd.org/publshrs/⟩.

Oard, D. W. (1997). Serving Users in Many Languages: Cross-Language Information Retrieval for Digital Libraries. *D-Lib Magazine*, December 1997. Available at ⟨http://www.dlib.org/dlib/december97/oard/12oard.html⟩.

OCLC. (2001a). WorldCat. Available from ⟨http://www.oclc.org/oclc/menu/colpro.htm⟩.

OCLC. (2001b). Persistent URL Home Page. Dublin, OH: OCLC Online Computer Library Center. Available from ⟨http://purl.oclc.org/⟩.

Ouksel, A. M., Sheth, A. P. (1999). Semantic Interoperability in Global Information Systems: A Brief Introduction to the Research Area. *SIGMOD Record* 28(1):5–12.

Powell, J., Fox, E. A. (1998). Multilingual Federated Searching Across Heterogeneous Collections. *D-Lib Magazine*, September 1998. Available at ⟨http://www.dlib.org/dlib/september98/powell/09powell.html⟩.

Severiens, T., Hohlfeld, M., Zimmermann, K., Hilf, E. R. (December, 2000). Phys-Doc—A distributed network of physics institutions documents: collecting, indexing, and searching high quality documents by using harvest. *D-Lib Magazine* 6(12). Available from ⟨http://www.dlib.org/dlib/december00/severiens/12severiens.html⟩.

VTLS. (2001a). Virtua ILS. Available from ⟨http://www.vtls.com/products/virtua/⟩.

VTLS. (2001b). VTLS Home Page. Available from ⟨http://www.vtls.com/⟩.

Witten, I. H., Boddie, S. J., Bainbridge, D., McNab, R. J. (2000). Greenstone: a comprehensive open-source digital library software system. In: Proceedings of the Fifth ACM Digital Libraries Conference, pp. 113–121.

Yan, T. W., Garcia-Molina, H. (1999). The SIFT Information Dissemination System. *ACM Transactions on Database Systems* 24(4):529–565

Young, J. A. (2001). NDLTD: Authority Linking Proposal. Dublin, OH: OCLC Online Computer Library Center. Available from ⟨http://alcme.oclc.org/ndltd/AuthLink.html⟩.

6

NDLTD Union Catalog Project

Hussein Suleman*

Virginia Polytechnic Institute and State University
Blacksburg, Virginia

DESCRIPTION

NDLTD is comprised of many individual member institutions and consortia, each of which has a process in place for archiving and distributing ETDs. The Union Catalog Project is an attempt to make these individual collections appear as one seamless digital library of ETDs to students and researchers seeking out theses and dissertations.

While ETDs are owned and maintained by the institutions at which they were produced or archived, it is possible to give searchers the appearance of a single collection by gathering all the metadata (title, author, etc.) into a central search engine. Then, when a potentially relevant document is found, the user will be redirected to the institution that contains the actual document.

This approach of making metadata available to aid in discovery of resources is supported by the Open Archives Initiative (OAI—http://www. openarchives.org), which has developed a protocol for exchanging such metadata. Using the OAI's Protocol for Metadata Harvesting (http://www.

Current affiliation: University of Capetown, Capetown, South Africa.

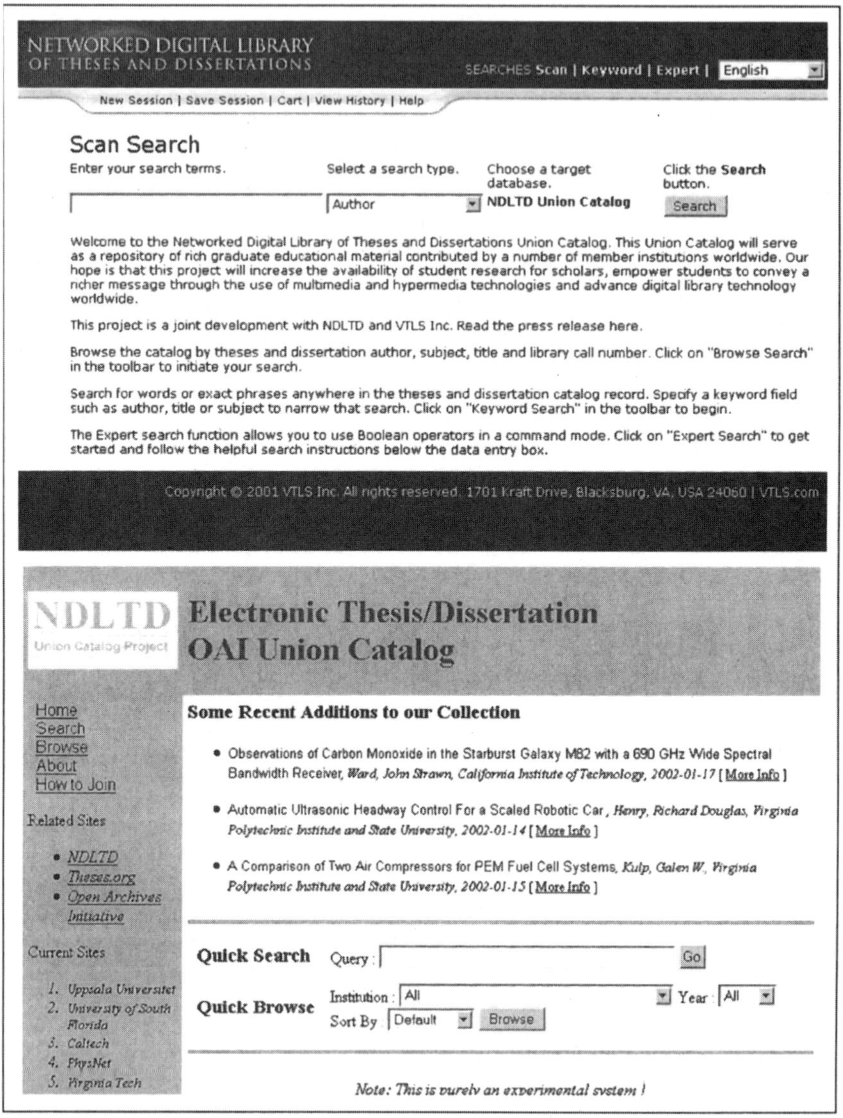

FIGURE 1   Union Catalog user interfaces (top: VTLS, bottom: OAI-based).

openarchives.org/OAI/openarchivesprotocol.html), individual sites can make their metadata accessible to providers of search and discovery services, while still maintaining complete control over the resources.

While membership in NDLTD does not require making metadata publicly available, it is highly recommended. NDLTD is currently developing global resource discovery services to promote the visibility of ETDs at individual member sites. Figure 1 shows the interfaces to two existing resource discovery systems based on the Union Archive: the NDLTD Union Catalog, operated by VTLS at http://www.vtls.com/ndltd, and the experimental OAI-based Union Catalog at http://purl.org/net/etdunion. The easiest and recommended way to contribute to these and future endeavors is by supporting the OAI protocol at individual institutions!

HOW TO MAKE A COLLECTION ACCESSIBLE

1. The individual in charge of a local ETD collection needs to decide to publicly export the metadata and settle on a set of rights and conditions under which this can be done. For most institutions this is usually a statement of the form "Metadata may be used for noncommercial purposes only" or "Metadata may be used for commercial and noncommercial purposes." (This statement is added onto all exported metadata.)

2. A technical person (programmer) needs to build support for the OAI Protocol for Metadata Harvesting http://www.openarchives.org/OAI/ openarchivesprotocol.html) into the archive. This protocol is a web-based service that can be implemented using CGI scripts, Java servlets, PHP scripts, ActiveX controls, or any other web server back-end processing mechanism. The following list recommends steps to follow to achieve OAI-compliance for various technologies upon which ETD collections could be based:

> *ETD-db software from Virginia Tech* (http://scholar.lib.vt.edu/ETD-db/ developer/). All recent versions have built-in OAI support. For those using an older version of ETD-db, there is a drop-in package available to easily add on OAI support for all versions of the software from v1.0 to v1.7 (and possibly beyond). Instructions and downloadable files can be found at http://www.dlib.vt.edu/projects/OAI/ software/ndltd/ndltd.html.
>
> *EPrints software from University of Southampton* (http://www.eprints. org). All versions of the EPrints software contain support for the OAI protocol. Check the website and documentation for more information. Note that in order to support version 1.1 of the OAI protocol, at least version 1.1.2 of the EPrints software must be installed. (Older versions can be upgraded.)

Custom-built or other database-driven software. The OAI website (at http://www.openarchives.org) has tools in various programming languages that may be used as templates or starting points in implementing the OAI protocol. Many of these templates require only modifications to access a local database and format the data appropriately. Any custom solution will require reading through and understanding the OAI Protocol for Metadata Harvesting. The most common implementation issues that arise include how to provide unique identifiers for each record, how to access records by the last modification date, how to convert/map the existing metadata into Dublin Core as required by the OAI protocol, and whether to divide the records into sets and, if so, how. Further assistance can be sought from members of the OAI implementation mailing list. See the OAI website for details on how to join.

Website (one or more HTML pages). The OAI protocol is primarily devised to share metadata contained in databases, but it is possible to use data from files if those files have a standard format. As before, the tools on the OAI website are useful as a starting point for any implementation. Another option is to create a database or set of XML files corresponding to the ETD collection website and then use standard OAI software tools.

3.   Implement support for the ETD-MS metadata format (as described at http://www.ndltd.org/standards/metadata/). This is a metadata format that is specific to ETDs and allows for the exporting of fields specific to ETDs, which are not common in other metadata formats. (The ETD-db OAI extension already has this support built-in.)

4.   Test your OAI interface with the Repository Explorer at http://purl.org/net/oai_explorer.

5.   Register your OAI interface with the OAI (at http://www.open-archives.org/) and with the NDLTD Union Catalog Project (by emailing your OAI baseURL to etdunion@oai.dlib.vt.edu).

6.   After your OAI interface is confirmed to be operational, your metadata will be harvested on a periodic basis into the OAI-based Union Archive, which provides a central merged metadata archive for service providers such as the NDLTD Union Catalog (at http://www.vtls.com/ndltd). *Note*: Since harvesting occurs on a periodic basis (usually daily), changes will not show up immediately.

HOW TO PROVIDE SERVICES

While it is not anticipated that many institutions will want to provide global resource discovery services, all NDLTD members are welcome to use the data in the Union Archive to supplement their own services or provide new and enhanced services to the NDLTD community. For example, disciplinary services could be built, such as a service handling the global collection of ETDs related to computing, physics, ecology, or bioengineering. To obtain the data, a service provider may use an OAI harvester (see OAI website) to periodically gather data from the Union Archive located at the baseURL: http://unionarchive.ndltd.org/cgi-bin/Union/union.pl.

REFERENCES

More information about this project can be found in the following articles on NDLTD in the September 2001 issue of D-Lib Magazine:

Networked Digital Library of Theses and Dissertations: Bridging the Gaps for Global Access—Part 1: Mission and Progress ⟨http://www. dlib.org/dlib/september01/suleman/09suleman-pt1.html⟩.
Networked Digital Library of Theses and Dissertations: Bridging the Gaps for Global Access—Part 2: Services and Research ⟨http://www.dlib.org/dlib/september01/suleman/09suleman-pt2.html⟩.

If you have comments, questions, or suggestions, contact *etdunion@oai.dlib. vt.edu*

7

ETDs: Structuring Elements of Scientific Research

Frédéric Potok and Marie-France Lebouc
Laval University
Quebec, Canada

While the debate about electronic theses and dissertations (ETDs) mainly deals with the advantages and difficulties in the cataloging and storage of electronic documents, we would like to underline some challenging elements in the production phase of theses. Although these elements may seem purely technical, they have important impact on strategic relations between students and theses supervisors and between students and their peers in their research field, and they also have epistemological consequences.

INTRODUCTION

The Internet and other new information production and broadcasting technologies are drastically changing traditional methods of getting and transmitting information. Theses and dissertations (TDs), as both results and means of scientific knowledge, seem particularly adapted for this new electronic medium. This growing tendency to electronic formatting of TDs leads us to rethink what TDs are and how they are produced. University authorities usually consider that, with regards to electronic formatting, TD production follows three main steps.

Step 1—Conceptualization, writing, and defense of the thesis, or the proper making of the TD

Step 2—Document formatting so that it is accepted by the School of Graduate Studies

Step 3—Cataloging and archiving (generally by academic libraries)

According to various reports on ETD projects, it seems that both the second and third steps cause much concern. Writers are preoccupied with technical questions, data processing, or even the need for competent human resources to help students, academics, and other administrative staff switch to electronic publishing. By contrast, the first step does not seem to have raised as many concerns so far. As a matter of fact, we found no publications on that question, except ones concerned with technical matters.[1] Existing papers could lead readers to think that writing TDs (step 1) and formatting them (step 2) are successive yet distinct and independent stages. However, this apparent disjunction is questionable. By bringing new opportunities, electronic formatting (step 3) might well influence steps 1 and 2, that is to say, the whole process of scientific knowledge production in TDs.

The present chapter aims at exploring the impact of a new technology on a particular process of scientific knowledge production: a doctoral thesis. We hypothesize that electronic format, through the technical opportunities it brings, helps structure the whole process of doctoral research and influences the way research objects are tackled and conceptualized. Traditionally, the production process of a thesis or dissertation is said to follow the following steps: first, choosing and conceptualizing a research object; second, collecting and analyzing data; third, writing the dissertation; and finally, defending and disseminating the thesis to committee members and the public. Yet the impacts are not only technical; they can also be strategic, political, and epistemological. In this chapter, we do not intend to cover all the potential effects of ETDs production, but rather to identify those that seem particularly relevant. In order to go from the most technical and frequently discussed aspects to the more unfamiliar ones, this chapter is organized following a double logic. First, we go backwards, from defense and diffusion, to writing and object investigation,[2] because discussions mainly deal with diffusion technical problems. Second, at each step a number of dimensions are noticeable, be they technical, political, or epistemological. Their importance varies according to the step we describe. Hence, this chapter has a matrix structure.[3]

Of course, what we put forward is valid only if a student wishes to fully use all of the opportunities the electronic medium offers, that is to say, if he or she is willing to do more than simply turn a document—usually already formatted with a word processor—into a new electronic format such as Standard General Markup Language (SGML) or Portable Document Format (PDF). In this case, changes would be slight and would only consist of technicalities in steps 2 and 3. While writing and typing, the student would have to follow a Document Type Definition (DTD) and save his or her work under a new format file. However, among other criteria, multimedia is an important reason why some universities choose SGML.[4] Hence, it is highly probable that students would want to do not only ETDs, but multimedia dissertations as well.

Furthermore, it is important to mention that neither author of this chapter is specialized in electronic publishing nor pretends to be. However, as Ph.D. students in social sciences, we have been both observers and actors in power relationships, negotiations, and conflicts within the scientific community. It is with this qualification that we intend to examine some impacts beyond the purely technical dimension.

TECHNICAL CHOICES AND POWER GAMES

When a university decides to implement a production procedure of ETDs, storage is usually well planned. For example, Virginia Tech allows terabytes of storage for its students' ETDs.[5] However, even before final archiving, students should be able to save their work throughout the elaboration process. When we take into consideration the storage capacity needed by sound, graphic, or video files, the final medium could be a CD-ROM or, more likely, a DVD. But such storage devices are not adapted for daily backup. The latter requires electronic equipment that is flexible enough for all three kinds of storage. Here is a double technical problem well known to ETD specialists: the diversity of storage equipment on the market and their availability in universities.

This problem, which seems merely technical, may cause tensions among faculty members, has consequences in power relationships, and influences strategies. Organizational behavior specialists refer to this kind of situation as resistance to change, and they have devoted considerable work to describing real difficulties associated with it, as well as possible remedies. Although this problem is not specific to ETDs, one should not overlook them. The following are three examples of the kinds of difficulties that could arise.

First, standardizing file formats and equipment means choosing among a variety of commercial products. What criteria will prevail? Once the choice is made, only the selected formats will be officially supported on the campus. Indeed, a mixed solution could work, yet perhaps at a cost unaffordable at a time of budgetary restrictions. This will increase competition among companies to win academic markets. The pressure IBM and Macintosh put on academic institutions is a good example. Such choices will affect relationships between members of the university community. Presently, almost each school, college, or even faculty member has its own equipment, chosen for performance considerations, even though it may differ from what is found elsewhere on the campus. None is willing to give up its up-to-date equipment if it is made obsolete by administrative decisions at the top level of university hierarchy. We must also consider that, for the moment, most of the universities listed in the Networked Digital Library of Theses and Dissertations have a technical vocation. On general campuses it will be even harder to obtain equipment homogeneity. Once the technical choice is made, people must very rapidly switch equipment, transfer files, and learn how to use new equipment. Thus, tensions and potential hard feelings are likely to build up among teachers, employees, and technicians.

A second element goes beyond technical aspects: once the electronic medium is selected, thesis committee members, including those from other universities (e.g., external reviewers), should be equipped and prepared to read the electronic document. As a matter of fact, not only should these persons be able to use the most widespread software, but it might be necessary for them to add plug-ins, to convert files, to use the Internet, an Intranet, and perhaps even to configure their computers. However, computer and multimedia knowledge varies greatly among supervisors; it is an understatement to say that some professors are uncomfortable with new technologies and their educational applications. Nevertheless, even if they are averse to the "technological era" and the use of "electronic gadgets" for education, and thus crystallized in a defensive position, these persons will still be willing to act as supervisors or committee members. One must keep in mind that supervision activities are part of the strategic game of relations among peers. Thus, for accepting someone as a supervisor or as a committee member, we should reckon with computer knowledge in addition to other traditional criteria such as competence in the student's field of interest, accessibility, research subsidies, and publishing activities.

Third, it is possible that all the computer equipment, multimedia normalization, ETD projects, and multimedia theses public defenses could be used to improve "institutional credibility." Equipment availability may be put forward to promote an image of up-to-date universities. The danger is that "hard" components of education, that is technology, will take precedence over "soft" components, such as teaching skills, methodological training, and access to faculty.[6] It is possible that some universities might consider ETDs as a marketing product to promote student applications and gain notoriety.

WRITING AND SUPERVISION

Electronic medium impacts are felt not only at the end of the production process, but also during writing. Therefore, ETDs have an impact on both thesis structure and supervision. Students may wish to take advantage of ETDs and vary the form of their works. Instead of a static and linear text, it is thus possible to construct texts containing hyperlinks, where interactions between sections are more frequent, making the text more dynamic. These links can refer to other sections in the same document, as well as to other files or programs. Such possibilities may radically change the way dissertations are written. One does not write a web page like a paper page; quite similarly, an ETD may or may not follow a classical logic structure. Here are three examples of what this structure may become.

First, it could be pyramidal. In this case, the reader might be able to choose between several depths of analysis. A linear reading may still be possible, but the reader would be in a position to read more thoroughly about a concept or a fact every time he or she wishes to do so. He or she would thus be able to read the same story at various levels of conceptualization or details. Second, it could be a "multiple choice path of reading." At the end of each section, the reader could choose among two or three following sections. The text should then be structured to help the reader jump from one section to another without having to follow the main linear path or missing any element. For example, this may be interesting to readers wishing to focus first on operational aspects of the research rather than on more conceptual ones. From introduction to conclusion, someone's "reading journey" could begin with the research problem, then the methodology, and end with the conceptual framework, while someone else's could be different. Third, the structure could mix the two previous ones and resemble electronic encyclopedias. In a dissertation there are numerous kinds of elements: concepts, data, examples, methodological indications, etc. In an encyclopedic structure, each of these elements can refer to a set of other items, within the same chapter or not. Hence, the reader would have a choice in terms of depth of analysis and of reading path.

Such transformations in the dissertation structure and process can dramatically alter the way a supervisor oversees the writing of a dissertation. This change is particularly important since the dissertation structure and the writing logic are the media of the demonstration: when an examiner reads a TD, not only does he evaluate the content (data, concepts, method), he also evaluates the way it is put together so as to convince him. Thus, presentation is part of demonstration. Writing a good linear demonstration is not easy, but when the writer allows several paths of reading, or several depths of analysis, he greatly complicates his task of having to reach a very high level of consistency and logic. Nevertheless, committee members must be aware of the technological illusion trap. Whether or not renewal of form may improve content, the latter remains the core element to evaluate. Committee members will have to be simultaneously more flexible and more rigorous to distinguish what may be a technical halo from an original and judicious use of technology.

TRANSLATION OF INVESTIGATION CHOICES FOR DIFFUSION

In the previous section, we saw how text structure is important; here we focus on text content. Writing, which Déry (1989) calls translation, represents the second stage of the knowledge-production process, where investigation of the object and diffusion to peers are, respectively, first and last. During translation, the student shapes her argumentation or proof. Translation is thus characterized by a retrospective look at the research object in order to describe it and a prospective look towards the readers. Not only must the student say what she found, but while reflecting on the research object, she must aim at convincing future readers. The question for the student is: "How can I best present what I found and know?" This stage of the knowledge-production process is marked by a tension between a descriptive logic and a strategic one.

From a descriptive point of view, in order to build knowledge about a research object, the student may choose between various methods. Then, she faces the problem of giving an account of the data she has collected. For example, one hour of audio or video recording entails several hours of transcription work. Transcription also means a loss of data richness, especially when the use of such methods is designed to capture information beyond verbal expression, such as nonverbal communication, settings, or other elements of context.

ETDs now make it possible to keep more raw data. For instance, when studying both metacommunicational elements and verbal communication during a negotiation process, a student may use video recording and then quote video excerpts. Results of surveys conducted at Virginia Tech (Kipp and McGonigle, 1997) showed the following: approximately 5% of attendees planned to include video clips, 8.3% planned to include sound clips, 47.2% planned to use scanned images, 25.0% intended using color images, and nearly 10% planned to include hypertext links. Also, 21.2% planned to include some feature of ETDs (e.g., hypertext) that would not be possible in a paper document. Of course, such inclusions are not necessarily an advantage. In certain instances current ways of translating or giving accounts of data are perfectly appropriate. Moreover, integral quotations do not lessen the work of analysis the student has to do. It might even increase the work allotted to committee members.

From a strategic point of view, important consequences derive from a possible inclusion of either databases, computerized simulations, and excerpts of video or audio recordings. The first obvious gains, as we just saw, are saved working time and a better preservation of data significance. Another set of consequences deals with convincing readers. The student may be more able to convince the committee by adding explicitness to the research and analysis process, although confidentiality and copyright can be problematic. The student has a chance not only to write what he found and knows, but also to show it. And the members of the committee have a chance not only to read but also to listen or see, and thus judge for themselves. So, inclusion of such raw data upon which the student built his interpretation or analysis could become the norm, and one or more members of his committee could make it compulsory.[7]

This increase in technical possibilities for exposing data has at least two kinds of major consequences. First, including raw data in ETDs raises the question of evaluating research and scientific criteria. Members of a committee are placed in a situation where they can, if necessary, refute the student's interpretation and analysis. It is the convergence of committee members' opinions that will validate analysis, even if this convergence is negotiated. This is fundamental. As a matter of fact, many social and human scientists claim that researchers in their fields should use, and students should be taught to use, the natural science model. They expect these sciences to help us explain, understand, predict, and control social phenomena. According to Kerlinger (1986), these are the aims of theories that scientific research strives at producing. It is not unanimously accepted that humanities have reached a postpositivist era where interpretative approaches are the utmost form of research. Far from wishing to go back to naïve inductivism or to forget the theory-ladenness of facts,[8] some researchers want more stress on research objects than on interpretation (Hunt, 1994a, 1994b).

Bunge's opinion (1991, 1992) shows how important it can be for many social and human scientists that science is supported by a set of rigorous standards, as shown by his conclusive moral: "Where anything goes, nothing goes well" (Bunge, 1992). Among these standards are internal and external validities. They are traditionally presented as exclusive (Campbell and Stanley, 1963). New information technologies applied to TDs could increase internal validity as they allow easier access to raw data—this is, what we called explicitness. At the same time, they could widen the proofs of generalizability of the results—external validity—because the document could refer to databanks, websites, or any other elements to which the theoretical part of the TD would apply in real time. For instance, a new financial theory could be validated thanks to a link to daily updated stock exchange databases. These researchers who stress the importance of such positivist criteria, as they are sometimes qualified, may find technical possibilities carried along with ETDs a warranty. From this point of view, ETDs and their material medium may become a powerful instrument of scientific checking and validation.

Including raw data may bring a second set of unexpected consequences. It may be a truism to specify that the nature of raw data collected depends on the tools used to collect them, but once the use of certain data-collecting methods is made easier, less time consuming, and more convincing, these methods could become more common and their use reinforced by committee acceptance or requirement of integral quotations—although usage does not mean legitimation. One can imagine how these changes could influence the "discovery" of new aspects of the research object or help put a new emphasis on traditionally less important aspects. Thus, on the one hand, new ETD presentation techniques are structuring research, in the sense that they simultaneously enable and constrain wording. On the other hand, they are structured by the researcher. The latter needs to find ways of presenting investigation results and of convincing readers: information technology specialists try to meet these needs by creating new tools.

CONCLUSION

The starting point for this chapter was to question the link between switching to an electronic format for disseminating and storing TDs and the general process of making TDs. Up to now, this relation did not seem to cause much concern except for technical problems. We mainly focused on political, strategic, and epistemological impacts. First, we think that ETDs, as new technical tools, will have an impact on power relations among faculty members because of the technical knowhow needed to supervise students who use new information technologies to do and to present their research. Second, ETDs will have an impact on the way students phrase investigation results to better convince their committees. The ordinary linear text could become obsolete as ETDs make it possible to include such features as hyperlinks or video clips. Third, when they are presented with raw data, such as integral video quotations or data bases, committee members will have to adapt their scientific validity criteria. That could have an influence on how research is evaluated in the future. Finally, we think that not only will ETDs affect presentation and validation, but that even the way we think about research objects could be indirectly modified when certain data-collecting methods become more commonly used, as these methods could help determine the emphasis on certain facets of the object. Hence, electronic medium is clearly a structuring element of doctoral research as it affects every stage of the knowledge-production process.

These influences may seem unexpected to people who focus on technical aspects of the subject. Further theoretical and empirical investigation will be possible in the years to come with the increase in the number of ETDs and the arrival of students who know from the start that they will be making an ETD.

While awaiting the results of such investigation, we hope that the present chapter, although linear and paper, may help widen the scope of the debate about ETDs.

REFERENCES

Bunge, M. (Dec 1991). A critical examination of the new sociology of science: Part I. *Philosophy of the Social Sciences* 21(4):524–560.

Bunge, M. (March 1992). A critical examination of the new sociology of science: Part II. *Philosophy of the Social Sciences* 22(1):46–76.

Campbell, D. T., Stanley, J. C. (1963). *Experimental and Quasi-Experimental Designs for Research*. Boston: Houghton Mifflin Company.

Déry, R. (1989). La structuration discursive de la problématique de la décision dans la revue Administrative Science, Quarterly: une contribution à l'épistémologie des sciences de l'organisation. Ph.D. Thesis, Faculté des sciences de l'administration, Université Laval, Quebec.

Hunt, S. D. (1994a). A realist theory of empirical testing: resolving the theory-ladenness/objectivity debate. *Philosophy of the Social Sciences* 24(2):133–158.

Hunt, S. D. (1994b). On the rhetoric of qualitative methods. *Journal of Management Inquiry* 3(3):221–234.

Kerlinger, F. N. (1986). *Foundations of Behavioral Research*. 3rd ed. Fort Worth, TX: Harcourt Brace Jovanovitch.

Kipp, N. A., McGonigle, T. P. (June 16, 1997). Grant Performance Report: Improving Graduate Education with a National Digital Library of Theses and Dissertations. U.S. Department of Education. See http://www.ndltd.org/pubs/FIPSEfr.pdf.

ENDNOTES

1. When such subjects are approached in discussion groups like "Electronic theses and dissertations in the humanities" ⟨http://etext.lib.virginia.edu/ETD/about⟩, participants question the lack of standardization for multimedia files and the high cost of purchasing or writing on electronic medium.
2. This division is largely inspired by Déry (1989).
3. We are well aware that no knowledge production process is so linear and that research is rather made of numerous feedback loops between theory and practice, conceptualization and analysis.
4. This criterion helped Laval University ETDs committee to select SGML as the cataloguing file format.
5. See "Frequently Asked Questions of the ETD Initiative" at Virginia Tech Web site: http://etd.vt.edu/faq/mmedia.html.
6. Lately, business schools have promoted teaching through communica-

tion networks and have made it compulsory for students to buy lap-top computers. Even though there is no proof so far of improved skills in either teaching or learning, the number of student applicants is significantly on the increase.

7. Certain paper journal editors and reviewers in operational research have already made such requests.

8. According to naive inductivism, science begins with observation, and observation is unbiased. This view is not taken seriously by contemporary philosophers of science. Since the 1960s, Kuhn and Feyerabend, among others, have put forward the opposite. Facts are not simply observed but perceived, and the language used to give an account of what is perceived relies on previously formed theories, hypotheses, expectations, or beliefs. This is called theory-ladenness of facts.

8

For Students: Dissertating on the Network

Joe Moxley
University of South Florida
Tampa, Florida

In past essays on the subject of electronic theses and dissertations, I have explored why universities should require ETDs for graduation ("Universities Should"), analyzed new ETD genres ("Graduate Education"), suggested research opportunities for scholars and researchers interested in new media scholarship, information literacy, and digital libraries ("New Media"), explored why American universities are falling behind other research universities world wide ("Academic Scholarship"), presented FAQs related to ETD efforts ("ETDs at USF"), and suggested ways in which rhetoricians and compositionists can contribute to ETD efforts ("Dissertating"). In addition, I helped edit and manage *The Guide for Electronic Theses and Dissertations*, an online resource published by UNESCO. All of these past essays, proposals, and online works have been designed to convince faculty and university administrators that they should adopt mandatory ETDs, mentor their students to author ETDs, and become involved in ETD initiatives as mentors and researchers.

In contrast, rather than invoking faculty as my audience—faculty who tend to be tied to preserving the status quo—in this chapter I'm writing for graduate students. Having worked with hundreds of graduate students as a professor of writing, research, and scholarly publishing (see http://joemoxley. org), I understand that many graduate students were raised with a remote in one hand and a mouse in another. Of course it is true that some graduate students use their word processors as glorified typewriters, yet many are designing hypertextual, multimedia theses and dissertations. Many graduate students are breaking new ground, showing us new ways to mentor, collaborate, research, and publish. As you might suspect, innovative graduate students are using software tools and the Internet to gather research and create new theses and dissertation genres. To contribute to these efforts, I focus on exploring the following issues and questions:

1. Why should you write an ETD?
2. What can you reasonably expect from committee members?
3. How are theses and dissertations evolving as a result of new software tools and digital libraries?
4. How can you find exemplary ETD models?
5. What do you need to know about Web design?
6. How can you use software tools to facilitate your research, scholarship, and interactions with mentors and peers?
7. Should you limit access to your work?

WHY SHOULD YOU WRITE AN ETD?

Writing an ETD will improve access to your work. According to Gail McMillan, Director of Virginia Tech's Digital Library and Archives, "an ETD collection 1/3 the size of the theses and dissertations available in 1998, circulated 100 times more in 2000/01." Virginia Tech's circulation records show that between 1990 and 1994, 15,335 theses and dissertations were approved, and 3967 of these works were checked out in 1998. In contrast, by 2000/01, Virginia Tech had 3393 ETDs in its collection and 1,565,151 PDFs were downloaded by users (largely ETDs). That remarkable increase clearly resulted from the university's shift to ETDs, as no other significant changes took place at Virginia Tech in the same period.

Writing an ETD will enable you to engage readers in new ways. Simon Pockley's ETD (http://www.cinemedia.net/FOD/), which has been accessed by more than one million distinct computers'[1], provides an excellent example of how ETDs can continue to evolve following "completion." Since 1998, Pockley has received hundreds of e-mails each day about his work, with comments ranging from the profound to the profoundly weird (http:// www.cinemedia.net/FOD/FOD0989.html#Richardson3).

If you don't provide an ETD, UMI will. The only problem is that UMI's scan of your thesis or dissertation will be inferior to the one you can prepare.

UMI, a private company that has been the central repository and dissem-
inator for North American print dissertations for the past 50 years, now scans
all the print dissertations it receives and converts them to Portable Document
Format (PDF) files of page images. Thanks to UMI's Current Research@
service (see http://wwwlib.umi.com/cresearch/gateway/main/), users can
search citations and abstracts of dissertations and theses and view 24-page
previews of dissertations published after 1996.

WHAT CAN YOU REASONABLY EXPECT FROM COMMITTEE MEMBERS?

Like everyone else, most faculty will want to review printed copies of texts.
When documents go over three pages, readability research has found that
people typically print the pages.

Admittedly, the traditional five-chapter dissertation took time to develop from the model of the first dissertation submitted in America—a six-
page, handwritten thesis at Yale University in 1860. We can't expect major
institutions to reinvent themselves overnight. Theses and dissertations are
cherished academic genres, so faculty are justifiably concerned about monitoring their evolution.

Understandably, many faculty and university leaders are unaware of the
benefits of new technologies, unsure of how to use software tools to mentor
students, format documents, or collaborate online. They are unsure of what
benefits, if any, might inure. As Kenneth Green's yearly survey of campus
technology trends has demonstrated, faculty are not always willing to use new
technologies: "I think it's fair to say that many faculty members have ceded to
their students the whole issue of technology skills" (see Olsen, 1999).

HOW ARE THESES AND DISSERTATIONS EVOLVING AS A RESULT OF SOFTWARE TOOLS AND DIGITAL LIBRARIES?

Clearly, new technologies are transforming our research, teaching, and
writing processes. They are also threatening our cherished conventions, such
as the five-chapter dissertation with one-inch margins. Christine Boese's
dissertation from Rensselaer Polytechnic Institute provides a glimpse that
might reflect a format checker's worst nightmare: "The Ballad of the Internet
Nutball: Chaining Rhetorical Visions from the Margins of the Margins to the
Mainstream in the Xenaverse" (1998–2000). Her jazzy topic, sexy images of
Xena, confusing navigation, use of sound files, interactive features (including
a forum and a survey), and the ongoing nature of the work provide yet
another glimpse of a new media dissertation.

Would it make a difference if the conversations with committee members were incorporated, perhaps hypertextually, into the thesis itself? How would our conception of the Ph.D. thesis change if it were to include not only the product of the student's research but the process as well? That is, what if readers could trace the project from inception to publication and, perhaps, even extend the research by adding comments of their own? What if the defense were held online as well, like Dene Grigar's (1997) online dissertation defense at Lingua MOO, or by incorporating audio and/or video files, asynchronous discussions (e.g., email discussion), or electronic marginalia into the work itself?

New media scholarship makes it possible to include many voices—in ways that may challenge our conception of authorship entirely. Of course, merely including other voices doesn't necessarily pose such a challenge, but experimentation with new forms may challenge us in other ways. Paulette Robinson, a student at Towson University, for example, completed her dissertation on student use of Web-based conferencing, replete with shockwave flash movies (well designed and conceived, but annoying after the first flush), student comments in both text and streaming audio, and a hypernews forum so well password-protected that interested readers cannot even access it. Her use of animated menus, image maps, and color-coded indexes to organize her work results in a dissertation that is game-like, but frustrating because of its lack of traditional cues.

What does it look like to think spatially in a network of connections? What would the conventions look like? Or, do there have to be conventions? How much cognitive bridging or conceptual mapping does the reader need to feel familiar and not confused or frustrated? Does the reader build comfort by revisiting the piece and begin to gain familiarity through visitations? How do we build new notational systems?

Part of the problem with dissertations such as Robinson's, which push the margins—literally—beyond the one-inch margins allowed by paper to the (more or less) limitless margins allowed in cyberspace, is that few of us are really comfortable reading these works. Casual readers may enjoy the sense of play and discovery, but serious readers may be frustrated by the limitations imposed on us by our training in linear forms. And yet, without such experimentation, how can we fulfill the needs of future readers, readers for whom traditional linear forms are quickly becoming archaic?

Simon Pockley's dissertation includes digitized images, animated graphics, and hypertextual links, yet there is nothing in the dissertation itself that couldn't have been presented in traditional print format. What does make this work unique, however, is the ongoing conversation that surrounds it, conversation that is encouraged by its publication online.

Keith Dorwick's (1996–1998) dissertation project at the University of Illinois at Chicago, "Building the Virtual Department: A Case Study of

Online Teaching and Research," uses frames, annoying pop-up windows, and, like Pockley, often-confusing navigational cues to present textual information that would have been easier to read in a traditional print format. However, Dorwick also includes software for both synchronous (i.e., real-time) and asynchronous communication along with Web-based forms as part of his dissertation project, so that his dissertation continues to grow as readers' responses are incorporated into the project. The conversations allowed by the software are an integral part of Dorwick's project—in some respects, the conversation *is* the project. So, while the metadiscussion Dorwick presents could easily have been presented in a more traditional format (i.e., print), the software not only requires electronic publication, it requires publication online.

Imagine, too, as graduate students and graduate faculty become comfortable with new writing and researching tools, online dissertations that incorporate animation, three-dimensional modeling, multimedia, and ongoing conversations, dissertations that cross space and time, that grow and change even years after the author has been awarded his or her degree—in short, imagine a dissertation that is more than just a ticket to the profession but that is a continuing contribution to the body of knowledge in a discipline, a work that can grow along with the career of its author.

HOW CAN YOU FIND EXEMPLARY ETD MODELS

The Guide for Electronic Theses and Dissertations, http://etdguide.org, provides an online, interactive database of exemplary ETDs. You can use the NDLTD union catalog or drill down into the ETD collections of universities: http://www.ndltd.org/browse.html.

WHAT DO YOU NEED TO KNOW ABOUT WEB DESIGN?

Web design has been an exciting topic for many Netdenizens. Consequently, you can find many online guides to writing HTML or working with Web editors. Below are links to sites that contain advice, tools, or tutorials that help with designing documents. New shareware tools and tutorials are readily available on the Internet, so you may be able to find additional resources by searching on popular search engines.

Usability and Interface Design Resources

Writing for the Web by Sun Microsystems, http://www.sun.com/980713/webwriting/

Based on its readability research, Sun Microsystems reports on guidelines that can be used to "double the usability of your web site." This is a very important essay for web designers to review, particularly beginners.

The Alert Box: Current Issues in Usability, http://www.useit.com/alertbox/
Links to Jakob Nielsen's biweekly columns on usability issues.

First Rule of Usability: Ignore the Users, http://www.useit.com/alertbox/20010805.html
Interesting essay on conducting usability research.

Usable Web, http://www.usableweb.com/
Created and maintained by Keith Instone, "Usable Web is a collection of links about information architecture, human factors, user interface issues, and usable design specific to the World Wide Web."

Writing for Readers Who Scan by Kathy Henning, http://www.clickz.com/design/onl_edit/article.php/836621
Short piece that advocates scannable documents.

How Users Read on the Web http://www.useit.com/alertbox/9710a.html
Interesting discussion of the effects of scannable prose, promotional prose, and objective prose on readability.

Web Design Resources

Yale Web Style Design Guide, http://info.med.yale.edu/caim/manual/
Excellent book-length, rhetorical treatment of web design. Includes sections on interface, site, and page design.

Monitoring Order, http://www.hu.mtu.edu/~awysocki/mOrder/mOrder0.html
Visual desire, the organization of Web pages, and teaching the rules of design. Originally published in Kairos 3.2.

Web Page Design for Designers, http://www.wpdfd.com
Excellent "megasite" with timely articles, editorials, and tutorials (with archives going back to 1998). Designed for web design professionals yet broad enough for the novice.

Web Pages that Suck, http://ww.webpagesthatsuck.com/ and Fixing Your Website, http://www.fixingyourwebsite.com/

Working in tandem, *Webpagesthatsuck* provides criticisms of poorly designed websites while *Fixingyourweblinks* provides advice on ways to improve web sites.

Graphics and Web Design Based on Edward Tufte's Principles, http://www.washington.edu/computing/training/560/zz-tufte.html
Published by the Department of Computing and Communications at the University of Washington, this site contains advice extracted from Edward Tufte's books on using visuals to illustrative quantitative relationships.

Demitry's Design Lab, http://www.webreference.com/dlab/
These articles written by Dmitry Kirsanov are for everyone interested in the important basics of design proper—design as art and science. Such design essentials as color, fonts, shape, texture, dynamism, the principles of using artwork, photography, and animation, plus some more specific issues such as web site navigation or logo design, are treated in detail and illustrated by case web design projects.

Web Developers (Virtual Library), Website Design, http://www.wdvl.com/Authoring/Design/
Megasite with links to essays on web design, including links to numerous essays on usability studies of particular web designs.

Web Design Guide, http://www.dreamink.com/
Good basic introduction to web design. Includes links to commercial sites.

Web Design Tips, http://www.colin.mackenzie.org/webdesign/
Although written in 1998, this tutorial on web design provides advice that is still helpful for beginning web designers.

Creating Killer Websites, 2nd ed., http://www.killersites.com
Beautiful site for those who favor Adobe and Macintosh tools; includes links to downloadable web design tools. Provides design tips and links to examples.

HTML Help by the Web Design Group, http://www.htmlhelp.com/design/style/
The Web Design Group has tutorials and advice for Web Designers as well as novices. Includes several style guides that focus on the

HTML coding. This site is geared toward coding as opposed to writing.

Page Resource, http://www.pageresource.com.
Extensive site written for web designers; includes some useful essays on web design http://www.pageresource.comgne/zine/index.html).

HOW YOU CAN USE SOFTWARE TOOLS TO FACILITATE YOUR RESEARCH AND SCHOLARSHIP?

You can help ensure you complete your coursework in a timely manner by developing an online portfolio at the beginning of your career and then using this online space to maintain an annotated bibliography, links to documents written during coursework, to online syllabi of coursework taken, and to archives of online conversations. Rather than receiving criticism from one professor at a time, you could post the work to a campus network, provide whatever document security you wished, and then your mentors and peers could access the work and post comments, criticisms, and suggestions. Below is a brief discussion of asynchronous communication tools and synchronous communication tools.

Asynchronous Communication Tools

Email, Discussion Forums, and Listservs

Interestingly, new technologies provide us with creative new ways to interact with our readers. We no longer need to intuit what our readers think of particular ideas or sentences. People are using email, discussion forums, and listservs to develop and disseminate ideas.

Find out what people are saying on topics by listening to online conversations. Using a search engine, you can find discussion groups on all conceivable topics, including entertainment, book reviews, and photography.

Incidentally, after finding a discussion forum on a topic of interest, you should first check its archives—that is, the record of past posts to the list. You can usually locate the archives by going to the FAQs for the discussion forum, if available, or by posting a query to folks on the list.

Tile.Net: Listserv Search Engine (search for listservs in your discipline?): http://www.tile.net

Google Groups: Usenet and Listserv Search Engine: http://groups.google.com/

Note: Immediately sending a query to a list can break with netiquette. Often lists are rich discussion forums "settled" by people who have come to know each other fairly well. When someone new comes on a list, starts asking questions without first listening to what people are discussing, asking questions completely out of turn or unrelated to the focus of the list, his or her queries for information may be ignored.

Receive Feedback from Readers by Placing Email Addresses, Discussion Forms or Feedback Forms at the End of Your Essay

In his essay "Networking on the Network," note how Professor Agee provides his email so readers can respond to his essay. He also acknowledges those who have helped shaped his essay over the past 8 years. Providing an email so readers can respond to you is an easy, low-tech solution (Networking on the Network, http://dlis.gseis.ucla.edu/people/pagre/network.html).

Many online journals also provide discussion forums that enable users to tag comments to specific essays. For example, readers of the online journal, The Technology Source, http://horizon.unc.edu/TS/, can respond to essays published in the journals, carrying on dialogs with other readers and the author of the essays. "You may print a printer-friendly version of the article, email the article to a colleague, take part in an online discussion about the article (and get a note if someone responds to your post), or see related articles, grouped by subject matter or section of TS. You may also search for any article in the TS archives." Incidentally, for a short while The Technology Source allowed readers to embed oral comments to essays, but they dropped this feature due to lack of use.

Questionnaires and Feedback Forms

You can also attach a survey to your document and solicit specific feedback. For example, when I was writing a grant proposal to the U.S. Department of Education (FIPSE Proposal 2001), I created a survey of questions that would provide answers needed to support the grant proposal: http://dmi.usf.edu/fipsedata.asp. I then went to appropriate lists and asked users to respond to the survey. Thirty-six people from universities around the world completed the survey, which I then used to revise the proposal. Also, I submitted the survey results as empirical support for the argument I was making in the proposal.

Database Approaches

Websites that enable users to suggest resources frequently are designed as a database. Users can input feedback, and it will immediately enter a database.

If desired, this feedback immediately becomes part of the website (see, for example, Wikipedia). Other examples are:

> UNESCO's The Guide for Electronic Theses and Dissertations enables users to nominate exemplary ETDs: http://etdguide.org/models/default.htm.
>
> The Online Writing Consortium's website enables users to suggest resources: http://owcc.colostate.edu/links.cfm.

In the past, people needed special training to develop databases. Web designers needed special training to write the code that would enable the database to work. Thanks to new tools, however, creating databases is quite simple.

Text Commenting and Track Change Features

Popular word processors, such as Word Perfect or Microsoft Word, enable users to attach comments and edits to particulars lines of texts—that is, to create "inline edits" just as you do with pen and pencil. In other words, a writer can circulate an electronic copy of a document and multiple users can insert their commentaries (See Figs. 1, 2).

Tutorials on Using Commenting or Track Changes Features

> Microsoft Word and the Writing Process. Sponsored by Microsoft < http://joemoxley.org/word >, this is a wonderful resource for users interested in ways to use writing collaboratively.

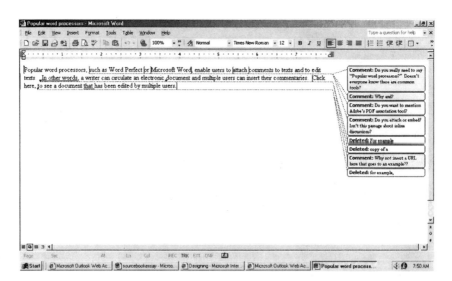

FIGURE 1   Commenting and Track Changes in Microsoft's Doc Format.

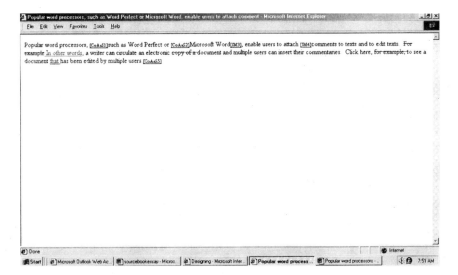

FIGURE 2   Commenting and Track Changes in .HTM Format.

Microsoft Word and the Writing Process, http://www.joemoxley.org/ word/Default.htm Sponsored by Microsoft, this Web site explores ways to use Word to introduce students to the writing process. See, e.g., Microsoft Word and the Writing Process (Doc).

Of course, useful alternatives exist for non-Microsoft users—alternatives that allow similar text-editing and commenting features.

The Paper Review Form, http://sites.unc.edu/tools/pr2.0/ Daniel Anderson's free web-based paper review tool.

Quick Topic, http://www.quicktopic.com/ "Upload any HTML document (Microsoft Word documents too) and Quick Topic's document review service gives you an instant private space for your reviewers to comment on it. QT inserts a comment link before each paragraph, or whatever items you choose. Comments are all kept in one private QT forum attached to your document, each linked back to the document."

E Quill, http://www.e-quill.com/ Complete editing tool designed with collaborative editing in mind. Very useful for businesses that want to exert strong control over corporate websites.

Users of Internet Explorer can embed inline comments using the Discuss Tool. In other words, after selecting the "Discuss" button on the IE toolbar, users can insert comments after every line break on every web page. This is a particularly useful tool for users who want to comment on specific websites. For example, a teacher could ask her students to respond to a course syllabus with this tool, which would yield detailed feedback.

Tutorials on Using Internet Explorer's Discuss Feature

How to Participate in a Discussion on an OSE-Extended Web
This is a very comprehensive article on using the discussion feature in IE
as well as Netscape.

Using the Discussion Feature in Internet Explorer
"This article explains how to use the Discussion feature in Microsoft
Internet Explorer when you are viewing files created in a Microsoft
Office 2000 product."

Web Folders

Web folders enable you to save documents to the web for critique and review, using Office 2000 tools, such as Microsoft Outlook or Microsoft FrontPage. Web folders can be used in conjunction with Track Changes, Commenting, or Discuss. For example, if you have access to an MS Office server, you can save a document to a web folder, invite participation, and then receive commentaries from Internet users. If users have access to Word, they can retrieve documents, make suggestions—using commenting and track changes—and then send the documents back to the web, saved, ideally, under a new name. Web folders provide a glimpse of how student writers work when they are assigned to review other students' documents.

Tutorials on Web Folders

Microsoft Word and the Writing Process,
http://www.joemoxley.org/word
Collaborating with Others Using Outlook 2002 and Exchange 2000,
http://www.microsoft.com/education/?ID = Outlook2002Tutorial

Synchronous Communications
Chat Rooms

Chat rooms enable people to talk with other people in real time. When people are collaborating in groups, they can keep the chat room running in the background, consulting it from time to time to see if colleagues have questions. Below are some popular chat rooms:

Chat Sites

Yahoo chat,
http://chat.yahoo.com

Excite chat,
http://www.excite.com/communities/chat/lite

TalkCity chat,
http://www.talkcity.com.

Essays on Chats

Tips on Online Chatting,
http://www.fullworld.com/chattips.html

Chat Danger
http://www.chatdanger.com

Instant Message/Chat Room Safety Tips
http://www.familyclick.com/internetsafety/index.cfm?page_load = featuredarticle/imchatips.cfm

Network Learning: Online Chatting Basics http://familyeducation. com/article/0,1120,1-4358,00.html

West Loogootee's Educational Chat Rooms
http://www.siec.k12.in.us/ ~ west/edu/chat.htm#safety

AOL's Instant Messenger Program

AOL's Instant Messenger program is exceedingly popular. In 2000, IM was the fastest growing communications function on the Internet, with more than 130 million users worldwide, and more than 3 million signing up every month. "Over 1 billion instant messages are sent every day, far more than the entire mail volume of the U.S. Postal Service..." ("Knocking on AIMs Door" by John Ochwat, http://www.openp2p.com/lpt/a/p2p/2000/10/27/aim.html).

According to the PEW American and Interent Life Project, 13 million American teenagers use IM everyday to communicate with friends—which constitutes 73% of kids ages 12–17. In fact, on college campuses, AOL's IM is so popular that it is actually interfering with students' ability to conduct work. Kids report they can express themselves using IM in ways that they feel uncomfortable with in face-to face situations.

Essays on IM

http://www.ultimateresourcesite.com/instantmessaging/main.htm

Instant Messaging Resources from About.com

http://netconference.about.com/cs/imresources/

http://www.pcworld.com/news/article/0,aid,53444,00.asp

http://www.usatoday.com/life/cyber/tech/review/crh643.htm

MOOs

Before the ubiquitousness of AOL's IM program or chat tools that allow for real-time audio and video, some netizens were fond of MOOs: multiuser, object-oriented environments. Like chat rooms, MOOs allow users to talk with one another in real time. In addition, MOOs are "architectural" spaces. Many MOOS "allow for such virtual reality features as blackboards and slide projectors, moderated panel discussions, and more. Further, MOOs allows teachers and/or students to build and customize the environment to suit their needs" (Walker and Moxley, 2002).

Connections MOO, http://www.nwe.ufl.edu/~tari/connections/index. html
Netoric Project's Tuesday's Cafe.

Lingua MOO, http://lingua.utdallas.edu/
Home to classes and the High Wired enCore interface; an academic virtual community) which is sponsored by Cynthia Haynes and Jan Rune Holmevik.

TappedIn, http://www.tappedin.org/
The Teacher Professional Development Institute.

Essays on MOOS

What is a MOO?, Athena University, http://www.athena.edu/campus/moo.html

Workshop on Synchronous Communication in the Language Arts Classroom, Janice Walker, http://www2.gasou.edu/facstaff/jwalker/tutorials/cte.html

SHOULD YOU LIMIT ACCESS TO YOUR WORK?

Universities typically allow students to limit access to their work to their home campuses—a move that some faculty champion for works that they hope will lead to journal articles, fearing that increased access constitutes prior publication. At Virginia Tech, at one point, one third of students required to submit ETDs elected to restrict public access to their work. No archival copies of their dissertations are available, nor does UMI receive a copy. Restrictions are renewable on a year-to-year basis. Students archiving their work at the NDLTD can put passwords on small sections of their work, on diagrams, or on whole chapters.

While I can understand password protecting work under development, I encourage graduate students to freely share their work online. After all, students must significantly revise their academic work, particularly the detailed account of their results, to accommodate the differences between academic and commercial publishing. Because hiring, tenure, and promotion committees value readership, citations, and influence on the field, they should prize a frequently accessed and cited thesis or dissertation.

REFERENCES

Beavers, T., Bruce, C., Database Editors. Mike, S., Design Editor. (2001). In: Moxley, J. M., Fox, E., Masiello, D., eds. *The Guide for Electronic Theses and Dissertations.* UNESCO.

Boese, C. (1998–2000). The Ballad of the Internet Nutball: Chaining Rhetorical Visions from the Margins of the Margins to the Mainstream in the Xenaverse. Diss. Rensselaer Polytechnic Institute. ⟨http://www.nutball.com/dissertation/index.htm⟩. Nov. 24, 2001.

Dorwick, K. (1996–1998). Building the Virtual Department: A Case Study of On-line Teaching and Research. Diss. University of Illinois at Chicago. ⟨http://www.uic.edu/depts/engl/projects/dissertations/kdorwick/toc.htm⟩. (Nov. 22, 2001).

Edminster, J., Moxley, J. (2002). Graduate education and the evolving genre of electronic theses and dissertations. *Computers and Composition* 19:89–104.

McMillan, G. (March 12, 2001). Personal email.

Moxley, J. M. (March/April 2000). Academic Scholarship in the Digital Age On the Horizon.

Moxley, J. M. (November/December 2001a). New media scholarship: a call for research. *Change: The Magazine of Higher Learning* pp.36–42.

Moxley, J. M. (2001b). American universities should require electronic theses and dissertations. *Educause Quarterly* 3:61–63.

Moxley, J. M. (2001c). ETDs (Electronic Theses and Dissertations) @ USF. Inquiry, Faculty Research and Creative Scholarship 4:1. USF Research Council: Inquiry, pp. 10–11.

Moxley, J. M. (In press). Texts and Technology. In: Walker, J., ed. *The Role of Compositionists in Creating the Networked Digital Library of Theses and Dissertations*. Hampton Press.

Olsen, F. (Oct. 29, 1999). Faculty Wariness of Technology Remains a Challenge, Computing Survey Finds. Chronicle of Higher Education. ⟨http://chronicle.com/weekly/v46/i10/10a06501.htm⟩. Nov. 28, 2001.

Pockley, S. (1995). The Flight of Ducks. Diss. Royal Melbourne Institute of Technology. ⟨http://www.cinemedia.net/FOD/⟩. Nov. 21, 2001.

Pockley, S. (1995, 2001). Killing the Duck to Keep the Quack: Networked Proliferation and Long-Term Access. ⟨http://www.cinemedia.net/FOD/FOD0055.html⟩. Nov. 21, 2001.

Pockley, S. (May 20, 2001). Personal email.

Robinson P. (Nov. 24, 2001). Within the Matrix: A Hermeneutic Phenomenological Investigation of Student Experiences in Web-Based Computer Conferencing. Towson, MD: Diss. Towson University. ⟨http://www.towson.edu/~probinso/Dissertation/⟩.

Walker, J., Moxley, J. M. (2002). Dissertating in a digital age: the future of composition scholarship. In: Carter-Tod, S., Latterell, C. G., Moore, C., Welch, N., eds. *Reinventing the Discipline in Composition and Rhetoric and a Site for Change*. Portsmouth, NH: Boynton/Cook Publishers, pp. 110–118.

ENDNOTES

1. Web server statistics for "Flight of the Ducks" are as follows: successful requests, 1,128,357; average successful requests per day, 2265; successful requests for pages, 533,057; average successful requests for pages per day, 1070; redirected requests, 81; data transferred, 9256 Gbytes, average data transferred per day, 19,032 Mbytes.

2. Each "tracked change" or "comment" is associated with a name—e.g., CoAaS1 or JM. These are the names of the computers on which people conducted the editing. In this manner, users can sort out comments from particular users, e.g., accepting all revisions from one user while rejecting all comments from another user.

9

Multimedia in ETDs

Stephan Fischer and Ralf Steinmetz
Technische Universität Darmstadt
Darmstadt, Germany

Conventional publications are restricted to media such as text and graphics. Electronic documents, however, allow authors to use audio and video, thus increasing the expressive capability of documents. Furthermore, an author can include support for interaction, resulting in interactive multimedia documents. For example, hyperlinks can be used to connect parts of documents as well as complete documents, establishing information networks that are much better suited to represent human knowledge than traditional sequential document structures (Neilsen, 1995).

This chapter recommends ways to publish electronic documents containing (hyper)text, images, video, audio, and animation. We explain, analyze, and compare authoring environments that can be used to create interactive multimedia documents. We assist in the process of selecting which authoring system to use. One of the most important choices to be made during the process of software development is which tools to use. For developers in the Microsoft Windows environment, this choice is particularly difficult because of the huge number of authoring systems and programming languages on the market, all of which are advertised as the definitive development tool, "tomorrow's software standard," "the ultimate hypermedia tool," or "the professional's choice." It cannot be our goal to recommend one specific authoring tool, because the choice depends on the special needs of the user. Our goal is hence to explain the different alternatives available today and the decisions necessary to compare different systems.

The chapter is structured as follows: following an explanation of interactive multimedia applications, off-line as well as on-line authoring environments are discussed in detail. Authoring environments can be subdivided into frame-based, icon-based, and timeline-based systems, which are explained next. They can be based on the World Wide Web with full multimedia component support, which we explain in the following. The section will also explain how to include interactive components based on Java and VRML. Finally, we identify the critical issues involved in choosing an appropriate authoring tool.

INTRODUCTION

During the creation process of multimedia applications, in which the crucial issue is the presentation of multimedia data, users commonly use authoring systems rather than classical programming languages. Authoring systems, often called *application generators*, can be utilized instead to specify and generate multimedia presentations, similar to the process of working with text within a word processing application (Jonassen, 1989).

Application generators often offer a proprietary or a standardized scripting language, which is designed specifically to customize the look and feel of an application. User-defined functions can be developed to support the user application, exploiting the strength of the scripting language.

The term multimedia programming often denotes the integration of multimedia data into an application. However, many more application development processes can be described using this term. Development tools have been utilized for many years to publish documents electronically or to create presentations. These allow authors who are not familiar with multimedia programming languages to create and modify such applications. In this context we also call these development tools *authoring systems*. Another approach to creating interactive documents is the use of visual programming tools that already contain easy-to-use interfaces for applying audiovisual techniques to improve the traditional process of software development.

An authoring system can be defined as a program that supports the development of interactive multimedia applications by offering a variety of preprogrammed elements, thus implementing a kind of application development environment for nonprogrammers (Barker, 1993). However, it would be wrong to state that only tools that require no coding from the author can be deemed to be authoring tools, because then popular tools such as Toolbook (see http://www.asymetrix.com/products/index.html), which use their own programming languages, would be ruled out. The important issue is hence that a nonprogrammer can learn to use such a tool in a very short time (relative to that taken to learn a conventional programming language, such as C, C++, or Java), and use it to produce high-quality applications.

Classifying and evaluating the currently available authoring systems is quite complex, as these are very different with regard to orientation, features, and learnability. An off-the-shelf "point-and-click" authoring system is not yet available. This chapter concentrates on authoring tools rather than programming languages. However, it should be mentioned that the line between tools and languages is becoming increasingly blurred by products such as Visual C++ (http://msdn.microsoft.com/visualc/) and Delphi (http://community.borland.com/), which are neither programming languages nor authoring tools in the pure sense. Despite this, as we still speak of programming, it is obvious that the functionality of the program including the underlying concepts and paradigms still has to be learned. In the following we analyze authoring system paradigms.

Authoring Systems

Many authoring systems are based on one of three main designs (Riley, 1994):

Card- or Script-Based Systems

The first authoring systems described in the literature were script- or card-based systems. Perhaps the best known card-based tools are Hypercard (Kahn, 1989), which was introduced in 1987 for the Macintosh, and Asymetrix Toolbook (see http://www.asymetrix.com/products/index.html and Figure 1) for Microsoft Windows. An application generated using a script-based system is made up of one or more stacks of cards, or pages, navigated using paging or hypertext links. They are particularly well suited to producing hypertext documents. If a user usually works with a lot of text in his or her applications, it is important to find out how the authoring system handles text imports and cut-and-paste operations from one card to the next. A powerful object-oriented language is in most cases the core of such a system. The editing of elements such as graphics, video, or audio is in most cases limited or impossible. Because scripting languages often are interpreted instead of compiled, their runtime behavior can be worse than that of other systems. Card-based systems are well suited for on-line publishing purposes because hypertext is one of the main reasons for the enormous success of the World Wide Web.

Script-based systems allow programmers without any knowledge of higher programming languages to create applications including text, graph-

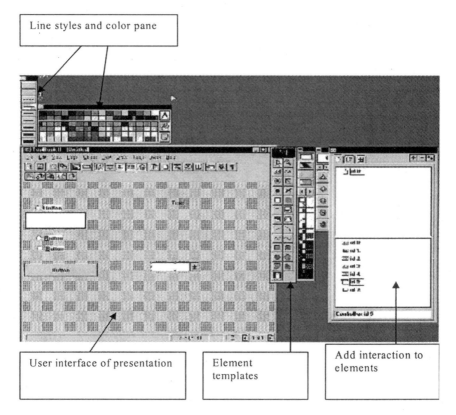

Line styles and color pane

User interface of presentation

Element templates

Add interaction to elements

FIGURE 1 Asymetrix Toolbook.

ics, and audio. Although an author has to write scripts similar to programming languages when using script-based authoring systems, system-based hardware details are completely hidden. The scripting language is focused on the creation of presentations and hence less complex than conventional programming languages. Script-based systems can be used easily to create applications in a universal and flexible way. However, the original intention, i.e., the optimal support of nonprogrammers, is neglected in these systems (Jonassen and Grabinger, 1990) because the user still has to learn a programming (scripting) language.

An interesting example of script-based systems is Macromedia's Director (see http://www.macromedia.com/software/director/), which uses a musical score metaphor. Elements parallel in time are simultaneously displayed in horizontal tracks with synchronization shown by lining up events vertically. A particular strength of the music metaphor is its ability to describe the behavior of each participant in a well-structured way (Oliveira, 1992). These programs are thus well suited to include animations or other applications where strict control of timing is essential. An example of a script-based presentation developed with Director is shown in Figure 2. It should be noted that Director is in fact a mixture of a script-based and a time-based authoring system. Time-based systems are explained below.

Icon-Based Systems

Icon-based systems use flow charts in which the developer places and connects icons to create program control flows (Brailsford and Davies, 1994). Icons are placeholders for animations, texts, or commands. The core of such programs is the Icon Palette, containing the possible functions/interactions of a program, and the Flow Line, which shows the actual links between the icons. An example of icon-based systems is Aimtech's IconAuthor (see http://www.asymetrix.com/products/index.html). The best known example of this type is Macromedia's Authorware (http://www.macromedia.com/software/authorware/), which is available for both Macintosh and IBM PC-compatible machines. In Authorware, for example, icons include display icons, in which

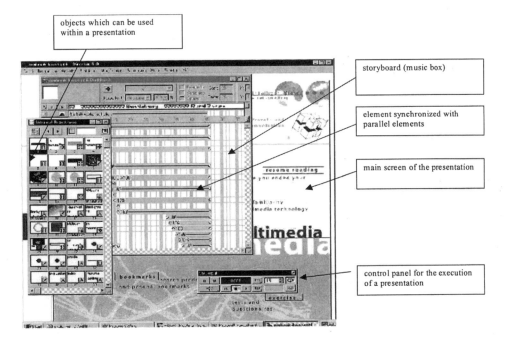

FIGURE 2 Macromedia's Director.

text and graphics can be added, as well as decision and branching icons, or animation and sound icons. Although these types of programs often can be used to generate simple applications quickly, more complex presentations require skill and planning.

Closely related to icon-based systems are authoring tools using the *frame paradigm*, where an icon palette is used. However, links between icons are conceptual and do not always represent the actual program flow. Most frame-based products integrate a compiler language, for example, Quest 5 for Windows (Allen Communications) or Apple's Apple Media Tool, which uses C as its scripting language.

Time-Based Systems

Time-based tools often use a visual time line on which multimedia events are placed to control the flow of the application. A great advantage of this kind of authoring tool is their comfortable usability. Symbolic information objects are placed on a time line, which represents the execution order of a presentation. Examples include Macromedia's Director and Action! In Figure 2 a storyboard is shown on which elements can be placed on time lines. Simple time-based tools often are used to generate multimedia presentations.

Many authoring packages also include a scripting language that increases flexibility. The scripting language may be used to launch other applications or keep track of variables. Although these are individual to each package and tailored to the functions they will most often be required to perform, they are usually based on a conventional programming language. Examples of scripting languages include OpenScript in ToolBook and LINGO in Director. Although most packages allow for the creation of content using their built-in tools, these tend to be rudimentary when compared with those available in dedicated programs. For more professional output, software dedicated to the creation and editing of a specific medium should be used. The content should then be imported/integrated into the multimedia program that has been designed using an authoring tool (see Fig. 3).

Other applications to be launched may include:

Paint or paint effect programs to create and work with graphics or images
Programs to digitize/sample and edit digital video, audio, and speech
Word processors to create and edit scripts as well as text
Programs to create and edit animations, for example, Java

Some authoring packages are driven solely by a scripting language. These differ from conventional programming languages in that they have been specifically designed to produce multimedia applications.

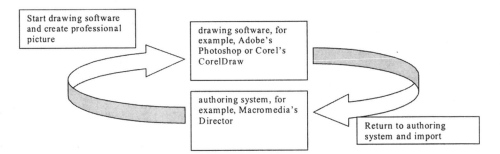

FIGURE 3   External creation of professional pictures for authoring presentations.

Visual Programming

Visual programming as well as the use of visual development frameworks support the intuitive development of software. A visual language manipulates visual information or supports visual interaction, i.e., it allows programming with visual expressions. The latter is taken to be the definition of visual programming languages. Visual programming languages may be further classified according to the type and extent of visual expression used in icon-based languages, form-based languages, and diagram languages, somewhat similar to the classification of authoring systems provided in the previous section. Visual C++ is one such language, an object-oriented language based on C++, designed to produce any sort of multimedia application. Although the code is oriented to authoring, it still requires an experienced programmer to produce good applications. Other examples of visual programming languages are products such as Visual Basic or Visual C. These are somewhere between a conventional language and an authoring system. They are very useful for rapid prototyping, as the "front end" is normally constructed by drawing onto the screen and then adding appropriate code to events such as buttons. Strictly speaking, these are not, however, visual programming languages, but rather textual languages with a graphical interface. True visual programming languages do not use code.

Current Developments

The borders between categories describing currently available authoring systems tend to disappear. Macromedia's Director, for example, is both a time-based as well as a script-based system. Applications generated using Director follow a strictly time- or event-based order, but Director also offers LINGO, a powerful programming language. Also, the transition to visual programming environments is gradual. The argument that inexperienced programmers could produce sophisticated presentations quickly seems to be rather optimistic.

Without any knowledge of the language and the concepts of an authoring system, a professional presentation cannot be generated. Also, extensions or changes of the architecture or language result in changes in the code generated outside the authoring environment. Extensions to mostly undocumented code that has not been created by the user can be very time-consuming. A user should thus be aware to what extent a programming language plays a role in the authoring system he or she wants to use. If the user is an inexperienced programmer, it would be useful to deploy an authoring system where programming or scripting is not one of the important features.

SELECTION OF AN AUTHORING SYSTEM

There is a great variety of authoring tools on the market, including off-line and on-line systems. The prospective software developer has to use stringent criteria to choose from among them. Many tools occupy a niche insofar as they are specifically designed to create and support certain types of applications. An example is NetObject's Fusion (http://www.netobjects.com/products/), which offers a rich functionality to create web sites, but only limited interfaces to import or export content. Rather than explore every specialist niche application, we focus on general-purpose authoring tools capable of creating a wide range of applications. General-purpose tools require more work from the author than niche tools and in particular require that the author acquires some application design/programming skills, but this is compensated for by their flexibility. In the following sections we analyze the requirements of authoring tools according to the following criteria: requirements of the developer, user interface, design, media, and information about the software product.

Requirements of the Developer

Working with an authoring system can be very annoying if the necessary previous planning step has not been organized well. Hence, the developer of interactive multimedia has to be aware of his or her skills and experience as well as the resources available. It should be clear what paradigm the authoring follows (for example, script-based, card-based, icon-based, or time-based) and which of them seem to fit the requirements of the developer. As already mentioned, some authoring tools assume programming experience. These tools work best if the author is already an experienced programmer, or if there is a realistic chance that he or she can acquire the necessary skills. Another important issue is the question as to whether an author wants to use an integrated package or a collection of tools to edit multimedia data. Integrated packages are convenient to use, but a collection of tools is in most cases the more powerful alternative. Certainly this is also a financial question as a collection of different tools is often much more expensive than an integrated solution containing, e.g., built-in editors for video or hypertext. Finally, the developer should not forget to check the available hardware in order to meet the requirements of the software considered. Most packages will give a recommended hardware specification including the processor type and speed, the necessary hard disk space for the installation and maybe additional space for files containing the multimedia presentation, the graphics requirements indicating how many colors and what resolution a graphics card can support, as well as additional necessary hardware such as sound card, video board, or a videodisc player.

After considering the expectations an application should be able to fulfill, it may even turn out that an authoring package does not have to be used at all. Many common packages, such as word processors, have macro languages and limited ability to handle multimedia. For example, many Microsoft Windows packages can make use of DDE (Dynamic Data Exchange) and OLE (Object Linking and Embedding) to add multimedia functionality. In some cases these may be all that is required to produce the interactive multimedia document the author has in mind.

Ease of Interface Design

Interface design is a critical issue both for the author developing an interactive multimedia application as well as for the user who will have to work with the final application. The author's expectations usually concern the comfortable use of the interface of the authoring tool itself. The user is interested in an application that is easy to use. The ease of use is thus indirectly dependent on the capabilities of the authoring tool because the author must be able to design high-quality and intuitive interfaces within the authoring system to offer a rich functionality to the user.

Thus, one general question an author should have in mind when comparing different authoring systems is whether he or she prefers to write code, for example, scripts, or if a graphical interface is more suitable. Almost every authoring tool available comes with some kind of scripting language, but the extent to which the author will need to use it will vary from package to package, also depending on the type of application to be created.

The interface the user of a final application will employ depends largely on the author of that application. However, some packages lend themselves more to one type of interface (e.g., card- or icon-based) than another. Keep in mind that users who are presented with a consistent interface, such as a standard Microsoft Windows interface, should experience a reduced cognitive load that aids concentration on the subject to be communicated. Some other features to bear in mind are:

> Communication abilities of the interface: Data exchange between the application created with the authoring system and other devices such as a palmtop or printer is very useful.
>
> The authoring system should offer screen design capabilities that are easy to use. Most modern development environments allow the developer to "draw" and manipulate objects like buttons or dialogues on a screen without having to write code for them. This makes the process of interface design and editing significantly easier.

Design

The design of any application is of particular importance as it directly influences user acceptance (Shneiderman, 1997). Systems with a bad or nonintuitive design often will be used only a few times if the user cannot be convinced that the "new" product is significantly better than that already in use. A well-defined and structured navigation is hence one of the critical issues an authoring system should be able to master (Kahn et al., 1995). Methods to navigate in a multimedia document may include menus, next/previous buttons, linked hypermedia, index lists, or site maps. Also, a powerful search facility and tools that control the navigation depending on the progress of the user (determined by user input) play an important role. A good authoring system should therefore provide tools to support the creation of structured navigation to avoid the lost-in-hyperspace problem (Kahn and Landow, 1993).

Media

The pedagogical strength of multimedia is that it uses the natural information-processing abilities that we already possess as humans. The old saying that "a picture is worth a thousand words" often understates the case, especially with regard to moving images, as our eyes are highly adapted by evolution to detecting and interpreting movement (Stonier, 1990). Different media such as text, video, audio, and animation are the basic components representing the particular strength of electronic books (Steinmetz and Nahrstedt, 1995). An authoring system should therefore provide either powerful tools to handle different media or well-defined interfaces to collaborate with external applications. This also includes data exchange with other applications or devices. Missing support can cause problems when importing data from other applications as well as difficulties concerning the output of a presentation. Some authoring systems use proprietary formats where an import of text documents is difficult, while others, especially web authoring systems, cannot be used to print a single document containing the entire web site. In the following we examine the requirements an authoring system should fulfill to support convenient work with different media.

Text

Word processing is especially important for electronic documents. If only short passages of text need to be used at a time, limited text facilities may be acceptable. In most cases, however, large bodies of text have to be incorporated, requiring the following features:

> *Import and export*: Importing and exporting documents already available should be supported by an authoring system, preserving the text formatting. The support of data exchange formats such as rich text (RTF) hence should be supported. This feature is a good criterion to evaluate authoring software products.
>
> *Text editing and processing*: Although many authoring systems include tools to edit text, there is no guarantee that features such as search and replace or spell checking are included. Especially authors who are mainly interested in writing and enhancing their material with other media need these advanced features.

Another important aspect of text processing is the ability of an authoring system to support hypertexts, as the link concept is a major advantage of electronic documents. Tools to ensure the comfortable handling of internal as well as external links hence should be part of an authoring system.

Graphics

A great number of common graphics formats are used nowadays, for example, JPEG, GIF, TIF, BMP, or EPS, to name a few (Steinmetz and Nahrstedt, 1995). Some of them are open standards, while others are proprietary. It is obvious that many authors depend on a good illustration of their material to communicate the document's content. The following graphics features should be kept in mind when analyzing the capabilities of an authoring system:

> *Data format*: The use of open, standard formats is no guarantee that graphics can be used in a specific authoring system. Tools may be needed to convert the data format in a way that graphics can be imported and exported into and from the authoring system.

Color depth: Many systems use a color depth of 8 bits, allowing 256 colors to be displayed. This can be an unfortunate failing if a large number of real-world images have to be used. A demonstration of the system can help indicate whether the system is suited to the user's needs. It also should be examined how an authoring system handles the display of two or more different pictures at the same time. Often only one of them will be properly presented, especially when the system uses private color maps.

Storage: Authoring systems store images either in separate files, for example, as assets in a pool of multimedia material, or internally in one main application file. The latter has the serious disadvantage that separate images cannot be loaded without running the authoring system. However, the overall administration of only one file is much easier than would be handling many different assets.

Video

Besides hypertext, a particular strength of electronic documents is the use of media components such as video, audio, and animation. Various video formats are available (for example, Motion-JPEG, MPEG or Apple's Quick-Time), which can be an integral part of a vivid presentation but which require in most cases external players. The application interface of an authoring system must hence provide facilities to interact with external players, including the overlay of video windows with other information using chromakey facilities as well as possibilities to control a movie. Some authoring systems also allow for controlling a video with an authoring language.

Audio

The issues to be addressed when considering the integration of sound into electronic documents are similar to those of video. Like graphics, sound files are stored in a number of different formats, for example, in SUN AU on UNIX platforms or in MP3 or WAV on PCs. It thus should be considered what formats an authoring system can import and how the playback is controlled, including facilities to control the playback volume and a random-access playback of selected parts of an audio file.

Animation

To animate something is, literally, to bring it to life. An animation covers all changes that have a visual effect (Foley et al., 1992). Visual effects might include time-varying positions (motion dynamics), shape, color, transparency, structure, and texture of an object (update dynamics), and changes in lighting, camera position, orientation, and focus. A computer-based animation is an animation performed by a computer using graphical tools to provide visual effects. Animation has gained increasing importance due to the fast growth of the World Wide Web together with emerging new languages like Java and VRML. Most authoring systems do not support Java, JavaScript, or VRML directly except through the integration of already existing components. An authoring system thus should be able to collaborate with developer tools like Symantec's VisualCafe (later available in WebGain Studio) or IBM's Visual-Age (see IBM WebSphere Studio) to enable the comfortable development of animation and its integration into the electronic document within the authoring system. Another possibility to enrich documents is to use built-in animation editors. Many packages provide some sort of animation editor. Usually this will involve moving a single image along a user-defined path. To produce more complex animations or video, external programs will be needed.

Some authors need to enrich a presentation with a significant amount of animation to visualize complex technical problems. Although animation can be generated in some packages, as always some tools will be better suited to this task than others. Again, the decision criterion is whether an authoring system should be used to define an animation, or whether an external application is better suited to perform this task.

External programs to create animation provide powerful means to write animation but may require a detailed understanding of a programming language, for example, Java. Animation created in authoring systems might not be that powerful but often is much easier to produce. Macromedia's Director, for example, can be used to define animation in a very easy way, which can even be included in on-line presentations using the Shockwave format. If an author needs an authoring system that supports the creation of animation, the package should be highly interactive. Another important issue is the definition of variables, allowing for conditional branching based on variables, or calculations regarding behavior when the animation is executed.

Product Information

Other topics related to the selection of a product include cost and distribution as well as actual and future support of an authoring system. Comparing the basic cost of different authoring systems is a difficult task, because these depend strongly on the features of the package. A rich set of tools, including a good documentation as well as comfortable handling of run-time licenses, must be kept in mind. Many, though not all, proprietary authoring environments require runtime modules (reduced versions of the environment with development functions removed) to be distributed with completed applications in order to "play" them, and the owner of the environment may charge royalties for the distribution of these modules or impose conditions on distribution and packaging.

It is also worthwhile to assess the current level of support for the package. An application with a large user base is likely to be around longer, and there will be more resources, such as mailing lists and user groups, to get help from. Another important question is the level of technical support the company provides. For some packages, such as Authorware and Toolbook, tutorial shells have been produced by a number of groups. These shells have the structure of a tutorial already created, allowing the user with a single application to only have to put in, or modify, the content.

A major worry with any proprietary development system is that it will become obsolete, especially as new versions appear, either through lack of support from the company or because the company goes out of business. This consideration encourages the use of tools that have large installed bases and discourages choosing newer authoring environments.

CONCLUSIONS

In this chapter we first explained, analyzed, and compared paradigms of authoring systems. We compared WYSIWYG (what-you-see-is what-you-get) interfaces with visual programming languages. In the second part of the chapter we elaborated criteria that can be used to analyze the capabilities of an authoring system and to select a product, for example, the requirements of the developer, the user interface, the design, the use of media, and the information about software products.

Considering how many different authoring systems are available for various operating systems, no general recommendation can be given. However, the reader should be able to analyze and select among the available products in order to produce a highly interactive ETD enriched by multimedia, exploiting to a maximal amount the capabilities of an authoring system.

REFERENCES

Barker, P. (1993). *Exploring Hypermedia*. London: Kogan Page.
Brailsford, T., Davies, P. (1994). *New Frontiers of Learning: Guidelines for Multimedia Courseware Developers in Higher Education*. ITTI: University of Nottingham.
Foley, J. D., van Dam, A., Feiner, S. K., Hughes, J. F. (1992). *Computer Graphics— Principles and Practice*. Reading, Massachusetts: Addison-Wesley.
Jonassen, D. H. (1989). *Hypertext/Hypermedia*. Englewood Cliffs, NJ: Educational Technology Publications.
Jonassen, D. H., Grabinger, R. S. (1990). Problems and issues in designing hypertext/ hypermedia for learning. In: Jonassen, D. H., Mandl, H., eds. *Designing Hyper-*

text/Hypermedia for Learning. (NATO ASI Series, Series F: Computer and Systems Sciences 67). Berlin, Germany: Springer-Verlag.

Kahn, P. (1989). Webs, trees, and stacks: how hypermedia system design effects hypermedia content. In: Salvendy, G., Smith, M. J., eds. *Designing and Using Human-Computer Interfaces and Knowledge Based Systems*. The Netherlands: Elsevier.

Kahn, P., Landow, G. P. (1993). The pleasures of possibilities: what is disorientation in hypertext? *Journal of Computing in Higher Education* 2(4):57–78.

Kahn, P., Peters, R., Landow, G. P. (1995). Three fundamental elements of visual rhetoric in hypertext. In: Schuler, W., Hannemann, J., Streitz, N. A., eds. *Designing User Interfaces for Hypermedia*. Research Reports ESPRIT, Springer-Verlag.

Nielsen, J. (1995). Multimedia and hypertext. The Internet and Beyond. Cambridge, Massachusetts: Academic Press.

Oliveira, A. (1992). Hypermedia and multimedia. In: Oliveira, A., ed. *Hypermedia Courseware: Structures of Communication and Intelligent Help* (NATO ASI Series. Series F: Computer and Systems Sciences). Berlin, Germany: Springer-Verlag.

Riley, F. (1994). *Understanding IT: A Review of Hypermedia Authoring Packages*. Sheffield: CVCP/USDU.

Shneiderman, B. (1997). *Designing the User Interface*. Reading, Massachusetts: Addison Wesley.

Steinmetz, R., Nahrstedt, K. (1995). *Multimedia: Computing, Communications and Applications*. Upper Saddle River, NJ: Prentice Hall.

Stonier, T. (1990). *Information and the Internal Structure of the Universe*. Berlin: Springer-Verlag.

10

XML—An Overview

Shahrooz Feizabadi
Virginia Polytechnic Institute and State University
Blacksburg, Virginia

INTRODUCTION

In the brief span of just over a decade since its inception, the World Wide Web has grown at an astounding rate. Near-ubiquitous internet accessibility, coupled with ever-increasing data transmission bandwidth, have made terms such as the "Web" or "surfing" part of the everyday American lexicon. With trillions of dollars in investments, the IT industry has come to be a corner stone of the Information Age economy.

As witnessed by the rapid rise of the "dot com" world, the unprecedented development of the information infrastructure created countless opportunities for the establishment of business enterprises. Backed by substantial investment capital, IT developers competed fiercely to venture into markets never before envisioned. While historically proven most efficient, this development model is not free of adverse side effects.

Many a novel and innovative solution has been devised by IT companies to address the technical challenges faced along the way. Not all solutions, however, are compatible, or even optimal. With the primary objective of capturing the widest market share and maximizing profitability, proprietary technologies abound. Given any internet development issue with a potential economic impact of consequence, any number of competing proprietary approaches are proposed—often cacophonous and nonconvergent. Developed in isolation and property of the patent holders, such solutions are often changed with no notification and manipulated to advance company objectives.

Enter the scene: W3C. To balance this environment, a group of individuals (including Tim Berners-Lee, the inventor of the World Wide Web), companies, and organizations founded the World Wide Web Consortium (W3C). The consortium now includes more than 500 organizations worldwide and has developed more than 35 technical specifications for the web since its establishment in 1994. W3C's development efforts advocate and adhere to open standards guidelines ensuring substantial community participation and non-proprietary practices such as internet RFCs (Request for Comments) and involvement with IETF (Internet Engineering Task Force). Their stated design principles are (1):

1. *Interoperability*: Specifications for the Web's languages and protocols must be compatible with one another and allow (any) hardware and software used to access the Web to work together.
2. *Evolution*: The Web must be able to accommodate future technologies. Design principles such as simplicity, modularity, and extensibility will increase the chances that the Web will work with emerging technologies such as mobile Web devices and digital television, as well as others to come.
3. *Decentralization*: Decentralization is without a doubt the newest principle and the most difficult to apply. To allow the Web to "scale" to worldwide proportions while resisting errors and breakdowns, the architecture (like the Internet) must limit or eliminate dependencies on central registries.

XML is one such technology conceived by the W3C.

WHAT IS XML?

W3C defines XML thus: "The eXtensible Markup Language (XML) is the universal format for structured documents and data on the Web" (2). While true, this definition is somewhat broad. Though it initially appears deceptively plain, XML is a multifaceted concept defying oversimplified definitions. The sections outlined below describe XML at different levels.

Metalanguge

Metadata

Abstractly, any type of digital information can be viewed as data and represented as a raw bit stream. The contents can be quite complex such as entire databanks, or a simple integer, such as:

0156904365

By itself, however, we know nothing of the meaning of this integer. Now suppose our integer appears in the context shown below:

Title	Author	ISBN
Four Ways to Forgiveness	Le Guin, Ursula K.	0575601752
Till We Have Faces	Lewis, C. S.	0156904365
. . .	. . .	. . .

The visual layout of a table readily conveys to us the relevant information needed to deduce the meaning of the specific piece of data. The data boundaries are clearly delineated by the table cell structure, and the column headings descriptively label contents. Positional information, coupled with descriptive column headings inherent in a table structure, allows us to intuitively establish context and deduce the semantics (meaning) of the data cells in the table.

Metadata are data about data. It is the descriptive information that makes data meaningful. Though implicit, the position of data within a table, along with the column headings, can be viewed as metadata.

The "table" data construct has been extensively used in databases. Visualizing data in this format is easy and intuitive. However, database management systems must internally represent this information. Oracle®, for instance, internally stores metadata in what is called *data dictionaries*. Microsoft® SQL Server® equivalently stores metadata in their *system tables*. Other proprietary internal data representation schemes exist.

Markup Languages

A *markup language* is, by definition, a method of adding labels (marks) to other contents that enhance the contents in some way (8). A familiar example of a markup language is the Hyper Text Markup Language (HTML). For example, our integer from the previous section can be marked up by adding the HTML boldface tags:

```
<b> 0156904365</b>
```

An HTML browser renders the contents thus:

0156904365

HTML is composed of a predefined set of tags used for marking up contents. An HTML browser is designed to understand and process these predefined tags, which make up the legal *vocabulary* of HTML. Though the markup enhanced the appearance of our integer, without the context we still know nothing of its meaning.

We learned from the previous section that our integer is actually the ISBN for C. S. Lewis's book "Till We Have Faces." Suppose we wish to use markup to enhance our data by attaching metadata to it, such as:

<ISBN> 0156904365 </ISBN>

While this is valid given the concept of markup, HTML would be incapable of accommodating it as it does not include an < ISBN > tag in its predefined vocabulary.

Grow-Your-Own Markup

The most applicable—and perhaps the most accurate—approach to understanding XML would be to view it as a standardized framework for creation of *self-describing* data (4). XML provides this capability by allowing creation and extension of markup languages—hence the name XML.

Adhering to a bare-bones set of syntax rules, one can produce a legal markup language under XML. Such a markup language is called an *XML application* or a *document type* (4,5). A *well-formed* XML application is one that conforms to these minimal set of syntax rules:

The document must have only one root element.
Proper nesting of all elements is strictly enforced.
All elements must have both start and end tags.
Start and end element tags must contain exactly the same element name.

Keeping to these rules, we can now create our first XML document:

```
<? xml version="1.0">
<library>
    <ISBN> 0156904365 </ISBN>
</library>
```

Though trivial, the above example demonstrates XML's ability to create self-describing data. From the outlined simple structure it is clear that the encapsulated data is an ISBN number, which in turn is itself a part of a library. Click, one huge step for standardized structuring and formatting of data! Incidentally, metadata association yields much more meaningful web search results as context is fetched along with the data.

We can expand our use of XML as a nonproprietary metadata representation by describing the table in the previous section using XML:

```
<?xml version="1.0">
<library>
    <book>
        <title> Four ways to Forgiveness </title>
        <author> Le Guin, Ursula K. </author>
        <ISBN> 0575601752 </ISBN>
    </book>
    <book>
        <title> Till We Have Faces </title>
        <author> Lewis, C. S. </author>
        <ISBN> 0156904365 </ISBN>
    </book>
</library>
```

The above example implicitly illustrates the elegant and intuitive simplicity of XML. Ease of use and flexibility as building blocks for many different types of information expression are among the advantages of XML (3,5,6).

Because metadata are data about data, a *metalanguage* is a language about a language. As such, XML can be viewed as a metalanguage. It provides a language to build home-grown markup languages. The objective of providing this capability is to maximize metadata flexibility for customized, domain-specific markup languages to describe the content they encapsulate (6–8).

Information Storage and Retrieval Philosophy

At a higher level, XML can be viewed as a configurable toolkit for structuring, storing, managing, and exchanging data (4,7). XML's objectives in this context are twofold: first, it intends to strip data of all but their essential attributes yielding the purest data format; second, it aims to impose a strict hierarchical structure on data.

Presentation/Semantics Decoupling

A document's *presentation* addresses issues regarding the appearance of the document. This would involve "aesthetics" such as font types, font colors, background images, table spacing, etc. The *semantics* of a document, on the other hand, strictly involves the meaning of the data contained in the document.

HTML contains tags that pertain to both presentation and semantics. For example, the < title > tag would be a part of document semantics, as it clearly describes the function of the data it encapsulates. The < font > tag, conversely, would be an example of a presentational tag, as it only conveys how the data it wraps should look, but nothing of its meaning.

Historically, HTML has its roots in SGML (Standard Generalized Markup Language, ISO 8879) (4,6). SGML is derived from a markup language originally designed at IBM for the production of technical manuals. SGML is itself a specification for design of specialized markup languages. As a "pure" markup language, it keeps styling information separate from document contents. To implement HTML across a distributed system, SGML had to be greatly simplified and "augmented." As a result, HTML drifted from the original design principles of SGML. To address the ever-increasing demand for more control over the display of web pages, style information was interwoven, and eventually tightly integrated into HTML specifications (4,6).

Advances in the state of the art, however, have allowed for regaining some of the functionality lost in HTML design compromises. An ambitious project was started to implement SGML over the web. This, however, was ruled out as too complex—for now. As a result, while staying true to the original design goals of SGML, a limited subset of it was adapted for the web. This SGML subset was later dubbed XML.

True to form, XML maintains a strict separation between document presentation and semantics. This allows for storage and manipulation of pure data unhindered by extraneous style information. This untangling of meaning from style affords information systems architects the freedom of abstract data types (ADTs). Once data systems are designed to satisfaction, presentation can be handled separately by a different system. XML's methods of data presentation are discussed later in this chapter.

Data Representation

Having disassociated ourselves from data presentation concerns, we can now focus on data structuring. Most data, by nature, can be represented hierarchically. A *tree* data structure best represents hierarchical data. A legal XML application must be, at a minimum, well formed. In order to be well formed, all document elements must be properly nested, and exactly one root element must exist per document. Combined, these two rules enforce a rooted tree structure over the XML document elements (5,8).

This fact is quite significant as trees are powerful and well-understood data structures. Insertion, search, and delete operations can readily and optimally be implemented for data thus represented. Furthermore, each element within the tree can be uniquely addressed. XML Pointer Language (XPointer) is the mechanism for addressing nodes of the tree structure comprising an XML document (4,7).

Add to this the concept of *namespaces* (a method of ensuring element-name collision resolution) and *URI*s (Unique Resource Identifiers) and click, we now have the unprecedented capability of uniquely addressing *each element* of *any* XML document—a finer level of granularity not possible before. The significance of this newly acquired capability is self-evident.

PRESENTATION

The XML document itself is designed to contain only data tagged with metadata. Presentation information for a document is stored elsewhere. This affords XML the flexibility to "dress up" the data in any desired output form. The association of contents and presentation information is achieved through the use of *stylesheets*. One-to-one and one-to-many mappings of styles and elements are allowed within a stylesheet (6,8).

Disassociation of style and meaning allows for creation of a "master" stylesheet that can be used with many documents. One needs only alter the master stylesheet to effect systemwide changes to output display of all associated XML files.

Using the master stylesheet concept, one can consistently display many XML files using the same presentation scheme. The opposite of this concept also holds true: using stylesheets, the data contents of one XML document can be presented in multiple, distinctly different output formats. Going back to our two-book library example from the previous section, we can design a stylesheet that would output the information about our books in an HTML table to be displayed on the web. Alternatively, we can use a different stylesheet to output the same table in PDF. The same contents can be read aloud using a stylesheet specific to a speech-synthesizing device (4,6).

We can wrap any style around the pure data extracted from the XML file. This offers us tremendous flexibility as we are not limited to any specific style vocabulary. Different presentation versions of the same data can be dynamically and simultaneously produced and displayed (Fig. 1).

XML provides a rich set of data-presentation tools. By and large, CSS (Cascading Style Sheets) is prominently used to associate presentational style information with XML-tagged data. Like CSS, CSS2 is a W3C specification that can potentially be used with XML (9).

Beyond CSS, XSL (Extensible Stylesheet Language) is used for advanced styling of documents. The term "styling," however, is used loosely here. XSL is capable of providing much more than simple styling for a

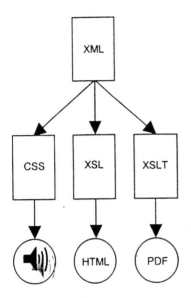

FIGURE 1   Different versions of pure data.

document. XSL is composed of three parts: XSL Transformation (described later in this chapter), XPath (a method of referring to specific parts of an XML document), and XSL-FO (XSL Formatting Objects).

XML PROCESSING

Extracting data from an XML document requires *processing*. A web browser capable of displaying XML documents is, in effect, an XML processor. The ASCII file containing XML code is a physical representation of the tree ADT (Abstract Data Type) underlying the document structure. *Parsing* XML is the process of decoding XML tags in the input file to internally reproduce in memory the same ADT present in the document. Once an XML document is parsed, its data elements are available for manipulation by other processes.

HTML parsers are designed to offer a great degree of flexibility. Handling of potential errors, such as missing end-tags, is left to the HTML parser. As HTML has come to be concerned mostly with presentation, parsers can make intelligent guesses as to how to handle errors. The parser can, for instance, implicitly assume a missing end-tag upon encountering a new start-tag. HTML parsing specifications are somewhat loosely defined and highly implementation dependent (4,6).

XML parsers, on the other hand, are designed to be quite strict and strongly enforce the language rules. A missing end-tag, in XML's case, would cause a fatal parsing error. Specifications are meant to ensure consistent processing. XML must work the same way, everywhere, every time (4).

DOCUMENT MODELING

As previously mentioned, a home-grown markup language using XML rules is called an *XML application* or a *document model* (see Figure 2). XML applications can conform to two different levels of syntax strictness. At a minimum, XML documents must be well formed. Documents conforming to the next level of syntactical strictness are considered valid (5).

Well-Formed XML

A well-formed XML document, as previously indicated, is one that minimally adheres to a set of rules on forming and using tags. The rules defining a well-formed document impose no restrictions on the vocabulary, grammar, or element attributes (5,6,10):

> One can use any element name, as long as the matching end-tag is supplied.
> No restrictions are imposed on what these elements can contain. They may be empty elements or contain anything.

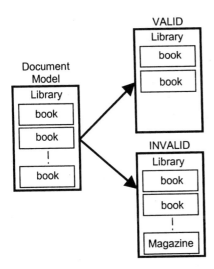

FIGURE 2   Document model, valid and invalid.

If optional element attributes are used, they need not conform to any predefined restrictions.
Elements may appear in any order.

Valid XML

Validity constraints impose a higher level of syntactic restriction on an XML application. The validation process involves the following steps:

1. XML rules are applied to create a markup language. This markup language is, in essence, a set of metadata tags that encapsulate the document's data contents.
2. Our freshly minted document model provides us with a finite vocabulary and a grammar specific to that vocabulary. This model serves as a blueprint of what other XML documents should contain.
3. Document instances structured upon this model are restricted to its finite vocabulary and grammar rules.
4. A new document conversant in this dialect of XML must use its vocabulary only and strictly adhere to its grammar rules to be considered valid.

A misspelled tag—as long as accompanied by its matching pair—is not marked as an error in a well-formed document. However, a validation check of the document would reject the misspelled tag as outside the allowable vocabulary for that document. Furthermore, document modeling ensures conformance to the intended document structure by tightly regulating elements, their attributes, and the order in which they appear within the document.

In short, XML document modeling is the formal definition of language elements and how they can be used. It defines what elements a document can contain, how these elements are named and structured, and what attributes they must have.

Currently, XML accomplishes document modeling through *DTDs* and *Schemas*.

DTD

Inherited almost intact from SGML, a Document Type Definition (DTD) describes the structure of an XML document using declarative rules. As previously mentioned, a document model provides the vocabulary and grammar for a document instance based upon a model. DTDs provide this capability in the following way (6,10):

1. The legal vocabulary for a document type is defined in a DTD. All element names are predefined here. A document instance using this DTD cannot contain elements names outside this finite set.

2. The DTD provides grammar rules on how the document's vocabulary can be combined and used. A *content model* is defined for each element specifying:

   a. What is allowed inside that element—whether data or other elements
   b. The order of appearance of the contents
   c. The numbers of each
   d. Whether they are required or optional

3. Attributes for each element are also defined here. The definition includes:

   a. The attribute name
   b. Optional default value for the attribute
   c. Whether the attribute is itself optional or required

4. Document structuring is further enhanced by DTD *modularization.* Consistent with software engineering principles, all or parts of external DTDs stored elsewhere can be imported and reused in a modular fashion. Large DTDs can often contain complex and numerous element and attribute declarations. Logically related elements can be grouped into functional subcomponents and stored separately. A DTD can then import and recombine these element declarations as needed (4,7).

Schema

Historically, DTDs were designed as a part of SGML to facilitate document management. In this role, DTDs function quite adequately within XML as well. However, as XML expands beyond document management into such arenas as e-commerce and application-to-application message exchange, limitations of DTDs become more apparent. Schemas are the next step beyond DTDs in the evolution of XML document modeling.

A significant enhancement in XML document modeling added by schemas is *strong typing.* A language in which every piece of data is associated with a single data type is considered strongly typed. Strong typing provides greatly improved validation, error-checking, and much finer-grain control over data. This allows XML processors to strictly enforce consistent data representation in heterogeneous environments, conforming to XML's design objective of high reliability (11,12).

Furthermore, XML schemas are themselves written in XML. This offers many advantages. Learning a separate DTD syntax is no longer necessary; the schema simply has to be well-formed XML. Also, as with any other XML document, standard XML tools can be used to edit schemas. Like XML documents, schemas can be used as components of a flexible systems architecture. Generic schemas can be devised once and retooled dynamically through XSLT transformations (described later in this chapter) to fit specific needs on demand (4,6,11).

As with DTDs, schemas also provide structure for an XML document. Borrowed from the world of object-oriented programming, a method of defining structure by example has been included with XML schemas. *Archetypes*, analogous to object super classes, can be defined in a schema. The specifications for this aspect of XML schemas have not yet been finalized, however, proposals include mechanisms for archetype refinement, analogous to method overrides in instantiated objects (12,13).

Examples of XML Applications

Rules of XML have been applied to generate many domain-specific markup languages (also known as XML applications or document models). Each such language is defined by a legal vocabulary and grammar through DTDs or schemas. XML-based markup languages have been adapted to address diverse needs (5):

> CML, the Chemical Markup Language, is used for describing and rendering molecular structures.
> XCI, the XML Court Interface, has been designed for legal document and information exchange.
> BSML, Bioinformatics Sequence Markup Language, is used to describe, encode, and display RNA, DNA, and protein sequence information.
> MusicML is used for composing sheet music.
> RETS, the Real Estate Transaction Standard, is used for exchange of real estate information.
> Vector Markup Language, VML, is used for storing vector graphics data.
> OFX, Open Financial Exchange, has been adopted as a data format by financial programs such as Quicken® and Microsoft® Money®.

Examples of XML applications are numerous and ever-expanding. Three of the more widely used document types are described below.

MathML

> MathML is intended to facilitate the use and re-use of mathematical and scientific content on the Web, and for other applications such as computer algebra systems, print typesetting, and voice synthesis. MathML can be used to encode both the presentation of mathematical notation for high-quality visual display, and mathematical content, for applications where the semantics plays more

of a key role such as scientific software or voice synthesis. MathML is cast as an application of XML. As such, with adequate style sheet support, it will ultimately be possible for browsers to natively render mathematical expressions. For the immediate future, several vendors offer applets and plug-ins which can render MathML in place in a browser. Translators and equation editors which can generate HTML pages where the math expressions are represented directly in MathML will be available soon. (14)

For example, Einstein's famous equation, $E = mc^2$, would be represented as:

```
<?xml version="1.0"?>
<math xmlns=http://www.w3c.org/TR/REC-MathML/>
    <mrow>
        <mi>E</mi>
        <mo>=</mo>
        <mrow>
            <mi>m</mi>
            <mo>&invisibleTimes;</mo>
            <apply>
                <power>
                    <mi>c</mi>
                    <mn>2</mn>
                </power>
            </apply>
        </mrow>
    </mrow>
</math>
```

XHTML

An XML-compliant reformulation of HTML, XHTML is almost the same as HTML 4. Strict XHTML excludes presentational tags and relies on external mapping of contents to styles (through such mechanisms as CSS) for output. The basic document type for this application is defined over a set of modules (8).

Consistent with XML metadata philosophy, all elements (tags) are designed to mark the semantic contents of the document. The "structure" module, for instance, consists of four tags: < body >, < head >, < html >, < title >. These tags clearly convey the semantics of the information they encapsulate.

Another example clearly illustrating this point is the < strong > tag included in the "text" module. Semantically, this tag is intended to indicate strong emphasis. Once processed for output presentation, the information encapsulated by this tag should be clearly distinguishable. The implementation, however, is not explicitly stated. Using stylesheets, one may choose to indicate strong emphasis by using boldfaced, underlined text. For example, the tagged word < strong > important < /strong > would appear as **important**. Another stylesheet, however, could map the same tag to italicized, boldfaced text, rendering it thus: ***important***. A third stylesheet might format the word to be pronounced slightly louder on a speech synthesizer.

DocBook

Designed for (but not limited to) software documentation and technical publications, DocBook is an XML application providing a rich vocabulary of several hundred elements. Widely adopted by open-source developers and publishers, this application has been designed to accommodate works even as large as multivolume book sets. A light-weight simplified version of DocBook is also publicly available. While maintaining upward compatibility, this small subset of the original DocBook DTD is intended for single, article-type documents (15).

TRANSFORMATION

Transformation is the process of rearranging the contents of an XML document to produce another XML document. Recall our simplistic two-book library example (4,6,16):

```
<?xml version="1.0">
<library>
    <book>
        <title> Four Ways to Forgiveness </title>
        <author> Le Guin, Ursula K. </author>
        <ISBN> 057601752 </ISBN>
    </book>
    <book>
        <title> Till We Have Faces </title>
        <author> Lewis, C. S. </author>
        <ISBN> 0156904365 </ISBN>
    </book>
</library>
```

The books in this example are sorted alphabetically by title. Suppose we want a sorting of our books based on ISBN. A transformation would produce the following XML document:

```
<?xml version="1.0">
<library>
    <book>
        <title> Till We Have Faces </title>
        <author> Lewis, C. S. </author>
        <ISBN> 0156904365 </ISBN>
    </book>
    <book>
        <title> Four Ways to Forgiveness </title>
        <author> Le Guin, Ursula K. </author>
        <ISBN> 057601752 </ISBN>
    </book>
</library>
```

Transformations can also be used to filter documents. Suppose we want only the book titles in our library. A transformation would produce:

```
<?xml version="1.0">
<library>
    <book>
        <title> Till We Have Faces </title>
    </book>
    <book>
        <title> Four Ways to Forgiveness </title>
    </book>
</library>
```

A transformation can be used to map one domain-specific XML vocabulary to another. Suppose we want to display the author names in our library. We can use a transformation that would filter out all but the author names, and then define a mapping to produce an XHTML document for output:

```
<?xml version="1.0">
<!DOCTYPE html
      PUBLIC "-//W3C//DTD XHTML 1.0 Stricy//EN"
      "http://www.w3c.org/TR/xhtml1/DTD/
      xhtml-strict.dtd">
<html
      xmlns="http://www.w3c.org/1999/xhtml"
      xml:lang="en" lang="en"
      <head>
          <title> My Authors </title>
      </head>
      <body>
          <br> Le Guin, Ursula K. </br>
          <br> Lewis, C. S. </br>
      </body>
</html>
```

XSLT (Extensible Stylesheet Language for Transformations) is a complex programming language offering a rich set of tools used for defining XML transformations. Publicly available transformation engines such as XT or Xalan can be used for XSLT processing.

RELATED TECHNOLOGIES

At the lowest level, XML can be viewed as a generic data representation scheme. Due to its self-describing (metadata) nature, an XML data stream embeds information about what the raw data traffic means. Though somewhat verbose, its standardized, human-readable form makes it a highly versatile building block for information management, and thus highly desirable.

Another open-source project related to XML from W3C is DOM, the Document Object Model. Addressing the need for standardization of dynamic web page content delivery, DOM is a "platform- and language-neutral interface that will allow programs and scripts to dynamically access and update the content, structure and style of documents. The document can be further processed and the results of that processing can be incorporated back into the presented page" (1).

XML's standardized format makes it particularly well suited for application-to-application communications and line-of-business data integration. Data exchange in a heterogeneous environment has been addressed in various contexts by such technologies as RPC (Remote Procedure Call) and CORBA (Common Object Request Broker Architecture). XML's inherent ability to maintain data structure integrity as it moves between environments implicitly addresses one of the thornier issues of interoperable data exchange.

Originally designed at Microsoft® and later placed in the open-source domain, SOAP 1.2 (Simple Object Access Protocol) is an XML-based remote object-invocation protocol designed for distributed systems. It defines a framework for structured and typed application-specific message exchange between collaborating peers in a heterogeneous networked environment (17). XML's family of Xlink, XPath, and XPointer technologies provide greatly expanded data addressing and querying capabilities.

Ultimately, XML code must be parsed and processed at the lower levels. To this end, SAX (Simple API for XML) provides an event-based application programming interface. As middleware, SAX handles reading input streams, parsing XML, and routing data to event handlers. Higher level constructs, such as event handlers, can then be made to interface with SAX underneath (4,6,7).

CONCLUSIONS

Quite young at version 1.0, XML has made significant inroads far and wide into the landscape of today's information technology. Its success is largely due to its simplicity, versatility, and self-consistency. A highly configurable data representation scheme, XML can be readily adapted as a vessel for virtually all hierarchical information. XML's tight definition and strict syntax enforcement have made it highly portable and error resistant. Its built-in support for Unicode allows it to more easily transcend geographical boundaries. Using families of technologies such as XSL, highly domain-specific behavior can be programmed in the XML framework. As Perl has come to be the duct tape of the internet, XML can potentially become the internet Swiss Army knife!

Though well received, XML is not devoid of controversy. A young family of technologies, many of XML's specifications are works in progress. Independent implementations of systems specifications drift apart due to (1) lack of a formal certification process and (2) the ever-evolving nature of the very specifications. Furthermore, high processing efficiency has been compromised to accommodate the necessarily verbose nature of XML.

REFERENCES

1. World Wide Web Consortium, http://www.w3.org/Consortium.
2. Extensible Markup Language (XML), http://www.w3.org/XML/#9802xml10.

3. Feldman, B. (1999). Get up to speed with XML, XML Magazine. http://www.fawcette.com/Archives/premier/mgznarch/xml/1999/01win99/bfwin99/bfwin99.asp.
4. Ray, E. T. (2001). *Learning XML*. Sebastopol, CA: O'Reilly and Associates.
5. Young, M. J. (2000). *Step by Step XML*. Redmond, WA: Microsoft Press.
6. Goldfarb, C. F., Prescod, P. (2000). *The XML Handbook*. 2nd ed. Upper Saddle River, NJ: Prentice Hall.
7. Harold, E. R., Means, S. (2001). *XML in a Nutshell*. Sebastopol, CA: O'Reilly and Associates.
8. Hunter, D., et al. (2001). *Beginning XML*. 2nd ed. Chicago, IL: Wrox Inc.
9. Gerlach, M. (2000). Abstracting the interface: building an adaptable Web app front end with XML and XSL, IBM DeveloperWorks. http://www-106.ibm.com/developerworks/library/x-abstract/index.html.
10. Wahlin, D. Back to basics: the XML fundamentals, XML Magazine. http://www.fawcette.com/archives/listissue.asp?pubID = 2&magIssueID = 432.
11. Williams, K. (2001). Soapbox: why XML schema beats DTDs hands-down for data: a look at some data features of XML Schema, IBM Developer Works. http://www-106.ibm.com/developerworks/xml/library/x-sbsch.html.
12. Radiya, A. (2000). The basics of using XML Schema to define elements, IBM DeveloperWorks. http://www-106.ibm.com/developerworks/library/xml-schema/index.html.
13. Mikula, N., Levy, K. (1999). Schemas take DTDs to the next level, XML Magazine. http://www.fawcette.com/Archives/premier/mgznarch/xml/1999/01win99/nmwin99/nmwin99.asp.
14. W3C's Math Home Page, http://www.w3.org/Math.
15. OASIS DocBook, http://www.oasis-open.org/docbook.
16. Colan, M. (2001). Putting XSL transformations to work, IBM Developer Works. http://www-106.ibm.com/developerworks/library/x-xsltwork/index.html.
17. W3C SOAP, http://www.w3.org/TR/2001/WD-soap12-part0-20011217.

11

Beyond the Paper Paradigm: ETD-ML and the Case for XML Markup

Neil Kipp and Shahrooz Feizabadi
KIPP Software
Denver, Colorado

INTRODUCTION

This chapter presents a discussion of different methodologies used in the generation of ETDs. The comparative merits of the underlying technologies are outlined and their suitability for the ETD project explored. ETD-ML, a proposed universal markup language for creation of ETDs, is discussed and evaluated.

MORE THAN PUTTING DOTS ON THE SCREEN

Information needs a face. If publishing is putting ink on paper, then electronic publishing is putting dots on the computer screen. The purpose of both is the same: information exchange. Electronic theses and dissertations (ETDs) explicate the research of the graduate student in an electronic medium. Having ETDs gives us the opportunity to exploit electronic media for the overall benefit of students, faculty, librarians, and library patrons, particularly by allowing automatic search and retrieval, machine indexing, and unlimited, perfect copying.

Indeed, electronic publishing can be more than putting dots on the screen. It can involve creating and manipulating ideas, having tools that search for terms and concepts, and *data mining* of documents to extract the knowledge they contain. And while the "page" is a convenient structuring device for printed artifacts, pages often have little to do with the semantic intent of the author, and can actually hinder the author's expression.

Unfortunately, the electronic medium can be problematic. If the electronic publication uses "virtual paper" like Adobe's Portable Document Format (PDF), then in many ways the ETD has some of the same disadvantages as paper—in other words, virtual paper can be just as restrictive a publication target as chiseled stone. Virtual paper is inflexible to reformat. Furthermore, we must teach the computer to "read" electronic paper in order to determine the difference between, for example, italicized book titles and foreign phrases. It is conceivable that authors could better express themselves electronically, but to do so we must escape the two-dimensional prison of the "page."

For ETDs we can leave the page metaphor and take advantage of a flexible electronic medium to archive students' research to be usable and reusable forever, especially in ways that we cannot predict. Facilitating this means that we must unglue ourselves from the paper paradigm and provide a way for students to prepare and submit ETDs.

Furthermore, tearing up the page metaphor gives digital libraries of ETDs the opportunity to:

1. Make searching the corpus easier, faster, and more precise
2. Provide unlimited circulation without risking damage to the information source (in this case, the ETD)
3. Accommodate the alternate needs of persons with disabilities
4. Perfectly preserve media for eternity by renewing the resource itself or by emulating tools used to manipulate the resource in newer contexts

The longevity of electronic formats is critical for ETDs. For example, Microsoft releases a new version of its page-based Word product every other year or so. If libraries are standardized on the Word format, then every document in the archive must be upgraded—at substantial cost—to keep up with new releases of the software. What about the TeX (or LaTeX) document formatting language? While new versions are less likely, it is still a page-based metaphor that does not take advantage of even the simplest use of the electronic medium such as hypertext. PDF is not ideal—once the document is in PDF, it is nearly immutable (feature for many; nightmare for archivists).

Therefore we ask: How can we capture the semantic intention of the author—as a "protodocument"—so that we can preserve it? And once captured and preserved, how do we generate from it the normal representations (such as PDF or paper) that are usefully readable this very minute? Representing with high fidelity the *semantic contents* of a document rather than one or more of its many possible faces is the deeper challenge faced by electronic archivists.

PROPOSED SOLUTION

Perhaps a *formal language* for the expression of ETD semantics will facilitate long-term preservation of ETDs. Such a language would capture the underlying intention of authors so that their ideas could be used and reused by themselves and others. The language would be primarily declarative; for example, it would include ways to express "This is my chapter," "I'm being *emphatic* here," and "Here I have cited an inspiring article published in the Journal of Psychotropic Xenomorphs, January 2001." Also, the language should be readable as plain text (like a programming language), processable by computers, and easy for ETD authors to understand and utilize.

One method of creating readable, declarative languages is the use of a "markup language." Historically, "markup" comes from the printing industry process by which editors give instructions to typesetters indicating that a data string should be formatted in a particular way. Similarly, electronic markup enhances the document's contents by denoting such information as type, function, structure, or relationship to other annotated data entities. Electronic markup first appeared in the late 1960s, where authors embedded markup characters as control codes into their electronic documents to make page printers behave in certain ways, instructing printers to "change to italics," "return the carriage," "switch back to roman," and so on. Languages such as TeX and troff well addressed text formatting issues and provided a high degree of control over how documents looked. Printed output, however, was less consistent. Control codes were not standard between printers; furthermore, some printers had features that others did not. As a result, document sharing and archiving became problematic because documents tended to outlive printer hardware.

Faced with the challenges of consistent content management and document presentation in a heterogeneous environment, the Graphic Communications Association (GCA) devised a preliminary solution. The problem was twofold: consistently *presenting* documents, while simultaneously providing a method for document *structuring*. The latter involved a decomposition of a document into its functional components and denoting them accordingly—a mailing address, for instance, would contain functional components such as city, state, and zip code. The structure of the document containing this mailing address would be enhanced if the components of the address were thus marked up. Absent this structural markup, a TEX document, for instance, would simply contain information about how the five-digit number (our zip code) should look but convey nothing of its semantics.

GenCode was CGA's solution to this problem. Generic coding principles called for establishment of a consistent set of "generic" markup tags capable of describing different types of documents. Components of a document could be descriptively tagged according to function, then reassembled into a cohesive whole. Though sometimes "busy," documents marked up in GenCode are human-readable. The markup is done in the same environment as the text editing. The final output, however, must be rendered. The markup tags have to be processed and translated into their presentational equivalents.

GenCode thus achieved an initial decoupling of a document's presentational formatting (syntax) and its functional meaning (semantics). The systems pertaining to each could now be developed separately. The informational contents of a document can now be treated abstractly as "pure" data and manipulated accordingly—stored in databases, processed by external algorithms, etc. The focus now becomes what the document contains, *not* how it looks. Freed from the "pint preview" mode, authors can concentrate on content quality.

Viewing GenCode as potentially promising, the IBM Corporation started the GML (Generalized Markup Language) project, keeping to GenCode's design principles. Charles Goldfarb and his team at IBM aimed to develop GML as a flexible document authoring system capable of functioning across systems of varying architecture and physical location. The project proved highly successful. Use of descriptive tags enabled parsing and processing of documents marked up in GML by a host of external applications. GML later became the official document authoring language for all of IBM's considerable body of technical literature.

Impressed with the innovation and versatility of GML, the American National Standards Institute (ANSI) considered it for adoption as a standard. SGML (Standard Generalized Markup Language), a refined version of GML, became an ANSI standard in early 1980s. Soon after, the Department of Defense as well as the Internal Revenue Service adopted SGML as their official documentation language.

From the late 1960s to the early 1980s, many electronic documents including theses and dissertations were "marked up" prior to printing using systems like Scribe. High-volume publishers continue to use markup languages for their automatic typesetting systems.

In the early 1980s, the "PostScript" page description language was released by Adobe Software, beginning the age of "virtual paper." While PostScript does have a markup language component (data strings are "annotated" with position and font information), it does not have a generic markup component. In other words, higher-level structures (like "chapters") cannot be represented easily using the structures provided by the PostScript language.

As computers came to the desktop, software tools and display devices for "desktop publishing" were becoming available that made document creation and printing more direct and usable. The "what-you-see-is-what-you-get" (WYSIWYG) paradigm emerged—a document's printed output is exactly the same as its screen display. The WYSIWYG way has fewer steps: because it is more direct, it is easier to learn and easier to use. It demands less from its users and gives them a natural way to make the pages that are familiar to them. So for the love of printed pages, generic markup was nearly forgotten.

Web pages, on the other hand, are not inextricably paper. Rather, "markup" is born again in the worldwide Hypertext Markup Language (HTML). HTML documents are served to different rendering devices (browsers instead of printers) and can be read aloud or rerouted to automatic Braille devices.

HTML itself is an adaptation of SGML for the web. Much of SGML's functionality, however, had to be simplified away to make it work over the web. What remains is about 100 markup elements to be used specifically for the presentation of web pages. As such, HTML is *not* a generic markup language.

Technological advances, however, have made possible a return to the original SGML design objectives. XML (Extensible Markup Language) was the result of the second major attempt at a web-enabled version of SGML. While still a narrow subset of SGML, XML is truly a generic markup language. One can use XML to create markup languages for a particular purpose, like ETD development and archiving. XML is a natural choice from which to derive our ETD markup language. (For a more detailed discussion of XML, see the previous chapter.) ETD-ML is an XML application with a markup vocabulary and grammar specifically designed for use with theses and dissertations.

Today, markup is used to protect documents from changes in the software industry. Different word processing documents have their own specific data storage formats, and when documents are transferred between computers, the specific software that processed those documents must follow, or the document will not be readable in the new context. While software is still required to read marked-up documents (like a printer was required to print them), a vendor-neutral interchange format helps ensure that the valuable information contained within the document can be used in other contexts.

There are several ways to prepare an ETD. The most common is to use a WYSIWYG editor (e.g., Word, WordPerfect) to generate virtual paper, specifically as PDF files. The next most common is to use a markup programming system like TeX or LaTeX to generate virtual paper. Specifically this involves creating a device-independent (DVI) file that can be converted automatically into PostScript or PDF (portable document format). Alternatively, one can use generic markup as ETD-ML to prepare the thesis, and then use style processing tools to generate readable output in a variety of formats. Using ETD-ML also means that more tools can be written easily to analyze, index, search, and process ETDs in ways we cannot yet foresee.

Students need to develop ETDs in ETD-ML without significant impact on their busy workweek and meager income. This involves having free software tools that work equally well on their home and laboratory computers. Students demand flexibility to create language constructs for their own purposes and yet keep a transparent interface between them and their research ideas. In this way, students can manage their ETD development as a component of their research project. An application of XML, ETD-ML allows authors to abstractly think of their work as independent information assets. A dissertation, for example, can be considered a compilation of its constituent components. Using tools such as XSL and XSLT, the same components can be transformed and reordered to appear in the format required by a journal article or a book chapter. The same information can be readily "repackaged" for multiple destinations. While using ETD-ML, students can learn about electronic publishing and republishing. They can gain confidence by generating documents with a "professional" look and feel.

Meanwhile the faculty will enjoy marking paper, at least until ETD-ML tools provide an annotation capability for document editing that rivals the natural usability of a professor's red pen. Tools to make this possible will emerge, but until that time an ETD-ML system must also include a component that can print an ETD directly to paper on which such marking can occur. Also important is a way to translate ETD-ML documents into the popular word processing formats, HTML, and PDF.

With ETD-ML, graduate schools that review ETDs can automate the enforcement of document structuring standards, saving them time and effort. All ETDs that are submitted in ETD-ML can be formatted professionally, and all follow the university style guidelines automatically. This will result in a faster, more accurate, less costly review of incoming ETDs and a higher-quality corpus should result. XML's strict enforcement of predefined document requirements ensure consistent format and close adherence to specifications across the board. Graduate schools can accept an ETD-ML validated document with a high degree of confidence regarding format fidelity. No personnel resources need be dedicated to manually validate format adherence.

Even so, librarians reap the ultimate benefit of ETD-ML. It is easier to archive and is more renewable than PDF. New styles can be written once, for the entire corpus, as new language constructs and presentation styles and formats emerge. Visually impaired patrons will be able to take advantage of the structural markup so that Braille display and automatically reading text aloud becomes more useful. Researchers using the library resources can take advantage of known constructs in ETD-ML to narrow their searches. Citation networks and maps can be generated from bibliographies in the corpus and merged with other online library resources. Hyperlinks can connect ETD-ML components (e.g., figures, tables) into aggregate documents such as for a topical literature survey. Finally, metadata from ETDs in ETD-ML will populate library indexes automatically upon submission. Searching, data mining, cross referencing, and document transformations are all greatly facilitated by ETD-ML.

ETD-ML and its role as part of the ETD development, submission, and archival process is described below. Some problems still remain to be solved, particularly:

1. As there is an initial learning curve involved, markup documents are more difficult to author.
2. Desktop tools for generic markup are rare and expensive and require some training to use.
3. The competition (WYSIWYG) is more attractive for students in the short term.
4. The language written today can never be complete—ETD-ML must be an extensible matrix so that ETDs of the future will benefit from it and not be restricted by it.

Markup has some drawbacks. To be deeply explanatory, markup must become verbose and is therefore difficult to author. On the other hand, if markup is terse, it cannot be particularly explanatory; it will provide but some of the structural information that the author might have intended. Another drawback is that markup is only useful as one component of a publishing system. While marked-up documents are directly readable as plain text, comfortable viewing demands that at least one formatting program be available for each document type. Because authors might not also be programmers, WYSIWYG document authoring systems are more "direct," and therefore are more attractive to users initially.

So actually, electronic publishing is much more than putting dots on the screen. It is making sense of those dots as information and being able to drive alternative displays and support alternative applications. In archival situations, republishing is important to keep the archive "fresh" as new devices for accessing the archive gain popularity. And for this all this to work smoothly, a stable, standard language for the annotating information is needed.

Generic markup is a powerful abstraction. Using it can benefit all the characters in the ETD submission story. With this in mind, let us proceed to the ETD-ML definition and how it is used in a document publishing system.

ETD-ML

One of the primary tenets in the ETD-ML design was that the entire system should be able to be learned by students in less than one hour. For this reason, TEI and ISO 12083 were rejected as base DTDs and ETD-ML was begun from scratch. Following this, many elements that could be in the language have been omitted. The language will need to be specialized for particular purposes, and certain specializations may be incorporated eventually into the base definition.

Electronic Thesis and Dissertation Markup Language

ETD-ML is an XML application. An XML application is also known as a "document type," which is perhaps more descriptive. Entire classes of documents can be defined using XML. By defining a document type, one defines a set of characteristics that all the *document instances* of that particular type must share. These common characteristics unambiguously define two things about a document: the markup tags used in the document and how the tags can be used. These two things establish the document's semantic and structural framework, respectively. The markup tags denote the semantics of the information they encapsulate, whereas the associated formal grammar clearly defines how the tags (and the data they describe) are ordered and structured.

Currently, two methods of document modeling exist. One can produce a DTD (Document Type Definition) for a class of document or, alternatively, a schema. Both serve as blueprints for constructing documents of that type. A DTD utilizes formal declarative rules, whereas a schema provides structure by example through templates.

ETD-ML (http://www.ndltd.org/etd/etd-ml) is defined using a DTD. This DTD (http://www.ndltd.org/etd/etd-ml/dtdetds.htm) rigorously defines a vocabulary and grammar specific to the domain of electronic theses and dissertations. ETDs in ETD-ML may contain (but are not limited to) abstracts, chapters, appendices, sections, paragraphs, emphasized phrases, tables, cross-references, and citations.

Styles

Once the ETD is expressed using ETD-ML, software programs can be run on the single source to give the ETD a "face," be it PDF, paper, or to make it into a Web site. In document formatting, titles might become large and centered. Running headers and footers might appear. Foreign words might become italicized. Such formatting is called applying a "style," and document styling is expressed either by "style sheets" using standards like CSS, XSLT, XSL, or DSSSL or by writing a special-purpose program or a desktop tool.

Each document may have one or more style sheets applied to it to achieve different formatting for different visual displays—devices or printers. For example, an ETD chapter would be styled differently for a book, journal, a magazine, or the Web—each demands a different presentation of the same basic information.

Style application for documents follows the "single source multiple target" paradigm shared by all XML documents. The document is not explicitly tied to a particular style and therefore can be processed in a number of different ways. This flexibility is important so that documents can get a facelift every few years and so that persons with a variety of disabilities will not be prevented from using the ETD. Comparatively, documents prepared in typical word processors have only one face, and changing that face and ensuring a consistent result is laborious.

The benefit for ETD authors is that when an automatic style is applied, it is applied the same way for each *document instance*. Thereby ETD-ML guarantees consistency across a document but also through the entire digital library. Consistent style application in formatting can be used to provide internal consistency with collections or so that users can select formatting preferences for certain document types.

Document preparation, parsing, and styling are all part of the XML publishing model that involves defining languages with DTDs, authoring document instances, creating style sheets and applying them, and generating formatted documents for editing or publication.

ETD-ML Publishing Model

In the ETD-ML publishing model, the graduate school and library settle on a document model—either ETD-ML as given or a dialect of ETD-ML—specialized for a particular university's needs. Style sheets are also provided but will change as library patrons' needs become more well known and new technologies emerge.

Authoring tools for the student include simple text editors such as Emacs, vi, Notepad, or WordPad, and complex XML editors including Arbortext Adept, SoftQuad Author/Editor, and Documentor. New versions of WordPerfect and Microsoft Word have some XML-generating capability.

Style sheets and styling software are available from the NDLTD. These include or will include "etd2html" (standalone program), "etd2html.xslt," "etd2html.as," or "etd2pdf.dsl" (style sheets), Adobe FrameMaker + XML templates, Arbortext Adept templates, SoftQuad XMetal templates, Documentor templates, and Word Perfect templates. With the variety of formatting targets, graduate schools, libraries, and students can choose the one that meets their needs.

The student submits the ETD source and at least one version of the formatted output to the graduate school for review. The graduate school reviews the ETDs, approves them, and passes them to the library for archiving. The library extracts the catalog data from the title page, archives the ETD, indexes its contents, and provides it for use. Meanwhile, they can collect document statistics and use the bibliography to add to their citation maps.

OTHER USES FOR MARKUP IN THE ETD PROCESS

Digital libraries can apply XML in many other ways besides ETD-ML. XML can be applied in the workflow of ETD acceptance and in digital library cataloging. XML has also been used to structure user interfaces to workflow processes as well. XML, therefore, is useful as ETDs are created, submitted, accepted, cataloged, and archived.

Workflow

Before electronic submission, theses and dissertations were led around by paper forms that denoted author's name, student number, date stamps, and notes that fees had been collected. In the ETD paradigm, an ETD "workflow" record in XML can be used in place of the paper form. As the ETD passes the various checkpoints, the workflow record is filled in appropriately. Workflow records can also maintain authors' current addresses and affiliations, references to derivative and related works, and even pointers to reflections and annotations by other scholars.

Dublin Core/ETD Extensions

ETDs can be classified and cataloged along many axes (especially beyond the Library of Congress system). The NDLTD has devised an extensive cataloging scheme based on the Dublin Core recommendation for metadata for electronic documents using XML syntax. More information is available from http://www.ndltd.org.

Markup in Digital Libraries

For libraries of ETD collections, hyperlinks can be used to manage cross-document glossaries, topical indexes (with hand-authored synonyms added), and topical webs. Annotations by other authors can be linked to one or more ETDs in the collection. Document and collection metadata can be organized, amended, and extended using hyperlinks.

ETDs benefit from hyperlinking. Authors can be more expressive, and users can find relevant components of ETDs more easily when hyperlinks are present. XML, XLink, and XPointer together make possible for ETD-ML a rich hyperlink capability that can be ported to various architectures and preserves authors' various intentions.

DISCUSSION

Why Not HTML?

Students and university administrators have inquired about using HTML as a standard submission format for ETDs, offering that HTML is immensely popular, and HTML browsers and authoring tools are nearly ubiquitous.

The negative argument is thus: graduate schools are committed to professionalism, and libraries are committed to long-term archiving of ETDs. HTML already has too many "flavors"—versions and extensions abound. Universities argue that their good intentions could be compromised by authors using browser-specific constructs (e.g., "center" elements and Active-X controls) that are not part of the HTML standard. Authors might be encouraged otherwise by particular authoring applications, and those approving ETDs would require expensive technical training to be able to determine ETD validity.

On the other hand, HTML offers a flexible medium for authors to be creative. Because HTML is a formal language (as an application of SGML), validators are easy to implement. University libraries already manage many HTML documents on their Web sites and can use the HTML "meta" element to handle document metadata appropriately. Furthermore, ETDs in HTML can be converted more easily to ETD-ML than ones in PDF. While the rigor of ETD-ML can prove advantageous in the long-term, the HTML solution has significant near-term benefits. Though standardization and integration would be complex, universities should consider allowing the submission of ETDs in HTML.

Document Structure versus Document Hyperstructure

In ETD-ML, authors may choose to keep all ETD front and body matter in one XML document. In this strategy, the document table of contents is generated automatically by the formatting program. Alternatively, authors may split their ETD into logical components and create a table of contents hyperlink to connect the ETD together. Hyperlinks allow a decoupling of a document's physical structure (where the files live) and its logical structure (how the pieces fit together). Authors can arrange and rearrange the logical structure of a document by adjusting its hyperlinks.

ETDs as Hyperdocuments

An ETD as an academic work is a webbing of references. Footnotes, tables, and figures all appear "near" the text that refers to them. Paragraphs in one chapter refer to sections in another. Abbreviated references appear in the body text—these are expanded in the bibliography. References to online documents can include "clickable" hyperlinks to online resources. Indeed, referencing (naming and hyperlinking) is the glue that holds the Web world together.

Links are simultaneously two things. First is what we see—the "hot blue text" over which we may place our mouse pointer and depress the selection button. The other denotes the semantic of "connectedness." Two resources are connected when there is a link between them. Authors create links, readers click on the links, and documents have the state of "being linked." Conceptually, a link connects two points: a source and a destination.

Creating a hyperlink is more complicated than typing simple text. One must appreciate four things. The "context" is where the link will appear; perhaps it is flowed within a paragraph or is one item of a bulleted list. The "icon" is the hint that the human reader sees that should indicate "clickability" and what will be displayed upon clicking. The "type" of link tells why, be it "seealso," "footref," or "tableref." The "address," of course, gives the full or relative name of the linked resource so that the system can go to that document when in the browsing system the link is selected.

Hyperlinks are familiar to most in the context of HTML. One can create links to HTML documents or other internet resources. However, to create a hyperlink to an internal part of an HTML document, a *named anchor* needs to be explicitly created for the destination point. The hyperlink at the source must then include a *fragment identifier* to specifically reference the intended piece of the HTML document.

XML expands HTML's hyperlinking capability. Due to its strict hierarchical structure, all internal fragments of an XML document are labeled and, therefore, inherently addressable. As all XML documents are tree representations of the data they contain, each node within the tree is reachable from the document's root element. XPointer is the technology that allows traversal of the document's tree structure. Using this mechanism, one can specifically access the document's internal elements. To ensure uniqueness of element names used within a document, XML uses the concept of *namespaces*. Names within a namespace are guaranteed to be unique. Namespaces themselves are also uniquely identified.

XML provides two methods of specifying resource: by location or by name. Specifying resources by name is done through the familiar URI (Universal Resource Identifier) mechanism. http://www.w3c.org/XML, for example, is a URI. Problems occur, however, when the destination resource moves. If our page moves to http://www.w3c.org/Markup/XML, for instance, all the links pointing to it are now broken. It has been proposed to provide the ability to uniquely name a resource and universally reference it by name alone. Not unlike DNS (Domain Name System), an independent "back-end" system would ensure location transparency by automatically mapping names to physical location of resources. FPI (Formal Public Identifier) is one such universal naming scheme proposed. XML has adopted FPI as its resource-by-name specification mechanism. FPI—and other proposals like it—are, however, in a state of development and not yet finalized.

XLink is another area where XML surpasses HTML in linking capability. In addition to HTML's basic unidirectional (source to destination) linking, XLink allows establishment of complex linking relationships between multiple resources. It also allows for association of metadata with links. Furthermore, the link's *behavior* (whether it presents as a link or pipes in the target contents) can be specified. ETD-ML uses XPointer and XLink for all its references—table, figure, footnote, section, bibliography. ETD-ML uses multiply ended links for its "table of contents" structure.

Markup languages have rich descriptive ability beyond document structure and hyperlinking. ETD authors can create "virtual worlds" to make their ETDs more expressive, perhaps using document interchange languages HyTime or VRML. Chemical compounds can be visualized, buildings can be designed, operas can be staged for performance. Moreover, virtual worlds that are encoded with markup languages can be reused, preserved, and converted much more easily than operating system-specific software programs designed to present the same things. In addition, the textual features of worlds can be indexed and glossaries made just the same as with text files. The ETD itself could be presented within a virtual world. For example, a three-dimensional setting with a study, a laboratory, and a section of beach could represent primary components of an ETD in biology.

CONCLUSION

Benefits

ETD-ML should benefit students: it is easy to create an electronic document for any research paper, and it teaches the importance and process of ensuring the longevity of information. The language should benefit faculty: it will become easier to review paper as a hypertext online, and an online system can collect annotations from faculty, with no more problems understanding the handwriting of the various editors. Graduate schools will spend less time checking margins and page numbers. Libraries benefit: they get the best archival format and multiple publication targets to serve different users' needs. Scholars everywhere: can download the most useful format of ETDs and can reuse experimental data and software within them most readily to verify results and to leverage all available prior work before proceeding with their own.

Furthermore, ETD-ML depends on nonproprietary and open source technologies not tied to the fortunes of any one company. This reliance on standardized IT methodologies alleviates the significant cost of acquisition, operations, maintenance, and upgrades incurred by vendor-specific packages. Students need not allocate often scarce financial resources for software purchases. XML is fast becoming an indispensable tool of the trade. As its syntax and inner workings become second-nature (as HTMLs once did), so too will the syntax of XML applications such as ETD-ML.

Universality

As theses and dissertations will always be a creative medium for a wide variety of students, trying to enforce an inflexible, universal ETD-ML is immediately resisted. However, ETD-ML is an excellent substrate from which to build different document types specific to genres, disciplines, or even a particular dissertation. It opens a robust architecture that makes multiply useful, long-lived ETDs possible. Authors appreciate its flexibility. Graduate schools appreciate its rigor. Libraries appreciate its openness. Implementers appreciate its simplicity.

When you weigh the case for markup for ETDs, please try to see beyond the paper paradigm. When you browse this ETD Sourcebook—be it formatted for seeing, hearing, or touching Braille—it has editors, authors, chapters, and paragraphs, none of which immediately depends on a page-oriented paper format. Trust the professional publishers. Trust the librarians. Side with markup for a long-term solution.

REFERENCES

1. Bayraktar, M (1998). Proceedings of Digital Libraries '98, the Third ACM Conference on Digital Libraries. Pittsburgh, PA.
2. The Electronic Thesis and Dissertation Markup Language. (1998). http://etd.vt.edu/etd-ml.
3. Extensible Markup Language (XML). (October 2000). http://www.w3.org/TR/REC-xml.
4. Goldfarb, C. F., Prescod, P. (2000). *The XML Handbook*. 2nd ed. Upper Saddle River, NJ: Prentice Hall.
5. Harold, E. R., Means, S. (2001). *XML in a Nutshell*. Sebastopol, CA: O'Reilly & Associates.

6. ISO 8879: Information Processing—Text and Office information Systems—Standard Generalized Markup Language (SGML). International Organization for Standardization, Geneva, Switzerland, 1986.
7. Networked Digital Library of Theses and Dissertations (NDLTD). (May 2003). http://www. ndltd.org.
8. Ray, E. T. (2001). *Learning XML*. Sebastopol, CA: O'Reilly & Associates.
9. The World Wide Web Consortium. (September 2003). http://www.w3.org.

12

Math*Diss* International

Günter Törner and Thorsten Bahne
Universität Duisberg-Essen
Duisberg, Germany

BACKGROUND

The development of a scientific community depends by and large on its scientific productivity. The actuality of research questions discussed within scientific communities and the work being done or completed on these research questions, especially in the mathmatical and science fields, is decisive for the technological development of our communities for tomorrow. This is underlined by the fact that mathematics has taken on the position of a key technology. Keeping pace with scientific research internationally is a challenge which has to be constantly strived for.

In this context, dissertations[1] present a significant indicator for scientific research. These scientific papers document actual research questions in the laboratories and on the writing desks, on the one hand, and on the other hand they reflect methods employed in research. Therefore, all science communities must have a vital interest to take in this information and equally to make it public so that it can serve as a basic product for innovation[2].

Information, however, entails the danger of being experienced by the individual as nothing else but an uncontrolled flood. Thus, concepts have to be developed enabling the individual scientist to come to terms more adequately with this enormous flow of information. This appears to be more a characteristic experienced in our western communities, whereas scientists from countries of the so-called Third World may be experiencing difficulties with the opposite situation, namely information not getting through to them. In this context mass electronic information and communication (IuK) plays a decisive role. It can compensate for the deficits at both ends: it can optimize precision selection of information, on the one hand, and on the other hand it can, with great ease, open information sources that by traditional methods would only be possible through great effort, if at all.

It therefore does not come as a surprise that particular academic communities for mathematics and the sciences in the Federal Republic of Germany have recognized the need to innovate in this field as well as to assess the possibilities. These communities founded the IuK-Initiative (http://www.iuk-initiative.org) to accompany and develop innovations in information and communication processes in academic disciplines—last but not least in the exact sciences—to be able to assist constructively and productively. A development example in the Deutsche Mathematiker Vereinigung (DMV) (http://www.mathematik.uni-bielefeld.de/DMV/mathnet_de.html) is Math-Net (http://www.Math-Net.org), an Internet information service for mathematicians, which serves as a reference source. Likewise, we would like to point out that PhysNet (http://physnet.uni-oldenburg.de/PhysNet/physnet.html), the Physics Department and Document Network, serves the same purpose for the Deutsche Physikalische Gesellschaft (DPG) (http://www.dpg-physik.de).

Within this process, scientists play a double role: they deliver information and they receive it. For the first time on the level of electronic communication, the mediating role of publishing companies and other producers of literature has been changed, in particular because financing library aquisitions is becoming increasingly too expensive for universities in Germany and elsewhere. It is thus good advice to encourage scientists to take some of their interests into their own hands. The DMV in cooperation with the Österreichische Mathematiker Gesellschaft (ÖMG) (http://www.mat.univie.ac.at/~oemg/) has given these questions an independent subject-specific platform (http://elib.zib.de/IuK-DMV/) catering to the individual sections of the annual conferences.

Electronically archived scientific and general documents play a decisive role here. The nonprofit sector opens possibilities for development and design whereby electronically represented doctoral dissertations are assigned a central, even an exemplary, role. For this purpose a new term has been established in the international context for the field of electronic papers: Electronic Theses and Dissertations (ETDs). On the one hand, ETDs are a suitable object for studying new workflow options and problems related to electronic publication, and on the other hand one is also dealing with scientifically substantial content in these documents. The annual ETD conferences of the Net-

worked Digital Library of Theses and Dissertations (NDLTD) (http://www.
ndltd.org) bear witness that these changes have been recognized by the communities and have themselves become the object of various surveys and research projects.

DISSERTATIONS ONLINE AND ITS RESULTS

The recently completed DFG project Dissertations Online (http://www.
dissonline.org), initiated and developed by the DMV, has developed solutions for electronically archiving and publishing dissertations. The project
focuses on

> Making digital dissertations accessible via metadata
> Adaptation of a search engine towards further metadata types
> Interdisciplinary networking of servers as search engines
> Development of document type definitions (DTDs) and automatic gen-
> eration of information for conversion to XML
> Inclusion of multimedia elements (chemistry) into digital dissertations
> Setup of a user-oriented information system
> Adaptation to present-day library techniques and procedures

During the execution of the project in the years 1998–2000, it became clear
that for the objective of reaching a unified solution for treating dissertations
electronically there exist barriers across all disciplines, not even taking into
consideration traditional criteria or procedures particular to disciplines for
defining dissertations, which we consider to be a marginal but solvable aspect.
The central problem still is the aspect of a variety of differing data formats.
The employed data formats are necessarily geared to presentation necessities
for the scientific results in question. One cannot expect uniformity here in the
middle term. Every doctorate will make use of a language appropriate to the
level of complexity of the subject matter in question. The central issue of
the above-mentioned project *Dissertationen Online* was documents compiled
under Microsoft Word, a system designed for format requirements in particular in the humanities. Thus, subsequent priority was given to working on
documents produced in the LaTeX format, the standard format for mathe-
matical-scientific documents.

SPECIFIC FEATURES OF MATHEMATICAL DISSERTATIONS

In the case of Word-based dissertations, one can assume that there are no
difficulties converting them into SGML as archive format when they do not
entail components of mathematical formulas. (Every new Word version entails new surprises here, however!) However, transformation of LaTeX
documents into SGML is possible at present only to a limited degree. On

the one hand, one notes that, e.g., formulas in relatively clear structured LaTeX degenerate to a long string of complex entities representing images and graphics. On the other hand, a mathematical dissertation sometimes consists of about 90% formulas, and thus it is clear that a transformation into SGML would create a complexity that cannot be desirable or practicable. This problem cannot be simply overlooked, as the actual September 2001 statistics in the University and Polytechnics sector registered at the Deutschen Bibliothek (DDB) (http://www.ddb.de) present a clear picture. The quota of online dissertations in mathematics is almost 20%, which is only surpassed by dissertations in chemistry (23%) and physics (22%). Altogether they constitute an interdisciplinary quota of about 10%.

This problematic condition is also being recognized more and more in international mathematics and science communities. The latest developments are taking this into account and are reducing the burden of publishing and making available mathematical and scientific contents on the World Wide Web (WWW), while at the same time preserving the semantic information of the LaTeX codes, e.g., OpenMath (http://www.nag.co.uk/projects/openmath/omsoc/) or MathML (Mathematical Markup Language) (http://www.w3.org/TR/REC-MathML/). An international congress held in Berkeley on the Future of Mathematical Communication (http://www.msri.org/activities/events/9900/fmc99/) demonstrated that these "languages" are being developed. As MathML, however, needs further semantic information not entailed in the LaTeX code, the presence of a mathematically correct and automatic conversion method is at present illusory. It will take a number of years before these languages have matured and reached the acceptance and the distribution (concerning science text compilation) already enjoyed by LaTeX in the scientific community today.

THE CONCEPT OF MATH*Diss* INTERNATIONAL

The state of the formats and the archiving of an optimum amount of information at present has to meet the demands of long-time archiving, and for the unforeseeable time in the future they will also have to contain ASCII-LaTeX files, which provisionally serve as source files and serve presentation purposes (and not (!) SGML derivatives). Even in the case of LaTeX files a problematic variety of formats is noted due to text authors referring to their self-developed input files. In all cases it is necessary here to discuss homogenization. Transitional solutions are being worked out by experts in the United States for preserving authentic LaTeX texts, as the translation of such texts into subsequent market-adequate products is viewed as a problem that will eventually be solved, as already recognized by the International Mathematical Union (IMU) (http://elib.zib.de/IMU/), the Committee on Electronic

Information and Communication (CEIC) (http://elib.zib.de/IMU/IMU_
Committees/CEIC.html) and the Los Alamos Servers (http://xxx.lanl.gov).
This led to the development of a machine on which electronic mathematics
and science papers are "conserved" in LaTeX format. Dissertations, however, play only a minor role on this server. Furthermore, the framework
conditions of this American machine by no means meet demands in Germany
concerning standards (metadata, authentification, etc.), agreed upon and
established with *Dissertationen Online* and science libraries, e.g., DDB und
SUB Göttingen.

File format not only has problematic consequences for long-time
archiving, but also plays a decisive role in the for automatic research of texts.
As a full text search is not an adequate substitute for text research but instead
more often than not leads to a flood of information, the Document Type
Definitions (DTDs) are of central importance alongside the original metadata. From a pragmatic point of view, one must require that such DTD
information is automatically compiled. Consequently, it would be necessary
to develop or adapt one's own tools for each and every text-producing
program (and possibly for every subsequent update).

In the project *Dissertationen Online* this has been successfully completed
for Word documents and has been achieved with limited success for LaTeX
documents, which were allocated secondary priority. A Word-parallel solution for LaTeX files was hereby sought to fundamentally guarantee compa-
rability with Word documents. Finally, it was not taken into consideration
that LaTeX has its own programming possibilities for generating metainfor-
mation. It was not possible to ignore the fact that, as a rule, Word is employed
in other academic fields, namely in the humanities, as compared to TeX or
LaTeX.

Once again it is apparent that a document server for a homogenous
science discipline as well as for a homogenous format in this context allows
simpler solutions when, during production of the document (i.e., through
specific indexing), appropriate preparations are made. It is conceivable that
on the level of the LaTeX language, glossaries, indexes, bibliographies, etc.,
can be exported relatively easily into a database, allowing exactly defined text
research and search methods. As the demands in such homogenous science
discipline worlds hardly differ on an international scale, one can expect a high
degree of international cooperation, which also has a synergistic side effect for
the development of professional conversion tools.

Building on the results of *Dissertationen Online,* these thoughts are
fundamental for setting up an international mathematics dissertation server
(Math*Diss* International) (http://www.ub.uni-duisburg.de/mathdiss/). This
project, sponsored by the Deutschen Forschungsgemeinschaft (DFG), is a
joint venture of the Institut für Mathematik at the Gerhard-Mercator-

Universität Duisburg and the Staats- and Universitätsbibliothek (SUB) of the
Bundesland Niedersachen in Göttingen (http://www.sub.uni-goettingen.de/).
The last mentioned will provide service and continue its development after
this present project phase has been completed.

OBJECTIVES AND IMPLEMENTATION OF THE PROJECT MATH*Diss* INTERNATIONAL

The objectives of the project can be divided into two areas.

Search Options

Subject-specific search in mathematical documents has changed over time.
Scientists do not employ other methods of literature research just because a
search medium or publication form has changed. In light of the functionalities
of the text set system LaTeX (assuming it is employed here), an adequate
search appears feasible. Viewing their use as most natural, these functionalities generate automatically new files that can be referred to for adequate retrieval of automatic content lists, for processing bibliographies with BibTeX,
for compiling an index with MakeIndex, etc. In particular, we are dealing with
information that could enhance retrieval relevance concerning the following
search options:

> Abstract
> Mathematical Subject Classification (MSC)
> Contents
> Bibliographies
> Index
> Key Words and Glossary

One aspect also has to be mentioned here. It is still necessary to "educate"
authors, i.e., doctoral candidates, to write at a literary level of high quality in
conjunction with their scientific activities. At the beginning of literary
production the candidate must be aware of the circumstances and the conditions to which the dissertation will later be subjected. In the case of electronic publication, the prerequisites for high-quality subject matter–specific
retrieval of sophisticated content have to be defined. This fundamental requirement, that is, source files enriched with information, leads us straight to
the next central issue.

Archiving Information

As already described, appropriate automatic conversion of archive formats
for mathematical documents is not without its difficulties. For this reason we

have to preserve all information available. This is only possible by storing the source file of all the required styles and by using package files.

One recognizes that participation in Math*Diss* International (as a library, an institution, or an individual) is linked to efforts that have to be worked out in advance. What are the advantages, however, that can be achieved by participation?

Dissertations passed on to this enterprise are stored in the linked Allegro database, which is fed with the generated metadata. These consist of the metadata that meet the requirements of the DDB for submitting electronic dissertations and the metadata that are automatically generated in agreement with the NDLTD initiative (http://www.ndltd.org). Thus, the dissertation can be found in both an international and an interdisciplinary data bank. This is of particular importance because actual reports or comments inform us that there is the possibility to refer to electronic dissertations independent of time or place. However, the quality of retrieval can suffer due to nonspecific search options (such as author or title only) or due to split searches onto different servers. Thanks to international links and the specialized focus of the services of Math*Diss* International, this constitutes a problem that we can come to terms with.

A further bonbon for doctorates can also be offered. Due to an agreement between the central publishing organ MATH (http://www.zblmath. fiz-karlsruhe.de/MATH/home) and the central publication of the European Mathematical Society (EMS) (http://www.emis.de/), all dissertations that meet the standards and demands of the project Math*Diss* International and its services are published and reviewed in the central periodical MATH. This also enables international recognition of the dissertations.

INTERNATIONAL COOPERATION

A further working aspect of our project is entailed in the naming of the project. The objective of internationality is to be fulfilled. For this purpose it has been and still is our intention to build up international cooperation. Besides the already mentioned cooperation with NDLTD and thus also with the Open Archives Initiative (OAI) (http://www.openarchives.org), further contacts have been established with other institutions, in particular with countries with German-speaking communities outside of Germany. To promote cooperation with Austria, appropriate steps have been initiated. However, we are still waiting for an official decision of the Austrian Government Ministry on this matter. In Switzerland a competent and prominent partner, namely ETH Zurich, has been won for this project. Alongside further contacts with other northern and eastern European states, we would also like to mention the cooperation with Cellule MathDoc from the French University of Grenoble, which publishes an annual list of mathematical dissertations in France (http://www-mathdoc.ujf-grenoble.fr/these.html). Further cooperation has been agreed upon with the University of Uppsala.

CONCLUSION

On the whole, one can assert that with Math*Diss* International an instrument of particular importance for mathematics and international mathematical research has been developed and implemented. The user aspect stands in the foreground of this initiative. The central organization structure of this service enables one to quickly obtain an overview of actual research results. This project is, however, not only conceived as a research project specific to mathematics, but also as a model for building a document server, homogeneous in subject matter and format, on an international level.

We invite all interested persons to constructively participate in the development of this service and would like to offer all doctorates of mathematics, wherever they may be in the world, the opportunity of publishing their dissertations on the Math*Diss* International server, including automatic referencing in the central publishing organ MATH.

Contact Persons

Prof. Dr. Günter Törner
toerner@math.uni-duisburg.de
Dipl.-Math. Thorsten Bahne
bahne@math.uni-duisburg.de
Gerhard-Mercator-Universität Duisburg
Fakultät 4—Naturwissenschaften; Institut für Mathematik
BD Hans-J. Becker
becker@mail.sub.uni-goettingen.de
Dr. Thomas Fischer
fischer@mail.sub.uni-goettingen.de
SUB Göttingen

URL for Math*Diss* International: http://www.ub.uni-duisburg.de/mathdiss/

ENDNOTES

1. The Deutsche Bibliothek (DDB) in the Federal Republic of Germany receives 20,000 copies pro annum.
2. To quote a program of the German federal government 1996–2000.

13

ETD-db

Anthony Atkins
Virginia Polytechnic Institute and State University
Blacksburg, Virginia

In the early 1990s, work began at Virginia Tech to examine the possibility of creating and maintaining a collection of electronic theses and dissertations. The early working group considered the issues facing students, faculty, graduate school personnel, librarians, and researchers wishing to access the finished works.

Based on the initial concerns of the working group, Peter Haggerty of the Scholarly Communications Project at Virginia Tech developed a series of Perl scripts that used the Common Gateway Interface (CGI) to allow authors, reviewers, and librarians to create and manage an ETD using any computer with an internet connection and a web browser. Initially, submission of an ETD was entirely voluntary. A few students chose to submit an ETD using the new process, and from their experiences much was learned about creating and managing complex content.

This submission process allowed authors to use a standard web browser to enter their title page information and to upload the files containing the full text of their thesis or dissertation. The author's title page information was converted into an HTML form, which was readable only by the graduate school and which provided a means to approve the finished work.

The graduate school reviewed this form using a standard web browser. The reviewer typically confirmed that the student's committee approved the work, that the work was of acceptable quality, that all the paperwork had been filled out, and that all fees had been paid. Once all of these conditions had been met, the graduate school reviewer used a button on the form to send the contents of the form to an approval script. The approval script generated yet another HTML form, which was placed in a directory readable by the catalog librarian.

The catalog librarian reviewed the title page using a standard web browser and constructed a catalog record by copying and pasting information from the title page into the catalog and adding additional information to make a complete catalog record. Once a catalog record was completed, the catalog librarian used a button on the form to send the contents of the form to a final script. During peak periods, the process of adding the works to the catalog could add a delay of 2–3 weeks between the time the work was approved by the graduate school and the time the work was added to the live collection.

The script that received works from the catalog librarian moved the directory containing the author's title page and materials into a directory appropriate to the level of access selected by the author. The script then generated a finished HTML title page in the new directory and added the work to a listing of ETDs available at the appropriate level of access.

The graduate school also managed the release of campus-restricted and patent-restricted ETDs. The early submission process could handle the release of restricted ETDs for wider access well enough. This worked for simple situations in which the author chose to restrict access initially and then release the work at a later time. All cases in which the author wished to restrict their work beyond its initial level of access required manual intervention. Because many authors would change their level of access two or three times, managing the levels of access was something of a full-time occupation in the weeks following each approval period.

These early scripts handled the initial process of submitting an ETD adequately but did not allow authors or reviewers to make even small changes to an ETD once it had been submitted. Even a minor change in spelling or punctuation required an author to submit from scratch.

The early scripts stored listings of author names and ETD titles as flat files, with authors appearing in the order in which their ETDs were approved. Third-party search engines provided full text searching of the collection, but browsing through the collection was less than ideal. Entities were listed in chronological order by default. Listings of ETDs by author name were generated manually and were difficult to keep current.

In short, the initial system made it relatively easy to create an ETD, but made it difficult to change the same ETD and its metadata over time. With an inflow of a few ETDs here and there, this was adequate to the task, but required a lot of manual intervention. In the spring semester of 1997, Virginia Tech began requiring its graduate students to submit their theses and dissertations electronically, and the number of incoming theses increased dramatically.

It soon became apparent that the existing scripts were inadequate to handle the expanding needs of ETD authors, the graduate school, the library, and researchers. So, over the summer of 1997, our group (Digital Library and Archives) was charged with developing a more robust solution for processing ETDs. Having just started my time with the Digital Library and Archives, I was excited by the opportunity to improve a new and vital function of the university.

This new system would address the same concerns that drove the development of the initial submission process, but would take advantage of a relational database to transform an ETD into a living document that could be managed effectively throughout its life cycle. After a few initial prototypes, the first version of the ETD-db was put into production at Virginia Tech during the fall semester. The conversion from the initial submission process to the ETD-db was relatively painless, requiring a limited amount of data entry and proofreading of converted records.

The ETD-db provides each party involved in the production of an ETD with the ability to enter and update appropriate information using any computer with an internet connection and a web browser. There are separate interfaces for authors, reviewers, catalog librarians, system maintainers, and researchers.

Like the previous submission process, the ETD-db author interface allows authors to enter their title page information and upload their files. Unlike the previous system, the author interface of the ETD-db is password-authenticated. The authentication mechanism is tied into the existing user accounts provided by the university, such that an author can connect and begin assembling their ETD without requesting a new account. Once an author's identity is verified, their unique username is associated with the ETD they create. Their unique username can be used to make changes to their ETD until it is approved and becomes part of the permanent collection.

The updated graduate school interface allows reviewers to see a list of ETDs waiting to be approved and to make changes to the ETDs as needed. Later versions added the ability to notify the author by mail of any problems with their ETD. The list of ETDs waiting to be approved clearly indicates to the reviewer which ETDs are waiting for author input and which ETDs have been updated by the author in response to a notice from the graduate school. When an ETD is prepared and all the necessary fees and paperwork are taken care of, the reviewer interface is used to add an ETD to the live collection.

The catalog librarian's interface to the ETD-db simply provides a list of ETDs that are waiting to be added to the card catalog. The catalog librarian adds the ETD to the card catalog and then flags the ETD as having been cataloged. The ETDs waiting to be cataloged are already available at the level of access selected by the author; there is no delay between the approval of an ETD and its addition to the live collection.

The system maintainer's interfaces to the ETD-db are used to update an ETD once it has been added to the live collection. Most commonly, these interfaces are used to change the level of access to an ETD. Because of the large volume of ETDs stored in the collection, the system maintainer interface also offers a rudimentary search of an author's title page information. Search results provide links to view or edit any ETD matching the search criteria.

Finally, the ETD-db provides end users with browse indexes and a rudimentary search mechanism. The search mechanism allows authors to find ETDs based on words contained in their title page information. The browse indexes allow end users to view ETDs by the author's last name or by the author's department. To reduce the processing load on the system, a script to generate static HTML versions of the browse indexes was later developed.

From the outset, the ETD-db has been geared towards open source software packages, all of which are freely available to educational institutions. This made it very easy to package the ETD-db for use at other NDLTD member institutions. An institution with a networked machine running most any variant of UNIX can set up a pilot project using the free ETD-db distribution, a freely available web server (Apache), a freely available database server (MySQL), the Perl scripting language, and a series of freely available Perl modules.

All public distributions of the ETD-db provided a complete copy of the ETD-db as used at Virginia Tech, which could be customized by a programmer familiar with Perl. Versions later than 1.5 separate all printed text into language files, so that implementers could more easily adapt the wording of the ETD-db to their environment. To date, this language mechanism has been used to provide a translation of the author interface into Spanish and to provide a complete translation of the ETD-db into German. In version 1.5, the interface between the Perl scripts and the database was further modularized, such that other databases (Oracle, Postgres) could be used instead of MySQL. All versions of the public distribution have included the most current documentation from the live ETD-db site.

Late in 2001, the software was updated to support the Open Archives Initiative http://www.openarchives.org Protocol for Metadata Handling. Thus, sites running this software can have their metadata harvested for inclusion in the NDLTD union collection, for example. An update or add-on package was also created by Hussein Suleman to provide this capability for other sites.

For more information about the ETD-db, please visit http://scholar.lib.vt.edu/ETD-db/. This site includes the software itself, as well as instructions to help install and customize the software. A full-functioning demonstration of the software is also available at http://lumiere.lib.vt.edu/ETD-db/.

14

Digital Document Durability*

H. M. Gladney
HMG Consulting
Saratoga, California, U.S.A.

The dramatic and continuing decrease in digital technology prices is encouraging institutions of widely varying size and funding levels to consider using digital library technology to manage multimedia collections. The ensuing technical attention has been focused on rapid, inexpensive document interchange, paying little attention to preserving documents for decades to centuries. This chapter examines long-term preservation of digital documents that include ETDs.

Authors might assume that their digital works, once deposited in an archive, will be available forever. As things currently stand, they would be mistaken. Missing are institutional commitment, funding, and library staff expertise. There are also technical challenges that are the principal topic of

---

* Although this chapter was written in mid-2001 and digital document preservation is a "hot" topic, most of what the chapter contains is still timely in mid-2003. This is partly because the discussion of technology needed is limited to aspects that end users and university administrations need to understand, and partly because the very difficult issues of intellectual property are left to other writings. Shortly before the chapter was released to the publisher, we did make modest changes that reflect recent developments. Some of these appear as footnotes intended to inform the reader where to find still-evolving information.

this chapter. Notwithstanding contrary voices (Guthrie, 2001), we believe these technical issues are on a sure path to resolution—something we would not have asserted as recently as 18 months ago. Furthermore, the research library community has begun to move towards institutional commitments and some generous funding has been granted (see Appendix).

This chapter is intended for graduate students who need to submit their theses in digital form between now and whenever format standards become settled and preparation tools become readily available. It is also intended for university administrators who need to establish institutional procedures and rules for digital dissertations and long-term preservation and who might want to participate in the ongoing standards and tools discussions.

TECHNICAL AND STANDARDS BACKGROUND

Functional Needs

Theses and dissertations are part of the much larger intellectual product of society. We neither need nor can afford to choose special methods to preserve ETDs. Thus, this chapter reflects preservation planning for all kinds of digital documents, focusing on creating archive-worthy representations of "born-digital" original works and essential metadata.*

Archivists insist that original documents should always be accompanied by metadata-related information describing creation and subsequent handling. Such ancillary information is the essential difference between a document of little evidentiary value and a record useful to an attorney or a historian.

> Records are documents accumulated in the course of practical activities. As instruments and byproducts of those activities, records constitute ... evidence about the activities and the actors involved in them. While records are often conceived in terms of textual documents, such as letters and reports, they can take any form. What differentiates records from documentary materials in general is not their form, but their connection to the activities in which they are made and received. If this link is broken, corrupted, or even ob-

---

* Within the topic of digital preservation, we discuss only the preservation of "born digital" documents. Converting material artifacts for digital preservation encounters many challenges that are outside our scope (see, e.g., Council on Library and Information Resources, 2001a).

scured, the information in the record may be preserved, but the record itself is lost (Thibodeau, 2001).*

Anyone who wants to create or obtain an archived document will be interested in three things, and only three things, about digital archives: (1) the content, structure, and syntax rules that authors should follow to make their work useful to eventual readers; (2) how to determine whether or not a repository will manage archived works well and responsibly—starting with the obvious, but not automatically kept, commitment not lose it; and (3) what interfaces—administrative and input-output—with repositories he or she must use. These topics can be treated within a requirements analysis, without straying much into implementation aspects that would be premature—even likely to become obsolete in the interval between submission and printing of what follows.

Digital authors would be mistaken even if they merely assumed a broad and sound consensus about what is needed. The prominent literature includes implicit assumptions that cannot survive careful examination.† Some of these should be abandoned because they are overly strong and thereby induce excessive cost risks. Others need to be more carefully interpreted than is commonly done, because they risk confounding what library patrons need to know and do with what librarians need to know and do. Still others need to be reconsidered because their style is subjective, making conformance testing impossible, when it could be objective, so that an independent auditor could report without controversy as to the facts.

---

* "For example, a map of [Belgrade] is a document, but a map of [Belgrade] known to have been used in making a targeting decision that led to the bombing of the Chinese Embassy is an essential record of that action. The key difference between the document and the record is the specification of the context of action in which the record was involved. To preserve authentic records entails preserving the documents themselves and also their connections to the activities in which they were used" (Thibodeau, 2001).

† Perhaps the most pervasive and risky unspoken assumption in the literature addressing digital preservation is that to make digital objects useful for many decades or centuries, the optimal topic is the structure and procedures of archival and library institutions. However, the question at hand is the survival of information in efficiently useful forms, not the survival and role of institutions or techniques. Libraries, librarians, and their procedures are merely means to accomplish this. Arguably, information producers and information consumers (the people libraries intend to serve) care most about three things: (1) that the eventual user can find the best information for her task of the moment, (2) that this information is intelligible or otherwise useful at least to the extent that its producer intended, and (3) that this information is sufficiently trustworthy for the application at hand. Library clients do not care how these properties are achieved, except that their access to these services is fast, convenient, and inexpensive. Gladney (2002–03) claims to show a digital preservation method that is more reliable and less expensive than the methods proposed in other articles.

Therefore, as much as we might like a simple tabulation of every need that the experts agree is important, even that is not yet possible. Instead, what follows is the author's assessment, contrasted with some commonly written opinions and the author's objections to or questions about the latter. Hopefully, this will prepare the reader to consider critically further requirements that are likely to appear in the next 2–3 years and to object whenever they do not speak to what he or she needs or wants.

Preserving ETDs as Multimedia Documents

An ETD collection is likely to be as broad as any other digital document collection. Even a small number of dissertations will probably include every data modality found in any collection whatsoever—not only text, graphics, images, soundtrack and video data, but also complex engineering drawings, geographic maps, scientific tables, computer programs that include simulations, and all manner of input-output. What follows is determined entirely by these factors and simple cost considerations, namely:

1. Digital documents chosen for preservation should be manageable by whatever digital services each institution has chosen for other applications.
2. No enterprise can afford more than one prescription for preparing archival documents.
3. Copying a digital document between possibly remote stores needs to be fail-safe, even if the communication channels are unreliable.
4. Preserved documents should be immediately useful in environments other than their source environments, e.g., across incompatible computer operating systems.
5. Modifying a document years after it is stored is unaffordable and risks translations errors that are unacceptable because they might not even be noticed.
6. Some readers will want to assure themselves that content they depend on, and its purported provenance, are authentic.

These factors suggest broad aspects of eventual satisfactory solutions:

1. Engineering for longevity must be independent of service environment architectures, i.e., longevity should be inherent in the content and format of the digital documents themselves.
2. A single scheme must accommodate all data types, including programs, except that extensions from base schema must support specialized needs, such as for different disciplines.

3. The stored representation of each document should be a single computer file if at all possible, with inherent redundancy for validity checking.*
4. Digital preservation schema must be the same as document interchange schema.
5. Each archived document must be sealed with a message authentication code (Schneier, 1996), whose key connects to a key chain leading to some credible authority.
6. Each document's content should ensure that it surely can be correctly interpreted or executed at unknown places and unknown times by people who cannot query their originators.

Notice the flavor of these requirements statements and solution characteristics. Each is meaningful to most end users, who should find it easy to determine to what extent their archive service subscribes to it and delivers conforming service. Each is independent of technological constraints that might be different in different countries or a decade from now; nevertheless, each can be reconciled to evolving international standards for document interchange and other likely constraints, such as rules for intellectual property management. Each permits relatively objective independent audit, in remarkable contrast to the criteria articulated in the latter half of (RLG-OCLC, 2001). Each immediately suggests the next level of detail to experienced software engineers who will, as part of their general expertise, understand the prevailing software standards and tools sufficiently to elaborate solutions that conform both to the abstract requirements and to those of their institutions' infrastructures. For those readers who happen to be software engineers, this extends to their being likely to design similar solutions to the one the author has in mind.[†]

Requirements discussions that touch on much of what is needed are lively in many communities, moving rapidly, and mostly accessible to anyone facile with the WWW and e-mail. They are also decentralized, i.e., anarchic and somewhat chaotic, so that it takes time and energy to decide which threads are worth following and more effort to extend from being a listener to becoming a contributor. This apparent chaos is, in fact, a productive one in which good proposals are rapidly displaced by better ones.

---

* However, some objects may be too large for operating systems to manage as single objects; these will have to be represented in multiple files that include robust representation of their interrelationships. Managing these will be more expensive than managing documents that can be handled as single files.
[†] This does not extend to syntactic details.

Consequently, what follows is a snapshot view of what is known and of discussion threads that seem likely to affect eventual outcomes. It suggests Web sites that will help readers track how current challenges are evolving towards solutions and new software tools almost as soon as they appear.

To readers who would prefer pointers to a sure "cookbook" for laying down a digital dissertation safely, we can offer optimism, but not yet certainty. Presuming that they are conforming to recent blob standards, such as MPEG for video, and XML schema being worked out in their discipline, they are unlikely to go far wrong. A complete solution is in sight but will probably take 2–3 years to emerge. Much of the software needed to make scholarly works archive-ready is already being made available inexpensively or even without cost to noncommercial users.

History

Starting about a decade ago and growing steadily ever since, immense expenditures of time and money have been applied to creating digital documents. In comparison, ridiculously little effort has been devoted to ensuring the long-term survival of some appropriate part of today's flood of business, scholarly, governmental, and cultural works (Gladney, 2000). Of course, some material is copied to paper and other analog media; however, the flood includes content that cannot be recorded on paper without information loss.*

The problem is partly institutional. Neither libraries nor other institutions have created needed infrastructure; they face practical issues: missing funding, authorization, staff training, technology, and legal uncertainties (Garrett et al., 1996). The shortfalls in systematic accumulation and management of digital holdings have recently been considered in two National Research Council reports, *The Digital Dilemma: Intellectual Property in the Information Age* (2000) and *LC21: A Digital Strategy for the Library of Congress* (Library of Congress, 2000). There is a bright side—massive loss of digital information probably has not yet occurred.

Contrary to naive opinion, the U.S. National Archives and Records Administration (NARA) and the Library of Congress (LC) do not come close to filling the gap, nor could they do so even with much increased resources.[†] Furthermore, their programs to date are mostly research programs, rather than service programs of significant scale. NARA has chosen to focus on analyzing the practical organization of archival digital storage (Gladney, 1993) doing that in a pilot project (Moore et al., 2000) that overlaps topics em-

---

* This is not strictly true. Huttenlocher teaches how to mark paper digitally. However, as far as we know, this proposal is not being taken up with a view to eventual product offerings.
[†] This chapter cites U.S. facts for illustration; the situation is similar or worse in other nations.

phasized below. In response to an LC request in early 2000, the U.S. Congress provided generous one-time funding for managing digital content (see Appendix), but details of how the funds will be used have not yet been revealed.

The best analysis of the challenges is by Garrett et al. (1996); we are not aware of any subsequent work that expresses them as broadly and effectively. What we know of today's circumstances suggests that they are qualitatively unchanged since 1995; later research projects (Beebe and Meyers, 1999; Hedstrom and Montgomery, 1998; National Library of Australia, 2000) confirm and broaden the 1996 assessment. Since then, research has increased, as has the library and archives community's awareness of the challenges (RLG DigiNews). We therefore simply summarize Garrett et al. (1996), acknowledging subsequent progress, but emphasizing that the resources applied have yet to eliminate any challenge. The business world includes a few substantial efforts, but these march to different drummers; there is regrettably little collaboration or even conversation between business and academic people with substantially similar interests.

The challenges are:

Administrative: research librarians were in 1995 mostly not authorized and not funded for digital archiving. Today, many research libraries acknowledge digital archiving as a responsibility.

Synergetic: universities face issues in deciding on how to share content. In traditional libraries, not everyone has equal access to collections.* Furthermore, many universities have long competed partly by offering unique research materials.

Ability: library staffs are not trained for digital serving and archiving.

Cultural: libraries need to change, but change usually happens slowly in large institutions (Drucker, 1999), especially for departments emphasizing client service along traditional lines.

Legal: libraries' liability as potential contributors to copyright infringement by their patrons is incompletely understood (*Digital Dilemma*, 2000) and apparently exacerbated by the Digital Millenium Copyright Act, if recent press is to be believed. The available software is insufficiently helpful towards controlling how and where materials

---

* Recall the Index Librorum Prohibitorum, as described in the Encyclopedia Britannica V, 327, 1976 edition. A current example is the British Library, which restricts access to its reading rooms to researchers who can demonstrate that they have exhausted other sources. See http://www.bl.uk/information/reader-admissions.html. Recently, Rayna Green reminded us of such practices (Council on Library and Information Resources, 2001b). How limitations of access are often forced on archives is described in (Seeger, 2001), which also recommends procedural steps for archivists, donors, and patrons. Such considerations are a source of requirements for provenance, copyright, and conditions metadata.

are reused, and there are unresolved tensions surrounding the "fair use" exemptions of the U.S. Copyright Act of 1976 (Gladney, 2001). Publishers are selling limited-period licenses for digital content, rather than selling physical carriers (books, etc.), and the pertinent contract law is unclear and changing (UCITA, 2000).

Selection: the number of new works is much larger than it was before "the information age," partly because prosperity has much expanded the population with the knowledge, resources, and leisure to create interesting material. Deciding what small fraction should be saved is a difficult community decision involving constituencies with different priorities, hidden politics, and philanthropists' preferences.

Costs and Funding: accessioning content often costs more than the content itself; on the other hand, the cost of accessioning digital works might prove to be much less than for traditional works once methodology has been decided and institutionalized.* That the research library community moans so much that funding is inadequate—an issue whose merit we do not question—makes it difficult to assess the situation relative to digital content. However, assertions that digital works will be more costly to take in than works on physical media might prove to be incorrect.[†]

Technical: assuming progress towards addressing the above challenges, there remain technical challenges.[‡] These can be partitioned into standards for metadata, saving blobs, ensuring that our successors will be able to read and play the blobs a century from now, and authenticity controls.

Digital technology and infrastructure are in their infancy compared with their counterparts for paper, which have been refined for about 3000

---

* That widely accepted estimates comparing digital library service costs with traditional service costs are not available seems to bedevil written worries about costs. The existing estimates exist are confounded with improvements in service and by transitional and "learning curve" costs that are surely much higher than steady state costs will prove to be.

[†] Comments on costs often exhibit one or more of the following blind spots: (1) ignoring the rapid improvements in the costs of technology—improvements that are expected to continue at least for the next 5–10 years; (2) overlooking possible efficiencies in managing digital collections differently from physical collections; e.g., it is not necessary for a library that owns a digital collection to have an internal computing service; and (3) confusing costs attributable to transition from paper to digital objects with ongoing running costs. Industry has long known that manufacturing and distribution costs can be managed downwards significantly as a product "matures." Given that this is called "the learning curve," it is ironic that academic institutions do not seem to understand it!

[‡] As of early 2003, we believe that all the technical problems are solved in principle, but that this needs to be demonstrated by prototypes and pilot installations, and that the purported solution needs to survive effective peer criticism (see Gladney, 2002–03).

years. Anyone who might otherwise think that digital information will soon displace paper-based information might consider that our largest civilian employer is devoted to moving paper; it is the U.S. Post Office, with over 700,000 employees.* (The Post Office does have a fledgling e-mail business, but it accounts for less than 1% of its total revenue.)

Current Discussions of Objectives, Norms, and Standards

Digital preservation of scholarly works began to receive attention in late 2000. What is written can be found either directly or by citation in the periodical literature of archivists, research librarians, and museum curators, especially *D-Lib Magazine* and *RLG DigiNews*. Arguably, however, these writings focus on the interests of cultural custodians to such an extent that they give insufficient attention to:

1. Helping content originators structure their output to be convenient both to custodians and eventual consumers
2. Helping scholars and students construct private catalogs (bibliographies) (Witten, 2001) that suit their work better than what libraries can afford to provide, e.g., coupling data imported from institutional and informal sources with their own topic structures[†]
3. Helping consumers judge information dependability by providing metadata certified through a public key infrastructure (NIST) to enable automatic testing
4. Working with commercial repositories, both for their methodologies and for the opportunities of coupling commercial information with public information[‡]
5. Adapting to economic and technological trends that might change libraries dramatically (Odlyzko, 1997)
6. Exploiting software produced by the giant, informal Internet community. This includes tools useful for academic research—tools available to private individuals or researchers for little or no cost.[§]

---

* See http://www.usps.gov/history/pfact98.htm.

[†] Assisting scholars, engineers, and business administrators in this way is an immense opportunity to improve their effectiveness and efficiency.

[‡] Hundreds of companies have private collections and might benefit immensely from coupling this content with publicly offered content and catalogs. The public value might be immense; for instance, the pharmaceutical industry is perpetually hungry for better ways of finding and reusing what is known.

[§] Many of the best tools, in fact, come from the academic community and are made available gratis either out of desire to contribute to the public good or because their potential markets are too small to merit the investment needed to produce and market commercial offerings. Some of this is government funded, with the deliberate intention of (1) reducing what governments need to pay for software and (2) furthering government-funded research.

This inattention is exacerbated by hidden assumptions that blind people to opportunities and optimizations. Little (if anything) is written without an unspoken assumption that digital services and organizational responsibilities will be distributed as a digital shadow of today's pattern. However, today's pattern is an artifact of printing press economics, not a law of nature. That big changes are likely is illustrated by the people's searching behavior, which has mostly shifted from libraries to Web indices accessed from offices and homes. But only recently—5 years after the shift started—have librarians started to discuss how to reorient the reference desk.

Consider what the research library community seems to be doing with a draft recommendation for space data system standards—the reference model for an Open Archival Information System (OAIS, 1999). It cites this often, without much extension of what was proposed in 1999, and with seemingly uncritical acceptance. That research libraries need to be flexible and inventive with OAIS is clear when one remembers that OAIS was devised for the internal needs of American and European space R&D agencies, and not for research, university, or public libraries.

The economic and administrative circumstances of the space R&D agencies differ from those of the academic research community in major ways that surely color their information–archiving approach. Space R&D agencies are large bureaucracies both needful of and capable of tight quality control of their information banks, since these hold their primary product—information gathered by satellites and ground sensors. They probably have two classes of users with radically different privileges: agency personnel and outsiders. Furthermore, they are much better funded than academic libraries, have been politically sensitized by publicity about massive data losses, such as inaccessibility of LandSat data, and control which small fraction of their content is made publicly available.

For such reasons, measures that might be overkill in academic libraries are mere prudence for space agencies. A wary attitude about expensive OAIS overspecification should be maintained.* We need to be alert for specifications of little relevance in research libraries and cultural archives and unmentioned design shortcuts that reduce complexity and cost. An example dominates half of a widely circulated first draft of an RLG-OCLC Report "building on the soon to be international standard of the OAIS Reference Model" A CPA/RLG call for comments elicited:

> You build forward from a careful analysis ... of the "Trusted Computing Base (TCB)." But TCB was designed for defense applications,

---

* This is not a criticism of OAIS, but rather a recognition that it is responsive to requirements different from those of academic collection management.

not for delivery of mostly public information. Starting with TCB ideas might lead the library community into adopting systems, infrastructure and internal methodology far more expensive than needed to achieve your objectives (RLG-OCLC, 2001).

In addition to being designed for military intelligence work, a TCB is intended for reliable execution of arbitrary programs whose results cannot be independently validated except by further expensive calculations. In contrast, archives have only two critical kinds of output: reproductions of the documents stored and search results. Well-known technologies, such as message authentication codes, would allow users and auditors to validate such outputs inexpensively (Schneier, 1996).

What archive users want is trustworthy information. They do not particularly care that any particular library service is trustworthy. (This does not imply that *librarians and other information* service *agents* can ignore repository trustworthiness, because it might reflect on the reputation of their institutions.) Proof of digital document authenticity and provenance can be achieved by message authentication codes signed by trusted institutions and included in the metadata integral to each document delivery. e.g., while I would value a reliable British Library signature certifying the authenticity and provenance of a document received, I won't much care whether the document came from a British Library repository or not.

Regrettably, the Research Library Group (RLG) contained other problems of similar magnitude.* Discovery that such large problems exist motivates the careful, but incomplete, analysis in the rest of this chapter.

The CCSDS OAIS Reference Model: A Framework

OAIS defines itself to be a reference model and articulates its purposes as follows (OAIS, 1999):

An OAIS is an archive, consisting of an organization of people and systems that has accepted the responsibility to preserve information and make it available for a Designated Community. It ... allows an OAIS archive to be distinguished from other uses of the term 'archive'. ...

---

* The issue here is not what RLG says. Between when this chapters was written and when it will appear in print, a new version of RLG will appear and is likely to be responsive to most of my October 2001 criticisms. Instead, my intention is to suggest how much change is needed in the consensus views about the role, objectives, and design of repository services.

The information being maintained has been deemed to need Long Term Preservation, even if the OAIS itself is not permanent. Long Term is long enough to be concerned with the impacts of changing technologies ... or with a changing user community. . . . This reference model:

- provides a framework for the understanding ... of concepts needed for Long Term digital information preservation and access; ...
- provides a framework, including terminology and concepts, for describing and comparing architectures and operations of existing and future archives;
- provides a framework for describing and comparing different long term preservation strategies and techniques;
- provides a basis for comparing the data models of digital information preserved by archives and; ...
- provides a foundation that may be expanded by other efforts ... [extending to] physical media and physical samples; ...
- guides the identification and production of OAIS-related standards.

. . . It identifies both internal and external interfaces ... and ... high-level services at these interfaces. . . . It defines a minimal set of responsibilities for an archive to be called an OAIS, and ... a maximal archive to provide a broad set of useful terms and concepts.

Here, the phrase "reference model" should be interpreted precisely, and the above statement is properly careful. It defines an ontology—interrelated terms of reference, words and phrases—to make it possible to discuss and compare with fewer communication misunderstandings than would occur without such a "reference model and framework." OAIS is not a design, or even an architecture. This distinction is easily overlooked, as arguably has occurred within the research library community.

Language—even formal and precise language—is subject to the limitations taught by the mathematical philosopher Ludwig Wittgenstein, whose lectures convey the care essential for the most fundamental concepts. Wittgenstein (1939) emphasizes and reiterates three teachings that suggest how carefully we should proceed:

1. Inattention to the meaning and intent of key words or sentences can make consequent reasoning and conclusions incorrect or misleading. This is particularly dangerous when it includes ill-founded assumptions about notions that are seemingly "obvious."

2. Words and sentences take meaning only from the contexts of which they are parts.
3. What is important is how words and sentences are used—and what we find useful.

We add a fourth lesson implicit in Wittgenstein's 40 years of analysis, namely, that whenever we try to communicate precisely and logically, we stand on a slippery slope. We therefore suggest that the reader be as carefully critical of what follows as we have tried to be with prior work.

We should not overinterpret OAIS, which emphasizes, "This reference model does not specify a design or an implementation. Actual implementations may group or break out functionality differently" (OAIS, 1999). The issue is making unspoken and incorrectly narrow assumptions that exclude potential solutions that are less costly than the "obvious" alternatives.

Recent work illustrates this and is susceptible to design alternatives to apparent consensus thinking.* Consider the "appropriate copy" problem (Beit-Arie et al., 2001; Caplan and Arms, 1999; Flecker, 2001), chosen here because it is part of a corpus that has been discussed widely, including with staff members of most Digital Library Federation institutions.[†] Even though the project has encountered unexpected complexity, we know of no publication questioning its underlying premises sufficiently to encourage alternative designs.

Applying the OAIS Model to Preserving Scholarly Works

Flecker's (2001) "archive design based on [the] Open Information System model" starts with the document flow shown in Figure 1. The figure says little. Even so, it allows one to overlook essential simplification because

---

* A serious issue is the danger of consensus fostered by excessive committee thinking. That a tight community representing prestigious institutions has not generated searching questions internally is not sufficient reason to accept its dominant opinions. Quality design rarely starts as committee action; it more frequently starts with a lonely thinker whose proposal is challenged by a skeptical community, sometimes fairly and sometimes in ad hominem attacks (see Marcum, 2000). The issue here is not merely academic. If the direction questioned in this chapter prevails, it will guide the expenditure of approximately $100 million of U.S. taxpayers' money (see the Appendix). The author is considering an article to take up this issue directly; to do so here would be premature and a distraction.

[†] Beit-Arie et al. (2001) communicate a key leg of the archives strategy of the following institutions: Ex Libris, Inc., Florida Center for Library Automation, the Ameri National Information Standards Organization (NISO), the Digital Library Foundation (DLF), the National Federation of Abstracting and Indexing Services (NFAIS), the Society for Scholarly Publishing, and the International Digital Identifier Foundation. They continue a series of articles that publicly develop a consensus direction starting in 1999 (Caplan and Arms, 1999).

deposit   *request*   **DESIGNATED**
CREATOR ——————→ **ARCHIVE** ←———————— **USER**
                                    distribution   **COMMUNITY**

FIGURE 1   Simple document flow in OAIS according to Flecker (2001).

OAIS, being focused on the archive, does not mention all document flows or external constraints. Figure 1 can also lull one into overlooking that documents sometimes flow out of archives without queries. We prefer to illustrate at the same detail level as shown in Figure 2. OAIS talks of "Submission Information Packages" (SIPs), "Archival Information Packages" (AIPs), and "Dissemination Archival Packages" (DIPs). Figure 2 immediately shows that SIP schema and DIP schema must work with all operating systems and be almost identical because a consumer would dislike having to interpret a document coming from a research library differently from the same document sent directly by its author. The only changes a research library is likely to feel it can appropriately make are additions clearly distinguishable as its own work—not the author's. In contrast, a repository department within a space agency might have the responsibility and authority to improve radically what it receives—far more radically than traditional practice in research libraries would permit.

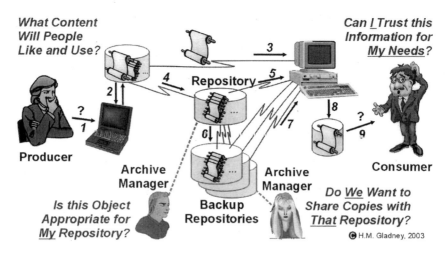

FIGURE 2   A better way of seeing document flow.

Figure 3 might tempt one to interpret the large box as an enterprise boundary because doing so suggests correctly how research libraries handle paper documents. However, OAIS does not require this. The slight changes depicted in Figure 4 encourage the reader to think more broadly and pro-ductively—"out of the box," as it were (Marcum, 2000). This figure not only removes the box, but suggests that each SIP must be forwarded intact into a DIP that is part of a historical and evidentiary trail. The archive staff might optionally festoon the SIP. The issue here is not a prohibition against an archive's creating new works that excerpt and embellish multiple SIPs. Such innovation is often a valuable service to client communities (and a profes-sional satisfaction to cultural custodians). However, historians, professional archivists, and governments have a more fundamental requirement. They would say that combining and embellishing documentary excerpts is merely "nice to have," whereas maintaining an audit trail of "the real McCoy" is essential.

Users mostly won't care about AIPs, since OAIS has AIPs flowing exclusively within archival custodians' loci of control. Fleischhauer et al. (2000) suggest AIPs to be SIPs extended by management information that mostly stays within library walls. However, they say nothing about constrain-ing most DIPs to be SIP extensions. The copyrights of many works will, in fact, restrict libraries to this; since space agency archives probably own most of their holdings, this restriction would not apply to them.

Figure 4 also illustrates that catalog queries need not be connected to document delivery orders. Furthermore, the archive catalog need not be

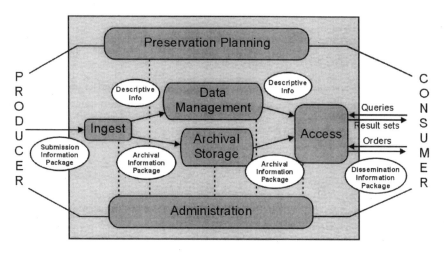

FIGURE 3 OAIS functional entities. (Adapted from OAIS, 1999.)

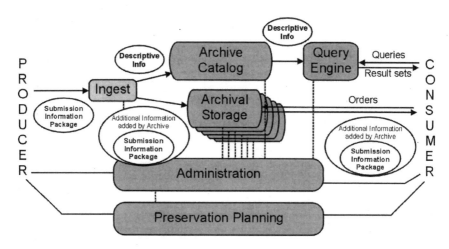

FIGURE 4   Proposed digital archive management.

located close to archival storage locations, and the latter can be distributed into sections under independent management control even for that elusive entity, "a single archive." Indeed, IBM Digital Library, which came into the market in 1993 and today is known as the IBM Content Manager product separated the catalog from the collection and allowed the collection to be distributed among remote sites in order to minimize network latencies.

Metadata for Dissertations

However librarians might treat other documents, they will will leave theses and dissertations in pristine condition apart from adding accession metadata. Each dissertation AIP will become the SIP augmented with no more than simple accession data that certifies the date received and other provenance information, and the corresponding DIP will be identical to the AIP. In fact, given where the expertise of any thesis resides and the economics (student time is not a university cost, whereas librarians' time is), perhaps the universities requiring or permitting electronic dissertation submission should require that students' submissions conform to METS and MODS metadata guidelines (Guenther and McCallum, 2003), starting with what Figure 5 suggests and continuing along the lines of Fleischhauer et al. (2000) adapted for dissertations. In addition, students and librarians should consider an extensively discussed minimum metadata schema known as the "Dublin Core" (Library of Congress, 2001; Weibel, 2000).

The Content Information subtree in Figure 5 will usually be provided by authors and editors; the Preservation Description Information is likely to be

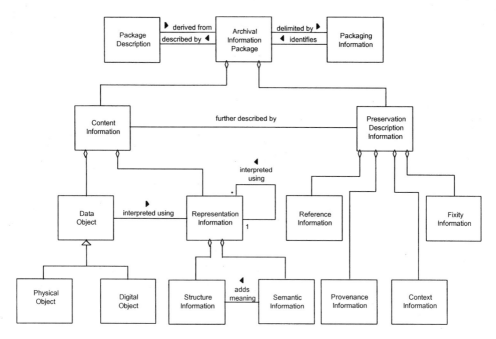

FIGURE 5 Archival information package, detailed view. (From OAIS, 1999.)

provided mostly by librarians. Although this seems a reasonable guess, metadata responsibilities might evolve differently; the topic is not yet much discussed. Proper metadata will follow discipline-specific schema, as illustrated in Table 1.

Discipline specificity in metadata is likely to extend to the "Representation Information" depicted in Figure 5. A few topical areas are already represented in proposed metadata schemata. All will need it.

FOR END USERS

Requirements

Most of OAIS addresses archivists' and librarians' needs—archive managers and those who design systems for them—rather than end users' needs. We need to pay more attention to the latter. What users will want is simple:

1. Archived blobs should survive storage and network failures, including improbable disasters.

TABLE 1 Preservation Description Information Types

Content information type	Reference	Provenance	Context	Fixity
Space Science Data	Object identifier Journal reference Mission, instrument, title, attribute set	Instrument description Processing history Sensor description instrument Instrument mode Decommutation map Software interface specification	Calibration history Related data sets Mission Funding history	CRC Checksum Reed-Solomon coding
Digital Library Collections	Bibliographical description Persistent identifier	For scanned collections: metadata about the digitization process pointer to master version For born-digital publications: pointer to the original metadata about the preservation process pointers to earlier versions of the item change history	Pointers to related documents in original environment at the time of publication	Digital signature Checksum Authenticity indicator
Software Package	Name Author/Originator Version number Serial number	Revision history License holder Registration Copyright	Help file User guide Related software Language	Certificate Checksum Encryption CRC

Source: OAIS, 1999.

2. End users should easily locate and copy digital documents. We don't address this.
3. End users should be able to read or fully use as otherwise intended any archived document, even though they cannot ask its originators to explain missing or obscure details. As suggested by Figure 6, everything needed should be packaged in a single blob (Kahn and Wilensky, 1995).
4. End users should be able to validate document authenticity and provenance as thoroughly as their application requires. Figure 7 suggests part of what is needed to accomplish this.
5. The end user needs instructions for constructing and submitting archive documents.

The first two needs will be met primarily by the operating procedures of network servers (see, e.g., Reich and Rosenthal, 2001). The third can be met by structuring each archived work to include *everything* that its end users might need to interpret and exploit them, except for information common to many document instances, which should be reliably and durably replicated. The final need can be met by applying public key encryption. (Menezes et al., 1997).

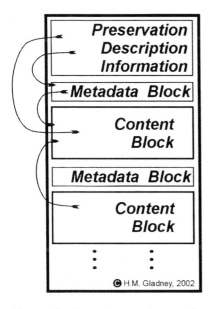

Preservation Description Information

Metadata Block

Content Block

Metadata Block

Content Block

© H.M. Gladney, 2002

FIGURE 6   Content, metadata, and preservation description information.

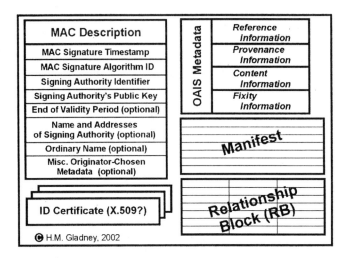

FIGURE 7   Detail of preservation description information for an ETD.

XML and Archiving Standards and Conventions

The favored language to express document structure and syntax will almost surely be XML. Although it is premature to be certain what other rules and schema major institutions will choose for what they accept into long-term, quality-controlled collections, XML seems sure to be required. Like HTML, it is a derivative of SGML, but HTML and XML have had different development dynamics that affect what each is good for. HTML developed rapidly in a highly competitive and chaotic marketplace with little influence from standards bodies or computer scientists. Standardization of HTML occurred to a large extent after widespread adoption and dealt with deficiencies and troublesome irregularities exposed by practical usage. In contrast, XML has had and continues to have the care of experts and widespread public comment on proposed design elements before they come into dominant usage. It is approximately an SGML subset constrained to simplify writing efficient parsers and other programs.

Using XML is not yet easy for novice computer users but seems likely to become so within 3 years. By then they will work with interactive tools that mostly hide underlying XML representations of digital objects from them, just as they today produce HTML pages without having learned HTML. Many such tools exist already, but they have not yet been woven into a complete fabric available at attractive prices. A few good tools are cost-free for individual private users, but it is unlikely that anyone will provide a cost-free integration of sufficient quality for authors and editors who fear that distraction by the mechanics of preparing XML documents will impact their productivity and focus.*

Users will also have to conform to discipline-specific metadata schema, as already suggested in Table 1, and to blob representation standards such as JPEG for images and MPEG for video clips. Since there are many of these and they are evolving rapidly, people who need them should either take the advice of computing support personnel or search for the latest and best pertinent stuff on the WWW. Table 2 suggests some current starting points for searching hierarchically.

Interpreting the Blobs in 10 Years or Much Later

The most difficult technical challenge for digital preservation is caused by obsolescence. When it comes time to exploit a blob, all computing systems that can interpret it may have vanished, not only locally, but throughout the world.

Archival documents will be represented as integrated objects whose components are metadata and content blocks (blobs) (Fig. 6); these will be set off from each other by punctuation defined by widely published XML schema. The metadata will be encoded in either ASCII or UNICODE representations of finite set members; some metadata will identify the data type of each blob, and other metadata will convey attribute values whose domains and meanings will be different for different blob types.

For each blob type, what remains is to define the attribute domains and the blob encoding, which might depend on the attribute values. For instance, digital audio information might require an attribute to indicate the encoding used—.mp3, .wav, .au, or some other format.

Many blob types will not be covered by reliable, formal, public standards. To understand this, consider a simple case—a single frame of black and white television represented as a raster image—and much more complex cases—programs such as computer games, editors, and even entire operating systems. A raster image file sufficiently orderly for a schema specification is demonstrably precise and complete and almost surely comprehensible a century from now. This specification will cover many billions of images, so that the effort for the single frame will be amortized over many frames, i.e.,

---

* I'm waiting and watching for an elegant "complete" package that seems durable and fits my budget. Here, "complete" is not well defined, but certainly includes the ability to import content represented in the data formats I depend on today and to export content in formats acceptable to my output targets. A purist might protest that it isn't fair to saddle a new offering with compatibility with the content products of less sophisticated predecessors. But fairness is irrelevant; consumer utility is the measure.

TABLE 2 Resources Identifying Standards, Tutorials, and XML Tools

Topics and their Web addresses	Description and comments
The XML Cover Pages, http://www.oasis-open.org/cover/sgml-xml.html. See also W3C's XML root page, http://www.w3.org/XML/	Is a comprehensive reference work for XML and SGML. It points to extensive documentation on the open, interoperable "markup language" standards, including XSL, XSLT, XPath, XLink, XPointer, HyTime, DSSSL, CSS, SPDL, CGM, ISO-HTML, MPEG-7, and others.
Resource Description Framework (RDF) http://www.w3.org/RDF/. See also The Semantic Web Community http://www.semanticweb.org/, a good site for thinking and tools about ontologies, RDF, and discipline-specific resources.	RDF integrates applications from library catalogs and Web directories to aggregation of news, software, and content to personal collections of music, photos, and events using XML as interchange syntax. It provides a lightweight ontology for the exchange of knowledge.
XML Resource Directory http://www.xmldir.com/. See also IBM XML Resources http://www.alphaworks.ibm.com/xml	Pointers to a cornucopia of XML tools and tutorials of interest to NDLTD members, such as signature support required below. For instance, IBM's XML Security Suite implements the latest draft of the XML Encryption specification. Many of the tools offered by IBM may be licensed without cost.
XML and Music, http://www.oasis-open.org/cover/xmlMusic.html	A complete MusicXML example of a classical song by Schubert, showing many MusicXML's features, including how multi-voice, multi-staff parts are represented.
Joint Picture Expert's Group (JPEG).[a] http://www.w3.org/Graphics/JPEG/itu-t81.pdf. The MPEG Home Page is at http://mpeg.telecomitalialab.com/.	JPEG was standardized by ISO in August 1990 for single compressed images. MPEG is partly standardized and partly evolving rapidly.

[a] In contrast, although TIFF (Tagged Image File Formal) is widely used and widely supported, no official group seems to recommend it to be a preservation standard, perhaps because Adobe Corp. holds the copyright to the TIFF specification. For pointers to information, see The Unofficial TIFF Home Page.

somebody can afford the careful work and testing needed to provide it. In contrast, the description of a computer program is approximately as complex as the program itself, and the notion of schema is not useful for programs; two programs that are similar can have radically different execution behaviors. Thus, some blob types will be covered by standards and others will need other schemes of durable representation (Huttenlocher and Moll, 2000). Although we know that raster images fall into the former class and most computer programs into the latter, we cannot say where the simple/complex boundary will lie. It will change with time as knowledge and economics change. Thus, a blob (Fig. 6) will be interpretable forever if its representation conforms to a machine-independent international standard, such as MPEG for video blobs. However, standards will be sufficiently reliable only for data types simple and useful enough to have been *completely* described in ISO specifications. For the blobs not so covered, some other mechanism is needed.

Some people put their hope in so-called active migration—converting the representation of every at-risk blob to whatever is supported by the hardware/software environment succeeding a fading environment. Lorie (2000) explains why this approach would be at best expensive and probably infeasible:*

1. To write and test a correct and complete conversion program is likely to be difficult and expensive. In a 100-year time span, it is likely to be required several times for any blob type.
2. Even if (1) is done carefully, there will remain substantial risk of undetected errors and oversights. These would accumulate over subsequent migrations, so that the affected content would gradually drift from what was laid down. Since the conversion programs are themselves likely to suffer obsolescence, retroactive correction of a 50-year old error, for instance, would be almost impossible.
3. Each conversion event would have to handle every affected blob, perhaps in all archives in the world, because if the expense of one conversion program instance is a serious obstacle, two programs doing the same thing will be judged unaffordable. This would re-quire careful administration by people not a priori trained for the task, standing in sharp contrast with preservation of paper records that works well with good humidity control and touching docu-ments only rarely.

---

* Everything in this section has been learned from Raymond Lorie. The critiques of inadequate approaches are synopses of his careful analyses that are partially represented in his writings, but might include elements we have discussed without his having published the complete arguments. The reader who wants to dig deeper than the current section provides is referred to Lorie (2000).

An emulation approach has been widely publicized by Rothenberg (Cullen et al., 2000). Its idea is to emulate obsolete machinery on the machinery available when a document's use is wanted, e.g., when some program written in 1999 is wanted in 2105, the user would have to find or write a M1999/M2105 emulator.* However, this proposal has two drawbacks—one merely economic and the other deadly. The economic problem is that the world would need an Mx/My emulator for every pair of Mx and My; Lorie's alternative is that the world could make do with much less software—one translator (like a compiler) for every Mx and one emulator for every My. The deadly problem is that one cannot write an Mx/My emulator until the My machine is available, and by that time it is unlikely that any Mx machine is available. Not only would it be very difficult to write the emulator from Mx specifications, one risks that the specifications are incomplete or contain subtle but deadly errors. Of course, by the time one notices any Mx specification error, anyone who might clarify the problem is likely to have forgotten the details or have been dead for 30 years! Since no Mx machine is available, it will be impossible to compare Mx executions with Mx/My-based emulations running on My.

Lorie avoids such problems in a subtly different approach: defining a Universal Virtual Computer (UVC) that is Turing-complete, i.e., able to execute any program that works on a stored program computer. The UVC need never be realized in hardware, but any Turing-complete real machine could emulate it. Furthermore, it is possible to specify a UVC that is sufficiently simple that its description can be demonstrated to be correct and complete. This could be done with a formal specification language, e.g., denotational semantics (Gordon, 1979). Writing the UVC definition in such a formal language can be used to make it comprehensible in the future, even though its user cannot ask any question of its architect.

Figure 8 suggests what current and future users will need to do for the case in which the archived object is a program. With UVC defined, today's user would translate the program of interest to be a UVC program (using well-known techniques of translating programs, such as compilation) that is archived. He or she would also create a UVC emulator on today's real machine—the same machine that is used for executing the conventionally compiled target program. The user could then compare UVC target program executions with conventional target program executions to validate the correctness of his UVC compiler.

---

* For brevity, we here use Mxxxx/Myyyy to denote an emulator of a xxxx A.D. computer that executes on the Myyyy computer available. (The notation could be extended to indicate which particular computer architectures were intended.)

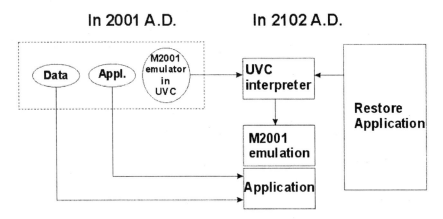

In 2001 A.D.   **In 2102 A.D.**

FIGURE 8   Saving a program today and emulating it in 100 years.

The future user would build an UVC emulator for his or her target machine and run the saved program on that machine. Presuming that the two UVC emulators—one on today's real machine and one on the future real machine—are correct, the UVC target program will behave identically today and in the future. All the necessary testing can be done when the needed real machines are available.*

Although Lorie seems correct and practical, until it is shown in realistic pilot installations we cannot persuasively assert that the problem is fully solved. So this defines three tasks ahead: (1) demonstrating that the UVC idea is correct and practical; (2) deciding whether each blob type we need is tractable by the standards approach or needs the UVC approach; and (3) demonstrating satisfactory archiving of documents containing all our blob types and essential metadata.

FOR ARCHIVE MANAGERS

Managing Blobs

Ensuring that blobs survive can be accomplished economically by combining:

1. Maximizing the durability of storage volumes (tapes or disks, each possibly carrying many blobs)

---

* This description is simplified from practical circumstances, in that few practical computers consist of only one processor. Although the elaboration presents software engineering challenges, we believe none of these to be a "show stopper."

2. Copying to new volume technologies as these replace older technologies*
3. Replicating within each storage services (backup)
4. Replicating to remote storage servers for protection against massive disasters[†]

An extensive literature addresses "best practices" for media durability (Gibson, 1997). Although the details are important to custodians of large collections, for smallholders they boil down to:

1. Keeping the media at uniform temperature and humidity comfortable for human beings (a little cooler and a little drier might be a little better)
2. Avoiding imposing physical stresses while the media are idle
3. Reading the data from the media only on properly maintained equipment
4. Reading the masters only to produce secondary copies for playback
5. Checking data correctness by sampling volumes periodically (e.g., annually)

Because magnetic disk technology is improving at about 26% p.a. (for the space that a dollar will buy), copying file collections gradually from expiring media to their replacements will be affordable.

Syntactic and Metadata Standards

Several independently started discussions are progressing towards de facto or de jure standards for interchange of multimedia data (e.g., National Library of Australia, 2000). Within 4 years we will have a broadly useful multimedia document interchange standard that uses XML for its packaging and structuring syntax. Since the current standards proposals do not explicitly mention long-term archiving, we need to investigate whether they are already adequate for it or need to be extended.

---

* Moore et al. (2000) are investigating migration. Smallholders will have to adapt what the large archives do to their own circumstances, and will be driven to migrate their holdings mostly by rapid technology evolution. Copying files from one volume to another is already easy; how and when to do it will probably be addressed from time to time in the PC trade literature. Migration from magnetic tape media to CD media is just now becoming inexpensive and timely.
† Reich and Rosenthal (2001) Reich eloquently argue the merits and methodology of distributing replica objects among mutually remote storage services. This might couple well with tactics by which each user would find and copy the least expensive instance of each work of interest (Beit-Ane et al., 2001). Integration of such technologies into complete, practical services has not yet occurred.

If standard metadata are held inside each digital object, a library can easily create catalog entries as part of accessioning objects. This proves to be the right thing to do for reasons of information integrity. Recent authors have persuasively argued the importance of document authenticity and trustworthy provenance information (Cullen et al., 2000; Lynch, 2001). Indeed, this is the central objective of archivists, who achieve it by rigorous controls and audit trails that bind each archive holding to historical events.*

Semantic Information and RDF

The above discussion does not extend beyond the syntax of information representation. It says nothing about information semantics, i.e., nothing about meaning or human interpretation. We draw the readers' attention to that, but limit what follows to recommending literature entries, because productive thinking about representing semantics in digital catalogs has only recently begun.

What has recently been written can be found on the WWW by searching on one or both of "ontologies" and "RDF." Today's inquiry into semantics can also be found at the W3C RDF thread, which "integrates a variety of web-based metadata activities including sitemaps, content ratings, stream channel definitions, search engine data collection (web crawling), digital library collections, and distributed authoring, using XML as an interchange syntax" (Resource Description Framework, 2000). RDF is part of the basis for the current ISO/IEC proposal (1999–2002) for a digital video and audio interchange standard. All this work originates in and conforms to the fundamental limitations of language and of formal logic first taught by Ludwig Wittgenstein.

DISCUSSION

The availability of the OAIS ISO proposal seems to have mesmerized a needy community. However, those dazzled by a brilliant flash find it hard to see what's in the shadows. Many optimizations are being overlooked. Seeing what's hidden might be difficult, but that's little excuse for not trying to do so.

---

* It is in this respect that the objectives and practices of archivists differ from those of librarians. To an archivist, the story told by a document is made valuable by the evidence that the document is what it purports to be and comes from the sources it purports to come from. In contrast, research librarians pay more attention to internal evidence in documents and its relationship to that in other documents. As will presently become clear, digital technology can much assist the archivist achieve his or her objectives.

The issue is not that OAIS says anything incorrect. As far as we know, what OAIS explicitly provides has no big problems. However, being a reference model and framework, all that OAIS provides is an ontology—a set of phrase definitions and depictions of how their authors intend them to interrelate. As an ontology, at worst OAIS could be irrelevant (*it isn't*); for it to be incorrect is *intrinsically* impossible.

> Suppose I said, "If you give different logical laws, you are giving the words the wrong meaning." This sounds absurd. What is the wrong meaning? Can a meaning be wrong? There's only one thing that can be wrong with the meaning of a word, and that is that it is unnatural. To give "not" the meaning of "and" and vice versa is not at all unnatural. But there are other things that are unnatural. For instance, we said we don't want to say "reddish-green". It is unnatural— unnatural for us—to use "red" and "green" in the way we're accustomed, and then to go on to talk of "reddish-green." And it is unnatural for us, 'though not for everyone in the world, to count: "one, two, three, four, five, many." We just don't go on in that way. (Wittgenstein, 1939)

Marcum's (2000) warning warrants careful consideration. An ancient joke recommends checking, if there are many ripples on the pond, whether or not they all come from the same rock. Among this chapter's citations, an incomplete tally of the authors that appear pairwise in at least one citation* is Arms, Beit-Arie, Blake, Caplan, Flecker, Fleischhauer, Lannom, Van de Sompel. Among colleagues that meet frequently and need to collaborate, criticism of opinions expressed tends to be muted.[†] Are we seeing independent opinions about digital archive design, or a single opinion?

The opinions at issue have been discussed in public seminars and in meetings in the authors' institutions. Among all the experts involved, ap-

---

* Starting with any author, such as Flecker, tabulate his coauthors; then tabulate the coauthors of everyone in {Flecker, (coauthors of Flecker); recurse *limiting this to this chapter's citations that have to do with OAIS*, because the objective is to suggest a shared or consensus opinion about digital archives design for scholarly content. If an author's spouse is a coauthor of a cited paper, that link merits inclusion also. Only citations from 1999 until now are counted.

† As well as being human nature, such caution is mere prudence because criticisms of professional opinions are often perceived as ad hominem criticisms, and because dealing with controversial issues carefully can cost much committee meeting time. There is also a cultural factor; research librarians value consensus highly. The behavior of a group of computer scientists tends to be quite different, partly because it is scientific tradition to confront technical disagreements not only directly, but sometimes loudly. (For cases of this extreme to the point of incivility, see Michael White, *Acid Tongues and Tranquil Dreamers*, Harper-Collins, 2001. Such cases are rare; scientists seem competent at avoiding ad hominem attacks.)

parently no voice questioned the consensus view loudly enough to have been heard outside. That might suggest that the consensus view is close to good enough for archive design in the near future, without risking design elements that are expensive to correct in production systems. If so, the warnings and opinions suggested above and in related publications are sounding alarms that are prudently ignored. If not, large public resources might be expended very inefficiently. The reader will have to form his or her own opinion.

CONCLUSIONS

Saving the bits will be accomplished by periodically copying every file onto new substrate. Creating and organizing metadata is well understood by research librarians and archivists; for digital records, standard XML will be used unless a better alternative appears. A practical multimedia archiving environment is being prototyped (Moore et al., 2000), but not carried to commercial software as of this writing. We even know in principle how to assure that the bits have meaning in some distant future (Lorie, 2000). However, the greatest challenges to implementations are not technical, but rather economic and political.

Knowing how to solve the technical problems is not enough. One has to do it, with the expectation that doing so will expose challenges of reduction to practice, definition of quality measures and assurance procedures, and training of staffs. Four great libraries, the British Library, the Royal Dutch Library, the National Archives and Records Administration, and the Library of Congress have recently made institutional commitments to address digital archiving; government libraries in Australia seem to be ahead (National Library of Australia, 2000). Notwithstanding such reasons for optimism, we must still assert that, with at most niche exceptions, nowhere in the world is a public digital preservation program growing at a breadth, pace, and scale commensurate with the private and public repositories.

Among originators, librarians and archivists, archives, and prospective consumers that include scholars, the natural units of information transfer are complete documents—documents with their essential metadata and fixed prior versions firmly attached. This fact, combined with continuing dramatic improvements in what digital technology dollars will buy, can be translated into radical improvements in scholars' and students' tools. It can also overcome much-discussed obstacles to digital libraries.

We (Raymond Lorie and I) are looking into questions implied by this chapter and will expose solution components to public critique as soon as we are confident they are correct and we have straightforward explanations. We do believe that all necessary invention has occurred, and are therefore optimistic that an overall digital preservation solution will emerge within 5 years. In the meantime, documents limited to the standardized subset of blob types can safely be archived.

This chapter raises technical questions about what seem to be consensus views—questions that apparently have not even been asked, much less answered. We suspect the existence of digital archive designs much more economical than the consensus approach that has been put in front of RLG members. We do not yet propose an alternative approach, because to do so would be premature.

ACKNOWLEDGMENTS

I gratefully acknowledge many detailed discussions with Raymond Lorie, an IBM Research Division colleague.

APPENDIX: U.S. GOVERNMENT SUPPORT FOR DIGITAL PRESERVATION

The largest U.S. initiative for digital preservation is called the National Digital Information Infrastructure Preservation Program (NDIIPP), and was authorized by legislation that reads:

> MAKING OMNIBUS CONSOLIDATED AND EMERGENCY SUPPLEMENTAL APPROPRIATIONS FOR FISCAL YEAR 2001 (Public Law 106-554) For the Library of Congress, $25,000,000, to remain available until expended, for necessary salaries and expenses of the National Digital Information Infrastructure and Preservation Program; and an additional $75,000,000 to remain available until expended, for such purposes: Provided, That the portion of such additional $75,000,000, which may be expended shall not exceed an amount equal to the matching contributions (including contributions other than money) for such purposes that (1) are received by the Librarian of Congress for the program from non-Federal sources, and (2) are received before March 31, 2003: Provided further, That such program shall be carried out in accordance with a plan or plans approved by the Committee on House Administration of the House of Representatives, the Committee on Rules and Administration of the Senate, the Committee on Appropriations of the House of Representatives, and the Committee on Appropriations of the Senate: Provided further, That of the total amount appropriated, $5,000,000 may be

expended before the approval of a plan to develop such a plan, and to collect or preserve essential digital information which otherwise would be uncollectible: Provided further, That the balance in excess of such $5,000,000 shall not be expended without approval in advance by the Committee on Appropriations of the House of Representatives and the Committee on Appropriations of the Senate: Provided further, That the plan under this heading shall be developed by the Librarian of Congress jointly with entities of the Federal government with expertise in telecommunications technology and electronic commerce policy (including the Secretary of Commerce and the Director of the White House Office of Science and Technology Policy) and the National Archives and Records Administration, and with the participation of representatives of other Federal, research, and private libraries and institutions with expertise in the collection and maintenance of archives of digital materials (including the National Library of Medicine, the National Agricultural Library, the National Institute of Standards and Technology, the Research Libraries Group, the Online Computer Library Center, and the Council on Library and Information Resources) and representatives of private business organizations which are involved in efforts to preserve, collect, and disseminate information in digital formats (including the Open e-Book Forum): Provided further, That notwithstanding any other provision of law, effective with the One Hundred Seventh Congress and each succeeding Congress the Chair of the Subcommittee on the Legislative Branch of the Committee on Appropriations of the House of Representatives shall serve as a member of the Joint Committee on the Library with respect to the Library's financial management, organization, budget development and implementation, and program development and administration, as well as any other element of the mission of the Library of Congress which is subject to the requirements of Federal law.

In February 2003, the Library of Congress released a preliminary plan (Campbell, 2003). Regrettably, its technical sections have not been helpful in refining this chapter.

REFERENCES

Beebe, L., Meyers, B. (June 1999). The unsettled state of archiving. *Journal of Electronic Publishing* 4(4).
Beit-Arie, O., Blake, M., Caplan, P., Flecker, D., Ingoldsby, T., Lannom, L. W.,

Mischo, W. H., Pentz, E., Rogers, S., Van de Sompel, H. (September 2001). Linking to the Appropriate Copy: Report of a DOI-Based Prototype. *D-Lib Magazine* 7(9). Over the past several years, substantial effort has gone into building an environment to support linking between the rapidly growing number of journal articles available on the web. As this environment developed, it became clear that the initial linking model required refinement to reflect the full range of service arrangements found across the information landscape today. In particular, the model worked well for articles served exclusively through a single delivery system, but not for those replicated in multiple service environments. The complexity inherent in having multiple online copies has become known as the "appropriate copy problem"; this paper describes a project demonstrating one solution to this problem.

Campbell, L., et al. (February 2003). Preserving Our Digital Heritage: Plan for the National Digital Information Infrastructure and Preservation Program. U.S. Library of Congress. Available via http://www.digitalpreservation.gov/ndiipp/repor/repor_plan.html.

Caplan, P., Arms, W. Y. (July/August 1999). Reference linking for journal articles. *D-Lib Magazine* 5(7/8). During the past year, great progress has been made in the field of reference linking, particularly in the important area of links to journal articles. This paper summarizes the current state of the art, describes a general model for static linking, compares several current implementations against the model, and discusses some of the required future work. Particular emphasis is given to the minimal set of metadata needed for reference linking and to selective resolution of identifiers, methods by which a client can specify which of several copies of an item is accessed.

Consultative Committee for Space Data Systems, Reference Model for an Open Archival Information System (OAIS), CCSDS 650.0-R-2 Red Book, May 1999. http://ftp.ccsds.org/documents/pdf/CCSDS-650.0-R-2.pdf. The purpose of this document is to define the International Organization for Standardization (ISO) Reference Model for an Open Archival Information System (OAIS). An OAIS is an archive, consisting of an organization of people and systems that has accepted the responsibility to preserve information and make it available for a Designated Community. It meets a set of such responsibilities as defined in this document, and this allows an OAIS archive to be distinguished from other uses of the term "archive." The term "Open" in OAIS is used to imply that this Recommendation, as well as future related Recommendations and standards, are developed in open forums, and it does not imply that access to the archive is unrestricted.

The information being maintained has been deemed to need Long Term Preservation, even if the OAIS itself is not permanent. Long Term is long enough to be concerned with the impacts of changing technologies, including support for new media and data formats, or with a changing user community. Long Term may extend indefinitely. In this reference model there is a particular focus on digital information, both as the primary forms of information held and as supporting information for both digitally and physically archived materials. Therefore, the model accommodates information that is inherently nondigital (e.g., a physical sample), but the modeling and preservation of such information is not addressed in detail. This reference model:

Provides a framework for the understanding and increased awareness of archival concepts needed for Long Term digital information preservation and access

Provides the concepts needed by nonarchival organizations to be effective participants in the preservation process

Provides a framework, including terminology and concepts, for describing and comparing architectures and operations of existing and future archives

Provides a framework for describing and comparing different long-term preservation strategies and techniques

Provides a basis for comparing the data models of digital information preserved by archives and for discussing how data models and the underlying information may change over time

Provides a foundation that may be expanded by other efforts to cover longterm preservation of information that is not in digital form (e.g., physical media and physical samples)

Expands consensus on the elements and processes for long-term digital information preservation and access, and promotes a larger market which vendors can support

Guides the identification and production of OAIS-related standards

Council on Library and Information Resources. (November 2001a). The Evidence in Hand: Report of the Task Force on the Artifact in Library Collections. CLIR Report pub103. Available at http://www.clir.org/pubs/reports/pub103/pub103.pdf.
Council on Library and Information Resources. (May 2001b) Folk Heritage Collections in Crisis, p. 47. http://www.clir.org/pubs/reports/pub96/contents.html.
Cullen, C. R., et al. (2000). Authenticity in a Digital Environment, published as CLIR Report pub92. (ISBN 1-887334-77-7). Available at: http://www.clir.org/pubs/abstract/pub92abst.html. On January 24, 2000, CLIR convened a group of experts from different domains of the information resources community to address the question: What is an authentic digital object? To prepare for the discussion, five individuals were asked to write position papers that identify the attributes that define authentic digital data over time. These papers, together with a brief reflection on the workshop, are presented here:

Authentication of Digital Objects: Lessons from a Historian's Research, by Charles T. Cullen

Archival Authenticity in a Digital Age, by Peter B. Hirtle

Where's Waldo? Reflections on Copies and Authenticity in a Digital Environment, by David M. Levy

Authenticity and Integrity in the Digital Environment: An Exploratory Analysis of the Central Role of Trust, by Clifford Lynch

Preserving Authentic Digital Information, by Jeff Rothenberg

Authenticity in Perspective, by Abby Smith

The Digital Dilemma: Intellectual Property in the Information Age. (2000). Computer Science and Telecommunications Board of the National Academies. Washington, D.C.: National Academy Press. http://books.nap.edu/html/digital_dilemma/.

Drucker, P. F. (1999). *Management Challenges for the 21st Century.* New York: Harper.

Flecker, D. (April 10, 2001). Nine E-Journal Archiving Issues, presentation related to Linking to the Appropriate Copy [Beit]. http://web.mit.edu/dspace/live/implementation/design_documents/ doso/OAIS-flecker.ppt. See also Dale Flecker, Larry Lannom, Rick Luce, Bill Mischo, and Ed Pentz, Localized Linking Prototype, http://www.crossref.org/CNI April 01(rev3).ppt.

Fleischhauer, C., et al. (2000). Archival Information Package (AIP) Design Study. http://www.loc.gov/rr/mopic/avprot/AIP-Study v19.pdf. This report documents a study of the technical issues surrounding the design of an Archival Information Package (AIP). It was prepared under Contract Number 00CLCDV4920 (continuation of 99CLCCT1097), Option Year 1—Lot 3—Task No. 7 of the Digital Audio-Visual Repository System (DAVRS) Prototyping Project. The Prototyping Project is a 3-year effort to study the feasibility of developing a digital repository system for the audio-visual collections at the Library of Congress (LC). The objectives of this study are:

> To analyze the technical issues related to the design of an Archival Information Package
>
> To develop a preliminary design of an AIP for LC digital AV collections
>
> To provide guidance for the development of a small sample of AIPs for feasibility testing

> An AIP is the digital equivalent of an archival item such as a book, a recording, or a motion picture. It consists of multiple data files that contain the digitized content of the archival item. In addition to the data files, the AIP contains metadata that describes the structure, content, and meaning of the data files. The data files and metadata are packaged (encapsulated) either logically or physically as an entity. AIPs are used to transmit and/or store archival objects within a digital repository system.

Garrett, J., Waters, D., Andre, P. Q. C., Besser, H., Elkington, N., Gladney, H. M., Hedstrom, M., Hirtle, P. B., Hunter, K., Kelly, R., Kresh, D., Lesk, M., Levering, M. B., Lougee, W., Lynch, C., Mandel, C., Mooney, S. B., Okerson, A., Neal, J. G., Rosenblatt, S., and Weibel, S. (May 1996). Preserving Digital Information: Report of the Task Force on Archiving of Digital Information, Commission on Preservation and Access and The Research Libraries Group. http://www.rlg.org/ArchTF/.

Gibson, G. (May 1997). Standards and Preservation of A/V Media and Data. International Preservation News: A Newsletter of the IFLA Core Programme for Preservation and Conservation (PAC). 14. ISSN 0890-4960.

Gladney, H. M. (1993). A storage subsystem for image and records management. *IBM Systems Journal* 32(3):512–540.

Gladney, H. M. (October 2000). Archiving the digital public record: an internet snail's pace. *iMP Magazine*.

Gladney, H. M. (2001). Digital intellectual property: controversial and international aspects. *Columbia-VLA Journal of Law and the Arts* 24(1): 47–92. http://home.-pacbell.net/hgladney/Columbia.htm. Intellectual property (IP) is the intangible product of the mind's work. Business and commerce involving digital or electronic intellectual property have become economically significant and are a growing component of the U.S. GDP and the international balance of payments.[*] Citizens whose livelihood depends on creating or managing digital IP should understand and possibly work to influence IP law and practice. Others who depend on IP less directly also might be interested, as might any citizen, since this area of law affects him as well. This article introduces some current issues surrounding digital IP and is written to help the reader locate additional sources with more depth and facts.[†] A National Academies' report, The Digital Dilemma: Intellectual Property in the Information Age,[‡] written by a study committee[§] ("the [IP] Committee" below), stimulated this paper. However, the views that the current article conveys are not always shared, but sometimes come into healthy conflict with those of my Committee colleagues.[¶]

Gladney, H. M. Trustworthy 100-Year Digital Objects, a series of articles being written in 2002–3. Where these will be published has not yet been decided. However, preliminary versions are being made available by the author to anyone who requests them. An up-to-date status report is available in the Digital Document Quarterly, accessible at http://home.pacbell.net/hgladney/ddg.htm.

---

[*] U.S. Department of Commerce, Digital Economy 2000, June 2000. To quantify the economic contribution of intellectual property is very difficult. The difficulties include identifying what should be counted and what should not. While the software industry, entertainment, and publishing should indubitably be in the count, some people would argue for inclusion of a portion of every high technology manufacture. However it is measured, IP business is immense and growing. See, for instance, Contributions of the Packaged Software Industry to the Global Economy, a study conducted by Pricewaterhouse-Coopers for the Business Software Alliance (BSA), April 1999.

[†] Paul D. Amrozowicz, When Law, Science and Technology Worlds Collide: Copyright Issues on the Internet, J. Patent and Trademark Office Society 81(2), 81–116 (1999) provides a good tutorial for newcomers to copyright law and practice. It concludes, "The Internet is truly... a legal frontier ... being expanded daily. Not far behind are the courts ... [y]et there still remains some uncertainty as to ... under what set of facts a court will find an ISP ... liable for direct, contributory, or vicarious infringement."

[‡] Computer Science and Telecommunications Board of the National Academies, The Digital Dilemma: Intellectual Property in the Information Age, National Academy Press, Washington, D.C. (2000).

[§] Appendix A identifies the members of the Study Committee on Intellectual Property Rights in the Emerging Information Infrastructure and their credentials.

[¶] Karen Hunter, Alan Inouye, Clifford Lynch, and Bernard R. Sorkin have each published views that go beyond The Digital Dilemma. See Against the Grain, v. 12 #3, June 3, 2000.

The abstract of the executive summary reads: "Preserving digital information has since 1996 received steadily increasing attention. Nevertheless, there has been little substantial progress against the key technical problems enunciated then and since."

The pertinent challenges include two computer science problems: (1) ensuring the future ability to execute today's computer programs on machines whose architecture cannot be known until they are built and to interpret data as its producers intended and (2) providing authenticity evidence so that each future user can prudently decide whether to trust saved information. End users-both information producers and information consumers—will further require that the components of a solution work in heterogeneous networks, are convenient and economical, and handle everything that machines can do and nothing but what machines can do.

We sketch how digital objects can be packaged to be trustworthy and reliably meaningful to their would-be users, no matter how distant these recipients are in time, space, and organization from the information sources. Our design works for all document types, independently of their purposes and data content types. Producers can prepare documents for archiving without permission from or synchronization with any authorities or service agents. Librarians can add metadata without communicating with producers. Consumers can test the authenticity and provenance of obtained documents without network interaction apart from what is needed to obtain cryptographic keys.

For context, we precede the solution by a summary of the organizational, funding, legal, and technical problems that must be solved to achieve a responsible international digital archiving program. This summary identifies the soundest writings that articulate the nontechnical components. Together with our solution, they identify a good start for comprehensive worldwide digital archiving., This Trustworthy series includes epistemological arguments for the completeness and optimality of the method proposed and preliminary design for a prototype and pilot installations.

Gordon, M. J. (1979). *The Denotational Description of Progamming Languages: An Introduction.* New York: Springer-Verlag. This book explains how to formally describe programming languages using the techniques of denotational semantics. The presentation is designed primarily for computer science students rather than for, say, mathematicians. No knowledge of the theory of computation is required, but it would help to have some acquaintance with high-level programming languages. The selection of material is based on an undergraduate semantics course taught at Edinburgh University for the last few years. Enough descriptive techniques are covered to handle all of ALGOL 60, PASCAL, and other similar languages.

Denotational semantics combines a powerful and lucid descriptive notation (due mainly to Strachey) with an elegant and rigorous theory (due to Scott). This book provides an introduction to the descriptive techniques without going into the background mathematics at all. In some ways this is very unsatisfactory; reliable reasoning about semantics (e.g., correctness proofs) cannot be done without knowing the underlying model, and so learning semantic notation without its model theory could be argued to be pointless. My own feeling is that there is plenty to be gained from acquiring a purely intuitive understanding of semantic concepts together with manipulative competence in the notation, for these equip one with a powerful conceptual framework—a framework enabling one to visualize languages and constructs in an elegant and machine-independent way. A good analogy would be with calculus: for many practical purposes (e.g., engineering calculations), an intuitive understanding of how to differentiate and integrate is all that is needed. Once the utility of the ideas and techniques are appreciated, it becomes much easier to motivate the underlying mathematical notions (like limits and continuity). Similarly, an intuitive understanding of the descriptive techniques of denotational semantics is valuable, both as a tool for understanding programming and as a motivation for the advanced theory.

Guenther, R., McCallum, S. (Jan. 2003). New metadata standards for digital resources: MODS and METS. *Bull. Am. Soc. Info. Science and Technology* 29(1):12–15.

Guthrie, K. M. (Nov/Dec 2001). Archiving in the digital age: there's a will, but is there a way? *Educause Review* 36(6): 56–65. With the increasing use of electronic and network technologies for scholarly communication, there is considerable and justifiable concern in the academic community about the challenges associated with protecting electronic information for future generations of scholars and students. Before the development of these technologies, the long-term availability of scholarly research was ensured through a system in which libraries—especially academic and research libraries—purchased, stored, and preserved books and journals in paper. There is not yet an equivalent system in place to protect the electroni literature being published today. How can we be sure that such a system will evolve? Where will the resources come from to support it on an ongoing basis? Who will accept responsibility and accountability for such a system? These are just some of the challenges that lie ahead if the academic community's commitment to archiving is to make the transition to the digital age.

Hedstrom, M., Montgomery, S. (December 1998). Digital Preservation Needs and Requirements in RLG Member Institutions. http://www.rlg.org/preserv/digpres.html.

Huttenlocher, D., Moll, A. (January 2000). On DigiPaper and the dissemination of electronic documents. *D-Lib Magazine* 6(1). Encoding electronic documents involves a tradeoff between maximizing the ease of dissemination and preserving the document appearance. For instance, a simple text file is the most easily and universally disseminated form of document, but it preserves none of the appearance. This paper proposes a new image-based document representation, called DigiPaper, which is designed to easily disseminate electronic documents with a guaranteed appearance, thus eliminating the tradeoff. DigiPaper provides fixed appearance by representing documents in image form, but uses new compression techniques to make the file size comparable to formats such as

Word, PowerPoint, or PDF. DigiPaper compression is based on two technologies: the Mixed Raster Content (MRC) color image model and token-compression. DigiPaper files are much smaller than current image formats used for scanning, achieving about a factor of 7 improvement in compression over TIFF Group 4 compressed images.

ISO/IEC JTC1/SC29 WG11, 1999 The MPEG Home Page, http://www.chiariglione. org/mpeg/index.htm.

Kahn, R., Wilensky, R. (May 1995). A Framework for Distributed Digital Object Services. cnri.dlib/tn95-01. This document describes fundamental aspects of an infrastructure that is open in its architecture and which supports a large and extensible class of distributed digital information services. Digital libraries are one example of such services; numerous other examples of such services may be found in emerging electronic commerce applications. Here we define basic entities to be found in such a system, in which information in the form of digital objects is stored, accessed, disseminated, and managed. We provide naming conventions for identifying and locating digital objects, describe a service for using object names to locate and disseminate objects, and provide elements of an access protocol.

Library of Congress, Committee on an Information Technology Strategy for the Library of Congress, Computer Science and Telecommunications Board, National Research Council. LC21: A Digital Strategy for the Library of Congress, July 2000. See especially Chapter 4, Preserving a Digital Heritage.http:// books.nap.edu/books/0309071445/html/73.html.

Library of Congress Network Development and MARC Standards Office. (March 2001) Dublin Core/MARC/GILS Crosswalk. http://www.loc.gov/marc/ dccross.html.

Lorie, R. (2000). Long-Term Archiving of Digital Information. IBM Research Report RJ 10185.

Lynch, C. A. (2001). When documents deceive: trust and provenance as new factors for information retrieval in a tangled web. *J. Am. Soc. Info. Sci.* 52(1):12–17. Historical information retrieval has focused on the indexing and retrieval of documents or surrogates from databases with little regard to how the indexing has been obtained or whether the surrogates are accurate. Information-retrieval systems have dealt with databases that are assumed to be well behaved, consistent, and often admission controlled, and questions of trust and data accuracy have been completely implicit, to the extent that they have been considered at all. This brief and somewhat informal article outlines a personal view of the changing framework for information retrieval suggested by the Web environment, and then goes on to speculate about how some of these changes may manifest in upcoming generations of information retrieval systems. It also sketches some ideas about the broader context of trust management infrastructure that will be needed to support these developments, and its points towards a number of new research agendas that will be critical during this decade. The pursuit of these agendas is going to call for new collaborations between information scientists and a wide range of other disciplines.

Marcum, D. B. (Nov./Dec. 2000). Too Much Consensus. CLIR Issues 18, available at http://www.clir.org/pubs/issues/issues18.html.

Menezes, A. J., van Oorschot, P. C., Vanstone, S. A. (1997). *Handbook of Applied Cryptography.* New York: CRC Press.

Moore, R., Baru, C., Rajasekar, A., Bertram, L., Marciano, R., Wan, M., Schroeder, W., Gupta, A. Collection-Based Persistent Digital Archives. D-Lib Magazine http://www.dlib.org/dlib/march00/moore/03moore-pt1.html and http://www.dlib.org/dlib/april00/moore/04moore-pt2.html.

National Library of Australia, The PANDORA Project (Preserving and Accessing Networked Documentary Resources of Australia) is a collaborative initiative that aims to develop policies and procedures for the selection, capture, and archiving of Australian electronic publications and the provision of long-term access to them. See http://pandora.nla.gov.au/documents.html, 2000. http://pandora.nla.gov.au/pandora/.

Odlyzko, A. M. (1997). Silicon Dreams and Silicon Bricks: The Continuing Evolution of Libraries. *Library Trens.* 46(1):152–167.

What seems not to be sufficiently emphasized in Daedalus 1996 are several key points that are likely to be crucial in determining the evolution of libraries:

(i) The ... inevitability of dramatic change. Printed matter will eventually be relegated to niche status.

(ii) The contemporary library is a relatively recent institution, resulting from a combination of the awkward print technology and the sizes of modern information collections.

(iii) Research and community libraries have different functions, and will be affected by the digital revolution on different time scales ...

(iv) Evolution of libraries will be determined by competition ... just as much as by technology itself.

(v) Adaptation to electronics is not a matter of one-time change, but an evolution that will take several decades. This implies prolonged upheaval and ... opportunity for gradual adjustment.(Andrew Odlyzko, The history of communications and its implications for the Internet, available at http://www.research.att.com/amoi.)

The Internet is the latest in a long succession of communication technologies. The goal of this work is to draw lessons from the evolution of all these services. Little attention is paid to technology as such, since that has changed radically many times. Instead, the stress is on the steady growth in volume of communication, the evolution in the type of traffic sent, the qualitative change this growth produces in how people treat communication, and the evolution of pricing. The focus is on the user, and in particular on how quality and price differentiation have been used by service providers to influence consumer behavior, and how consumers have reacted.

There are repeating patterns in the histories of communication technologies, including ordinary mail, the telegraph, the telephone, and the Internet. In particular, the typical story for each service is that quality rises, prices decrease, and usage increases to produce increased total revenues. At the same time, prices become simpler. The historical analogies of this paper suggest that the Internet will evolve in a similar way, towards simplicity. The schemes that aim to provide differentiated service levels and sophisticated pricing schemes are unlikely to be widely adopted. Price and quality differentiation are valuable tools that can provide higher revenues and increase utilization efficiency of a network, and thus in general increase social welfare. Such measures, most noticeable in airline pricing, are spreading to many services and products, especially high-tech ones. However, it appears that as communication services become less expensive and are used more frequently, those arguments lose out to customers' desire for simplicity. In practice, user preferences express themselves through willingness to pay more for simple pricing plans. In addition, there is a strong "threshold" effect to usage-sensitive billing. Even tiny charges based on utilization decrease usage substantially. In a rapidly growing market, it is in the service providers' interest to encourage usage, and that argues for simple, preferably flat rate, pricing. Historical evidence suggests that when service costs decrease, such arguments prevail over the need to operate a network at high utilization levels and to extract the highest possible revenues.

Communication services have long exhibited many characteristics of modern high-tech industries, namely high fixed costs, network effects, and difficulty in allocating costs among many products and services. Therefore, the historical lessons of this paper are likely to be applicable to many pricing situations in the future. When prices are high, and purchases infrequent, airline-style "yield management" is likely to dominate. On the other hand, when prices are low and a service is used many times a day, simple pricing and uniformly high quality are likely to be more common. Historical analogies as well as current expenditure data also suggest that in the "digital convergence" of broadcasting and point-to-point communications, it is the latter that will dominate in shaping the evolution of the Internet. The current preoccupation with professionally produced "content" is probably more a distraction than help in planning for the future. Content has never been king, it is not king now, and most likely will not be king in the future. The development of the Internet is likely to be determined by the same growth of the myriad unpredictable commercial and social interactions that have fueled other communication services.

The reference model addresses a full range of archival information preservation functions, including ingest, archival storage, data management, access, and dissemination. It also addresses the migration of digital information to new media and forms, the data models used to represent the information, the role of software in information preservation, and the exchange of digital information among archives. It identifies both internal and external interfaces to the archive functions, and it identifies a number of high-level services at these interfaces. It provides various illustrative examples and some "best practice" recommendations. It defines a minimal set of responsibilities for an archive to be called an OAIS, and it also defines a maximal archive to provide a broad set of useful terms and concepts.

Reich, V., Rosenthal, D. S. H. LOCKSS: A Permanent Web Publishing and Access System. D-Lib Magazine. LOCKSS (Lots Of Copies Keep Stuff Safe) is a tool designed for libraries to use to ensure their community's continued access to web-published scientific journals. LOCKSS allows libraries to take custody of the material to which they subscribe, in the same way they do for paper, and to preserve it. By preserving it they ensure that, for their community, links and searches continue to resolve to the published material even if it is no longer available from the publisher. Think of it as the digital equivalent of stacks where an authoritative copy of material is always available rather than the digital equivalent of an archive.

LOCKSS allows libraries to run web caches for specific journals. These caches collect content as it is published and are never flushed. They cooperate in a peer-to-peer network to detect and repair damaged or missing pages. The caches run on generic PC hardware using open-source software and require almost no skilled administration, making the cost of preserving a journal manageable.

LOCKSS is currently being tested at 40+ libraries worldwide with the support of 30+ publishers.

Archiving for permanent retention is facing some major challenges as we move into the next millennium. These include issues relating to selection from a burgeoning mass of information being produced in a wide range of formats, issues relating to media longevity and equipment obsolescence, migrating information across formats, the commercialization of activities, the growing impact of IT requirements, and the complexity of copyright and other rights in digital materials.

RLG DigiNews (http://www.rlg.org/preserv/diginews/issues.html) is a bimonthly web-based newsletter directed primarily at members of the Research Library Group.

RLG-OCLC Working Group, Attributes of a Trusted Digital Repository: Meeting the Needs of Research Resources, Draft for Public Comment, August 2001. The CPA/RLG report recommended "a dialogue among the appropriate organizations and individuals on the standards, criteria and mechanisms needed to certify repositories of digital information as archives." This report answers that directive and:

Proposes a definition of a trusted digital repository (for community response/agreement)
Identifies the primary attributes of a trusted digital repository
Articulates a framework for the development of a certification program
Identifies the responsibilities of an OAIS-compliant digital repository
Makes several recommendations for follow-on work.

Resource Description Framework (RDF) Schema Specification 1.0, W3C Candidate Recommendation 27 March 2000. See also W3C Committee for RDF, Semantic Web Activity: Resource Description Framework (RDF), http://www.w3.org/RDF/.

Schneier, B. (1996). *Applied Cryptography: Protocols, Algorithms, and Source Code in C.* 2nd ed. New York: John Wiley & Sons. ISBN 0471117099.

Seeger, A. (2001). Intellectual Property and Audiovisual Archives and Collections, in Folk Heritage Collections in Crisis.

The NIST PKI Program, in http://csrc.nist.gov/pki/.

Thibodeau, K. Building the Archives of the Future: Advances in Preserving Electronic Records at the National Archives and Records Administration. D-Lib Magazine. http://www.dlib.org/dlib/february01/thibodeau/02thibodeau.html.

UCITA. (2000). Computer Professionals for Social Responsibility. UCITA Fact Sheet. http://www.badsoftware.com/uccindex.htm, http://archive.infoworld.com/ucita.

Weibel, S. L. (December 2000). The Dublin Core Metadata Initiative: Mission, Current Activities, and Future Directions. *D-Lib Magazine* 6(12).

Witten, I. H. (University of Waikato). (2001). How to Build a Digital Library Using Open-Source Software, Joint Conf. on Digital Libraries. See also Ian H. Witten, David Bainbridge, Stefan J. Boddie. Greenstone: Open-Source Digital Library Software, D-Lib Magazine 7(10), October 2001.

This tutorial describes how to build a digital library using the Greenstone digital library software, a comprehensive, open-source system for constructing, presenting, and maintaining information collections. Collections built automatically include effective full-text searching and metadata-based browsing facilities that are attractive and easy to use. They are easily maintainable and can be rebuilt entirely automatically. Searching is full-text, and different indexes can be constructed (including metadata indexes). Browsing utilizes hierarchical structures that are created automatically from metadata associated with the source documents. Collections can include text, pictures, audio, and video, formed using an easy to use tool called the Collector. Documents can be in any language: Chinese and Arabic interfaces exist. Although primarily designed for Web access, collections can be made available, in precisely the same form, on CD-ROM or DVD. The system is extensible: software "plug-ins" accommodate different document and metadata types. The Greenstone software runs under both Unix and Windows and is issued as source code under the GNU Public license.

Greenstone incorporates an interface that makes it easy for people to create their own library collections. Collections may be built and served locally from the user's own web server or (given appropriate permissions) remotely on a shared digital library host. End users can easily build new collections styled after existing ones from material on the Web or from their local files (or both), and collections can be updated and new ones brought on-line at any time.

Wittgenstein, L., Wittgenstein, C., ed. (1939). *Wittgenstein's Lectures on the Foundations of Mathematics.* Cambridge. From the Notes of R.G. Bosanquet, Norman Malcolm, Rush Rhees, and Yorick Smythies, 1989.

15

OpenURL-Aware ETDs

Eric F. Van de Velde and Betsy Coles
California Institute of Technology
Pasadena, California

One of the significant advantages of ETDs over printed theses is the ability to incorporate active web links in ETDs. OpenURL technology amplifies this advantage by increasing the power of these web links. Already, an OpenURL-aware ETD may offer the following features:

1. Link each citation in the bibliography to a menu of services appropriate to the citation and to the reader of the ETD. For example, a citation to a journal article might be linked to:

    The full text of the article (if the reader has licensed access to the full text)
    Document-fulfillmentservices that the reader is allowed to use
    Online catalogs of libraries appropriate to the reader
    Abstracting and indexing services in which the article may be cited and where the reader may find additional related literature.

2.   Increase the longevity of the links by decreasing the reliance on
     static URLs, using metadata to describe the cited works instead.

The current state of the art is only the beginning. We expect Open-
URL technology to expand beyond the world of bibliographic citations. It
could be used to increase the functionality of subject headings and of references to chemical formulas, genomic sequences, or products. For example,
a biology ETD on a particular gene might be linked to all other scholarly
works that refer to this gene, whether or not the scholarly works existed
at the time of writing the ETD, whether or not the author was aware of
these other scholarly works. However, before OpenURL can be used for
these applications, significant additional development is required. For now,
we focus our attention on the application of OpenURLs to bibliographic
citations.

WHAT IS AN OPENURL?

A bibliographic citation describes a *referent*, which may be a journal article, a
book, a technical report, or some other work. When the citation to the
referent occurs within an electronic document like an ETD, it makes sense to
embed the URL of the referent in the ETD so that the referent is only a mouse
click away from the citation. In OpenURL terminology, the person who clicks
on that link is called the *requester*. In an ETD context, any reader of the ETD
is a potential requester.
     Embedding URLs has some disadvantages, however. For example:

     The URL becomes effectively useless when the location of the referent
          changes.
     Not all referents have URLs. For example, nondigital works do not
          have a URL.
     Some referents are associated with more than one URL, only one of
          which may be appropriate for the requester. For example, if the
          referent is part of a licensed resource, requesters need the URL of
          that version to which they have access.
     Requesters may be interested in more than just the referent: they may
          want services related to the referent. For example, they may want to
          check whether a book is available in their institute libraries.

     In the OpenURL approach, an indirect link replaces the direct link from
citation to referent. The appropriately formatted citation is transported to a
resolver, which transforms the citation into one or more URLs and/or into a
menu of services. Because the resolver performs this transformation when the
ETD is read, it is able to use information that was not known by the author of
the ETD. This includes the identity of the requester, current URLs of

referents, and scholarly information produced since the ETD was written. To implement this basic idea, we must

1. Cast the citation into a *format* that can be parsed by an automated service. This machine-readable format organizes the *metadata* obtained from the citation and from the context in which this citation occurs.
2. *Transport* the metadata via the web to the resolver.
3. Build a resolver that transforms metadata into services and/or URLs.

An OpenURL is a web-transportable metadata format. It is only concerned with steps 1 and 2 of the above process. While OpenURL is an enabling technology for linking services to citations, it is not concerned with the nature of these services or with the methods by which the metadata contained in the OpenURL are transformed into services. That belongs in the realm of resolvers. Whereas resolvers can be proprietary and closed systems, it is expected that OpenURL will become an open standard.

Draft guidelines for constructing OpenURLs are already freely available (Van de Sompel, et al., 2000, web site), and a formal standardization process has started under the aegis of NISO (NISO Committee AX, web site).

The number of available OpenURL resolvers is growing rapidly. Currently, they include:

SFX *[Ex Libris (USA), Inc. SFX]* was the first OpenURL resolver. In fact, the SFX resolver predates OpenURL. Van de Sompel and Hochstenbach developed the SFX resolver and the OpenURL concepts as part of their research on context-sensitive linking (Van de Sompel and Hochstenbach 1999a, b, c).

1Cate, jake.openly.com, and link.openly.com (Openly Informatics, Inc., web site).

LinkFinderPlus (Endeavor Information Systems, Inc., web site).

Open Linking Technology (Fretwell-Downing, Inc., web site).

Powell's OpenResolver (Powell, 2001) is available under the GNU open-source license.

DEMONSTRATION AND TECHNICAL DETAILS

Consider the following citation:

> Van de Sompel, Herbert and Beit-Arie, Oren. 2001. Open Linking in the Scholarly Information Environment Using the OpenURL Framework. D-Lib Magazine. 7(3).

EXAMPLE 1   A typical conventional citation to a journal article.

---

http://sfx.caltech.edu:8088/caltech?genre = article&atitle = Open%20
Linking%20in%20the%20Scholarly%20Information%20Environ
ment%20Using%20the%20OpenURL%20Framework&title = D-Lib
%20Magazine&issn = 1082-9873&date = 2001-03&volume = 7&issue
= 3&aulast = Van%20de%20Sompel

EXAMPLE 2   Example 1 formatted as an HTTP-encoded OpenURL.

Using the draft OpenURL specifications (Van de Sompel, et al., 2000, web site), the OpenURL version of this citation could take the form displayed in Example 2.

In other words, an OpenURL can take the form of a familiar HTTP GET and/or HTTP POST request. The part before the question mark is the URL of Caltech's SFX resolver (Ex Libris (USA), Inc. SFX, web site). The part following the question mark is the metadata describing the referent. In other words, this part is nothing but the citation in machine-readable form.

When the requester clicks on the above link, the requester's browser jumps to the URL of the resolver, and the metadata is transported to the resolver. What the resolver does with this information is not standardized in any way: resolver behavior is limited only by the imagination of resolver developers. In our example, the resolver produces a list of services appropriate to this particular citation. Figure 1 displays the list of services produced by the Caltech SFX resolver at the time of writing the current document. (Since the resolver and the database behind the resolver change over time, the list of services changes over time.)

The mechanism as explained thus far is inadequate. For example:

Non-Caltech requesters are referred to Caltech resources, such as the document-delivery system Ibid or the catalog of the Caltech Library System.

Documents containing links like those in Example 2 must be updated every time the URL of the resolver changes.

The resolver should be determined at the time when the requester clicks on the link. This can be achieved in several ways. Unfortunately, elegant solutions require web-browser modification, and we cannot wait for that to happen. For now, we must settle for pragmatic approaches, each of which has some drawbacks. For example, the URL of the resolver could be stored in a user profile. This works well for systems that require users to log in, but it does not work for ETD collections that are free and open to the public. In this case, one may have to resort (somewhat reluctantly) to web-browser cookies. This is not the proper forum to examine all possible approaches to resolver selection.

SFX Services for this record

Title   Open Linking in the Scholarly Information Environment Using the OpenURL Framework
Source D-LIB MAGAZINE [1082-9873]
        yr: 2001 vol: 7 iss: 3

Get Caltech-licensed full-text from **D-Lib Magazine**
year 2001 issue 3
Check holdings in **Caltech's Library catalog (CLAS)**

Request delivery via **IBID**

Search author in **Web of Science**
Name: Van de Sompel,
Lookup as cited author in **Web of Science**
Name: Van de Sompel,
Lookup as cited reference in **Web of Science**
Citation: Van de Sompel 2001 ...
Send feedback to **Caltech Library System staff**

Get the **Caltech SFX FAQ**

Search the **Web**
Google
Search: Open Linking in the Scholarly Informati

© 2001 SFX by Ex Libris (USA) Inc.

FIGURE 1   List of services produced by Caltech's SFX resolver with the metadata of Examples 1 or 2 as input.

However, it is instructive to examine the Cookie Pusher mechanism, first proposed by Van de Sompel and Hochstenbach (2000, web site).

Before they can use the resolver, requesters must browse to a particular web page in order to set a cookie that contains the URL of the resolver. This one visit activates their access to the resolver until the cookie is deleted. If this cookie is not set, the data provider (in our case, the ETD collection) assumes the requester does not have access to an OpenURL resolver and either does not provide resolver functionality or (if available) uses a free resolver that may be used by anyone.

For simplicity, we assume that the cookie has been set and that the ETD is formatted in HTML. Since we have no prior knowledge of the URL of the resolver, it is impossible to embed in the ETD an HTTP link like the one of Example 2. Instead, we have to retrieve the cookie, construct the

HTTP request, and process the HTTP request. In an HTML-formatted ETD, this activity is "hidden" behind a button placed next to the citation as in Example 3.

Van de Sompel, Herbert and Beit-Arie, Oren. 2001. Open Linking in the Scholarly Information Environment Using the OpenURL Framework. D-Lib Magazine. 7(3). **⑤ SFX**

EXAMPLE 3   An "OpenURL Aware" Citation to a Journal Article

Typically, a program written in a browser-compatible language such as Java or JavaScript performs all of the actions required. Ex Libris (USA), Inc. (JavaScript, web site) provides such a script for the SFX environment. The script reads the user's cookie, determines the appropriate resolver, and defines an SFXButton function that can be invoked in an HTML page. If the ETD includes this JavaScript, then the OpenURL-Aware citation of Example 3 can be encoded in HTML as shown in Example 4.

```
<P> Van de Sompel, Herbert and Beit-Arie, Oren. 2001. Open
Linking in the Scholarly Information Environment Using the Open-
URL Framework. D-Lib Magazine. 7(3).
   <SCRIPT TYPE = "text/javascript" >
SFXButton(
"genre = article&
atitle = Open%20Linking%20in%20the%20Scholarly%20In
formation%20Environment%20Using%20the%20OpenURL%20
Framework&
title = D-Lib%20Magazine&issn = 1082-9873&
date = 2001&
volume = 7&
issue = 3&
aulast = Van%20de%20Sompel&
auinit = H")
   </SCRIPT > </P >
```

EXAMPLE 4   HTML Representation of an OpenURL-Aware Citation

With this script in place, requesters who click on the "SFX button" are directed to the appropriate resolver and receive a tailored menu of services.

The bibliography of the online version of this chapter (Van de Velde and Coles, 2002) shows this technique in action. For demonstration purposes, requesters without a cookie are given access to the Caltech SFX resolver. (This works for this particular online bibliography only. Access to the resolver may be temporary. Only Caltech-affiliated requesters have access to the services offered in the SFX menu.)

OPENURL STANDARDIZATION

In February 2001, NISO formed NISO Committee AX and started the OpenURL standardization process. At the time of writing this, no NISO membership votes had been taken. What follows is an outline of the status of discussions within NISO Committee AX around the middle of January 2002, which is not endorsed by NISO or the NISO membership. For recent updates on the OpenURL standardization process, please check the NISO web site (NISO) or the NISO Committee AX web site (NISO Committee AX).

The Committee adopted both a short-term and a long-term approach. In the short term, it wanted to encourage early adoption of OpenURL by assuring reasonable stability to early adopters. In addition, the committee recognized that the OpenURL guidelines (Van de Sompel, et al., 2002, web site) are a great success both in number of early adopters and the quality of the applications. The Committee, therefore, recommended that draft without amendments or modifications as Version 0.1 of the OpenURL standard. OpenURLs without a version number will be interpreted according to these draft specifications. This should assure early adopters that the standardiza-tion process would not undermine their efforts.

In the long term, only an evolving OpenURL standard can be successful: it must continually adapt to new technologies. It is easy to get caught up in the minutiae of encoding issues. However, encoding is intimately tied to current technology and is, therefore, not the proper foundation for a long-term evolutionary process. For Version 1.0, the committee intends to put in place the theoretical and fundamental concepts that are independent of technology.

At the core, the fundamental issue is which metadata of which possible entities need to be described. In turn, this depends on what an OpenURL is supposed to be. The initial discussions led to the following definition of an OpenURL:

> An OpenURL is a transportation mechanism for metadata that describe one or more referents and zero or more other entities that

define the context in which the reference to the referents occurs or in which the transportation of metadata takes place.

This framed the discussion and led to the following result:

In an OpenURL, we must be able to describe the following entities: referent, resolver, requester, referrer, referring entity, service-type.

Each of these entities can potentially be described in several different ways. The fundamental metadata-description mechanisms (or descriptors) include:

Identifier
(By-Value) Metadata-description
(By-Reference) Metadata
Private-data

For each entity type, a menu of appropriate descriptors will be available. For example, it is likely that the resolver must be described by means of the id descriptor. That would be overly restrictive for the referent, and it is likely the referent may be described by any of the four available descriptors. For details, please consult NISO Committee AX documents (NISO Committee AX, web site) and Van de Sompel and Beit-Arie's theoretical OpenURL framework (Van de Sompel and Beit-Arie, 2001), which formed the basis of Committee discussions.

CONCLUSION

OpenURL is the beginning of an evolution that will increase the power of web links. With OpenURL, web links are context sensitive, deliver narrowly targeted and appropriate services, have a longer useful life, and provide connections to services and information that did not yet exist at the time of writing the documents.

Right now, OpenURL improves the functionality of bibliographies. In the future, it will improve the functionality of the complete ETD, because one can provide services not only for citations but also for subject headings, chemical formulas, genomes, products, patents, etc.

OpenURL is only one of the fundamental reasons why the scholarly record should be preserved in well-constructed OpenURL-aware electronic documents. Because beginning researchers are not only open to using these new technologies, but eager to, ETDs are the best place to start this (r)evolution.

RELATED WEB SITES

Endeavor Information Systems, Inc. LinkFinderPlus.
   http://www.endinfosys.com/prods/lfwhatis.htm

Ex Libris (USA), Inc. SFX.http://www.sfxit.com/
Ex Libris (USA), Inc. OpenURL JavaScript.
  http://demo.exlibrisgroup. com:8888/OpenURL/javascript.html
Fretwell-Downing, Inc. Open Linking Technology.
  http://www.fdusa.com/products/olt.html
NISO. The web site of NISO.http://www.niso.org
NISO Committee AX. The web site of NISO Committee AX on OpenURL
  Standardization.http://library.caltech.edu/openurl
Openly Informatics, Inc. 1Cate, jake.openly.com, and link.openly.com.
  http://www.openly.com
Van de Sompel, Herbert and Hochstenbach, Patrick. 2000. Cookiepusher
  document.http://www.sfxit.com/openurl/cookiepusher.html
Van de Sompel, Herbert; Hochstenbach, Patrick and Beit-Arie, Oren. May
  2000. OpenURL syntax description.http://www.sfxit.com/openurl/open
  url.html or http://library.caltech.edu/openurl/Documents/OpenURL_
  Version_ 0.1.mht

REFERENCES

Powell, A. (June 22, 2001). Open Resolver: A simple OpenURL Resolver. Ariadne.
  Issue 28. http://www.ariadne.ac.uk/issue28/resolver/intro.html.
Van de Sompel, H., Beit-Arie, O. (2001). Generalizing the OpenURL framework
  beyond references to Scholarly Works, the Bison-Futé Model. *D-Lib Magazine*
  7(7). http://www.dlib.org/dlib/july01/vandesompel/07vandesompel. html.
Van de Sompel, H., Hochstenbach, P. (1999a). Reference linking in a hybrid library
  environment. Part 1: Frameworks for Linking. *D-Lib Magazine* 5(4). http://
  www. dlib.org/dlib/april99/van_de_sompel/04van_de_sompel-pt1.html.
Van de Sompel, H., Hochstenbach, P. (1999b). Reference linking in a hybrid library
  environment. Part 2: SFX, a generic linking solution. *D-Lib Magazine* 5(4).
  http://www.dlib.org/dlib/april99/van_de_sompel/04van_de_ sompel-pt2.html.
Van de Sompel, H., Hochstenbach, P. (1999c). Reference hinking in a hybrid library
  envi-ronment. Part 3: Generalizing the SFX solution in the "SFX@ Ghent &
  SFX@LANL" experiment. *D-Lib Magazine* 5(10). http://www.dlib.- org/dlib/
  october99/van_de_sompel/10van_de_sompel.html.
Van de Velde, E. F., Coles, B. (January 2002). OpenURL-Aware ETDs, Caltech
  Library System Papers and Publications. http://resolver.library.caltech. edu/
  caltechLIB:2002.002.

16

ETD-ms: An Interoperability Metadata Standard for Electronic Theses and Dissertations

Anthony Atkins, Edward A. Fox,
Robert K. France, and Hussein Suleman*
Virginia Polytechnic Institute and State University
Blacksburg, Virginia

INTRODUCTION

This document defines a standard set of metadata elements used to describe an electronic thesis or dissertation.

Institutions dealing with electronic theses and dissertations have all developed their own standards or adapted existing metadata standards. These metadata standards all attempt to describe the author, the work, and the context in which the work was produced in a way that will be useful to the researcher as well as the librarians and/or technical staff maintaining the work in its electronic form.

This document is not a replacement for the metadata schemes developed for a particular university or environment. Rather, this document

Current affiliation: University of Capetown, Capetown, South Africa should be used as a guideline to develop a faithful cross-walk between local metadata standards and a single standard used for sharing information about ETDs.

AUTHORITIES

Each reference to an individual or institution in any field should contain a string representing the name of the individual or institution as it appears in the work. The reference may also contain a URI, which points to an authoritative record for that individual or institution.

METADATA ELEMENTS

The following is a description of the common Dublin Core metadata elements (and a new element specifically for theses). Guidelines are given as to which information related to an ETD belongs in each element.

If a more general element is described as *mandatory*, it should be specified fully, even if qualified elements are also specified. If a more general element is repeatable, it should be assumed that subelements are also repeatable. If an element contains free text, it must be repeatable to allow for ETDs that provide metadata in more than one language.

The ETD-MS group provides a "Vanilla" encoding of the standard set into XML and a recommended encoding into MARC-21. The XML encoding follows Dublin Core standards everywhere that the abstract metadata set follows Dublin Core elements. The MARC-21 recommendations follow AACR-2 policies and procedures for common bibliographic elements like title and publisher, with additions for elements particular to electronic theses and dissertations. A third encoding of the element set, into RDF, is envisioned. As this version goes public, that encoding has not yet been completed.

"Vanilla" XML Encoding

XML is the carrier for both a "Vanilla" encoding and for an extended encoding that also builds on the Resource Description Framework (RDF). The Vanilla encoding is a straightforward application of unqualified Dublin Core, with the "thesis" element added.

Sample Record

The following is the metadata for an ETD from the Virginia Tech ETD collection presented in one possible XML encoding based on this standard. It would certainly be possible to develop alternate encodings in XML, or encodings in RDF. The XML schema used can be found at http://www.ndltd.org/standards/metadata/etdms/1.0/etdms.xsd.

```
<thesis xmlns= "http://www.ndltd.org/standards/
metadata/etdms/1.0/" xsi:schemaLocation= "http://
www.ndltd.o0rg/standards/metadata/etdms/1.0/ http://
www.ndltd.org/standards/metadata/etdms/1.0/etdms.xsd">
```

```
<title>Conceptual Development and Empirical Testing of an
Outdoor Recreation Experience Model: The Recreation Expe-
rience Matrix (REM)</title>
```

```
<creator>Walker, Gordon James</creator>
```

```
<subject>outdoor recreation</subject>
```

```
<subject>recreation experience preference scales
</subject>
```

```
<subject>recreation experience matrix</subject>
```

```
<subject>recreation opportunity spectrum</subject>
```

```
<description>This dissertation examines four issues, in-
cluding: (a) whether outdoor recreation experiences not
included in the Recreation Experience Preference (REP)
scales exist; (b) whether these experiences can be catego-
rized using a framework called the Recreation Experience
Matrix (REM); (c) how well the Recreation Opportunity
Spectrum (ROS) variables of activity, setting, and exper-
tise explain the types of experiences outdoor recreation-
ists receive; and (d) how well two new variables—primary
mode and mode dependence—explain the types of experiences
outdoor recreationists receive. In order to address these
issues, an on-site questionnaire was distributed at Mount
Rogers National Recreation Area in Virginia during October
and November, 1995. A total of 410 people completed this
questionnaire. Of these, 336 provided useable addresses
for a follow-up mail-out questionnaire, with 169 (50.3%)
actually returning it. After performing a variety of
statistical analyses, it was found that: (a) some outdoor
recreationists did report having non-REP experiences in-
volving identity, cognition, absorption, and self-con-
cept; (b) indirect support does exist for classifying
outdoor recreation experiences using the REM framework;
and (c) the ROS variables of activity, setting, and
expertise, do explain some outdoor recreation experiences,
as do the new variables of primary mode and mode depend-
ence.</description>
```

```
<publisher>Virginia Polytechnic Institute and State Uni-
versity</publisher>

<contributor role="committee_member">Daniel R. Wil-
liams</contributor>

<contributor role="committee_member">K. Jill Kiecolt
</contributor>

<contributor role="committee_member">Bradley R. Hertel
</contributor>

<contributor role="chair">Joseph W. Roggenbuck
</contributor>

<contributor role="chair">R. Bruce Hull</contributor>

<date>1997-03-31</date>

<type>Electronic Thesis or Dissertation</type>

<format>application/pdf</format>

<identifier>http://scholar.lib.vt.edu/theses/
available/etd-3345131939761081/</identifier>

<language>en</language>

<rights>unrestricted</rights>

<rights>I hereby grant to Virginia Tech or its agents the
right to archive and to make available my thesis or
dissertation in whole or in part in the University Libra-
ries in all forms of media, now or hereafter known. I retain
all proprietary rights, such as patent rights. I also
retain the right to use in future works (such as articles
or books) all or part of this thesis or dissertation.
</rights>

<degree>
<name>PHD</name>

<level>doctoral</level>

<discipline>Forestry</discipline>

<grantor>Virginia Polytechnic Institute and State Univer-
sity</grantor>
</degree>
</thesis>
```

DOCUMENT HISTORY

This document is based primarily on the work of the Dublin Core Metadata Initiative and the proposed set of qualifiers put forward by the DC Date Working Group. The version of this document dated 06-05-2001 was prepared in response to comments made by users of the NDLTD-standards mailing list (see below for contributor information). The version of this document dated 01-10-2001 was produced as a result of a two-day meeting that took place at OCLC in Dublin Ohio on January 9-10 of 2001 (see below for contributor information).

This document is also a distillation of the discussions that took place at the workshop "DTDs and the Usage of New XML-Technologies for Electronic Theses and Dissertations" held in May 2000 at Humboldt University in Berlin. A list of the participants is included in the next section. More information regarding this workshop can be found at: http://dochost.rz.hu-berlin.de/epdiss/dtd-workshop/.

This document is also based in part on a prior document entitled "NDLTD Metadata" drafted by Gail McMillan and Paul Mather.

CONTRIBUTORS

The version of this document dated 06-05-2001 was prepared in response to comments made by users of the NDLTD-standards mailing list, including Tony Cargnelutti, Elaine Henjum, and Priscilla Caplan.

The version of this document dated 01-10-2001 was discussed and prepared as part of the "ETD Standards Meeting" held on January 9–10, 2001, at OCLC Online Computer Library Center, Inc. in Dublin, Ohio. The following people attended the meeting:

> Anthony Atkins, Virginia Tech
> Thorsten Bahne, Gerhard-Mercator-Universität (Germany)
> Eric Childress, OCLC
> John Espley, VTLS
> Ed Fox, Virginia Tech
> Robert France, Virginia Tech
> Nuno Freire, Portuguese National Library
> Thom Hickey, OCLC
> Sarantos Kapidakis, National Documentation Centre (Greece)
> Sunny Kim, Academy of Korean Studies/Virginia Tech
> Mann-Ho Lee, Chungnam National University (Korea)/Virginia Tech
> Akira Maeda, Nara Institute of Science & Technology (Japan)/Virginia Tech

Eric Miller, OCLC
Ed O'Neill, OCLC
Shalini Urs, University of Mysore (India)/Virginia Tech
Diane Vizine-Goetz, OCLC
Stu Weibel, OCLC

The following individuals and groups contributed to the previous draft of this document:

Edward Fox, Director, Networked Digital Library of Theses and Dissertations
Gail McMillan, Director Digital Library and Archives
Anthony Atkins, Technical Director, Digital Library and Archives

The following people participated in the metadata discussion led by Nuno Freire and Thorsten Bahne, which was part of the workshop "DTDs and the Usage of new XML-Technologies for Electronic Theses and Dissertations" held at Humboldt University in Berlin in May 2000:

Per Åkerlund, SLU (Swedish University of Agricultural Sciences) Libraries, SWEDEN, Per.Akerlund@bibul.slu.se
Anthony Atkins, Virginia Polytechnic Institute and State University, University Libraries, USA, anthony.atkins@vt.edu
Thorsten Bahne, Mathematics, University of Duisburg, Dissertation Online Project, GERMANY, bahne@math.uni-duisburg.de
Viviane Bouletreau, Sentiers, Université Lumiére, Lyon 2, FRANCE, vboletr@univ-lyon2.fr
Wolfgang Coy, School of Informatics, Humboldt-University Berlin, GERMANY, coy@informatik.hu-berlin.de
Peter Diepold, Humboldt-University Berlin, School of Educational Science, GERMANY, diepold@educat.hu-berlin.de
Susanne Dobratz, Humboldt-University Berlin, Computing Center, GERMANY, dobratz@rz.hu-berlin.de
Havard Fosseng, University of Oslo, Center for Information Technology Services, NORWAY, havard.fosseng@usit.uio.no
Nuno Freire, National Library Portugal, PORTUGAL, nuno freire@ext.bn.pt
Martin Hess, Informatik Uni Frankfurt: GERMANY, hess@tm.informatik.uni-frankfurt.de
Uwe Müller, Humboldt-University Berlin, Computing Center, GERMANY, u.mueller@rz.hu-berlin.de
Phil Potter, University of Iowa, Academic Technologies (part of Information Technology Services), USA, phil-potter@uiowa.edu
Sebastian Rahtz, TeX User Group, UK, sebastian.rahtz@computing-services.oxford.ac.uk

Paul W. Schaffner, University of Michigan at Ann Arbor, Library, USA, pfs@umich.edu

Matthias Schulz, Humboldt-University Berlin, Computing Center, GERMANY, matthias.schulz.1@rz.hu-berlin.de

Peter Schirmbacher, Humboldt-University Berlin, Computing Center, GERMANY, schirmbacher@rz.hu-berlin.de

Tuija Sonkkila, Helsinki University of Technology, Library, FINLAND, sonkkila@cc.hut.fi

Christof Steinbeck, Mack-Planck Institute of Chemical Ecology, Jena, GERMANY, steinbeck@ice.mpg.de

Kerstin Zimmermann, University of Oldenburg, Department of Physics, GERMANY, kerstin@merlin.physik.uni-oldenburg.de

dc.title

Element	Description	Notes
dc.title	A name given to the resource. In the case of theses and dissertations, this is the title of the work as it appears on the title page or equivalent.	Mandatory, repeatable
dc.title.alternative	Alternative title of the thesis or dissertation	Optional, repeatable

dc.creator

Element	Description	Notes
dc.creator	An entity primarily responsible for making the content of the resource. In the case of theses or dissertations, this field is appropriate for the author(s) of the work. Like other names and	Mandatory, repeatable

Element	Description	Notes
	institutions, this field should be entered in free text form as it appears on the title page or equivalent, with a link to an authority record if available.	

dc.subject

Element	Description	Notes
dc.subject	The topic of the content of the resource. In the case of theses and dissertations, keywords or subjects listed on the title page can be entered as free text. The scheme qualifier should be used to indicate a controlled vocabulary.	Mandatory, repeatable

dc.description

Element	Description	Notes
dc.description	An account of the content of the resource. In the case of theses and dissertations, this is the full text of the abstract. Note: dc.description is interchangeable with the qualified element dc.description.abstract.	Optional, repeatable
dc.description.abstract	The full text of the abstract.	Optional, repeatable
dc.description.note	Additional information regarding the thesis or dissertation. *Example: acceptance note of the department.*	Optional, repeatable
dc.description.release	Description of the version of the work. Should only be used for errata, etc.	Optional, repeatable

dc.publisher

Element	Description	Notes
dc.publisher	An entity responsible for making the resource available. This is typically the group most directly responsible for digitizing and/or archiving the work. The publisher may or may not be exactly the same as thesis.degree.grantor. Like other names and institutions, this field should be entered in free text form as it appears on the title page or equivalent, with a link to an authority record if available.	Optional, repeatable

dc.contributor

Element	Description	Notes
dc.contributor	An entity responsible for making contributions to the content of the resource. Typical use would be for co-authors of parts of the work as well as advisors or committee members. Coauthors of the entire work would be more appropriate for the dc.creator field.	Optional, repeatable
dc.contributor.role	Role the person played in the creation or approval of the work. Examples: advisor, committee member, chair, co-chair, referree, juror.	Optional

dc.date

Element	Description	Notes
dc.date	A date associated with an event in the life cycle of the resource. In the case of theses and dissertations, this should be the date that appears on the title page or equivalent of the work. Should be recorded as defined in ISO 8601 and the profile recommended for implementing ISO 8601 dates in Dublin Core.	Mandatory

dc.type

Element	Description	Notes
dc.type	The nature or genre of the content of a resource. This field is used to distinguish the resource from works in other genres and to identify the types of content included in the resource. The string "Electronic Thesis or Dissertation" is recommended as one of the repeatable values for this element. In addition, specify types of content using the standard vocabulary found at: http:// dublincore.org/documents/dcmi-type-vocabulary/. Degree and Education Level are now handled by the thesis.degree field.	Mandatory, repeatable

dc.format

Element	Description	Notes
dc.format	The physical or digital manifestation of the resource. In the case of an electronic thesis or dissertation, this should contain a list of the electronic format(s) in which the work is stored and/or delivered. Use the standard MIME type whenever possible (for a list of "registered" MIME types, visit ftp://ftp.isi.edu/in-notes/iana/assignments/media-types/media-types). List as "unknown" if no format information is available, omit if the work is not available in electronic form.	Optional, repeatable

dc.indentifier

Element	Description	Notes
dc.identifier	An unambiguous reference to the resource within a given context. This can and should be used to provide a URI where the work can be viewed or downloaded. Persistent URNs such as PURLs	Mandatory, repeatable

Element	Description	Notes
	(http://purl.org/) or Handles (http://handle.net) are recommended.	

dc.language

Element	Description	Notes
dc.language	A language of the intellectual content of the resource. This should be the primary language in which the work is recorded. Portions of the larger work that appear in other languages should use the lang qualifier. Language names themselves should be recorded using ISO 639-2 (or RFC 1766). If the language is not specified, it is assumed to be English (en).	Optional, repeatable

dc.coverage

Element	Description	Notes
dc.coverage	The extent or scope of the content of the resource. This element should be used for time periods or spatial regions. For any other type of "coverage," use dc.subject.	Optional, repeatable

dc.rights

Element	Description	Notes
dc.rights	Information about rights held in and over the resource. Typically, this describes the conditions under which the work may be distributed, reproduced, etc., how these conditions may change over time, and whom to contact regarding the copyright of the work.	Optional, repeatable

thesis.degree

Element	Description	Notes
thesis.degree.name	Name of the degree associated with the work as it appears within the work. Example: Masters in Operations Research.	Optional, repeatable
thesis.degree.level	Level of education associated with the document. Examples: bachelor's, master's, doctoral, postdoctoral, other.	Optional, repeatable
thesis.degree.discipline	Area of study of the intellectual content of the document. Usually, this will be the name of a program or department.	Optional, repeatable
thesis.degree.grantor	Institution granting the degree associated with the work. Like other names and institutions, this field should be entered in free text form as it appears on the title page or equivalent, with a link to an authority record if available.	Optional, repeatable

GLOBAL QUALIFIERS

In addition to the attributes specified for various elements, there are also a handful of global attributes that can be specified for any element.

lang: An indication of the language in which the value of a field is written. This is entirely separate from the dc.language element, which indicates the primary language of the work itself.

translated: An empty element that indicates that the value of a field is a translation provided by someone other than the author. For translations provided by the author, simply indicate the language of the field itself (using the "lang" attribute).

scheme: Description of the vocabulary or scheme used to determine the subject(s).

ENCODINGS

The abstract set of elements defined in this document can be encoded in a variety of standard formats. Two of particular interest to the digital library community are the MARC standard common to library catalog systems and the XML data markup language.

17

Phases and Issues in the Transition to ETDs

Martin J. Bunch* and Christine Jewell
University of Waterloo
Waterloo, Canada

INTRODUCTION

This chapter outlines phases through which an institution is likely to pass when adopting electronic theses and dissertations (ETDs) in addition to, or in place of, traditional (paper) forms of submission, storage, provision of access to, and distribution of theses and dissertations. Four phases are identified in this process: exploration, experimentation, transition, and institutionalization. Other chapters in this volume address technical aspects of ETDs. Thus, recommendations are not made in this chapter regarding details of ETD submissions, file formats, and the like. Rather this chapter addresses the process of investigation and adoption of ETDs at a university and presents an itinerary of issues that are likely to arise along the way. We hope that this discussion will be useful to those beginning an exploration into ETDs as a possible medium for theses and dissertations.

* *Current affiliation*: York University, Toronto, Canada

The body of this chapter is divided into six sections. The first section, *Background*, offers an overview of the activities of the University of Waterloo Electronic Thesis Project Team. It is on the basis of the authors' experience as members of this team and the results of its survey and widespread communications with individuals from other institutions involved in ETD projects that this generalization of the.phases of an ETD project is made. *Relevant Groups and Project Team Composition* describes the composition of a typical ETD project team. Composition may vary depending on the developmental phase at which the ETD project has arrived. *Exploration* covers aspects of the initial phase of an ETD project. The next section deals with the *Experimentation Phase*, where planning and implementation of a pilot project are discussed. The following section looks at the *Transition Phase*, and the final section touches on the final *Institutionalization Phase*.

In addition to detailed descriptions of the components of ETD project phases, most sections contain information relating to the University of Waterloo Electronic Thesis Project. The text boxes are intended to provide concrete examples and illustrations of the particular phase being described.

BACKGROUND

The University of Waterloo Electronic Thesis Project Team began meeting in the fall of 1996. The team was formed to explore issues relating to electronic theses and to investigate the technical feasibility of electronic submission, access, distribution, and storage of theses at the University of Waterloo (Waterloo, Ontario, Canada). Team members included representatives from the university's graduate studies office, library, the information systems and technology department, the university's graphic services department, faculty, and graduate students.

Early in the team's work, issues associated with ETDs were found to fall within several main areas: governance, intellectual property, submission, access/distribution, storage/preservation, and associated social and philosophical considerations (see below). As a tool to explore these issues, and to investigate the progress of ETD projects at other postsecondary institutions, the University of Waterloo Electronic Thesis Project Team developed an ETD survey (University of Waterloo Electronic Theses Project Team, 1997a). Information regarding ETDs and ETD projects generated by this survey tool, together with knowledge derived from other activities in the project team's investigation of ETD issues, provided a basis for the team to proceed to an experimentation phase. During this phase a pilot project was undertaken to determine the feasibility of electronic access and distribution of theses at the University of Waterloo.

The University of Waterloo is currently in a transition phase, accepting both paper and electronic thesis submissions. To provide access to ETDs, the university has established an E-thesis database (available at http://www.lib. uwaterloo.ca/ETD/etheses.html), which contains theses from the ETD project team's pilot project, numerous theses previously submitted to the Graduate Studies Office through traditional procedures and later converted to electronic format, and theses that have since been submitted to the graduate office as ETDs.

RELEVANT GROUPS AND PROJECT TEAM COMPOSITION

An ETD project team should include representatives from relevant and interested groups. These may include representatives from the library, the graduate studies office, computer and technology support departments, graduate students, and faculty. The work of such a composite group will be a collaborative effort, with cooperative association among a variety of people from across campus. Membership will not necessarily remain static. Depending on the project's developmental phase and immediate focus at any given time, active contribution from one group or another may not be essential. However, members should continue to participate, filling the role of consultants, and serving as informed representatives, willing to contribute as necessary as the project develops.

The immediate objective of a newly formed ETD project team will be to become familiar with the issues of this highly technical topic. It would be useful if the team members also had expertise or experience in some area relating to ETDs. This could range from technical expertise in computing to knowledge of intellectual property issues.

The promise of the electronic information revolution may provide the context for initial discussions about ETDs. A wide range of individuals and constituencies at a post-secondary institution may wish to see ETDs realized on campus for a variety of reasons. Increasingly, members of postsecondary institutions are working with electronic reference resources, journals, and texts. Electronic theses share the many advantages of these information resources. Some of these are outlined in Table 1.

Direction of the team should come from either the library or the graduate office, since these units are most directly involved with governance and handling of theses and dissertations (e.g., setting submission procedures, enforcement of thesis regulations, provision of access and distribution). A representative from the library computing department and/or the university's computing department can contribute technical expertise to the project. Graduate student and faculty members will provide representation of their constituent groups on campus (fulfilling a communication role) as well as making contributions based on whatever personal expertise and experience they bring to the group.

TABLE 1 Potential Benefits of ETDs

Benefits as seen by librarians	Benefits as seen by graduate officers	Benefits as seen by graduate students	Benefits as seen by researchers
Increased access to theses and dissertations	Reduced paper handling	Increased exposure of research	Metadata search for Ph.D. and master's research
Reduced physical storage requirements	Speedier procedures	Reduced costs from binding, printing, and photocopying of theses	Full text World Wide Web access to graduate research
Enhanced searching capabilities	Reduced costs of submission (e.g., post) to national libraries	Potential to include nontraditional components such as video, sound, and executable files	Potential for electronic full text searching in the text of ETDs

Participation of relevant stakeholders, from the students generating theses to those governing them, is crucial for two reasons. Participation of relevant stakeholders provides multiple perspectives on processes and technology to be adopted. This will reduce the possibility of overlooking important issues or stumbling into unforseen problems. Also, empowered participation translates to ownership of the process by groups likely to be affected by changes in policy process and technology. The transition to ETDs is likely to be more speedy, conflict-free, and effective if its implementation is undertaken in a participatory, rather than a command, mode.

Retaining a core membership, a project team may at times expand to include members such as research assistants and additional technical consultants. For example, depending on the specifics of the experimentation phase (e.g., the size of a pilot project, software and electronic formats being tested), it may be appropriate to invite participation from the unit at the institution which handles reproduction of teaching and other materials. Team membership may also shift in the transition phase because more work will be required of library and graduate office representatives at this time. Increased communication and demonstrations to the university community at large might also necessitate expanding the team. For example, graduate students and faculty members can undertake a liaison role, ensuring that policy changes are well known and understood throughout the institution. In addition, cooperative efforts with other institutions might effect ETD team composition.

EXPLORATION PHASE

Terms of Reference and Objectives

A clear Terms of Reference for the ETD project and an explicit set of objectives for the exploration phase will help to structure investigation of ETD issues. A Terms of Reference will indicate the scope of the inquiry and lay out the mandate of the project team. It should include a statement of the overall goal or purpose of the project and set specific objectives with a projected timeline where possible. Names and contact information for individuals involved in the project should be attached.

The initial phase of an ETD project will be concerned with information gathering in order to (1) familiarize team members with issues having to do with ETDs and (2) inform recommendations and actions for the next phase in the team's work. Objectives for the exploration phase may be usefully directed toward production of an interim report focused on key issues as identified by the project team.

Issues

A variety of issues must be explored before the feasibility of an ETD program at a post-secondary institution can be determined. Developing an understanding of the issues involved is probably the most substantial portion of the area under the learning curve for a newcomer to ETDs. A useful categorization of issues related to ETDs at a post-secondary institution is:

> Governance issues
> Intellectual property
> Submission of ETDs
> Access to ETDs
> Storage and preservation of ETDs
> Social and philosophical considerations

An exploration of governance issues begins with a review of an institution's current policy, regulations, and guidelines regarding theses. In addition, the set of actors involved in dealing with theses should be reviewed, from the graduate student who submits the thesis to governing bodies responsible for setting policy. For example, actors might be identified for such roles as storage of the official copy of theses, approval of the final form of theses for submission, and provision of access to theses.

Governance issues should be approached with an eye to changes in the roles of these actors. Adoption of ETDs, if it were to occur at an institution, will result in changes to policy, regulations, and procedures that will change the way that staff, students, and faculty handle theses. This suggests that consideration must be given to education, training, and facilities to support the handling of ETDs. Also, pertinent parties should be kept informed of the progress of, if not actively involved in, the ETD project. Participation of actors and stakeholders tends to increase the effectiveness of projects as well as smooth implementation of their recommendations.

Intellectual property issues deal with a variety of difficult and often controversial aspects of ETDs and electronic publishing. For example, the possibility of copyright violations associated with improved access to electronic theses leads to concerns about the currently confused state of intellectual property law with respect to electronic media and the World Wide Web and the difficulty in policing possible IP infractions. Also, although there seems to be no legal difference between providing access to theses in paper versus electronic format, the potential increase in access to the work has led some academic publishers to indicate discomfort in what they perceive as republishing material already made easily accessible electronically (e.g., through the World Wide Web).

Submission issues are fairly straightforward, but very important. This general category focuses investigation on such issues as acceptable formats for electronic submission of theses, the appointment of responsibility for preparing electronic theses in a manner suitable for submission, determination of necessary support personnel, equipment, and space to facilitate this, and the logistics of determining that an electronic thesis meets the published regulations and guidelines of the institution. In addition, it must be determined whether theses with nonstandard components such as video, audio, hypertext, and hyperlinks will be allowed, and the acceptable form and format for such must be ascertained.

The generation and dissemination of knowledge is a main role of universities. The possibilities for improved access to theses and dissertations in electronic form can greatly enhance the knowledge dissemination function. Some issues related to access of ETDs include decisions regarding who is to be allowed access to ETDs (e.g., the university community versus researchers outside the university community), whether this access should be free of charge, the availability of thesis records and abstracts through an electronic catalogue and/or the World Wide Web, the means of delivery of ETDs, media and formats employed for access and distribution purposes, and the responsibility for provision of access to ETDs.

The counterpart to these issues pertains to longer-term storage and preservation of theses and dissertations. Such issues include consideration of media and formats used to store ETDs for archival purposes, procedures to ensure preservation of the "official" or "canonical" copy of theses and dissertations, location of storage of the canonical copy, and the responsibility for long-term storage and preservation of ETDs.

Finally, social and philosophical issues will surface in an exploration of ETDs. One of the most important issues in this category involves the question: What is a thesis? The use of electronic technology opens up the possibility of radical evolution of the form and content of theses and dissertations. Decisions will have to be made as to whether to permit nontraditional components such as audio, video, virtual reality, compiled and executable code, hyperlinks, hypertext, as well as other unforeseen possibilities that the future may bring. Another important issue is the impact on, and reaction of, faculty and graduate students who will be affected by any changes in university regulation on theses and dissertations. It is important that the opinions of these groups be canvassed and that these constituencies be kept informed of the ETD project and its recommendations. As noted above, such groups should be represented within the project itself.

EXPERIMENTATION PHASE

With the completion of the information-gathering phase, an ETD team may experiment with ETD generation, submission, storage, and distribution. In the experimentation phase the ETD team will:

1. Attempt to resolve issues and test assumptions identified in the exploration phase
2. Develop technical knowledge and gain practical experience working with ETDs
3. Identify concrete problems
4. Recommend further action related to ETDs

These objectives may be accomplished by conducting one or more pilot projects. A pilot project that has clearly defined objectives and the support of all concerned parties can substantially facilitate adoption of ETDs at an institution.

To simplify such a project, it is a good idea to provide it with a primary objective. It is likely that a pilot project will provide valuable information relating to all ETD issues. However, a limited focus may result in a smoother project, particularly if those conducting the project will be experiencing a steep learning curve with respect to the technical aspects of ETDs.

A variety of factors will determine the appropriate focus for an institution:

1. Activities of other institutions (cooperative efforts will minimize overlap)

2. Immediate needs (e.g., the pilot may respond to requests already received for electronic submission)
3. Areas of responsibility (e.g., access may be a local responsibility, but long-term storage a national one)

A concise project proposal is needed to obtain official sanction for the project. The proposal should contain some background information, explaining the progress made by the ETD team throughout the information-gathering phase. The Terms of Reference for the ETD team should be included. The proposal should indicate the primary goal of the pilot project and identify specific objectives, as well as including a budget, time line, and date for submission of a final report summarizing the project results and recommendations.

Hardware, software, and personnel requirements and estimated expenses should be itemized in the proposal budget. As an ETD team is typically a cooperative effort across many departments on campus, support may be found from these departments in the form of staff assistance and computer hardware and software. Ideally, funds will be provided to support research assistants for work on the project.

With the completion of the pilot project, the ETD team will be able to make recommendations regarding hardware, software, personnel, organizational, and policy changes required to transition to ETDs. Also, some human capacity (and perhaps infrastructure) for ETD adoption will have been developed at the institution through the pilot project itself.

TRANSITION PHASE

A transition phase allows a timed phase-in of electronic submission, storage, preservation, access, and distribution of theses and dissertations and a corresponding phase-out of traditional bound paper documents. This phase begins with officially sanctioned preparations to accept the first submission of an electronic thesis at the university and ends with the last official submission of a paper thesis (or the routine conversion of all theses submitted on paper into electronic documents for storage, access, and distribution purposes).

Objectives in a transition phase will relate to the implementation of recommendations from the pilot project report and will be tailored to the situation of individual institutions. However, such goals will likely have to do with changes in policy to accommodate ETDs, the development of institutional capacity to handle ETDs, education and dissemination of information to the university community, commencement of the acceptance by the university of theses submitted in electronic format, as well as provision of access to ETDs by the university.

Changes in policy to accommodate ETDs will be necessary for universities to accept theses and dissertations submitted electronically. Changes may have to be made to university policy and to regulations associated with them by the appropriate governing body.

Development of institutional capacity will likely involve the development of human resources, such as training of staff to approve the form of ETDs when they are submitted. University staff will have to be trained in the use of appropriate software and instructed in submission procedures for electronic documents. Similarly, graduate students will require training in the handling of electronic documents. Periodic workshops and the development of on-line resources for the creation of ETDs would support graduate students in this task.

The development of physical capacity is also important. The university must acquire the appropriate tools, both hardware and software, to handle ETDs. Some tasks may be undertaken by outsourcing or in cooperation with other institutions. For example, access to ETDs may be provided though cooperative projects such as the Networked Digital Library of Theses and Dissertations (NDLTD) or commercial services such as those provided by UMI (see the relevant chapters in this volume).

INSTITUTIONALIZATION PHASE

Institutionalization is a return to normality, except that the normal way of doing things related to theses and dissertations assumes that these are (or may be) in electronic form. At this point, policy and regulations have been modified to incorporate ETDs, the institution has the physical and human capacity to deal with ETDs, procedures for handling them have been devised and the wrinkles worked out, ETDs are being submitted, handled, and stored, and access to them provided electronically.

ETDs will require a continued commitment from the institution throughout the institutionalization phase into the foreseeable future. Science and society are advancing ever more quickly, and this implies that the technology associated with ETDs such as file formats and media types are likely to become outdated rather quickly. This will also impact associated procedures developed to deal with ETDs in an institution. As a result, institutions must be prepared to periodically review regulations and procedures regarding ETDs and to commit to ongoing maintenance of the physical and human capacity to handle ETDs. Such tasks as upgrading of hardware will be required at the very least. Note, however, that changes associated with ETDs are likely also to support other educational and research activities, so costs may be shared.

Moreover, technology will likely advance in surprising ways, and theses and dissertations themselves will continue to evolve in form, placing new demands on the capacity of the institutions that generate them. For this reason it is important to make well-considered choices in earlier phases of the transition regarding the means of implementing ETDs at an institution. This should not be intended to fix technologies, procedures, and regulations associated with ETDs once and for all time, but rather in an attempt to reduce the frequency of required upgrades and changes to these in the future.

CONCLUSIONS

Based on the experience and research of members of the Electronic Theses Project Team at the University of Waterloo, this chapter has presented a guide to the process and structure of an ETD project, which is appropriate for newcomers to the topic of electronic theses and dissertations at postsecondary institutions. Four general phases in an ETD project have been identified: exploration, experimentation, transition, and institutionalization. One may take comfort in the observation that these phases are obvious for a project oriented toward the adoption of new technologies. Together with an itinerary of issues and considerations regarding ETDs for each of these phases, a framework has been presented that may be adopted and modified to guide an ETD project.

The process described begins with an exploration of issues variously associated with governance, intellectual property, submission of ETDs, access to ETDs, storage and preservation of ETDs, and social and philosophical considerations. Once ETD project team members are familiar with the issues and know, in general, in which direction they wish the project to proceed, they may validate the technology during an exploration phase. This can be done by implementing a pilot project. Providing the exploration phase has been fruitful, the institution may decide to accept—and provide access to—theses as electronic documents. Transition to ETDs from traditional forms of theses and dissertations will involve the modification of policy and regulations, the development of human and institutional capacity for ETDs, and education and dissemination of information to the university community. If ETDs become the norm, the project will have entered the institutionalization phase. It should be noted, however, that society and its technologies will continue to advance, requiring that these issues be revisited periodically.

Project team composition and communication with the university community at large are important considerations. Efforts should be made to involve all relevant groups in an ETD project. It is recommended that core team membership be composed of representatives of the university library, graduate studies office, computing and technology support units, and faculty and graduate student constituencies. Other individuals may be involved as appropriate, and relevant constituencies should be kept informed of the progress of the project.

At the University of Waterloo, the dean of graduate studies and the university librarian agreed to form a committee to investigate electronic theses. A librarian was asked to facilitate the project. The team for the exploration phase consisted of the facilitator (from the library), a member of the library systems department, a representative from the graduate studies office, several graduate students (for their assistance and perspective), a staff member from the computing department (for technical expertise), and a faculty representative.

Membership varied throughout the existence of the project team. Such variations have occurred as a result of changing project objectives and conflicting commitments of individual team members. For example, the ETD team expanded when it drew upon expertise (in electronic document production, publication, and conversion) from several members of the university's graphic services department for a pilot project conducted during the exploration phase of the ETD project.

The University of Waterloo is currently operating in a transition phase. The university began accepting an electronic version as the official thesis submission in November 1999. Eight ETDs were submitted in 1999, 26 in 2000, and 35 by mid-December 2001. The 2001 figure was close to 10% of the total number of theses and dissertations submitted. It is anticipated that the popularity of the electronic submission option will continue to increase.

The general objectives of the University of Waterloo's ETD team (University of Waterloo Electronic Theses Project Team, 1997c) during the initial exploration phase of the project, which should be generally applicable to any ETD project in its early stages, are as follows:

Review the current process for submitting a thesis
Investigate issues, costs, advantages, and disadvantages of ETDs
Research similar projects occurring at other institutions
Build and maintain contacts with individuals involved in similar
    projects
Solicit feedback from interested parties

The University of Waterloo Electronic Thesis Project Team proposed that UW conduct an ETD pilot project. For the purposes of this pilot, the team focused primarily on electronic access and distribution issues. The main components of the pilot project as given in the proposal (University of Waterloo Electronic Thesis Project Team, 1997b) are summarized below.

Goal

To determine the feasibility of providing electronic access to, and distribution of, theses.

Objectives

To select 20 test theses from a variety of academic departments,
    covering a range of types, including hard copy as well as theses
    with nontraditional components
To convert the theses into the distribution formats to be tested
To provide campus-wide Web access to the test theses
To solicit feedback from student/authors, researchers, library,
    and graduate office staff

Resource requirements

Library
    Project coordination
    Technical expertise
    Meeting facilities
    Office supplies (laser printing of reports, etc.)
Information Systems and Technology
    Technical expertise
    Electronic storage (disk space)
    Access to graphics facilities
    File conversion
    Optical character recognition (OCR) for full-text searching
Research Assistant

Web site construction and maintenance
Evaluation of Web interfaces for the pilot theses
Monitoring and analysis of WWW access
Preparing documents in portable document format (PDF)
Optical character recognition (OCR) and manipulation
Common gateway interface (CGI) scripting
Report on technical issues associated with distribution
Equipment
A mid- to high-end computer with large RAM and SCSI hard drive storage capacity
Color scanner
Adobe Acrobat software
Ethernet connection (to the university network and WWW)

Report

Following the completion of the pilot project, a report provided descriptions of the project procedures, details of hurdles and solutions found or tried, and recommendations regarding the future of ETDs at UW (University of Waterloo Electronic Thesis Project Team, 1997e).

At the University of Waterloo, thesis standards are governed by the senate graduate council and disseminated by the graduate studies office in a document entitled "Graduate Thesis Regulations" (Graduate Studies Office, University of Waterloo, 2001a). The regulations were originally oriented toward submission of traditional paper theses. For example, section 5.4 of the regulations deals specifically with the color, composition, and size of paper used for a thesis. In May 1999, the senate graduate council agreed to a revision of the thesis submission regulations to accommodate an electronic submission option. Electronic submission regulations are published in a document entitled "Electronic Thesis Submissions" (Graduate Studies Office, University of Waterloo, 2001b).

REFERENCES

Graduate Studies Office, University of Waterloo. Graduate Thesis Regulations 2001a, Online, accessed 13 December 2001. http://www.grad.uwaterloo.ca/General_info/Thesis_Regs/thesistofc.html.
Graduate Studies Office, University of Waterloo. Electronic Thesis Submissions,

2001b. Online, accessed 13 December 2001. http://www.grad.uwaterloo.ca/General_info/Thesis_Regs/EThesis/index.html.

University of Waterloo Electronic Theses Project Team University of Waterloo Electronic Theses Project Team: ETD Questionnaire Results, 1997a. Online, revised 15 April 1997. http://www.lib.uwaterloo.ca/ETD.

University of Waterloo Electronic Theses Project Team. Report on Phase I of the UW Electronic Thesis Project: Appendix D—Pilot project proposal, 1997b. Online, revised 29 April 1997. http://www.lib.uwaterloo.ca/ETD.

University of Waterloo Electronic Thesis Project Team. University of Waterloo Electronic Thesis Project Team: Terms of Reference and Team Members, 1997c. Online, revised October 1997. http://www.lib.uwaterloo.ca/ETD.

University of Waterloo Electronic Theses Project Team. ETD Pilot Project: UW Electronic Theses and Dissertations Server, 1997d. Online, revised 07 October, 1997. http://www.lib.uwaterloo.ca/ETD.

University of Waterloo Electronic Theses Project Team. University of Waterloo Electronic Thesis Project: ETD Pilot Project Summary Report, 1997e. Online, revised October 1997. http://www.lib.uwaterloo.ca/ETD.

18

Electronic Theses and Dissertations: Two Surveys of Editors and Publishers

Joan T. Dalton
University of Windsor
Windsor, Canada

Nancy H. Seamans
Virginia Polytechnic Institute and State University
Blacksburg, Virginia

At the 2nd Symposium on Electronic Theses and Dissertations in May 1999 in Virginia, it became evident that several issues or "controversies" had been identified in the discussions surrounding electronic publishing in general and electronic dissertations specifically. Some of the issues included:

The question of long-term preservation and transfer of content to future formats

Concerns about how electronic access might facilitate plagiarism

The need for training graduate students to use the technology

Implementation strategies needed to launch a project at academic institutions

One of the most important issues identified pertained to the level of awareness and acceptance of electronically distributed dissertations by the scholarly publishing community and how the members of this community were responding to the question of prior publication in cases where derivative articles or portions of electronic dissertations were being submitted for publication to scholarly journals.

At Virginia Tech, where it was mandated in 1997 that dissertations be submitted in electronic format, concerns were expressed by both faculty and doctoral students. Their concerns pertained to the wide dissemination of doctoral research through the web and potential effects this might have on future publication opportunities. In response to these concerns, Virginia Tech offered students several options for restricting access to their work. Students could choose to offer full access to their electronic dissertation without any restrictions, restrict access to the campus community, restrict access for a specific period of time, or restrict access entirely, which was desirable in specific cases such as with patent applications pending. These access choices have been used to varying degrees as additional institutions have started up ETD programs, with 11 institutions requiring ETDs of at least some of their students as of 2002.

While a range of options for restriction has been made available in many cases, the wide unfettered accessibility of ETDs remains the preferred option by the founders of the project, in keeping with the mission of the Networked Digital Library of Theses and Dissertations (NDLTD) based at Virginia Tech. Edward Fox, one of the principal investigators of the NDLTD Project Team, contacted several publishers in 1997 to solicit support for electronic dissertations and to request policy statements on the question of prior publication in the case of ETDs. Several of the publishers that were contacted supported the initiative, as evidenced by the letters received from the Association for Computing Machinery (ACM), the Entomological Society of

Table 1 Survey Results from Virginia Tech Regarding Access to ETDs, 1997–1999

Level of electronic access
   48% of the students chose for their ETDs to have unrestricted access
   33% of the students chose to restrict access to their university community
   19% of the students made their ETDs inaccessible to all
Graduate student survey
   78% of students decided to limit access to their ETDs on advice of faculty
   13% of students decided to limit access to their ETDs on advice of publishers
Alumni survey
   43% of alumni successfully published derivative works
   100% of alumni found no resistance from publishers

America, and Elsevier Science (NDLTD, July 1999). There still seemed to be hesitation by doctoral students, however (see Table 1), as seen in the results of several surveys done on the Virginia Tech Campus between 1997 and 1999.

According to the results from the survey of Virginia Tech alumni, it seemed the perception that publishers would reject submissions derived from ETDs was stronger than the reality. But perception is everything where there is little hard evidence from which to draw.

We felt that by soliciting responses directly from the scholarly publishing community by means of a survey, a picture might begin to emerge of where opinion was leaning with respect to widely disseminated ETDs and the question of prior publication. The broader question of what it means to publish in the electronic scholarly environment is paramount here.

2000 SURVEY (DALTON)

The approach in choosing which journal editors and publishers to contact reflects certain parameters. Because issues surrounding e-publishing were more relevant in the periodical publishing cycle, the survey was limited to publishers and editors of academic scholarly journals. It was deemed important to have representation from the for-profit and nonprofit sectors, as well as to include the publications committees of scholarly societies (see Table 2). A presurvey review of the editorial statements in dozens of journals revealed that editorial policy was set at either the level of the publisher or the society or at the editorial level for a specific journal. There seemed to be no significant

Table 2 Selected Publishers Included in the 2000 ETD Survey Population

Academic Press
American Chemical Society
American Psychological Association
American Society for Microbiology
American Society of Mechanical Engineers
Blackwell Science
Cambridge University Press
Elsevier Science
FASEB Societies
IEEE
Institute of Physics Journals
MCB University Press
University of Chicago Press
Wiley & Sons

pattern that could be discerned here, but it became apparent that examples of both should be represented in the audience to be polled.

Information was drawn from journal homepages on the web, where parallel electronic versions of established scholarly journals have proliferated in recent years. Individual journals were chosen by first identifying large academic publishers or scholarly societies and viewing the homepages for the journals that they published. Journal homepages on the web typically offer the same information as their print counterparts, including a listing of the members of the editorial board and—essential for this review—the "Instructions to Authors" or "Instructions to Contributors" statement.

The content of the final database created as a result of this review contained information drawn from 200 unique journals. Included in this database were the names of editors, publishers, and publication committee chairs, their email addresses, and relevant excerpts from the "Instruction to Authors" pages where specific reference is made to prior publication. In some cases, separate editorial policy statements proved relevant to the question of web-based documents and prior publication.

2001 SURVEY (SEAMANS)

Much of the work of the 2001 survey was based on what was addressed in the 2000 survey, with the primary difference being the way that the journal editors and publishers were identified. Faculty and students in Virginia Tech's interdisciplinary Science and Technology Studies (STS) graduate program were concerned about the impact of ETDs on their publishing opportunities. They compiled a list of places where they were most likely to publish. The list consisted of 133 journals, 18 academic presses, and 9 commercial presses. The majority were academic in focus. Also on the list, however, were popular titles such as *Harper's Magazine, The Nation, Smithsonian Magazine, The Atlantic Monthly,* and *Wired Magazine* (see Table 3).

I did only a cursory presurvey review of the editorial statements of these entities, since the survey instrument queried the respondents about the level at which editorial policy was set. I then identified an electronic means for contacting the journals and presses. Ten journals and two presses were dropped from the list, either because they had ceased publication (journals) or could not be identified from the information supplied. Presses were added to the list when a connection became apparent between several journal titles and those presses, making their absence from the initial list appear to be an oversight.

The final list of 148 contacts—entities where an email contact could be identified—included 121 journal titles, 18 academic presses, and 9 commercial presses. Seven emails were returned as undeliverable, so a total of 141 journals

Table 3 Selected Journals and Presses
Included in the 2001 ETD Survey
Population

Annals of Science
Canadian Bulletin of Medical History
Duke University Press
Edinburgh University Press
Feminist Studies
History and Technology
Johns Hopkins University Press
Journal of Social History
Kluwer Academic Press
Minerva
Perspectives on Science
The Philosophical Review
Postmodern Culture
Research Policy
Science, Technology, and Human Values
Techné: Journal of Technology
Technology and Culture Studies
Technology Review

---

or presses were contacted and asked to complete a survey. The instrument used was basically the same used by Dalton, with a few minor modifications to accommodate the difference in the population to be contacted. (Dalton had contacted only journal editors, whereas I also was querying editors for presses.)

To date, journal policy statements that include reference to ETDs have only appeared in a handful of cases, so it becomes necessary to track policies that are emerging with respect to electronically available research and the question of prior publication in more general terms, with an eye for how this might apply in the specific case of ETDs. It is our argument that by examining the policies emerging as scholarly publishers grapple with a coherent response to electronically available research and prior publication, we can extrapolate the path of developing policies to include electronic dissertations—a unique but significant genre in scholarly publishing. A review of the policy statements of the 200 journals identified in the 2000 survey yielded some interesting results.

In reviewing the policies stated under the "Instructions to Authors" pages and elsewhere on the journal web sites, the statements regarding manuscript acceptance and prior publication seem to fall easily into one of four specific categories. By far the largest number of journals gave the familiar and standard statement, an example of which would read "Manuscripts are accepted for review with the understanding that the same work has not been published, that it is not under consideration for publication elsewhere, and that its submission for publication has been approved by all of the listed authors and by the institutions where the work was carried out." With only slight textual variations among them, this was the most prevalent statement found regarding prior publication in 49% of the 200 journals selected (see Table 4).

Surprisingly, 15% of the journals had no specific reference to prior or simultaneous publication. However, 21% of the journals gave the standard policy with certain exceptions noted, often in reference to electronic documents. In this group there were several statements that specifically allowed posting on personal websites or an internal institutional website. In several cases, policies required that if on the web, the research must be labeled a "draft" and subsequently be removed upon acceptance for publication in the journal. Finally, 15% of the policies had restrictions based on prior publication, which were extended to specifically include research that may have been previously available in electronic format.

In this final group of statements, although "prior publication in electronic format" was the official restriction, it seemed that there was difficulty in defining what it meant to be "published" in electronic format. At least nine distinct definitions of electronic publication could be identified in this group of policy statements. In one case the definition identified "material in a public database system", which speaks to potential wide accessibility. In another case, the simple "electronic posting of a manuscript" is identified as a barrier for submission on the grounds of prior publication, without reference to location or level of accessibility. The lack of consensus in attempting to define what it means to publish in an electronic environment is worth noting. If the scholarly publishing community has difficulty defining what it means to publish in electronic format, how can it hope to adequately deal with all the issues that arise from communicating in this new medium?

In an important article on scholarly electronic publishing (1999), Rob Kling and Geoffrey McKim of the Center for Social Informatics at Indiana

Table 4   2000 Survey—Review of Stated Policies on Prior Publication Drawn from Journal Homepages

15%—no specific statement on prior or simultaneous publication
49%—standard statement
21%—standard statement with specific exceptions noted
15%—standard statement with specific inclusions outlined and described

University points to the lack of consensus in defining electronic publishing, in particular electronic journals. He attempts to bring some clarity to the effort by defining and classifying the different varieties of electronically available research in scholarly publishing into three categories:

1. Hybrid Paper-Electronic Journal: a package of peer-reviewed articles available through electronic channels, but whose primary distribution channels are paper-based (e.g., *Journal of Neuroscience, The Journal of Biological Chemistry*).

2. Electronic Working Articles: electronic scholarly communications that are not peer reviewed and are given a variety of labels: e-prints, working papers, pre-prints, e-magazines (e.g., *Los Alamos National Library Pre-Print Archive*).

3. Electronic Journals: defined as a package of articles that is distributed to most or all of its subscribers in electronic form. Often, no parallel paper format exists. (e.g., *Psycholoquy, Journal of the Association for Information Science*).

Kling and McKim note that in the current discussion of electronic scholarly publishing, these types of distinctions among electronically available research articles are rarely made. This leads him to the conclusion that "reports of the exponential growth of e-journals really mean exponential growth of the hybrid Paper-Electronic or PE journals." And while the hybrid Paper-Electronic journals "bring their reputations [and] review practices that they established in the paper world and some of their readership to their electronic versions," true electronic journals, those that have no paper parallel, "face more daunting problems in establishing their legitimacy, and risk a higher failure rate." (Kling and McKim, 1999)

Martin Blume, editor for the American Physical Society, tackled this question in a presentation at a workshop on developing practices and standards for e-publishing in science (Blume, 1998). In his presentation he reflects beliefs commonly held by the physics community, namely that the dissemination of research, either in print or electronically, will not preclude its acceptance for review and eventual publication.

Blume distinguishes between that which is published (small p) as a preprint, nonrefereed manuscript and that which is Published (large P) as an article that has undergone the peer review process. For Blume's audience, the distinction is a crucial one in defining what it means to be published. However, peer review is not the only criterion by which some publishers and editors define prior publication in the case of electronically available research. In many cases other criteria seem to be more dominant in determining a status of prior publication—thus we can detect a lack of consensus in the scholarly publishing community, which is where we begin examining the question.

2000 SURVEY: PROCEDURE

An identical email cover letter was sent to either the editor, publisher, or publications committee chair for all 200 identified journal titles, introducing the topic and requesting their participation in the online survey, which they could easily access through a hypertext link embedded in the email message. The survey was designed using a template located on a server at Virginia Tech and with the generous assistance of Anthony Atkins, the technical director of the Digital Library and Archives at Virginia Tech. The response rate reached 27%, with 46 actual surveys being completed (see Table 5). There were also eight personal email responses to the general question as it was presented in the cover letter by people who wished to comment but chose not to complete the survey.

In an effort to acknowledge the significant variations in the scholarly publishing cycle between academic disciplines, the survey results in some cases were examined through an imposed grouping of broad subject disciplines: physical sciences, life sciences, medical sciences, and social sciences. For the purpose of informing doctoral students and their advisors, a view of how electronic publishing issues are being addressed in their specific disciplines is helpful. Policy development with respect to electronic publishing will be shaped by the parameters unique to each discipline.

The first question was designed to gather information about the respondents and the journals with which they were affiliated (see Table 6). Respondents were then asked about the editorial policies of their journals, with specific reference to policies on prior publication. While in most cases there were stated policies on prior publication, far fewer had made explicit reference to research that may have been accessible on the web (see Table 7).

Review of Responses

A specific question on identifying what constitutes prior publication in **electronic** format listed several possible responses (see Table 8). Respondents

Table 5 Survey 2000—Questionnaire Return Rate

Editors and publishers were contacted by email, given a brief background on ETDs and the NDLTD, and asked to participate in the online survey titled "Electronic Theses & Dissertations: A Survey of Editors and Publishers" available at http://lumiere.lib.vt.edu/surveys/
- 46 responded by completing the survey
- 8 offered opinions by email without completing the survey
- Response rate: 27%

Table 6 Survey 2000—Characteristics of Survey Respondents

95%—Editor, associate editor, or editorial director
 4%—Publisher
 1%—Publications chair or officer
73%—Not-for-profit publications
27%—For-profit publications
39%—Physical sciences (includes: physics, chemistry, engineering, astronomy)
34%—Life sciences (includes biology, biochemistry, biophysics, genetics, mycology)
10%—Medical sciences (includes physiology, neurology, immunology)
 9%—Social sciences (including psychology, business, marketing)

were instructed to identify as many choices as were applicable according to the editorial practices of their journals. Included in the question was the opportunity to identify other forms of electronic publications, with a text box for comments.

Responses to Question 3A

Choices made by the respondents indicate that online conference proceedings and preprint articles are in many cases likely to receive the classification of prior publication. However, in the case of online theses and dissertations, only 9% of the responses would classify widely available ETDs as prior publication, and only 1% of the responses indicated that ETDs with limited availability would be considered previously published (see Table 9).

Looking at the responses to Question 3A through the broad discipline groupings identified earlier, it becomes clear that journals in the physical sciences are the most lenient in defining what constitutes prior publication in an electronic environment, with over half of the responses in this subgroup indicating that none of the choices given would be considered prior publication. Within this same subgroup, only 5% of the responses identified ETDs as examples of prior publication. However, in the other three disciplines (life sciences, medical sciences and social sciences), widely available

Table 7 Survey 2000—Policies on Prior Publication

94% of respondents stated that the journal(s) had a policy on prior publication explicitly stated in "Guidelines to Contributors" pages.
68% of respondents stated that the published policies **did not** specifically refer to work posted on the web or otherwise made electronically available.

Table 8   Survey 2000—Question 3A: What Constitutes Prior Publication in Electronic Publishing?

Online thesis or dissertation widely available through a web-based archive
Online thesis or dissertation with access limited to campus or institution
Research results available through a preprint server (e.g., Los Alamos server)
Research results available on a personal homepage prior to peer review
Conference proceedings available through a web-based server
All of the above
None of the above
Other—please elaborate

ETDs were identified as examples of prior publication at a rate of 25% in each case, potentially impacting the acceptability of derived manuscripts for publication.

Respondents were given the opportunity to offer their opinions in a free-text format, and many of the comments proved revealing in helping to understand what criteria the respondents were using to define prior publication in an electronic environment (see Table 10). In reviewing the responses to the survey question along with the textual comments, it became evident that four distinct criteria were being used to define prior publication in electronic publishing.

When examining the four identified criteria in light of the discipline groupings, the results show that although policies in physical science journals seem the least restrictive in terms of defining what is "published," the primary criteria used to do so is peer review. In the life sciences and medical sciences, the dominant criterion for defining "publication" seemed to be tied to the level of accessibility or exposure the material may have received as a result of

Table 9   Survey 2000—Responses to Question 3A: What Constitutes Prior Publication in Electronic Publishing?

20%—Conference proceedings available through a web-based server
13%—Research results available through a preprint server (e.g., Los Alamos server)
9%—Online thesis or dissertation widely available through a web-based archive
6%—Research results available on a personal homepage prior to peer review
1%—Online thesis or dissertation with access limited to campus or institution
19%—None of the above
2%—All of the above
30%—Other (see comments)

Table 10 Survey 2000—Criteria Identified—Prior Publication in Electronic Format

Criterion	Comment
Peer review	"Anything that has been peer-reviewed prior to publication"
Level of access/dissemination	"I would consider web-based publishing to be publishing since it is 'broadcasting' information."
Lack of content revision	"If [any electronically available material] is essentially identical to the manuscript submitted, it would represent prior publication."
Stability/Legitimacy of electronic format	"We do not recognize web-based publication as formerly published. Web-based publication does not constitute a stable form of publication that is citable as a reference."

being posted on the web. In the group of journals categorized in the social sciences, at least half of the responses to the question indicated that research available through either a preprint server or a personal web page posting would be considered "published," The issue of content revision was raised in the comments for this discipline, however. The point was made that as long as manuscript submissions were "derived from" but not identical to electronically posted materials (dissertations or otherwise), they would be acceptable for submission.

In another question, the respondents were asked more pointedly about the admissibility of content from web-based dissertations for submission to their respective journals (see Table 11). Respondents were asked to base their answers on existing policies of the journals for which they acted as editors or publishers in considering the question.

The responses to Question 5A (see Table 12) reveal that only 4% of those queried would refuse to consider submissions derived from dissertations, whether in print or electronically available, on the basis of prior publication. Nineteen percent of the respondents indicated that they would consider such submissions on an individual basis, and, even more heartening, a full 47% answered that they would welcome submissions for publication that were derived from web-based dissertations.

With a combined total of 66% of the responses indicating that manuscripts derived from web-based dissertations would be either welcomed or considered on an individual basis, these results should prove encouraging for

Table 11   Survey 2000—Question 5A: When Is Submission from Web-Based Dissertation Acceptable?

Under no circumstances. Manuscripts derived from dissertations would be considered previously published, regardless of format.
Under no circumstances. Research made widely available via the WWW would be considered previously published.
Only if the online dissertation has access limited to the campus or institution where it was completed.
Only if the contents and conclusions in the manuscript were substantially different from the dissertation.
Manuscripts derived from web-based dissertations would be considered on an individual basis.
Manuscripts derived from web-based dissertations would be welcomed for submission.
Other—please elaborate.

many doctoral students and their advisors on the issue of manuscript submission subsequent to web posting.

A review of the responses based on subject discipline reveals that in all areas other than the medical sciences, manuscripts derived from web-based dissertations would be either welcomed for submission or at least considered on an individual basis 73% of the time. Those respondents representing journals in the medical sciences would consider such submissions 50% of the time based on the responses to this question.

Table 12   Survey 2000—Responses to Question 5A

47%—Manuscripts derived from web-based dissertations would be welcomed for submission.
19%—Manuscripts derived from web-based dissertations would be considered on an individual basis.
19%—Other—please elaborate.
6%—Only if the online dissertation has access limited to the campus or institution where it was completed.
6%—Only if the contents and conclusions in the manuscript were substantially different from the dissertation.
4%—Under no circumstances. Manuscripts derived from dissertations would be considered previously published, regardless of format.
0%—Under no circumstances. Research made widely available via the WWW would be considered previously published.

Several comments offered by the respondents (to whom anonymity was assured) reveal the reasoning behind the policies they endorse as editors and publishers on the issues surrounding ETDs and prior publication policies. For example:

I view theses as a completely different form of publication. We expect that the results will eventually be published and do not discriminate against the student because the thesis is widely available.

We believe that distribution as a dissertation is sufficiently different from a publication in a refereed journal as to not be of concern.

I would see electronic availability of a thesis as only equivalent to what has long been available through microfilm and as not constituting prior publication.

. . . anyone can post anything they want on the web without compromising the acceptability of that material for subsequent submission to the . . . [journal], unless posting on the site requires that the material pass through some kind of peer-review. In this case, it becomes no longer acceptable for submission.

Communication in science and medicine will not be well served by standing in the way of publication in many versions, and the . . . [journal] is willing to consider for publication e-prints that have been posted on websites so long as their status as e-prints is clear. In the meantime, authors, editors and publishers have more work to do to make the status of articles entirely clear. This is the age of transparency rather than paternalism

Such comments seem to indicate that, regardless of format, if a paper had been refereed, it was considered previously published. However, based on the survey responses, this criterion was not the dominant one in all disciplines. In the life sciences and medical sciences, a work that had been made widely available through posting on a website was in some cases considered to have been "published" based on electronic accessibility alone and, therefore, subject to possible rejection for publication in an established print journal on this basis.

As members of the various academic disciplines begin discussing the issues surrounding electronic publishing and its application to the scholarly communication process in their own academic communities, it is expected that the trends toward acceptance and adoption will increase. It should be noted that disciplinary distinctions are important to make in considering the issues. Kling and McKim (1999) point out that the current discussion about electronic publishing does not go far enough in acknowledging the disciplinary differences in scholarly communication.

Unfortunately, few analyses of scholarly e-publishing explicitly acknowledge thedifferences in communication practices from field to field. Terms like "being published" are treated as categorical. However, the actual communicative practices that constitute publishing vary from one field to another (Kling and McKim).

2001 SURVEY: PROCEDURE

As with the 2000 survey, an email cover letter was sent to the editor, publisher, or publications committee chair for the 141 journals and presses identified. The topic of ETDs as prior publications was presented, and participation in the online survey was requested. A hypertext link to the survey was embedded in the email message. The first message was sent on January 22, 2001, and a reminder was sent on February 6, 2001.

The response rate reached 33%, with 46 actual surveys being completed (see Table 13). There were also 36 personal email responses to the general question as it was presented in the cover letter by people who wished to comment but chose not to complete the survey.

The first question gathered information about the respondents and the journals with which they were affiliated (see Table 14). The question about the broad subject areas of the journals and publishers revealed that the majority were more interdisciplinary than in the 2000 survey. (Respondents were asked to identify as many of the possible answers as they felt were appropriate to the question. Therefore, percentages reflect responses, not individual respondents.)

Extrapolating from the data, the general categories were:

Physics, Mathematics, and Statistics—6%
Chemistry, Biology, and Biochemistry—8%

Table 13 Survey 2001—Summary of Responses

As with the first survey, editors and publishers were contacted by email, given a brief background on ETDs and the NDLTD, and asked to participate in the online survey titled "Electronic Theses & Dissertations: 2001 Survey of Editors and Publishers," available at http://lumiere.lib.vt.edu/surveys/
- 46 responded by completing the survey
- 36 offered opinions by email without completing the survey
- Response rate: 58%

Table 14 Survey 2001—Characteristics of Survey
Respondents

62%—Editor, associate editor, or editorial director
10%—Publisher
28%—Other
74%—Not-for-profit publications
26%—For-profit publications

> Engineering, Environmental Studies—12%
> Social Science—16%
> Life Sciences, Health and Medicine, Psychology—14%
> Other—44%

Those who selected **Other** identified their journals or presses as covering such diverse areas as history, history of medicine, humanities, and philosophy, as well as an array of additional topics.

Respondents were asked for information on the editorial policies of their journals or presses, with specific reference to policies on prior publication. As with the 2000 study, most had stated policies on prior publication, but fewer had addressed the idea of research that had been made accessible on the web (see Table 15).

Review of Responses

Question 3A was intended to identifying what constituted prior publication in electronic format for the journal or press. Respondents were asked to identify as many choices as were applicable, as determined by the editorial policies for the journal or press. Included in the question was the opportunity to identify 'other' forms of electronic publications, with a text-box for comments (see Table 16).

Comments made by the respondents revealed that for some this was a new area that had not previously been considered, e.g., "We don't have a

Table 15 2001 Survey—Policies on Prior Publication

56% of respondents stated that the journal or press had a policy on prior publication specifically stated in the "Guidelines to Contributors" or as a statement of editorial policy.
72% of respondents stated that these policies did not specifically refer to work that may have been made electronically accessible on the web.

Table 16   Survey 2001—Question 3A: What Constitutes Prior Publication?

5%—Online thesis or dissertation with access limited to campus or institution
8%—Research results available on a personal homepage prior to peer review
10%—Research results available through a preprint server (e.g., Los Alamos server)
15%—Conference proceedings available through a web-based server
15%—Online thesis or dissertation widely available through a web-based archive
3%—All of the above
16%—None of the above
28%—Other—please elaborate

policy about any form of e-publication, so this is just my guess about where we'd come down . . . " Others indicated that they would expect a submission to their journal to be different from a thesis or dissertation, e.g., "Dissertations are too long for published articles and must be rewritten, thus would not necessarily count as previously published." Another respondent wrote, "Before publication, a thesis undergoes extensive revisions. The resulting book is an entirely new work and, therefore, e-posting of the original thesis does not constitute publication."

Another question asked the respondents specifically about circumstances in which a manuscript derived from an ETD would be considered for publication (see Table 17). By combining the two most frequent responses, the results show that in 62% of the cases, respondents would either welcome manuscripts derived from web-based dissertations or at least consider such manuscripts on a case-by-case basis. Once again, the comments made in response to this question are particularly telling, for example:

Please note "derived from"—it does not have to be substantially different but it must be reworked.

Again, we've yet to set policy on this. My guess is that how we'll come down depends on our assessment of (1) whether our review process involves substantially more peer review than is typically applied to dissertations, and (2) the difference between the amount of exposure afforded by the prior availability of the dissertation online and the amount of exposure any derivative paper would receive via publication in our journal. It might turn out that our policy would be to decide on a case by case basis.

General comments received both as part of the 2001 survey and as email sent in lieu of completing the survey provide a narrative that illustrates the

Table 17   Survey 2001—Question 5A: According to the Editorial Policy Governing the Enterprise (Journal or Press) Identified, Under Which Circumstances Would a Manuscript Derived from a Web-Based Dissertation Be Considered for Publication?

33%—Manuscripts derived from web-based dissertations are welcome for submission.

29%—Manuscripts derived from web-based dissertations are considered on an individual basis.

27%—Other—please elaborate

6%—Only if the contents and conclusions in the manuscript were substantially different from the dissertation.

2%—Under no circumstances. Manuscripts derived from research published as part of a dissertation are considered previously published, regardless of format.

2%—Under no circumstances. Manuscripts derived from research made widely available via the web are considered previously published, regardless of format.

0%—Only if the online dissertation has access limited to the campus or institution where it was completed.

issues that interest or concern those who are, in many cases, just realizing that electronic publishing is changing the face of scholarly communication:

> In the emerging electronic environment, the very meaning of "publication" is obviously undergoing significant change. Nevertheless, the central issue is public access to the finished work. If that is available, then the work does not require another outlet—hence it is published. Virginia Tech is doing its students considerable harm by ignoring the central concept behind publication.

> Issue also need to be addressed—article already published before thesis concluded, so journal owns copyright; does copyright then have to be released to allow for electronic publication? I don't know.

> We are dealing with a universe of people with limited means. If they can get something for free on the web, why should they buy it? These web dissertations seriously cut into the market for books by presses that are hanging on, financially, by their fingernails. . . .

> Your email message was passed on to me for response. Please note that we do indeed consider posted electronic theses and dissertations to be previously published material and would not accept them as original publications.

Other comments indicate that the word "derived" made a significant amount of difference for the respondents:

> Manuscripts derived from dissertations, web or print form, would be sent for peer reviews, and revisions would be expected prior to publication.

> Any book that we publish goes through an extensive review process, often with several rounds of revision. In cases where the project originated as a dissertation, the final book is generally three or four years of work away from that dissertation. A dissertation is written with the author knowing the entire audience, and with the assurance that the audience will read it (indeed they are paid to do so by the institution). The whole structure of argument in a book, where the audience is anything but assured, is completely different.

> I consider papers based on chapters of a thesis or dissertation to be appropriate submissions to my journal. Chapters in theses and dissertations invariably need a lot of additional work to turn them into publishable papers. Typically a chapter submitted as a paper is not adequately self-contained. References to other chapters, for example, need to be removed and some substantial amount of discussion or argument needs to be put in their places. The author may also wish to rewrite simply because new ideas, arguments, or perspectives came up after the thesis or dissertation was written. Submitting papers based on chapters in theses and dissertations is a good first step in a young scholars career. The appearance of a paper on the web is irrelevant since such postings are unlikely to be permanent.

CONCLUSIONS

The policies of many journals with regard to Internet posting and prior publication are still in flux, as evidenced by many of the responses to these two surveys. When pressed to define prior publication in the electronic medium, many publishers and editors naturally draw from standard practice in print publishing and identify peer review as the one element that determines the publication status of written research. Though this is obviously still an unresolved issue, the number of responses indicating that an ETD will not preclude book or journal publication of research should encourage students and their faculty advisors who are working in an increasingly electronic environment.

A comparison of the results from the 2000 and 2001 surveys (see Table 18) seems to offer some concrete evidence to doctoral students and their

Table 18 Comparison of Questionnaire Results

Question 3A: What constitutes prior publication in electronic publishing?	2000	2001
Online thesis or dissertation widely available through web-based archive	9%	15%
Online thesis or dissertation with access limited to campus or institution	1%	5%
Research results available through a preprint server	13%	10%
Research results available on a personal homepage prior to peer review	6%	8%
Conference proceedings available through a web-based server	20%	15%
All of the above	2%	3%
None of the above	19%	15%
Other	30%	28%
Question 5A: When is a submission from an electronic dissertation acceptable?	2000	2001
Under no circumstances. Manuscripts derived from dissertations would be considered previously published, regardless of format.	4%	2%
Under no circumstances. Research made widely available via the WWW would be considered previously published.	0%	2%
Only if the online dissertation has access limited to the campus or institution where it was completed.	6%	0%
Only if contents and conclusions in the manuscript were substantially different from the dissertation.	6%	6%
Manuscripts derived from web-based dissertations would be considered on an individual basis.	19%	29%
Manuscripts derived from web-based dissertations would be welcomed for submission.	47%	33%
Other	19%	27%

advisors that the perception of rejection by the scholarly community of manuscripts derived from web-based dissertations is stronger than the reality.

As with any new and significantly different pattern of communication, there is a need to continue to build a picture of where opinion is heading with respect to widely disseminated ETDs and their status as "publications." The discussion and the collection of data must continue so that a more comprehensive view of the role of ETDs in scholarly communication can be determined. It is only by ongoing discussion and debate that students and their advisors, along with editors and publishers, can determine the most appropriate roles for technology in scholarly communications.

REFERENCES

Blume, M. (1998). What Constitutes "Publication" in Electronic Media? AAAS/UNESCO/ICSU Workshop on Developing Practices and Standards for Electronic Publishing in Science. From http://www.aaas.org/spp/dspp/sfri/projects/epub/ses1/blume.htm.

Kling, R., McKim, G. (1999). Scholarly communication and the continuum of electronic publishing. *Journal of the American Society for Information Science* 50(10):890–906.

Kling, R., McKim, G. (2000). Not just a matter of time: field differences and the shaping of electronic media in supporting scientific communication. *Journal of the American Society for Information Science* 51(14):1306–1320.

Publishers and the NDLTD. Retrieved May 2000 from http://www.ndltd.org/publshrs/index.htm.

19

Rhetoric, Reality, and the Digital Publication of Ph.D. Dissertations and Master's Theses

William E. Savage

ProQuest Information and Learning
Ann Arbor, Michigan

INTRODUCTION

The recent interest in digital technology has inspired a number of projects to explore the publication of Master's theses and Ph.D. dissertations in digital format. I will not examine each of those efforts in detail. Rather, my purpose here is to briefly critique some of their claims and then to present a position on digital publishing based on empirical evidence and users' needs. To do so, it is necessary to first place the idea of digital publication in a broader context. These projects often appear in discussions of the development of digital libraries as the sites from which scholarly communication is conducted. I shall first conduct a cursory overview of that context and then look more closely into some of those publishing projects.

DIGITAL LIBRARIES

Much of the literature on the digitization of scholarly communication has sprung from the serials subscription crisis of the past several years where rocketing journal subscription prices have eroded library budgets and resulted in subscription cancellations and dwindling monograph purchases (Association of Research Libraries, 1997). The exploration of publishing alternatives to current journal literature coupled with the emergence of World Wide Web technologies have led to the development of preprint Web postings, electronic journals, and institutional self-publishing over the Web. Activity in these areas continues and increases. As new initiatives are announced, studies undertaken, findings reported, and conference proceedings are published, the reader is treated to extensive visions of a digital future. We are often presented with enthusiastic portrayals of digital library scenarios, the virtual spaces where future academic activity and scholarly communication take place.

While speculation on future developments can be exciting, recent research into the organizational issues involved in the development of digital libraries also provides sobering insight into the creation of these resources. One survey indicates that university investment activity often takes place outside of a comprehensive university plan. Investment in digital library resources simply drifts toward greater expenditures with little oversight or control. The driving forces propelling these development efforts have devolved to departmental or local campus forces outside of central management (Covi and Kling, 1996). Another study reinforces the view that some digital library development activities are not part of focused, coherent strategies. It appears that, in response to the demand for digital resources, some development programs have involved little more than the provision of digital holdings and digital tools for storage and access. Complex issues involving organizational change or practice to support the digital library received little attention. In these cases, development appears to be a process of "muddling through" (Travica, 1997).

The application of digital technologies to libraries and library use remain comfortably familiar when they rest on the paradigm of the paper-based library and traditional views of scholarship. Our grasp of the future seems a bit surer when "the poetics of the future are guided by metaphors from the past" (Lyman, 1998). So, for example, it has been observed that general conceptions of the future role of digital libraries often derive from prevailing assumptions about and idealizations of traditional libraries. The digital library is regularly conceived of as little more than a container for a digital collection (Lyman, 1997). Further, digital library collections are routinely described in terms of static, permanently stored documents. The dominant metaphor seems to be that the collection strategy for a digital library should somehow mirror a traditional library. Certainly, elements of a digital library collection can be analogous to paper texts. However, this ignores one of the more exciting potential uses of the digital format. A digital library collection is also capable of accommodating expanding electronic texts, collections of texts and dynamic connections between texts. Single canonical texts or a writer's complete *oeuvre* can be embedded with variants, footnotes, commentaries and indices allowing researchers single site access to those texts and the growing corpus of research that surrounds them (Hockey, 1997). These capabilities of the digital collection are sometimes overlooked in discussion.

Another tendency is to focus on the library as based only on digital technologies, containing only digital materials. This scenario appears to derive from a simplified view of the traditional library in which the content of the paper-based library is presumed to be only paper. The logical outcome of this view is that the future will see digital-only and nondigital libraries existing in separate spaces: one virtual, one actual. The weakness of this bifurcation of information into separate libraries is that it impoverishes the idea of the library. Library collections have always contained a variety of formats, from paper to microform to parchment. Each has its uses, and each is used. The development of a digital library should be the addition of one more component to a collection, not the exclusion of all other components. A more appealing vision of the future is one in which "libraries will contain digital and non-digital material—in which case 'digital library' is a misnomer, and certainly not synonymous with 'the library of the future' " (Levy and Marshall, 1995).

Occasionally, opinions as to how a digital library could be used spring from simplified views of user community behavior. In some cases it is assumed that the digital library will be used by individual researchers who work alone, a parallel to the cloistered scholar poring over a leather-bound manuscript. In other cases, the assumption swings to the opposite extreme. In this alternative formulation, users are part of collaborative efforts in the laboratory and workplace where project teams are scattered around a building, a campus or the world with distributed access to the same digital archive. Research activity in both academia and industry is far more varied than these assumptions allow. Information seeking in a digital environment can be a team's complicated search of a national database or an individual's e-mail message to a colleague with similar interests. A more useful perception of a digital library's capabilities should include its ability to support all its users at as many levels of research activity as they wish to use.

When elements of the past are uncritically superimposed upon visions of the future, these simplifications can impoverish the potential of the digital library and disregard what is good and useful about traditional library collections. These observations should remind us that library collections serve us well because of their diversity and their ready means of access to information. As the future extends from a distant horizon to become the foreground of our daily activity, our prospects for an information-rich environment increase when we can draw upon library collections with a range of digital and nondigital components that are flexible and open to all avenues of research and inquiry.

DIGITAL PUBLISHING

The preceding observations are useful lessons as we review proposals for the digital publication of dissertations and master's theses. Surveying those proposals, we find recurring themes that do color debate and cast visions of the future in specific, value-laden terms. Studies of the rhetoric surrounding the application of information technology provide our critical tools. One study categorizes a number of positions regarding the application of technology. In this analysis, each perspective exhibits characteristic attitudes toward the difficulties involved in technological development, the ability of individuals to understand and use technologies, the role of technology in social change, the potential for conflict within social change, what constitutes sufficient evidence in argumentation, and time orientation (Kling and Lamb, 1996).

Most discussions of digital publishing are dominated by a "technological utopian" perspective. This perspective assumes that the social benefits derived from the application of technology surpass any difficulty that may be encountered. Argumentation usually proceeds through the depiction of future scenarios. Conflicting interests within those scenarios are minimized or nonexistent. If conflict is encountered in practice, its origins seem difficult to grasp, its persistence a mystery. It is presumed that all people have the skills necessary to benefit from technological change. Moreover, contingencies on both individual and societal levels remain suppressed in the background of discourse. Instead, the presumption is that the conditions necessary for the effective application of technology already exist (Kling, 1996; Shenk, 1997). If expectations are not met, if technology somehow fails today, assurances are made that the required change, upgrade or revision is just around the corner. In effect, we are told, "Not to worry, it's inevitable." Then, when you point out a shortcoming in the application of technology, you usually receive the "great technological handwave" (Crawford, 1998).

To differing degrees, many current proposals for the digital publication of Ph.D. dissertations and master's theses exhibit facets of the technological utopian perspective. A critical reading of these proposals provides a core of common themes. The most prominent theme is economic; digital publication will result in substantial savings for authors and institutions. It is assumed that digital publication will eliminate all of the handling, production, and distribution costs associated with paper publication (University of Texas at Austin, 1996; Joint Electronic Thesis, University of Toronto, 1997). A collateral benefit is that paperless publishing is environmentally friendly.

Then, as virtual collections in digital libraries replace actual shelves and book stacks, further savings will be realized through reduced library storage (University of South Florida, 1997). Another benefit is that digital publication will result in increased access to and use of materials published in this format. In this view, access to information will be faster and more convenient through searches over the World Wide Web, uncovering hitherto inaccessible, hidden research (Fox et al., 1996, 1997). (See also relevant chapters in this volume.) Finally, it is assumed that conversion to digital publishing enjoys a unilateral applicability, benefiting authors, administrators, researchers, and librarians. The argument seems to be that since dissertations and master's theses are already in digital format at their creation, digital publication is the relatively simple process of converting to an appropriate delivery format and making documents available through a digital library site (Weisser and Walker 1997; University of Waterloo 1997).

Does publication of a document in digital format eliminate paper and reduce concomitant costs? The conclusions of the TULIP (The University Licensing Program) study, a 3-year project involving nine universities and Elsevier Science Publishing, provide empirical data that seem to contradict this assumption. One of the goals of the study was to ascertain the feasibility of networked distribution of journal information to and across institutions. Throughout the course of the study, it was clear that a user's first impulse was to print the delivered information (Tulip Final Report, 1996). While access to the information was digital, paper was the preferred medium of use. In two completely separate studies of work practice, both professional information analysts and academic researchers also demonstrated a clear preference for paper, even when most of the information seeking and retrieval activity was through digital sources (Levy and Marshall, 1995; Kling and Covi, 1997).

Do collections of digital documents reduce library storage costs? Carnegie Mellon University, one of the institutions participating in the Tulip study, concluded that no savings would be realized. In fact, quite the opposite was expected: "Based on a ten year replacement cycle, digital storage and access will cost academic libraries 16 times as much as print to store locally. . .the necessity to repeat capital expenditures on servers and storage will not encourage the development of digital libraries, even though hardware is becoming more of a commodity and storage costs may be trivial in the not-too-distant future" (Tulip Final Report, 1996). Hardware and storage costs have decreased since the results of this study were published; however, so has the accepted replacement cycle for digital preservation. A study on digital preservation commissioned by the Commission on Preservation and Access and the Research Libraries Group used a model in which equipment and software were capitalized over a 5-year period. After that time, both equipment and software are assumed to be obsolete (Task Force on Archiving of

Digital Information, 1996). Hence, it is difficult to see where digital publication offers anywhere near the savings that have been promised.

What about researchers and dissertation authors? Is digital publication any more beneficial for those who generate and use this information? On its face, the opinion that the speed and convenience of information available over the World Wide Web can only increase access to dissertation research does make sense. Still, there are nuances to acquiring information over the Web that are often overlooked in these sweeping statements. The Web is a superb tool for accessing and reading screen-sized bits of information. Accessing and acquiring a 300-page monograph is a very different activity. Several studies cited above have made it clear that readers are reluctant to spend an inordinate amount of time reading a document on a computer monitor. Hence, after accessing a monographic document, the next task in acquiring that information would be to download it to a hard drive and then to print it out. Here, some proposals tend to gloss over the requisite steps involved in information delivery over the Web.

In many discussions of digital publication, there is continued confusion between access to electronic documents and delivery of the information they contain. Access and delivery are often conflated and spoken of as if they were a single state of affairs. Looking at title lists that result from a search is not equivalent to reading the books. Calling up the title page of a monographic document on a screen is not information delivery. Many more intervening steps are required to have the document in hand, where it can be used. Without a high capacity link to the Web and a connection to a production printer, downloading a document and placing it on paper, in whole or in part, will be tedious at best. Moreover, no matter who prints the document nor where it is printed, there will be costs associated with that activity. Many proposals for digital publication fail to recognize that increased access to digital information must be supported by the increased ability to deliver that information. The claim that availability over the Web will increase use of information is no longer coherent. Increased access to information does not necessarily entail increased delivery and use, nor does it eliminate or even substantially reduce the costs associated with paper.

Another recurring claim for digital publication is that Web searching provides researchers with much more information, unlocking hidden research lying in moldy basements. These striking images rest on the rather weak assumption that Web and Internet infrastructures are equivalent to a library environment. In fact, query and retrieval on the Web still have a long way to go to be as efficient and effective as the specialized databases and searching resources available in libraries. A recent study estimates that the best Web search engine covers little more than one third of the indexable Web pages

(Lawrence and Giles, 1998). At the same time, a single, centralized database of dissertation research is already in use in practically every major research library in the world. Library users can search over 1.6 million citations to obtain far more efficient results than those currently available on the Web. An uncritical reliance on an inferior service does little to further good research.

Is it a valid position that digital publication will somehow "unlock" dissertation research and make it more widely known? Merrill Lynch recently announced a $50,000 award for the top dissertation within their Innovation Grants Competition (*Lingua franca*, 1998). Wall Street clearly recognizes the value of graduate research. If dissertations and master's theses remain underappreciated within academe, perhaps improving instruction in research tools and methods would be more effective than digital publication. Should one encounter collections of dissertations and theses in moldy basements, building maintenance and collection conservation appear to be more appropriate solutions.

Here, it is apropos to mention that publication of journal articles and the implementation of a digital publication program can and do result in competing interests that place student authors in difficult positions. When authors choose to publish portions of their dissertations in scholarly journals, digital prepublication of the dissertation threatens the timeliness of the journal article and has revenue implications for journal publishers. Hence, some journal publishers are reluctant to publish portions of dissertations or master's theses that have appeared on the Web through a digital publishing program. At the same time, it may be a graduate school requirement that the student submit and publish in digital format. Caught between fulfilling requirements for graduation and the need to embark upon future professional activity, student authors have had to make hard choices about the distribution of their work. In one case, rather than reclaiming an institution's intellectual property, digital publication has resulted in the restricted distribution of over 40% of a collection of digital dissertations and theses to campus or graduate school access only (Virginia Tech, 1998).

Finally, it is assumed that a digital publishing model is applicable to the creation and distribution of all dissertations and master's theses. The argument seems to be that all documents are created in digital format; hence, it is simply a matter of reformatting them into the appropriate distribution format. This assumes that all documents are equally amenable to reformatting into a distribution format and that all authors have the skills necessary to accomplish reformatting. Neither assumption is accurate. Dissertation literature is not as uniform as one might presume. Certainly, not all authors are prepared to make those conversions.

From these brief observations, it would seem that digital publication of Ph.D. dissertations and master's theses does not provide the clear benefits to authors, researchers, or libraries that have been claimed. The next question, then, should concern the nature of dissertations and master's theses. Does the nature and use of these documents require that they be in digital format?

THE DISSERTATION AS A DOCUMENT AND AS A LITERATURE

Throughout the graduate school community, there is general agreement that a dissertation should demonstrate a student's competence to employ the research procedures used within a discipline. Further, the research should be a significant and original contribution to knowledge (LaPidus, 1998). How those specific terms are to be understood for a definition of the dissertation is not clear. In practice, a single definition may not be necessary. The Council of Graduate Schools has rejected the notion of a single definition applicable to all disciplines; instead, it emphasizes a less constraining approach: "Disciplinary diversity affects the dissertation process and product. Any set of university-wide standards and requirements must acknowledge and accommodate the differences in how scholars in different disciplines conduct their work and how this diversity is reflected in expectations for the Ph.D. dissertation." It is recommended that graduate schools recognize and encourage differences between disciplines, and this results in functional expectations for the dissertation and dissertation research. "Dissertation research should provide students with hands-on, directed experience in primary research methods of the discipline. The dissertation should prepare students for the type of research/scholarship that will be expected of them after they receive the Ph.D. degree" (Council of Graduate Schools, 1991).

When the dissertation is seen as the result of a course of study within a discipline, there is nothing inherent in that view of a dissertation that necessitates electronic publication, nor is there a single defining feature of all dissertations that requires them to be in digital format. Hence, if a dissertation or thesis employs the standard structure of introduction, statement of the problem, literature review, text, conclusion, and end notes, there is no compelling reason to create, store, and distribute it solely as a digital document. If, on the other hand, the primary work in the student's discipline is being done in multimedia formats and massive databases amenable only to computerized searching, then it makes sense for the student to create a document in that format. Those decisions should be left to the student and the student's advisor and department.

In addition to transcripts and other elements of a student's administrative record, the dissertation forms part of the published record of a student's graduate education. Taken as a whole, the annual national output of dissertations is a body of literature that exhibits many of the trends or movements within academe. Dissertation literature, of course, mirrors the growth of the sciences and engineering that began in the 1980s. Nearly 60% of the dissertations published in the United States today are in those disciplines. The increasing emphasis on the currency of scientific information also finds expression in dissertation literature. A growing amount of the information that appears in science dissertations is first distributed through professional society and other specialized publications. Ten to fifteen percent of the science dissertations published annually are composites of previously published articles with little more than a narrative thread to hold them together. When science dissertations are published, they may remain current and in demand for 6 months to a year. Demand declines precipitously after that time. On the other hand, dissertations in the social sciences and humanities remain extended monographic studies of 250 pages or more. Publication as journal articles or books takes place long after the dissertation has been published. Dissertation research in the humanities, particularly in music, history, art, and literature, stays in demand for decades.

Observing the proliferation of professional scientists in positions such as provost or vice-president of research, one graduate dean has remarked, "the scientific model is becoming the default value in the university." Further, she notes that the role dissertation literature plays in scholarly communication has also begun to exhibit a divergence along disciplinary lines. For some advanced fields within the sciences and engineering, the use value of dissertation publication may be minimal, while its archival value remains important. The humanities and social sciences, on the other hand, find publication of dissertation literature valuable for both use in research and archival purposes (Sullivan, 1997). These keen observations of campus trends help us appreciate the strength and urgency of arguments for extending a digital publishing paradigm to the publication of the entire dissertation literature.

We have shown that the nature of the Ph.D. dissertation (and by extension, the master's thesis) does not require publication in digital format. We have also shown that dissertations comprise a diverse body of literature representing a range of disciplinary values as to how scholarly communication is best carried out. Finally, it appears that this literature may be influenced by the current trends within academe to adopt a single paradigm for scholarship and publication. These considerations lead to the next set of questions. If dissertations and theses are to be disseminated for use in research and archivally stored, what publishing services should be available? Collection, dissemination, and storage activities should encompass what options?

THE UMI POSITION

Since 1938, UMI® Dissertations Publishing, a division of ProQuest Information and Learning, has been providing the academic community with dissertation archiving, reference, and on-demand copy services. UMI's publishing activities now approach capturing North American doctoral scholarship in its entirety. With coverage that extends back to 1861, the UMI Dissertation Abstracts database contains over 1.6 million citations. Over one million full text titles are stored in UMI's microform vaults and are made available in paper, microfilm, or microfiche formats. Adding over 55,000 titles annually, nearly every degree-granting institution in the United States and Canada is represented in UMI's Dissertation Abstracts database and microform archive. UMI's database and microform archive also contains substantial representation of graduate institutions throughout Europe, Africa, the Middle East, and the Far East.

It is UMI's position that the creation of a sustainable communication environment with digital and nondigital components would provide maximum benefits for the international academic community—authors, researchers, graduate institutions, and academic libraries. To that end, UMI has reaffirmed its commitment to maintaining a permanent microform archive of Ph.D. dissertations and master's theses and to provide convenient, multiformat access and reference services to that archive. In addition, substantial resources have been committed to the development of a digital component of this communication environment. *ProQuest* Digital Dissertations is a major new program that opens UMI's archives to the international academic community by providing World Wide Web access to both the Dissertation Abstracts database and the full text of all new dissertations and theses submitted to UMI. UMI has begun by defining and implementing new World Wide Web services.

> Regardless of how dissertations and Master's theses were submitted, in paper or in digital format, the full text of documents received from 1997 forward is available now at the UMI Web site. Over 100,000 documents are available in either of two formats:
>
> > Those institutions that submit documents electronically will see them in full PDF; those institutions that submit in paper will see their documents as TIFF images wrapped in PDF.

Access to a single, central source for dissertation research is also available over the Web. The most current 2 years of the Dissertation Abstracts database, over 100,000 citations and abstracts, are freely available for searching.

Boolean operators, keyword, and field searching are all supported.
On-line ordering of an electronic or paper copy is available through a link to UMI's *Dissertation Express.*

In addition to World Wide Web access to the Dissertation Abstracts database and on-line access to the full text of new dissertations and master's theses, *ProQuest* Digital Dissertations offers the following services at no charge to researchers, submitting institutions, or academic libraries:

Free 24-page previews of dissertations and theses submitted from 1997 forward.
Each institution publishing with UMI receives free campus-wide online access to the full text of dissertations and theses submitted by that institution.
Each institution publishing with UMI receives a free Web URL that links a listing of citations, abstracts, and 24-page previews of current dissertations and theses submitted by that institution.

Current Research @ is updated monthly, providing a graduate institution with an additional presence on the World Wide Web showcasing research at that institution.

Free MARC records of dissertations and theses to submitting institutions.

In February 1999, UMI Dissertations Publishing and the U.S. Library of Congress completed an agreement providing on-site users at the Library of Congress with access to UMI's *ProQuest* Digital Dissertations. UMI Dissertations Publishing has guaranteed the Library permanent access to this digital collection. Hence, the Library of Congress has recognized the *ProQuest* Digital Dissertations collection as a remotely located collection of the Library of Congress. Under contract with the National Library of Canada, UMI Dissertations Publishing also carries out the collection, preservation, and dissemination of the Canadian national production of Ph.D. dissertations and master's theses, maintaining collections in both permanent microform and digital archives.

It is the goal of UMI Dissertations Publishing to provide products and services that facilitate worldwide scholarly communication and academic activity through the collection, provision of access, dissemination and archival storage of Ph.D. dissertations and master's theses. *ProQuest* Digital Dissertations was developed as a single component within that larger strategy. *ProQuest* Digital Dissertations provides the international academic community with economical digital publishing, easy bibliographic and full text access, value-added services benefiting individual authors and graduate institutions, and a permanent digital archive. When it is combined with UMI's traditional microform and paper publishing activities, UMI is able to offer a flexible publishing program that answers users' requirements for the widest possible range of products and services in all formats for all users.

CONCLUSION

The emergence of new publishing and distribution technologies has rendered the current systems of scholarly communication increasingly transitional. The once simple process of creating, distributing, and archiving printed paper has become an ever-shifting complex of publishing and distribution options. Authors and researchers may now choose to create and receive information in a variety of preprints, e-prints, digital documents, and archives as well as established analog formats. The situation will remain fluid as these technologies evolve into industries and mature to become institutions. In the meantime, perhaps the most appropriate tactic is to proceed as if there is no single, "silver bullet" solution to managing the complexities of scholarly communication in this transitional era. Rather, maintaining the flexibility to accommodate diverse publishing requirements and moving forward with a studied, deliberate transition to new technologies will afford us the best prospect of realizing the potential of scholarly communication in the future information environment.

REFERENCES

Association of Research Libraries. (1997). Scholarly Communication and the Need for Collective Action. ARL Discussion Paper. 1997. Available at http://www.arl.org/sparc/discuss.html

Council of Graduate Schools. (1991). *The Role and Nature of the Doctoral Dissertation: A Policy Statement*. Washington, D.C.

Covi L., Kling, R. (January, 1996). Digital Shift or Digital Drift?: Conceptualizing Transitions from Paper Media to Electronic Publishing and Digital Libraries in North American Universities. Center for Social Informatics, School of Information and Library Science, Indiana University. Available at http://www.slis. indiana.edu/~kling/pubs/ais95dig.html

Crawford, W. (January 1998). Paper Persists: Why Physical Library Collections Still Matter. *ONLINE*. Available at http://www.onlineinc.com/onlinemag/ JanOL98/crawford1.html.

Fox, E. A., Eaton, J. L., McMillan, G., Kipp, N. A., Mather, P., McGonigle, T., Schweiker, W., DeVane, B. (September 1997). Networked Digital Library of Theses and Dissertations: An International Effort Unlocking University Resources. *D-Lib Magazine*. Available at: http://www.dlib.org/dlib/september97/ theses/09fox.html

Fox, E. A., Eaton, J. L., McMillan, G., Kipp, N. A., Weiss, L., Arce, E., Guyer, S. (September 1996). National Library of Theses and Dissertations: A Scalable and Sustainable Approach to Unlock University Resources. *D-Lib Magazine*. Available at: http://www.dlib.org/dlib/september96/theses/09fox.html

Hockey, S. (1997). Electronic Texts: The Promise and the Reality. *American Council of Learned Societies Newsletter* 4(4):1–6.

Joint Electronic Thesis and Dissertation Project of the Faculty of Information Studies at the University of Toronto, University of Toronto Libraries and York University Libraries. (1997). "Paper Thesis and Dissertation Workflow Report." Available at: http://wwwfis.utoronto.ca/etd/report2.htm

Kling, R. (1996). Hopes and Horrors: Technological Utopianism and Anti-Utopianism in Narratives of Computerization. *Computerization and Controversy*. San Diego: Academic Press, pp 40–58.

Kling, R., Covi, L. (1997). "Digital Libraries and the Practices of Scholarly Communication." Report of a Project (October 1, 1994–September 30, 1996). Available at http://www-slis.lib.indiana.edu/~kling/SCIT/SCIT97.HTM.

Kling, R., Lamb, R. (1996). Analyzing Alternative Visions of Electronic Publishing and Digital Libraries. In: Peek, R.P., Newby, G.B., eds. *Scholarly Publishing: The Electronic Frontier*. Cambridge, MA: The MIT Press, pp 17–54. In a related development, a group of technology journalists and computing specialists recently established an organization and Web site to promote a balanced, anlaytic view of the role of technology in society. Some of the principles supporting their position are applicable to our present discussion of digital publishing. From the position of these individuals who style themselves "techno-realists,"

"Technologies are not neutral
The Internet is revolutionary, not Utopian
Information is not knowledge
Wiring the schools will not save them."

Available at http://www.technorealism.org/

LaPidus, J. (1998). "The Role of Theses and Dissertations as Independent Works of Scholarship." Paper presented at Seminar Series: Scholarship in the Electronic World, March 2, Virginia Polytechnic Institute and State University.

Lawrence, S., Lee, G.C. (1998). Searching the World Wide Web. *Science* 280:98–100.

Levy, D. M., Marshall, C. C. (1995). Going Digital: A Look at Assumptions Underlying Digital Libraries. *Communications of the ACM* 38:77–84.

Lingua franca. (1998). February 8(1):8–9.

Lyman, P. (1997). "Digital Documents and the Future of the Academic Community," Paper presented at Scholarly Communication and Technology, a conference organized by the Andrew W. Mellon Foundation, April 24–25, Emory University. Available at http://arl.cni.org/scomm/scat/lyman.html.

Lyman, P. (1998). "The Use and Abuse of Metaphor in Intellectual Property Policy: The Poetics of Information Highways, Digital Libraries, and Virtual Communities." Paper presented at Technological Visions: Utopian and Dystopian Perspectives, a conference sponsored by the Annenberg Center for Communication, November 6–7, University of Southern California. Abstract available at http://www.metamorph.org/confer/.

Shenk, D. (1997). Data Smog: Surviving the Information Glut. San Francisco: Harper Edge, pp 59–76.

Sullivan, T. (1997). The Future of the Genre. *The Specialized Scholarly Monograph in Crisis Or How Can I Get Tenure if You Won't Publish My Book.* AAUP seminar publications. Available at http://www.arl.org/scomm/epub/papers/sullivan. html, 1–7, 2.

Task Force on Archiving of Digital Information. (1996). *Preserving Digital Information.* A Report of the Task Force on Archiving of Digital Information commissioned by The Commission on Preservation and Access and The Research Libraries Group. Available at http://www.rlg.org/ArchTF/.

Travica, B. (April 1997). Organizational Aspects of the Virtual/Digital Library: A Survey of Academic Libraries. Indiana University School of Library and Information Science. Indiana University: Available at http://www-slis.indiana. edu/CSI/wp97-05.html.

TULIP Final Report. (1996). New York: Elsevier Science. TULIP was a three-year study among nine universities and Elsevier publishing. The goals were threefold: to determine the technical feasibility of networked distribution of journal information to and across institutions, to understand "economically and functionally acceptable" electronic distribution scenarios, to study reader usage. Institutions involved were; Carnegie Mellon University, Cornell University, Georgia Institute of Technology, Massachusetts Institute of Technology, University of California (all campuses), University of Michigan, University of Tennessee, University of Washington and Virginia Polytechnic Institute and State University (Virginia Tech). Levy and Marshall 1995 came to similar conclusions about the preference for paper. "In spite of organizational efforts to make all sources available through digital means and all composition and final production digital, analysts still make extensive use of paper as the principle interpretive medium."

The University of South Florida, "Electronic Publications of Theses and Dissertations. (1997). " Available at: http://www.usf.edu/ ~ writing/questions.html.

The University of Texas at Austin. (1996). "Report of the Ad hoc Committee on Digital Dissertations." Available at: http://www.utexas.edu/ogs/organizations/ ga/cd/dissertations.html.

The University of Waterloo, Electronic Thesis Project. (1997) "ETD Pilot Project Summary Report." Available at: http://www.lib.uwaterloo.ca/ ~ uw-etpt/summary.html

Virginia Tech. (1998). As of November 4, 1998, the Virginia Tech ETD Web site indicated there were 1,046 stored titles and 435 titles restricted to campus or graduate school access only. Available at http://scholar.lib.vt.edu/theses/temp-list.html

Weisser, C. R., Walker, J. R. (1997). Electronic Theses and Dissertations: Digitizing Scholarship for Its Own Sake. *Journal of Electronic Publishing*. University of Michigan Press, 3, no. 2. Available at http://www.press.umich.edu/jep/03-02/etd.html

20

Copyright in the Computer Age

Robert N. Diotalevi
Florida Gulf Coast University
Fort Myers, Florida

THE DIGITAL MILLENNIUM COPYRIGHT ACT

Overview

The information age has produced many concerns about copyright legalities. The Digital Millennium Copyright Act (DMCA) was actually designed to make copyright easy. President Clinton signed the bill October 28, 1998. It provides new game rules for the treatment and respecting of online copyrighted material. *The Digital Millennium Copyright Act,* Pub. L. No. 105-304, 112 Stat. 2860, served as the subject of debate for many interested in copyright law. Both houses of the one hundred and fifth Congress gave it the green light earlier in the month of October.

The DMCA adds two new chapters to Title 17 as it strengthens international law worldwide and protects domestic technology (Table 1).

The DMCA in Depth

Specifically, the Digital Millennium Copyright Act:

1. Limits copyright infringement liability for Internet Service Providers (ISPs) for the mere transmission of information as a con-

TABLE 1 Title 17, New Chapters

Title I: Implementation of two (2) treaties dealing with digital issues, copyright protection and management systems (The WIPO Copyright Treaty Act and the WIPO Performances and Phonograms Treaty).

Title II: Limitation of online infringement liability for ISPs (Internet Service Providers) (reducing legal uncertainties regarding such items as digital networks, strengthening anti-online piracy, outlining copyright owners' notification procedures, defining university liability, and creating a "safe harbor" for ISPs in four (4) situational activities):

1. Conduits (provision of materials transmission, routing and connections)
2. System Caching (temporary or intermediate materials storage to improve user performance and reduce congestion)
3. User Storage (materials storage on systems or networks at the direction of users)
4. Information Locators (linkage tools by service providers such as directories, pointers and/or hyperlinks to facilitate material access)

Note: 1 and 2: transmission must be initiated by a third party.
3 and 4: requires the ISP to be without knowledge or having reason to know of any infringement, to obtain no direct financial benefit and to not change the materials.

Title III: "The Computer Maintenance Competition Assurance Act" (formerly H.R. 72) (creation of an exception for temporary computer program reproduction in maintenance/repair).

Title IV: "Miscellaneous Provisions" (distance education, exemption for libraries/archives, ephemeral (momentary) recordings).

Title V: "The Vessel Hull Design Protection Act" (formerly H.R. 2696) (creation of new, sui generis protections for boat hull designs, in a new Chapter entitled Chapter 13 of Title 17 of the U.S. Code, effective for two years) [39].

[a] Except for Title I (Treaty), each was effective upon enactment.

   duit or transient host, provided no knowledge or financial gain is present.

2. Establishes guidelines for the removal by ISPs of material from the Internet that appears to be an infringement upon the knowledge by the ISP.

3. Limits liability against institutions when faculty members use educational facilities in order to publish materials electronically.

4. Makes criminal the circumvention of antipiracy devices, also known as "little black boxes."

5. Outlaws code-cracking devices but not ones being employed for research, testing, law enforcement activities, and related legal means.

6. States that the fair use doctrine remains a *viable defense* in copyright infringement matters, but does not go into much detail.
7. Updates the library exemption for facilities to take advantage of digital technology while engaging in activities similar to those for nondigital methodologies.
8. Directs The Register of Copyright to consult with educators, copyright owners, and libraries, and to submit recommendations for the promotion of distance education through digital means.
9. Implements two treaties regarding the respecting of copyright laws internationally.

The legislation has significant impact on our international status. Although technically the Senate still must ratify international pacts before governments of the world give credence to the measure, the law does prepare for the ratification and execution of two treaties regarding The World Intellectual Property Organization (WIPO). In December 1996, over 150 countries agreed on WIPO at a conference on digital information and copyrights in Geneva. The first treaty addresses digital authors' rights. The second pact focuses upon The Internet and sound recordings. Many members of the academic and research communities have mixed feelings about the measure. Some claim the DMCA would hinder concepts of fair use and other acceptable means of validly utilizing copyrighted materials. Concerns regarding educational use continue as a result. There are those who also claim that measure stifles operation, free thought, expression, system corrections, etc. Most library organizations oppose the measure, stating it does not contain many desired provisions. For example, among the changes for libraries, Section 108 of the DMCA now allows libraries to make up to three digital archival copies of published and unpublished materials for storage and retrieval. Previously one copy was allowed. However, the DMCA does not provide that these digital copies be made accessible to the public away from library grounds. The copy sent must arrive in analog form, and any copyright notice originally on a work should be included on the copy. If not, the library must give a legend stating that copyright law possibly protects the work.

The New Millennium Institutional Service Provider: Is It Fair?

The DMCA clearly does not mandate universities and colleges to become commercial ISPs or Online Service Providers (OSPs). But liability may result if institutions allow impropriety over their computer systems. It may very well be advisable to register an agent with The Copyright Office for the receipt of claims regarding potential copyright infringement. Among the schools that have done so are Northeast State Technical Community College in Blountville, Tennessee, The University of Nebraska in Lincoln, Nebraska, UCLA in

Los Angeles, California, and The University of Chicago in Illinois. Other facilities are quickly following suit.

Fair use is still somewhat convoluted. Fair use is an exception to normal copyright legalities. It allows, in a limited manner, use of copyrighted protected materials in itemsfor purposes of parody, news reports, comedic acts, research, and education. Fair use is on a case-by-case basis. The law considers four factors in determining if fair use isapplicable as a defense. The case of *Campbell v. Acuff-Rose Music, Inc.,* 510 U.S. 569, 114 S. Ct. 1164(1994), demonstrates this. Those factors include:

1. The *purpose and character* of the use, including whether use is of a commercial nature or is for nonprofit educational purposes.
2. The *nature* of the copyrighted work.
3. The *amount and substantiality* of the *portion used* in relation to the copyrighted work as a whole.
4. The *effect* of the use *upon the potential market* for or value of the copyrighted work.

In the Campbell v. Acuff-Rose case, The Supreme Court reversed the Sixth Circuit Court, claiming that it erred in finding copyright infringement against 2 Live Crew. The petitioners were band members Luther R. Campbell, Christopher Wongwon, Mark Ross, and David Hobbs. The group parodied Roy Orbison's "Oh, Pretty Woman" in a song Campbell entitled "Pretty Woman." After nearly a quarter of a million copies of the recording had been sold, Acuff-Rose sued 2 Live Crew and its record company, Luke Skywalker Records.

The Supreme Court applied the four-factor test summarized as follows:

1. The purpose and character of the use was a parody.
2. The nature of the copyrighted song does not prevent commercial use of a parody.
3. The portion used was only the necessary amount, as no more of the lyrics were taken than was necessary in relation to the parodic purpose.
4. The parody was unlikely to have a large effect on the marketplace.

Now it is unclear as to what constitutes fair use. Also complicating the matter are new and challenging digital advancements. Section 110(1) of the Copyright Act permits most face-to-face uses. However, copyright holders have exclusive rights to public display and public performance of their works. We glean some common classroom allowed and disallowed activities from our current statutes as well as recent case law (Table 2).

TABLE 2   Classroom Uses from Current and Case Law

Permissible uses	Impermissible uses
Unlimited, nondramatic performances of music or literature (i.e., reading novel excerpts and musical lines)	Dramatic performances of musicals or literary works
Unlimited displaying of charts, graphs, or photographs, including stills of motion pictures (distance education included)	Copying coursepacks for class distribution without meeting fair use criteria for each material used
Copying out-of-print-books	Out-of-print-book (placement on Web)
Journal article posted to Web page (restricted access, students and faculty)	Textbook photocopying and placement on Web (even if password or pin provided)
Placement of book on reserve in library	Copying of book and placement on reserve in library
Showing videotape for classroom instruction	Copying videotape for classroom instruction and/or charging fees
Broadcast or rebroadcast of classroom presentation to home or office (including the showing of another's video if permission is obtained)	
Videotaping of classroom (teacher's or student's presentation)	
Text, video, audio, and/or photographs used in telecourse for enrolled students	
Telecourse via cable television if institution-controlled audience (i.e., student body)	
Remote access of searchable database via the Internet if institution-controlled audience	
Student project placed on the Internet with restricted access to other students	
Use of commercial, instructional videotape on cable television or two-way interactive video	
Use of commercial, instructional videotape on cable television or two-way interactive video (via Internet, access restricted)	

TABLE 2 Continued

Permissible uses	Impermissible uses
Taping on-air television program to be shown on cable television or via two-way interactive video (remote sites allowed to record class to avoid possible technical difficulties)	

Overall it is extremely difficult to address specific concerns since the DMCA only provides that The Copyright Office consult with affected parties and make recommendations to Congress on how to promote distance education through digital technologies. Among the things that Congress desires in its report are:

The need for exemptions

Categories of works which would be included in an exception

Appropriate limitations on portions of works that may be used under any exemptions adopted

The parties eligible under exemptions

The extent to which use of technological protection measures should be mandated as a condition of eligibility for any exemption

The extent to which the availability of licenses should be considered in assessing the eligibility of any exemption

Other appropriate issues

In 1999 Congress received the final report from The United States Copyright Office (see Report on Copyright and Digital Distance Education, U.S. Copyright Office, May 26,1999 < http://lcweb.loc.gov/copyright/disted>). The Report advises that §110(2) be updated. Also, the report recommends clarification regarding the term "transmission," which should apply to digital as well as analog. Regarding fair use, the report claims that it is "technology-neutral" and must be defined in explicit language in order avoid further confusion. Thus, it was said that if Congress approved the recommendations, the law would let professors teaching classes over the Web at nonprofit institutions show a variety of interesting items, including but not limited to, movie clips or play parts of musical recordings. (*See, in general, id.* at 154-159; *see also U.S. Copyright Proposal Supports Distance Learning,* by Pamela Mendels, *New York Times,* May 29, 1999 and *Copyright Office Releases Proposal for On-Line Distance Education,* by Kelly McCollum, *The Chronicle of Higher Education,* Vol. XLV, No. 41, June 18, 1999.)

Criminal Consequences and Liability in the Digital Age

Civil plaintiffs recovering successfully for wrongdoing under the DMCA have the choice of illegally obtained profits, statutory damages, or injunctive relief. The most alarming fact is that copyright infringers can go to jail for violations. According to The Software Publishers Association, copyright piracy costs over $18 billion worldwide. (<http://www.spa.org/govmnt/iprt/wipotalk.htm>) The DMCA is filled with penalties as well as liabilities for those tempted to go astray. In general, the DMCA Sections 1203 and 1204 impose updated standards and gives guidance for works on the Net, especially regarding criminality. It will be unlawful to create or sell any technology used to break copyright protection devices. Illegal circumvention, i.e., those acts that constitute piracy of another's work, will carry statutory damages of twenty-five hundred dollars. (*See, e.g., Digital copyright bill becomes law*, by Courtney Macavinta, CNET NEWS.com, (October 28, 1998 <http://www.news.com/News/Item/0,4,28060,00.html?owv>.) And those committing illegal acts in a willful and purposeful manner will face serious criminal penalties of several hundred thousand dollars for each violation. A University of Oregon student was sentenced to two years probation and limited Internet access for illegally distributing copyrighted materials via a campus computer network. (*Oregon Student Sentenced to 2 Years' Probation in Copyright Case*, by Kelly McCollum, *The Chronicle of Higher Education*, December1, 1999 <http://chronicle.com/free/99/12/99120101t.htm>. *See also How Forcefully Should Universities Enforce Copyright Law on Audio Files?* by Kelly McCollum, *The Chronicle of Higher Education*, November 19, 1999 <http://chronicle.com/free/v46/i13/13a05901.htm>.)

Is It "My" Internet Course?

How does one know if one owns the course he or she created on the Net? An agreement between the parties is helpful, but it is not necessarily the determining factor. In fact, *control* itself is. The courts have looked at the employer's power over the employee and the work performed in deciding who retains ownership. Note that the term "employee" is interpreted according to general common law principles, which include:

The skill level involved in carrying out the task(s)
The source of tools/materials used by the person employed
The duration of relationship between the parties
The location of the work
The determination of the length of the arrangement
The method of payment
Whether or not the person working is self-employed

TABLE 3 Guidelines by Institution

University	Notes	URLs
University of Georgia	"The Regents Guide to Understanding Copyright and Educatoinal Fair Use"	http://www.usg.edu/admin/legal/copyright/ and http://www.peachnet.edu/admin/legal/copyright/copy.html (accessed November 15, 2002)
Indiana University–Purdue University Indianapolis and Indiana University	The Copyright Management Center serves both institutions. It has everything from fair use to distance education to library issues and special media issues. Indiana University offers policies as well as sample forms for faculty regarding distance learning and research considerations in general	http://copyright.iupui.edu/ (accessed November 15, 2002) http://www.indiana.edu/~rugs/respol/intprop.html (accessed November 15, 2002)
The University of Texas	"Guidelines for Classroom Copyrighting of Books and Periodicals," adapted from the Association of American Publishers and The Author's League of America.	http://www.utsystems.edu/OGC/IntellectualProperty/clasguid.htm (accessed November 15, 2002)
	The University System also has wonderful copyright presentations via the Web. Check out "Copyright Law in Cyberspace" at the above site with /nacua.htm finishing the web address after the intellectualproperty. Be sure to visit the copyright management information site at the preceding address, onding in copymgt.htm Finally, for the beginner, UT has a great site called "Crash Course in Copyright"	http://www.utsystems.edu/OGC/INTELLECTUALPROPERTY/cprtindx.htm#top (accessed November 15, 2002)
Rensselaer Polytechnic Institute		http://www.lib.rpi.edu/services/policies/lawhighlights.html (accessed November 16, 2002)

TABLE 3   Continued

University	Notes	URLs
Massachusetts Institute of Technology		http://web.mit.edu/policies/13.1.html (accessed November 15, 2002)
The University of Kansas	Found in Part 8 of the document	http://www.kansasregents.org/ academic/policy/academic.html (accessed November 15, 2002)
Massachusetts Institute of Technology	MIT also has a good site regarding frequently asked questions on copyright.	http://web.mit.edu/policies/13.1.html (accessed Jan. 14, 2001) http://web.mit/cwis/copyright/ faq.html (accessed Jan. 14, 1999) (dated 1995)
North Carolina State University		http://www.lib.ncsu.edu/scc/copyright/ copyrightmenu.html (accessed November 15, 2202)
Princeton University		http://www.wfubmc.edu/neurology/ copyright/princeton.html (accessed November 16, 2002) (dated 2000)
Cornell University	Also, Cornell is one of the best resources in copyright research	http://www.research.cornell.edu/ CRF/policies/copyright.html (accessed November 15, 2002) http://www.law.cornell.edu/topics/ copyright.html (accessed November 15, 2002)
Stanford University	Stanford also has excellent guidelines on fair use.	http://fairuse.stanford.edu/ (accessed November 15, 2002)
Yale University	"Copyright Resources Online" is a fantastic summary for anyone interested in these and related issues.	http://www.library.yale.edu/~okerson/ copyproj.html (accessed November 15, 2002)
The University of Tennessee		http://toltec.lib.utk.edu/~gco/ copyright.html (accessed November 15, 2002)
The University of Canada at Alberta	"Copying Right"	www.library.ualberta.ca/ copyright/_copyingright/index.cfm (accessed November 15, 2002) (dated 1994)
The University of Chicago	"Policy Guidlines for Publishing Networked Information"	http://www.uchicago.edu/docs/ policies/publishing-policy.html (accessed November 15, 2002) (dated May 30, 2000)

The payment of benefits by the employer

The payment of taxes by the employer (social security, worker's comp, etc.)

The power by the employed individual to hire an assistant or coworker

Community for Creative Non-Violence v. Reid, (490 U.S. 739, 109 S. Ct. 2166,1989) establishes a three-prong test for ownership rights, including control by the employer over the work, control by the employer over the employee, and the status and conduct of the employee. (*See also "When Professors Create Software, Do They Own It, or Do Their Colleges?*, by Scott Carlson, *The Chronicle of Higher Education*, July 21, 2000 <http://chronicle. com/free/v46/i46/46a02901.htm>.) Many institutions have created their own guidelines in dealing with these and other related copyright issues (Table 3).

THE TEACH ACT: TEACHING OLD DOGS NEW CLICKS

Overview

On November 2, 2002, President Bush signed into law the 21st Century Department of Justice Appropriations Authorization Act (H.R. 2215), which includes the Technology, Education, and Copyright Harmonization (TEACH) Act of 2001 with technical amendments to the Copyright Act. The text of the TEACH Act, Pub. L. 107-273, is available at the U.S. Copyright Office web site <http://thomas.loc.gov/cgi-bin/query/ z?c107:S.487.ES:>.

On March 13, 2001, The United States Senate Judiciary Committtee met to discuss the measure, S. 487 (the Copyright Technical Corrections Act, previously introduced as H.R. 614). Senators Hatch of Utah and Leahy of Vermont cowrote the bill in order to amend sections 112 and 110 of Title 17 of the United States Code. It gives credence to the report by Marybeth Peters, Register of Copyrights, to extend fair use regarding distance education. The Senate passed the measure in June 2001. (*See* Dale Carnevale, *Senate Passes a Bill Extending Copyright Exemption to Online Courses*, The Chronicle of Higher Education, June 12, 2001, at <http://chronicle.com/free/2001/06/ 2001061201u.htm>.) Again, the U.S. House followed suit in July 2001. (*See also* Andrea Foster, *House Committee Votes to Ease Copyright Restrictions on Distance Education*, The Chronicle of Higher Education, July 18, 2002, at <http://chronicle.com/free/2002/07/2002071801t.htm>.)

Section 110 of the U.S. Copyright Act includes 10 subsections. However, subsections one and two have the most impact regarding the new law.

(*See* The Software & Information Industry Association (SIIA) at <http://www.siia.net/sharedcontent/press/2002/11-4-02.html>.)

TEACH In Depth

The TEACH Act calls for safeguards against retention or distribution of copies other than as needed to teach and against interference with technological measures used by the copyright owner as well as permitting institutions to upload a copyright work onto a server under specific instances as defined by the Act and set out below. This will afford opportunities to allow certain schools to show audio-visual works via the Internet and other related means. Let us examine how this is to be achieved.

The TEACH Act repeals the former Section 110(2), which allowed educators the performance of limited works as well as transmissions to classroom settings. Thus, present concerns regarding digital or computerized transmissions required a change in the law. The Act extends Section 110 as to the expansion of uses allowed to include the performance and display of more works in the distance educational realm, by analog (physical) as well as digital means. [*See* the U.S. Copyright Office at <http://www.copyright.gov/tittle17/92chap1.html#110> (scroll down to section 110), The Copyright Managment Center at Indiana University-Purdue University at <http://www/copyright.iupui.edu/sec110(2).htm> and Cornell University School of Law's Legal Information Institute at <http://www4.law.cornell.edu/uscode/17/110.html>.] The act also amends Sec. 110(2) to broaden permitted uses to include the performance of any work by "reasonable and limited" portions. It also gets rids of the need for a physical classroom, a sort of neutral application regarding medium of information transmission so to speak. Again the act clears up instructional activities exempted in Sec. 110(2) as applicable to analog and digital transmissions, allowing in a limited fashion the reproduction and distribution of copies created as part of the automated process of digital transmissions. It also applies technological measures for unauthorized using and access thereto and permits safeguards for copyright owners by requiring institutions using the exemption to promote comliance with copyright law. [*See also* Educause at: <http://www.educause.edu/ir/library/pdf/ERM01610.pdf> and the America Library Association at <http://www. ala.org/washoff/teach.pdf>, <http://www.ala.org/washoff/disted.html>, as well as <http://www.11.georgetown.edu/allwash/ib0720013.html>. *See generally* The Technology, Education and Harmonization Act, S. 487, H.R. 614, incorporated into H.R. 2215, 21st Century Department of Justice Appropriations Authorization Act, at <http://thomas.loc.gov/cgi-bin/query/z?c107:S.487.ES> and <http://www.

copyright.gov/legislation/> . Stanford University Libraries has a good summary of recent copyright law and policy at <http://www-sul.standford.edu/geninfo/Provost_Copyright_Reminder.html>. For a comparison of the old and new law, see the chart by UNC Chapel Hill's Laura Gassaway at <http://www.unc.edu/~unclng/TEACH.htm>.]

Such groups as The American Library Association, The Association of American Universities, and The American Association ofUniversity Professors have praised the measure. [*See* The Association of American Universities at <http://www.aau.edu/intellect/copyri.html> and <http://www.aau.edu/intellect/SA487Test6.27.01.html> ; *see also* The American Association of Law Libraries at <http://www.11.georgetown.edu/aa11wash/ib0720013.html.>. The American Library Association's Washington office has a paper written by Professor Kenneth Crews, Director, Copyright Management Center Indiana University School of Law–Indianapolis, that summarizes the new standards and requirements established by the TEACH Act at <http://www.ala.org/washoff/teach.html>.]

However, the act is far from sweeping and certainly not a cure-all fro educators. It provides flexibility only for accredited, nonprofit educational institutions as part of "mediated instructional activities" to utilize Internet sources in the provision of copyrighted materials to distance education students. This means that the materials used directly relate to and/or are used for assistance in teaching the particular subject matter or course content. TEACH affords rights and protections but in somewhat of a limited manner. The type and amount of materials proscribed by the new law consist of whole performances of nondramatic literary and musical works, "reasonable and limited" portions of dramatic literary, musical, or audiovisual works, and displays or works, such as images, in amounts similar to typical displays in face-to-face teaching (i.e. stills, e.g.). [*See* The State University of Texas at
<http://www.utsystem.edu/ogc/intellectualproperty/teachact.htm> .]

There are indeed qualifications to the applicability of the new law. The following eight points summarize them:

1   When digitizing analog works, the law mandates that no digital version is available, and it must be free from technological protections that would prevent their uses as authorized.
2. Materials may be uploaded onto a serve to be disseminated only to students enrolled in a secure course in accordance with Section 110.
3. Materials cannot be for the public, especially while the regular course is not in session. They should be made available during "classtime."

4. Retention of materials by the institution is permitted to the extent it is necessary for asynchronous instruction thereof.
5. The Act amends Section 112 regarding ephemeral recordings, i.e., copies can be kept solely for transmission purposes pursuant to Section 110(2).
6. Faculty involved in the process must be educated about copyright law.
7. Supervision and policing by the school and instructor are deemed crucial so as to protect the rights of the copyright holder regarding performance or display at the institution.
8. The institution must provide notice that materials are or may be copyrighted as well as informational materials concerning copyright law. The State University of Texas provides a handy checklist to judge if an institution is ready to make use of the TEACH Act.

CONCLUSION

The copyright debate has taken yet another turn. The DMCA and TEACH Act are composed of complex rules and regulations and will face heavy testing in courts around the nation. It is too early to tell how these battles will affect copyright on the whole. Perhaps amendments or further statutory interpretations will be necessary by the federal legislature in order to alleviate concerns. Among the problems is the applicability of the fair use exception so heavily relied upon by educators and others. However, if we are to advance in the digital millennium, we must cut a compromise between right and rule, between freethinking and structured regulation. Only time will tell as to how these changes in copyright law will ultimately affect our activities in the electronic era.

REFERENCES

AALL: The American Association of Law Libraries, <http://www.11.georgetown.edu/aallwash/ib0720013.html>.
AAU: The Association of American Universities, <http://www.aau.edu/intellect/copyri.html>, <http://www.aau.edu/intellect/copyri.htmland> and <http://www.aau.edu/intellect/SA487Test6.27.01.html>.
ALA: The American Library Association, <http://www/ala.org/washoff/teach.pdf> and <http://www.ala.org/washoff/disted.html>.
ALA's New and Views, June 10, 1998, <http://www.ala.org>.

Association of Research Libraries. Washington, D.C. Press Release, Sept. 29, 1998, <http://arl.cni.org>.

Carlson, S. (July 21, 2000). When Professors Create Software, Do They Own It, or Do Their Colleges? The Chronicle of Higher Education, <http://chronicle.com/free/v46/i46/46a02901.htm>.

Carnevale, D. (June 12, 2001). Senate Passes a Bill Extending Copyright Exemption to Online Courses. The Chronicle of Higher Education, <http://chronicle.com/free/2001/06/2001061201u.htm>.

Copyright Management Center, The Indiana University–Purdue University, <http://www.copyright.iupui.edu>.

Cornell University School of Law, <http://supct.law.cornell.edu/supct/html> and <http:/www4.law.cornell.edu//uscode/17/110.html>.

Crews, K. (2002). New Copyright Law for Distance Education: The Meaning and Importance of the TEACH Act, <http://www.copyright.iupui.edu/teach_summary.htm>.

DFC: The Digital Future Coalition at http://www.dfc.org/dfc1/Archives/wipo/pr101698.html>.

Foster, A. (July 18, 2002). House Committee Votes to Ease Copyright Restrictions on Distance Education, The Chronicle of Higher Education, <http://chronicle.com/free/2002/07/2002071801t.htm>.

Gassaway, L. UNC Chapel Hill, <http://www.unc.edu/~unclng/TEACH.htm>.

John Marshall University Law School at http://www.jmls.edu/cyber/others.html.

Litman, J. (1994). The exclusive Right to Read. 13 Cardozo Arts & Ent. L.J. 29, <http://www.msen.com/~litman/read.htm>.

McCollum, K. (June 18, 1999a). Copyright Office Releases Proposal for On-Line Distance Education. The Chronicle of Higher Education, Vol. XLV No. 41.

McCollum, K. (November 19, 1999b). How Forcefully Should Universities Enforce Copyright Law on Audio Files? The Chronicle of Higher Education, <http://chronicle.com/free/v46/i13/13a05901.htm>.

McCollum, K. (December 1, 1999c). Oregon Student Sentenced to 2 Years' Probation in Copyright Case, The Chronicle of Higher Education, <http://chronicle.com/free/99/12/99120101t.htm>.

Mendels, P. (May 29, 1999). U.S. Copyright Proposal Supports Distance Learning. *New York Times.*

Office of the President's Press Secretary, The White House "Statement by the President." October 12, 1998, formerly at <ftp://ftp.aimnet.com/pub/users/carroll/law/copyright/h2281-res.txt> (currently unavailable).

Software & Information Industry Association, The (SIIA), <http://www.siia.net/sharedcontent/press/2002/11-4-02.html>.

Stanford University Libraries, <http://www-sul.stanford.edu/geninfo/Provost_Copyright_Reminder.html>.

State University of Texas, The, <http://www.utsystem.edu/ogc/intellectualproperty/teachact.htm>.

TEACH Act, The (Technology, Education and Harmonization Act) S. 487, H.R.

614, incorporated into H.R. 2215, 21st Century Department of Justice Appropriations Authorization Ac <http://thomas.loc.gov/cgi-bin/query/z?c107:S.487.ES> and <http://www.copyright.gov/legislation/>.

University of Texas, <http://www.utsystems.edu/OGC/intellectualproperty/cpttindx.htm> and <http://www.utsystems.edu/ogc/intellectualproperty/teachact.htm>.

U.S. Copyright Office, The <http://www.copyright.gov/title17/92chap1.html#110>.

21

ETDs as an Innovation: Using Theory to Grow an ETD Program

Suzie Allard
University of Tennessee
Knoxville, Tennessee

INTRODUCTION

ETDs help students gain a new perspective on scholarship by encouraging them to step beyond the traditional role of being electronic *document consumers* to become electronic *document creators*, who author and self-archive the documents they compose. The role of electronic document creator also allows students to extend the way in which they present and disseminate their research by utilizing technological skills and tools, some of which may be new to the student. However, while ETDs offer students significant advantages over traditional theses and dissertations, the rate at which students adopt this innovation may vary considerably. Additionally, as with any innovation, the success level of implementation is contingent on the acceptance and utilization of the process by the target community, which in this case is students.

Finding ways to increase the rate of adoption of ETD creation among students will help a university's ETD program grow more quickly and efficiently. To do this, it is useful to gain an understanding of the students who are among the first to participate in a university's ETD initiative and to focus strategic planning on encouraging higher levels of voluntary participation in

299

the future. This chapter will present some basic concepts about innovation adoption that can be helpful to ETD planning committees, and it will review the preliminary findings of some pertinent research conducted with students who participated in an ETD pilot program at the University of Kentucky (UK).

ENCOURAGING ETD CREATION UNIVERSITYWIDE

While many universities are encouraging or even requiring ETDs, students are still likely to perceive that the ETD is a "new" idea or innovation when it is offered at their university. Additionally, because students who create an ETD, particularly for completion of a Ph.D., are likely to be leaving the community of students, they will not be part of the social system supporting the innovation's introduction to new students. This situation places special emphasis on those students who are "innovators" or "early adopters" since they will be an important core group in any given year.

For ETD planning committees this unique situation of a quickly maturing target community that exits the environment places a focus on two basic issues that have been identified by diffusion of innovation scholars: (1) How do early adopters differ from later adopters? and (2) How does the perceived attributes of the innovation itself affect its adoption? Both of these issues are pertinent when introducing and implementing an ETD program since expanding the program will require attracting more than just those students who fit the profile of adventurous innovators. In terms of students, it is essential to find ways to reach the opinion leaders who are willing to try something new but are regarded as making solid decisions that are low in risk. The second dimension, focusing on the ETDs themselves, suggests that effectively informing students of the ETD's advantages could be another key to increasing participation in the program.

Three very useful lessons can be gleaned from diffusion of innovation research:

> The first centers on the stages an individual passes through when making the decision to adopt an innovation.
> The second focuses on the innovation's characteristics.
> The third describes how individuals may be classified into adopter categories.

While diffusion of innovation research has not been conducted specifically with ETDs, each of these concepts is still useful in helping to define the course of action for introduction and implementation of the ETD program.

An individual can be thought of as passing through several different stages when making the decision whether to adopt or reject an innovation (Rogers, 1995). For example, the first step in the innovation process is that a person needs to gain knowledge about the innovation. The university's ETD planning committee could address this information need with a campaign to announce and provide information about ETDs, their place in the university system, and their role in the future of scholarship. Similarly, there are planning implications entailed in the other four stages in the innovation process (see Table 1), which include the individual forming an attitude about ETDs, making the choice about whether to adopt or reject ETD creation, implementing (creating) ETDs, and gaining confirming input about the ETD after creating it. When developing strategies for a university's ETD program, it is useful to discuss the impact each of the stages may have on how the program is approached and promoted.

Other planning considerations come to the forefront when looking at the different dimensions of an ETD through the five characteristics used to describe innovations (Rogers, 1995). These five characteristics are relative

TABLE 1   Five Stages of the Innovation Process

Innovation stage	Possible actions the committee can take to address the stage
1. Knowledge: The student learns about the existence and details of the program.	Campaign to announce the ETD program Resources to provide information about the program
2. Persuasion: The student begins to form an attitude about ETDs.	Putting a "face on the campaign" to help students learn about the experiences of others Providing outreach programs featuring readily accessible information Offering training programs to help students feel comfortable with associated technologies
3. Decision: The student makes a choice to adopt or reject creating an ETD.	Training and information provision support programs for those who adopt Continued exposure of students who have successfully completed an ETD
4. Implementation: The student constructs an ETD.	Training and information provision support programs for those who adopt
5. Confirmation: The student gains positive input after creating the ETD.	Student has opportunity to become a featured ETD success story ETD is added to collection

advantage over the old technology, compatibility to the needs and experiences of the adopters, complexity of learning and using the innovation, trialability in terms of experimenting with the technology, and observability, which refers to the degree that others see the results of the innovation. Therefore, it could be assumed that a student would be more likely to create an ETD if the document is perceived as being much better than the traditional version, which might be expressed in terms of the potential for content representation, dissemination, cost, and/or ease of use. Thus, the ETD planning committee could focus their energies on identifying and addressing the key relative advantage issues for their graduate students.

The issue of relating the ETD's compatibility to the needs and experiences of the students is also very important. Each community of students will have different levels of technological expertise, which would suggest what type of actions should be taken such as the type of technological support that should be provided. Additionally, the concept of observability might suggest finding ways to highlight the program and the resulting ETDs so that students are aware of the program long before they have reached the stage of actually writing their thesis or dissertation.

In terms of gaining an understanding of the kinds of students who may be the first or the most motivated to create ETDs, once again diffusion of innovation research provides some useful concepts. This research has produced extensive empirical data that have been used to build conceptualizations of "ideal types" for five categories of adopters (Rogers, 1995). While reality produces exceptions to these conceptualizations, the ideal types can still provide some useful information about the innovativeness of graduate students who choose to create an ETD. Therefore, a committee might expect that when a program is introduced, the first students who choose to create an ETD would fit the profile of "innovators" who are very excited by new ideas and have a spirit of adventure. While this group will leap at the opportunity to try an innovation, they tend not to have a leadership role with their peers and can be thought of as gatekeepers. Thus, if this group has a positive experience with the introduction of ETDs, it can help the ETD concept gain greater awareness among graduate students, but it is the next group, the "early adopters," who have the greatest impact on their peers.

Early adopters are not as adventurous as innovators, but their peers respect them for making judicious decisions, and they often are regarded as role models. The concept of early adopters is important since these are the students whose belief in the ETD's value can provide an important boost to the acceptance of an ETD program. While it may be difficult to identify exactly who these students will be, a program can be sure that it is designed to address those who want to reduce uncertainty rather than just aiming at those who are ready for a new adventure. It is the early adopters who greatly influence the next group—the early majority. While early majority students are not opinion leaders among their peers, they account for nearly a third of the target population.

The final two groups are likely to be much more difficult to reach with a voluntary ETD program. For example, the late majority tends to adopt an innovation only when it becomes an economic necessity and when there is significant pressure from their peers among the early majority. The final group, the laggards, have a profile that suggests they can only be reached through mandatory ETD programs.

This overview only provides a glimpse of the rich material supplied by diffusion of innovation research, but it offers ETD committees a framework to help focus their efforts when assessing the situation at their university and planning for the introduction and implementation of an ETD program. The application of this framework is demonstrated by some pilot research conducted with University of Kentucky graduate students who participated in the university's Pilot Project.

THE UNIVERSITY OF KENTUCKY EXPERIENCE

In January 2000, the University of Kentucky formed a committee to explore the feasibility of introducing an ETD initiative at UK. This eight-member committee was chaired by the associate dean of the Graduate School and consisted of the university's associate general consul, three professors from a variety of disciplines, an electronic resources librarian from university libraries, the Graduate School's web coordinator, and a doctoral student. The committee began biweekly meetings in February and by April 2000, the UK-ETD Pilot Project was announced to the university community.

The Pilot Project sought 10–30 students who would complete their thesis or dissertation during the fall 2000 or spring 2001 semesters. Students were told that they would work with the Graduate School to test implementation procedures, and those who were interested in creating documents with multimedia components were especially encouraged to participate. In addition, the UK Graduate School presented the first 20 confirmed participants with a preparation grant of $100 each, but no other support, either technical or monetary, was offered. By August 2000, 43 students expressed an interest in participating, although by mid-September, only 25 students had filed intent forms that confirmed their interest in creating an ETD. By December 2000, the Graduate School had accepted its first ETD, and by the following fall 24 ETDs were accepted and online.

The 22 students who filed intent forms were of special interest to the ETD committee, since they were the individuals who were willing to step outside their normal peer groups and face the uncertainty of participating in a new and evolving program at the university. Of these 22 students, 11 completed and submitted an ETD.

It was believed that by learning more about these 22 volunteers, strategic planning for the future of the UK-ETD program could be improved so that it could begin to build momentum by attracting the next wave of ETD creators as predicted by the diffusion of innovation theory. Innovators are especially important in the diffusion process because they are the key players in "importing" an innovation into their social group groups (Rogers, 1995) and serving as gatekeepers. In terms of the student community, these social groups may reflect discipline or academic program. Therefore, a simple study was conducted to contact student innovators.

In September 2000, the associate dean of the Graduate School announced the research project via the UK-ETD discussion list that included all the student Pilot Project volunteers. The researcher also invited each of the students to participate via personal email. Those who volunteered to participate were sent the Awareness and Adoption Digital Library (AADL) instrument in either an electronic or paper-based version (see Appendix). After several months, students who answered the AADL were sent a follow-up set of three questions. In accordance with the request of the Graduate School to minimize inconvenience to students, the researcher only contacted each student one time at each phase. The research, which was named *Metamorphosis* in order to represent the student transition from document consumer to document creator, was conceived with two purposes:

1. To explore individual reaction to the introduction of electronic document creation and archiving from affective, cognitive, and behavioral perspectives.
2. To assess student response to the introduction of an ETD initiative at the University of Kentucky.

The AADL instrument was designed specifically for the Metamorphosis project. Acceptance and adoption of digital library technologies, particularly among graduate students, has not been extensively studied; but there is a large body of research focusing on information technology acceptance and adoption in the business environment. This technology acceptance research is theoretically rooted in several well-established models used to describe human behavior, including the theory of reasoned action, social presence theory, and social influence. Each of these threads approaches technology adoption from a different perspective, including personal motivation, social influence, uncertainty reduction, personal efficacy with the technology, and the technology's capacity to perform the task. For example, a study based on Bandura's Social Cognitive Theory took a closer look at an individual's perception of self in relation to technology (Compeau et al. 1999). This study found that a person's self-efficacy with computers is positively correlated with outcome expectations and negatively correlated with technological anxiety. Self-efficacy in this environment is defined as one's belief in his or her own ability to perform a distinct technological behavior. The ETD concept of making graduate students prepare an electronic document encourages individuals to operate autonomously, therefore, the perception of self is likely to play heavily into the likelihood of adoption. Management Information Systems research also targeted users' general attitudes towards computers, satisfaction with information technology, and workers' patterns of computer usage (Delone and McLean, 1992; Etezadi-Amoli and Farhoomand, 1996; Robey, 1979; Szajna, 1996; Torkzadeh and Dwyer, 1994).

However, the review of technology adoption literature did not reveal an instrument designed specifically for the type of electronic environment represented by the ETD. Therefore, while the AADL incorporated some well-established measures used for technology adoption of software programs, it also included some new measures that directly addressed digital library and ETD issues. The instrument consisted of 18 questions, including a demographic profile. A key section focused on student reaction to the ETD concept, including the tolerance level they had for difficulty in creating an ETD. Another important focus of the survey was on student use of and reaction to digital library technology in general since DL technology is the foundation of the ETD environment.

Other AADL measures focused on the individuals' technological knowledge and their general attitudes towards technology, including the degree to which the student believes technology enhances his or her work or school performance. Students were also asked to commit to a position regarding their comfort with technology. Other issues that were explored were student knowledge of electronic resources and student opinions about the relationship between technology and the educational experience.

WHAT WE HAVE LEARNED

At the time that this chapter was written, Metamorphosis was still in a pilot phase, and clearly a better understanding could be gained through administration of the survey at other universities. Additionally, the sample is quite small, with slightly more than a quarter of the Pilot Project students returning a Metamorphosis survey, but some measures were so consistent across all respondents that the results can begin to guide the sketching out of a profile of UK student ETD innovators. Noting these limitations, the Metamorphosis findings provided insights that were useful for the UK program and that can offer some guidelines for what should be considered when doing strategic planning of an ETD program. Most importantly, it appears that the introduction of this ETD program attracted students who have a taste for adventure and a basic level of technical proficiency initiative rather than students with exceptional technological expertise. The following observations are the key points that have emerged so far from the Metamorphosis study, and listed with each are some strategic actions that have been fashioned to address that observation.

Pilot Project Participants Were Adventurous

While most of these students were not aware of the Networked Digital Library of Theses and Dissertations and many had never turned in e-documents for class assignments, they still voluntarily decided to create an ETD. While it seems surprising that someone would choose to make an ETD their first academic electronic document, this finding is consistent with the characteristics of innovators who tend to be adventurous because they are more tolerant of any setbacks (Rogers, 1995). What this suggests is that to increase the level of ETD participation, an effort must be made to reach less adventurous students. This could be accomplished through publicity and information forums aimed at both students and their advisors. Additionally, it suggests that ETD participation is not limited by technical expertise of the graduate student body, although participation may be facilitated by reducing individual's uncertainty with required technology.

Pilot Project Participants Were Not "Techies"

Based on several AADL measures, it was apparent that students saw technology as a tool that allowed them to improve what they did, but technology was not a prime focus of their interest. In fact, students expressed a significant level of frustration with learning new programs. Other measures indicated that few students read technology magazines and most would not change their personal computer as long as it served their needs. This profile was somewhat surprising, since it had been expected that this first group of graduate students would represent those who are most technologically inclined. However, this survey indicated that it could be very important to make other students aware that it does not take extensive technological expertise to successfully complete an ETD. One way the UK committee addressed this issue was to institute a program that would "put a face" on the ETD process by creating a library of testimonials of successful ETD creators, each of which would be encouraged to discuss the level of their technological expertise.

Pilot Project Participants Had Some Experience with a Wide Range of Standard Applications

All had used email and most also had coded in HTML, designed a database, and used presentation software such as PowerPoint. However, there was no acquaintance with programming or applications that required more extensive expertise. These results confirmed that the ETD innovators were proficient with technology but not experts. It also suggested that technology support in terms of training could focus on skills that are specifically linked with ETD submission at the university, such as the creation of documents in PDF.

Pilot Project Participants Had a Positive Attitude Towards Technology, but It Was Not a Substantial Part of Their Image

In spite of noting frustrations with technologies, overall, these innovators believed technology was easy to use. Once again this seems consistent with the idea that innovators are tolerant of setbacks. However, these students did not see technology use as being prestigious and didn't feel their peers thought it was prestigious. This suggests that the value of ETDs to these students went beyond simply using new technology to the core issues of content representation and ease of dissemination. Clearly, it would be useful to find the specific issues that attracted these Pilot Project participants. It is interesting to note that these core issues are traditional scholarly dimensions. Addressing these dimensions very directly in the university's program materials could be an avenue to reaching the early adopters who are looking for a better way to tackle traditional activities.

Creating an ETD Is Especially Attractive If the Process of Creating One Takes No More Effort Than Producing a Traditional Thesis or Dissertation

These students were embarking on creating an ETD, and they still strongly believed that it was important that the process be no more difficult than the traditional way. Students did feel that copyright issues and cost were important considerations in their decision to create an ETD. This suggests that resource materials clearly address these issues and that students be provided with the means to learn about copyright—both in terms of what they can use and the protection provided to their own work. Additional emphasis should be placed on these and other important issues in terms of establishing the ETD's relative advantage over a traditional theses or dissertation. Finally, the university ETD submission process should not be more complex or difficult than the traditional method.

Women Were Not as Participatory in the Initiative as Men

This observation did not rely on self-reporting, but was a result of tracking the ultimate disposition of students who expressed an interest in the Pilot Program. There was a significant difference in the proportion of women students who showed an interest in participating in the UK Pilot Project and those who actually submitted an ETD. While 30% of the students who expressed an interest in submitting an ETD were women, only 19% of the ETDs submitted were created by women. Improving uptake among women could be addressed by being sure that women are included in the ETD testimonial collection.

CONCLUSION

Introducing and growing an ETD program is a challenging task that requires planning committees to efficiently channel their efforts to introduce the innovation in a manner that answers the needs of their graduate student community. Diffusion of innovation theory and research offers some concepts that can help guide strategic planning in terms of identifying what issues should be addressed and providing some insight into how these issues should be approached. One can gain an understanding of the stages an individual goes through during the innovation decision-making process that may illuminate points at which the ETD program should provide information or offer support. Also, the ETD can be discussed in terms of several dimensions, such as relative advantage and compatibility, that may indicate how the ETD program should be fashioned to best match a specific university's unique student characteristics. Finally, understanding the adopter categories can help a committee determine the focus of their program and what support may be needed to facilitate its success. Using these concepts to spark creative planning can help an ETD committee frame their program in a way that promotes the use of resources, both monetary and human, in a manner that benefits the student community most effectively.

APPENDIX: AWARENESS AND ADOPTION DIGITAL LIBRARY INSTRUMENT

1. For each of these questions check the appropriate answer.

	Yes	No
Are you currently a graduate student at (university name)?	☐	☐

If yes, what degree are you pursuing?

Masters	Doctorate	Other
☐	☐	☐

In what area are you specializing?

2. Here is a list of technological tools. For each please indicate if you use this tool, and where you use it. (mark as many circles as apply for each tool)

		Use computer at:			Do not use this tool
		Home	**School**	**Work**	
a.	Word processor (Word, WordPerfect, etc.)	☐	☐	☐	☐
b.	Spreadsheet (Excel , Lotus, etc.)	☐	☐	☐	☐
c.	Presentation software (PowerPoint, etc.)	☐	☐	☐	☐
d.	Database software (Access, Filemaker, etc.)	☐	☐	☐	☐
e.	Internet (shopping, getting information, playing games)	☐	☐	☐	☐
f.	E-mail	☐	☐	☐	☐
g.	Drawing software (Illustrator, Corel Draw, etc.)	☐	☐	☐	☐
h.	Desktop publishing (Publisher, Pagemaker, etc.)	☐	☐	☐	☐
i.	Photo software (PhotoShop, etc.)	☐	☐	☐	☐
j.	Game software (playing games of any type)	☐	☐	☐	☐
k.	Website production software (FrontPage, PageMill, etc.)	☐	☐	☐	☐
l.	Listserv	☐	☐	☐	☐
m.	Chat room	☐	☐	☐	☐

3. For those technological tools you have used, please show how frequently you have used them in the last two weeks. Was it daily, every other day, every third day, once a week, or once during the two-week period? (make a mark in one circle for each tool)

		Daily	**Every other day**	**Every third day**	**Once a week**	**Once in 2 weeks**	**Did not use this tool**
a.	Word processor (Word, WordPerfect, etc.)	☐	☐	☐	☐	☐	☐

		Daily	**Every other day**	**Every third day**	**Once a week**	**Once in 2 weeks**	**Did not use this tool**
b.	Spreadsheet (Excel, Lotus, etc.)	☐	☐	☐	☐	☐	☐
c.	Presentation software (PowerPoint, etc.)	☐	☐	☐	☐	☐	☐
d.	Database software (Access, Filemaker, etc.)	☐	☐	☐	☐	☐	☐
e.	Internet (shopping, getting information, playing games)	☐	☐	☐	☐	☐	☐
f.	E-mail	☐	☐	☐	☐	☐	☐
g.	Drawing software (Illustrator, Corel Draw, etc.)	☐	☐	☐	☐	☐	☐
h.	Desktop publishing (Publisher, Pagemaker, etc.)	☐	☐	☐	☐	☐	☐
i.	Photo software (PhotoShop, etc.)	☐	☐	☐	☐	☐	☐
j.	Game software (playing games of any type)	☐	☐	☐	☐	☐	☐
k.	Website production software (FrontPage, PageMill, etc.)	☐	☐	☐	☐	☐	☐

	Daily	Every other day	Every third day	Once a week	Once in 2 weeks	Did not use this tool
l. Listserv	☐	☐	☐	☐	☐	☐
m. Chat room	☐	☐	☐	☐	☐	☐

4. Thinking about the kinds of technological tools mentioned above, how much do you agree with each of these statements? (mark the appropriate number)

	Strongly disagree				Strongly agree
a. Technology has made it easier to do my job and/or schoolwork.	1	2	3	4	5
b. Technology has complicated my life.	1	2	3	4	5
c. Technology helps me get more done in a day.	1	2	3	4	5
d. I prefer to keep using a program I know rather than learn a new one even if the new one would make my job easier.	1	2	3	4	5
e. I like working with many different types of software.	1	2	3	4	5
f. I usually try to get the upgrades for my programs.	1	2	3	4	5
g. I find learning new programs very frustrating.	1	2	3	4	5
h. I read technology-oriented magazines and journals.	1	2	3	4	5

5. Once again think of the technological tools mentioned above. How much do you agree with each of these statements about technology, and how it has affected you at work or school? (mark the appropriate number)

	Strongly disagree				Strongly agree
a. Using technology improved the quality of some tasks for school or work	1	2	3	4	5

		Strongly disagree				Strongly agree
b.	Technology gave me control over my work or study.	1	2	3	4	5
c.	Technology enabled me to accomplish some tasks more quickly.	1	2	3	4	5
d.	Technology enabled me to accomplish some tasks more quickly.	1	2	3	4	5
e.	Using technology improved my performance in some tasks of my work or study.	1	2	3	4	5
f.	Using technology enhanced my effectiveness on some tasks of my work or study.	1	2	3	4	5

6.   Imagine that there is a new computer for sale that is faster and has greater storage than your present home computer. Which statement best describes your feelings? (check one)

I want to buy the more powerful computer as soon as possible.
I want to buy the more powerful computer but will wait until it has been around a while.
I would stay with my present computer as long as it seemed to serve my needs.
I don't think the more powerful computer is necessary.
I never make computer-purchasing decisions because someone else in my family does.
I don't make computer-purchasing decisions because I don't know what to buy.

---

7.   How much do you agree with each of these statements about the use of technology? (mark the appropriate number)

		Strongly disagree				Strongly agree
a.	I believe technology is cumbersome to use.	1	2	3	4	5
b.	Learning to use technology is easy/fun for me.	1	2	3	4	5
c.	Using technology is often frustrating.	1	2	3	4	5

		Strongly disagree				Strongly agree
d.	I believe that it is easy to get technology to do what I want it to do for work and school.	1	2	3	4	5
e.	It is easy for me to remember how to perform tasks using technology.	1	2	3	4	5
f.	While at work or school, the technology system requires a lot of mental effort.	1	2	3	4	5
g.	Overall I believe technology is easy to use.	1	2	3	4	5

8.   Here are some information resources that may be available to you. Please indicate if you have heard of each of these resources. For each resource that you are familiar with, please circle the number indicating how helpful you find it, 0 being no help and 5 being very helpful. If you are not familiar with the resource, place a check mark in the circle below Don't know.

		Not helpful					Very Helpful	Don't know
a.	University's on-line library catalog.	0	1	2	3	4	5	☐
b.	Networked Digital Library of Theses and Dissertations.	0	1	2	3	4	5	☐
c.	[insert name of digital library associated with nearest state].	0	1	2	3	4	5	☐

9.   Here are some educational technologies that may or may not have been part of your graduate school experience. For those you have seen, please assess how much it helped your educational experience with 0 being no help

and 5 being very helpful. If it has not been part of your experience place a check mark in the circle below Not used.

		Not helpful					Very helpful	Not used
a.	Online syllabus	0	1	2	3	4	5	☐
b.	Online quizzes	0	1	2	3	4	5	☐
c.	Listserv	0	1	2	3	4	5	☐
d.	E-mail	0	1	2	3	4	5	☐
e.	Lecture notes online	0	1	2	3	4	5	☐
f.	Turn-in home work as e-documents	0	1	2	3	4	5	☐

10. How would you rate the importance of using information technology in education?

(check one)
☐ Very important
☐ Somewhat important
☐ Not important

11. Thinking about your program of study, how much do you disagree or agree with each of these statements? (mark the appropriate number)

		Strongly disagree				Strongly agree
a.	People in my program who use technology have more prestige than those who do not.	1	2	3	4	5
b.	People in my program who use technology have a high profile.	1	2	3	4	5
c.	Using technology is a status symbol in my program.	1	2	3	4	5

12. There are many different interactive opportunities open to information technology users. Please indicate which of these activities you have done.

		Have done	Have not done
a.	E-mail group mailing	☐	☐
b.	HTML coding	☐	☐
c.	Writing Java applets	☐	☐
d.	Writing CGI scripts	☐	☐
e.	XML coding	☐	☐
f.	SGML coding	☐	☐
g.	Designing a database	☐	☐
h.	Presentation creation	☐	☐

13. Digital libraries are an on-line information source that allow users to navigate many databases that may include full-text books and articles as well as images and other media. Have you used a digital library?

If yes, please answer questions 14 and 15
If no, skip questions 14 and 15; go to question 16.

14. If you have used a digital library, how much do you agree with each of these statements about using digital libraries? (mark the appropriate number)

		Strongly disagree				Strongly agree
a.	It was time well spent.	1	2	3	4	5
b.	It was too difficult to find what I wanted.	1	2	3	4	5
c.	There was more information available than I expected.	1	2	3	4	5
d.	I found the information I wanted.	1	2	3	4	5
e.	I prefer going to a library on campus.	1	2	3	4	5
f.	I would like to get better acquainted with the navigation tools.	1	2	3	4	5

15. Do you recall the name(s) of the Digital Library(ies) you visited? List the names of as many as you can recall. If you have one particular favorite, place a check next to that name.

_____

_____

_____

_____

_____

_____

16. If security, copyright, and cost were not issues, how interested would you be in having your thesis or dissertation included in a digital library that could be accessed by scholars from around the world? (mark only one)

☐ Very interested.
☐ Only interested if it's not too much work.
☐ Would be interested if my cohort was participating.
☐ Not interested at all.

17. Suppose a software program was available that allowed you to create an electronic version of your thesis or dissertation with about the same level of effort as making a presentation file with software such as PowerPoint. How likely would you be to use it? (mark only one)

☐ I would definitely use it.
☐ I might use it.
☐ Not at all interested.

18. Students have mentioned several reasons for submitting their thesis or dissertation electronically versus in the traditional manner. How important do you think each reason is? (mark the appropriate number)

		Not important				Very important
		1	2	3	4	5
a.	More people will be able to access my thesis or dissertation.	1	2	3	4	5

	Not important				Very important
b. My work could be cited more frequently by others.	1	2	3	4	5
c. People working on similar issues will see my work and contact me.	1	2	3	4	5
d. The electronic format allows me to include aspects of my work that can't be captured on paper, such as simulations.	1	2	3	4	5

19. Please answer the following questions for classification purposes.

Your age:_____	Your gender:	Male ☐	Female ☐	
Student status:	Full time ☐	Part time ☐		
Do you have a job?	Yes, on campus ☐	Yes, off campus ☐	No ☐	
What is the title or nature of your job?_____				
How soon will you complete your degree?	Fall ☐	Spring ☐	Summer ☐	Year: _____

REFERENCES

Compeau, D., Higgins, C. A., Huff, S. (1999). Social cognitive theory and individual reactions to computing technology: a longitudinal study. *MIS Quarterly* 23(2):145:158.

Delone, W. H., McLean, E. R. (1992). Information systems success: the quest of the dependent variable. *Information Systems Research* (3):60–95.

Etezadi-Amoli, J., Farhoomand, A. (1996). A structural model of end-user computing satisfaction and user performance. *Information and Management* 30(2): 65–73.

Robey, D. (1979). User attitudes and management information systems use. *Academic Management Journal* 22(3):527–538.

Rogers, E. M. (1995). *Diffusion of Innovations*. 4th ed. New York: The Free Press.

Szajna, B. (1996). Empirical evaluation of the revised technology acceptance model. *Management Science* 42(1):85–92.

Torkzadeh, G., Dwyer, D. J. (1994). A path of anaylytic study of determinants of information system usage. *OMEGA International Journal of Management Science* 22(4):339–348.

22

Implementing ETD Services in the Library

Gail McMillan
Virginia Polytechnic Institute and State University
Blacksburg, Virginia

INTRODUCTION

When a university considers the option of or requirement for electronic theses and dissertations (ETDs), the library can take the opportunity to address a whole cadre of issues and responsibilities. Some of these include improving the quality and timeliness of access to information, maintaining the information server, and archiving. Students and faculty must be introduced to the library's new information resource, students as authors must be assisted or trained in online publishing, and faculty can be assisted to change their workflow for the online editing of digital works. Faculty fears of publisher's censorship can also be addressed. Some of these issues present new roles for libraries, and some require mapping traditional services and resources to digital resources and electronic services.

While the goals of ETD projects frequently focus on preparing graduate students to readily and actively participate in the Information Age, libraries can also gain a tremendous amount from such activities. Through ETD initiatives, libraries can become better stocked digital libraries, provide more timely access to information resources, serve more users with fewer staff, and reduce physical space requirements (i.e., shelves and buildings).

IMPROVED ACCESS TO INFORMATION RESOURCES

Universities are unlocking their intellectual property through ETDs. Previously, the research described in theses and dissertations was inadvertently hidden on the shelves of the library, as evidenced by their infrequent circulation. Check-out statistics (see http://scholar.lib.vt.edu/theses/data/ and http://scholar.lib.vt.edu/theses/data/somefacts.html) gathered during the early 1990s revealed that Virginia Tech's theses circulated about 2.25 times per year during the first 4 years they were available on the library's shelves. Dissertations, perhaps because of additional notoriety through such resources as UMI's *Dissertation Abstracts,* circulated 3.25 times during the same 4-year period. From UMI we know that few dissertations were requested often enough to warrant royalty payments prior to 2000. However, once online, this traditional inactivity gives way. ETDs are available to a wider community of users beyond the hours the library is open and are used far more frequently than were the paper versions. See Figure 1 for U.S. requests for VT ETDs.

The most popular ETD in 1997 was accessed 9,923 times (*Analysis and Reduction of Moire Patterns in Scanned Halftone Pictures* by Xiangdong Liu,

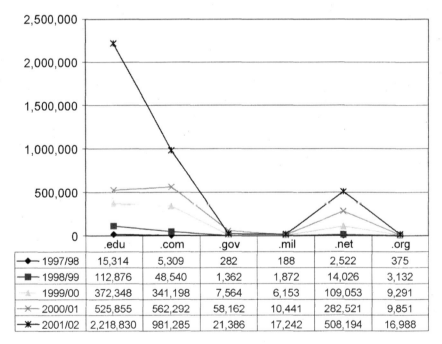

FIGURE 1   Requests for VT ETDs from U.S. Domains, 1997/98–2001/02.

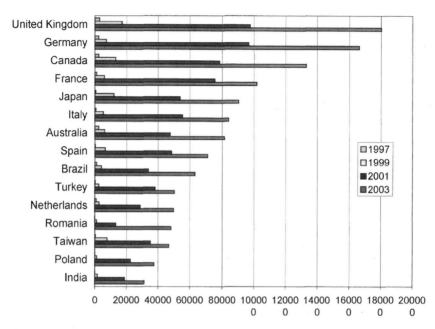

FIGURE 2 International requests for VT ETDs, 1997–2003.

Ph.D. 1996) (see links from http://scholar.lib.vt.edu/theses/data/some-facts.html#popular). In 1998 the most popular ETD was accessed 75,340 times (*Advanced Time Domain Sensing for Active Structural Acoustic Control* by Julien Maillard, Ph.D. 1997). In 1999, the most accessed ETD, *Novel Adaptive Array Algorithms and Their Impact on Cellular System Capacity* by Paul Petrus (Ph.D. 1997), was downloaded 22,682 times. Fiscal year 2000/01 saw Taehyung Park's ETD (Ph.D. 1998), *Network Design and Analysis Problems in Telecommunication, Location–Allocation, and Intelligent Transportation Systems Degree,* downloaded 25,982 times. Computer log files reveal that not only does the library provide increased access to its ETDs, but its clientele is broader than the local community, reaching not only government domains, but also the international community. See Figure 2 for international requests for VT ETDs.

UNIVERSITYWIDE COST SAVINGS

ETDs can also be economical for students to produce and for universities to process. When libraries or computing centers provide the necessary software, students do not have to purchase it, nor do they have to purchase special paper (rag or bond) or have multiple copies printed. Students may be required to pay archiving fees, but these can replace the binding fees they previously paid.

Reduced manual processing results in real savings for libraries. Even without deriving the cataloging record from the online text, Virginia Tech estimated that eliminating shelving, circulating, binding, and mailing costs could save 73.3% of the cost of processing paper theses and dissertations. Additionally, increased use does not require increased library staff time because ETDs do not have to be bound, labeled, security stripped, barcoded, checked out, checked in, shelved, and reshelved. Computer programs have been written that "move" submitted works through the approval process to availability, including making security copies and archiving them. Instead of mailing UMI a copy to be microfilmed, programmatically generated email messages announce that another ETD is available for processing (i.e., downloading, printing, microfilming, distribution, etc.). Automated scripts generate email notifications to authors and committee chairs when the students/authors' works have been approved.

Another problem avoided by ETDs is the one title–one user limitations of works on paper and microfilm. One of the true advantages of digital libraries is access to information when library buildings are closed, when someone has taken the volume from the shelf, and when a work is not returned when recalled. While theses and dissertations were not in tremendous demand (see circulation averages above), the one you wanted always seemed to be the one missing from the shelf when you arrived at the library. In addition to constant access, an ETD is simultaneously accessible by multiple users.

Libraries still need to provide access to ETDs from within their buildings, however, for those who do not have Internet and Web access in their homes or workplaces. Libraries at research universities also often provide faster downloading times due to high-speed campus networks. Throughout their systems, research libraries have installed Internet workstations (including at on and off campus branch libraries) for students to access completed ETDs; this often includes supporting computer labs for authors to prepare ETDs. University faculty must also have access to both works in progress and completed works, typically through their office computers on campus networks.

SOFTWARE STANDARDS

In the future, libraries may be the principal locale for the variety of software necessary to read all aspects of an ETD. Standards for software and multimedia used by ETD authors are developing by default, rather than through mandates or requirements. See Table 1 for recommended multimedia formats used in ETDs.

TABLE 1   Glossary of Multimedia Formats Used in VT ETDs

File type	Extension	Format
AIFF: Macintosh audio standard	**aif**	**audio**
ASCII: American Standard for Information Interchange	txt	text
Audio Video Interleaved (Microsoft)	**avi**	**video**
Authorware	**a5r, a5e, a5***	multimedia authoring
AutoCAD	dxf	
CD-ROM/XA	pics	
Compact Disc Digital Audio	[CD-DA]	audio
Computer Graphics Metafile	cgm	image (vector)
Device-independent bitmap (Windows)	bmp	image
Director	mmm, pics	interactive graphics/Web
Document (Microsoft)	doc	text
Encapsulated Postscript	eps	image
ETD markup language	[ETD-ML]	text
Excel	xls, xcl	spreadsheet, chart
Extensible Markup Language	xml	text
Graphic Image File	**gif**	**image**
Hypertext Markup Language	**html, htm**	**text**
Joint Photographic Experts Group	**jpeg, jpg**	**image**
Macintosh sound files	snd	audio
Microsoft Audio	wav	audio
Microsoft Excel	xls, xcl	spreadsheet, chart
Motion Picture Experts	**mpeg, mpg**	**video**
Moving Pictures and Associated Audio for Digital Storage Media	mpeg3, mp3	audio
Musical Instrument Digital Interface	midi	audio
PhotoCD (Kodak)	**pcd**	image
Portable Document Format	**pdf**	**text, image**
QuickTime	**qt, mov**	**video**
Standard Generalized Markup Language	**sgml, sgm**	**text**
Tagged Image/Interchange File Format	**tiff, tif**	**image**

TABLE 1 Continued

File type	Extension	Format
Virtual Reality Markup Language		VRML
Wave: Microsoft/Windows audio	**wav**	**audio**
Medium	**Recommended**	**Others used**
Image	bmp, gif, jpg, tif	cgm, dxf, pdf, PhotoCD, eps
Sound	aif, wav	CD-DA, CD-ROM/XA, midi, MPEG-2, snd, mcd
Movie	avi, mov, mpg, mpeg, qt	mjpeg
Other	SGML, XML	Macromedia (Authorware, Director)
Text	pdf, html, UNICODE	ASCII, SGML, ETD-ML, txt

Recommended formats are in bold. Formats that authors have included are not highlighted.

Some library users are uncomfortable when libraries have only ETDs and do not have additional copies in other formats (paper and/or microfilm). Over time they will become accustomed to this situation, especially when they realize the benefits that online works have, such as multiple copies of every work being stored in multiple places, both on and off site. The current trade-off is that libraries stop losing materials that are regularly mutilated, destroyed, and stolen, resulting in expensive replacements or elimination of the works from the library's collections. With ETDs, improved security measures easily become standard operating procedures. The security of multiple copies of every electronic work can help alleviate the tension created by not having paper on the shelf (see also below).

TIMELY ACCESS TO INFORMATION

Once the appropriate university unit, often the Graduate School, completes the evaluation of a thesis or dissertation, ETDs can become accessible immediately. Typically, hard copy theses and dissertations are bound and cataloged before being shelved and made available to the public; this usually takes a few months. Improved and timely access to ETDs is a result of libraries rethinking processes and workflow and creating Internet and Web access.

Libraries in the Networked Digital Library of Theses and Dissertations (NDLTD) and other institutions have constructed databases for ETDs so that access by author, title, and other distinctive elements from the title page information can be programmatically derived for online user browsing. (Some links to these are available at http://www.ndltd.org/members/.) In addition, a library's database of ETDs can be reindexed frequently so users can search, typically, on any word from the title page and abstract, if not the entire document. Cataloging records for theses and dissertations have improved. The records can include more information without more work by the catalogers, who can copy and paste in authors' abstracts. Some libraries have given the authors responsibility for providing keywords for indexing so that catalogers do not spend the extensive time often required to assign authoritative subject headings from controlled vocabularies. Many library systems can programmatically derive the cataloging records directly from the digital works, and with more computing power some institutions will index entire ETDs and every word in these works will be a point of discovery.

SECURITY

Prior to accepting the first ETD in 1995 and with paper copies stored in the university archives, security was known to be an extremely important issue. With Virginia Tech's decision in 1997 to require electronic submission of theses and dissertations came the decision that the library would receive, provide access to, and preserve only one format—digital. Fortunately, the library had foreseen the need to have secure and unimpeachable archives, having addressed the problems years earlier with ejournals and EReserves.

Security begins with authors being verified that they are, indeed, students of the degree-granting institution. This function can be easily incorporated when students are supplied with a PID—personal identifier—and password at the beginning of their graduate careers. With this already being a standard requirement for remote access to many licensed library resources and a function of campuses that support electronic mail services for their university communities, the library does not need to establish and maintain a separate system just to verify students submitting ETDs. Kerberos, a popular verification system already in use at many universities, can provide secure use by qualified systems personnel in the library.

The personnel who evaluate and approve the final work must also be verified and supplied with secure access to submitted ETDs. We have established separate and unique passwords for graduate school personnel who perform this function. Students can alter submitted works just until their works receive final approval. At that point, the work is considered a finished product, just like a bound volume. However, there is the occasional need to make a small change to the completed work—correcting typographical errors on the title page, for example. In the paper system, theses reviewers usually would ask the author to submit a new page. Now, appropriate personnel can make changes when deemed necessary by the approving unit.

Virginia Tech's Graduate School personnel must have PIDs and passwords that allow them not only to approve (and, therefore, store) the work, but to alter the type of access accorded the work. Typically, when ETDs are submitted for approval, authors designate the categories of access for their works—unlimited, limited, or withhold access. Limited and denied access categories will change over time to open access, and an ETD administrator must be able to change the level of access when needed. At least, initially administrators typically want changes in access to be a manual process so that opening an ETD to worldwide access has the full consent of at least the author, and often, the approval of the author's ETD advisor as well.

ARCHIVING

While libraries improve workflow and take advantage of the ease of providing prompt access to ETDs, they also have the continuing responsibility of maintaining this access for the long term and of archiving these works in their final and approved form. At some universities, computing centers or other information systems units are responsible for long-term archiving (and security). Libraries that have a tradition of strong, internal systems support, such as the University Libraries at Virginia Tech, will more readily assume responsibility for preserving ETDs and other original digital works. Many libraries will do so out of a greater sense of responsibility than is typically found in their information systems units (e.g., computing centers), which are not accustomed to providing long-term preservation/archiving services simultaneously with constant customer support.

Maintaining the server for ETDs need not be a huge added responsibility for libraries that already maintain computers for storage and access to other digital works. Virginia Tech's Digital Library and Archives (DLA, formerly the Scholarly Communications Project), for example, provides online journals, digital campus publications, and the electronic reserve system. Therefore, additional equipment, software, and staff were not necessary to begin an ETD project (i.e., to receive and process about 2 years' worth of voluntary submissions and to meet the needs of the first few years of storage and access). As universities joined the NDLTD, the programs written by DLA staff to process ETDs at Virginia Tech became available to NDLTD members without charge. Additionally, Adobe provided early NDLTD members with free Acrobat software and later decided to continue this practice for members of the organization.

A new challenge with ETDs is archiving and long-term preservation. Paper and microforms have known shelf lives. We know about problems with computer-generated works being stored off-line and the software and hardware that created them becoming museum showpieces, rather than working systems. We are also aware of early problems with compact disks that had labels that destroyed disk readability. One way to avoid these problems (considered an indefinite solution) is to not take ETDs offline—let them live and be actively available on a public server. One of the best security and archiving practices is for multiple agencies to reciprocate online archives, and the most effective way of doing this is through "mirroring." But well-managed, time-delayed copies can also effectively back up online resources. While this has not yet been formalized, it is a concept under discussion between several members of the NDLTD.

Some people are uncomfortable when ETDs are available only through proprietary software such as that from Adobe. The problem is not actually the format, however, because the code for reading Acrobat's PDF (portable document format) is publicly available. The real problem may be when improved formats become available and the resources to migrate existing works to the new formats are not available. Many of us are operating on the "good faith" promises from our university administrators that, as needed, resources will be found to restore information resources such as ETDs, truly unique works, and products of the home institutions.

Libraries are also working with their computer science departments where research and development in digital libraries holds great promise for the future. But even so, the fact that PDF is a pervasive format used heavily by our federal government as well as many commercial publishers means that university libraries will not be alone in trying to solve future migration issues. I believe that we will not be in a "misery loves company" situation but rather one of "many hands make light work."

LIBRARIES AS TRAINING FACILITIES

While the library is a traditional source of information, it has not necessarily established itself as the locale for computer training. This, of course, is changing not because of, but along with, the advent of ETDs. There are typically two types of library computer labs: those supporting access and those supporting training and resource development. Some libraries provide both, separately or together. Among those that provide access to digital works, printing often becomes more cost recovery based and centralized, with payment often handled by an auxiliary service in much the same way as photocopying—when it is a nonprofit, fee-based service.

Libraries often house computer labs. Many labs have evolved into busy environments where students send and receive email, search databases, access the Internet and the Web, as well as prepare files with word processors and spreadsheet programs, sometimes converting them to PDF. More sophisticated labs also provide programs for creating and manipulating graphics, digitizing audio recordings, etc. It can be "one-stop shopping," but often these labs do not provide trained staff, whose responsibilities include helping users learn new software programs. Many universities provide additional computer labs that serve as classrooms for instructor-directed training and development of individual projects.

PREPARING AUTHORS

Library computer labs now provide the opportunities for librarians to work with graduate students to assist them in using appropriate software and Internet resources to develop their class assignments and, eventually, their ETDs. This is an expanded role, but it is not inconceivable that librarians would assist their clientele throughout the information cycle, from discovering ideas; communicating them through text, graphics, and audio programs; and submitting them for online access—whether by their instructors, by journal editors, or as finished products to be read by library and Internet users. In addition, library labs can familiarize graduate students with asynchronous collaboration tools, enabling them to work with local as well as remote readers. One might assume that as graduate students become more sophisticated computer users (as are today's incoming university freshmen), libraries will perhaps provide authoring spaces with less professional intervention.

Graduate students who develop ETDs will be better prepared to enter academia in the Information Age. They will be more sophisticated digital library users, accustomed to creating online resources in addition to accessing them. They will be better prepared to submit articles electronically if they have developed and submitted their graduate works similarly. Libraries can be the locale where the full cycle of information takes place, from creation to access.

CONCLUSION

Libraries expand their traditional resources and services through digital initiatives such as electronic theses and dissertations. Because they generally are already providing their users with online information resources through commercial vendors, it is a relatively easy progression to receive and provide access to locally created resources. Servers, programmers, and Web interfaces can be modified to accommodate receipt, storage, and access to ETDs without requiring major capital outlay, as was done at Virginia Tech.

The scholarly community (as well as government and commercial users) should be praising university libraries for reducing by months the time it takes to process new theses and dissertations. The speed with which such information becomes available, combined with easy access on the Internet and Web, has resulted in many graduate works getting early exposure and the use they deserve. While many are anxious about the unanswered questions remaining (such as the "shelf" life of online works), many more are satisfied that ETDs are receiving greater use. Today's ETDs are being far more widely used while libraries continue to store thousands of theses and dissertations that languish and gather dust from lack of use.

By November 2001, over 100 universities throughout the United States and internationally had committed to electronic theses and dissertations by joining the NDLTD. Their libraries and others are adapting traditional procedures and workflow to incorporate local authors' direct submissions into timely, worldwide access to ETDs. Libraries are leading the way, providing training to authors as well as access to researchers to create effective ETDs. Libraries are also addressing the difficult issues of security and preservation. Clearly, without libraries ETDs would not have evolved into the timely resources that they are today and academia would not be resolving the issues crucial to digital libraries.

23

Electronic Scholarship and Citations: Documentation and ETDs

Janice R. Walker

Georgia Southern University
Statesboro, Georgia

Although copies of theses and dissertations have long been available to researchers through interlibrary loan services or through such commercial services as Bell and Howell Learning Company (formerly known as University Microforms International, or UMI), online publication of these works makes them quicker and easier to search and access. As a recent article in *The Chronicle of Higher Education* says, "scholarship stands to gain as it becomes easier for more scholars to read the latest dissertations and theses." (1) For instance, Virginia Tech's Scholarly Communications Project, with over 2800 electronic theses and dissertations (ETDs), published on its site as of 2001, boasts some ETDs that have already received thousands of hits (or visits). (2) Obviously, few paper Ph.D. or master's theses receive this kind of attention. Increased accessibility means that more and more of these works may actually be read, which, in turn, "is going to make us pay more attention to the quality of what gets in our dissertations." (3)

Many graduate departments and committees remain conservative, however; even those scholars who take advantage of electronic formats must produce work that will be approved by their graduate committees. It is unlikely, therefore, that the institution of hypertext ETDs will effect radical change in the substance or the form of these works in the near future. Graduate schools have long provided guidelines for formatting theses and dissertations along very traditional lines, and scholars have come to depend on these traditional formats to help determine the authority of a given text. Sloppy formatting may often be equated—consciously or not—with sloppy thinking. However, for the most part, these formats were developed for print publication. To date, no standards for producing and formatting electronic documents have been agreed upon. One source that is attempting to help formulate such guidelines for electronic publications is *The Columbia Guide to Online Style*, which argues, "If the production and dissemination of online academic writing is truly to redefine scholarship, it must first successfully negotiate a transitional period of legitimization. . . . Standardization of online style is a necessary first step in negotiating this transition." (4)

Developing standards for how to cite ETDs published electronically—on the World Wide Web, on CD-ROM, via UMI, or other electronic forms—is, therefore, one step toward authorizing these important works of scholarship. Moreover, students producing ETDs also need guidelines for documenting sources used in *producing* electronic scholarship, guidelines that make sense for online publication and acknowledge the differences between writing for print and writing for electronic distribution. In addition to standards for citation of ETDs in print scholarship, authors of ETDs may need to cite graphics, links, video and audio files, frames, document information screens, document source code, other ETDs, or whatever elements they may include that have not been addressed by any of the major documentation styles. In this chapter, I present some suggestions for how to cite electronic sources based on Columbia Online Style (COS) as presented in *The Columbia Guide to Online Style* by the author and Todd Taylor, as well as some suggestions for ways that authors of ETDs and other forms of electronic scholarship can handle links to volatile electronically published sources that may be prone to appearing, disappearing, or morphing at a moment's notice (or less).

AUTHORIZING SCHOLARSHIP IN THE ELECTRONIC AGE

Requiring electronic publication of theses and dissertations may ultimately lead to changes in how we define the dissertation itself and, hence, in our definition and conception of scholarly publication. According to Gary A. Olson and Julie Drew, "the fact remains that the conventionally published scholarly monograph continues to be the cultural capital with which to obtain tenure and promotion (and sometimes even a job) in the academy." (5) How will hiring committees and tenure and promotion review committees value electronic publication of these works? Even though more universities—teachers and students—are using the Internet as an integral part of the educational environment, for the most part electronic sources are approached with extreme caution by scholars. For example, the Modern Language Association (MLA) cautions authors that "Electronic media . . . lack agreed-on means of organizing works. Moreover, electronic texts are not as fixed and stable as their print counterparts. References to electronic works therefore must provide more information than print citations generally offer." (6)

MLA's bias against electronic sources is, of course, readily apparent: "These recommendations are aimed not at specialists in academic computing but primarily at scholars in the field of literature and language who use ideas and facts from electronic sources *to complement those derived from traditional print sources*" (emphasis added). This privileging of print (or print-based) scholarship extends to their treatment of how to cite electronically accessed work; MLA limits their recommendations for how to cite electronic material to those types of sites that have obvious "scholarly" credibility.

Thus, most current style manuals include only a limited number of examples for citations of electronic sources. The most current version of the APA manual now lists 16 types of electronic sources (up from only 6 in its previous edition), (7) the newly revised *MLA Style Manual* contains 48, (8) and other style manuals, such as the influential *Chicago Manual of Style*, include few if any examples of newly emerging electronic publications. (9) Furthermore, with the exception of *The Columbia Guide to Online Style,* which includes 63 examples organized by type of access, these manuals present electronic sources in a way that presupposes the superiority of certain types of publications (i.e., print-based ones) over others (electronic publications). By treating electronic sources differently from print-based ones for purposes of citation and providing only a limited number of examples, they effectively discourage use of these works.

The *MLA Style Manual*, for example, presents electronic sources based on the credibility of the site that supports their publication. That is, they privilege those works that are sponsored by already-recognized organizations or institutions. Of course, noting whether an online publication is sponsored by credible authorities can be useful in helping to evaluate the information it contains. Nonetheless, differentiating between types of sources based on a site's sponsorship can often be difficult for researchers, especially in new media such as online spaces. Obviously this is an attempt to authorize certain types of sources as more credible than others, just as in print-based work we privilege works published by a university press over those available from commercial or vanity presses. However, by so doing, these styles ignore that important information can be found even in such unlikely sources as comic books and video games, as well as personal home pages on the WWW, and all of these sources need to be adequately cited in our scholarship.

The complexity of most recommendations for citing electronic scholarship further discourages their use. Should authors link directly to discrete files or to the main page of a Web site? Is a journal published on the Web merely a copy of a print journal (in which case, researchers should attempt to locate the original—or printed—source)? Or is it a discrete edition that requires inclusion of previous (print) publication information in addition to the electronic publication information? What about a Web site that collects essays or other works of various authors? How is this different from a print anthology or collection? These questions point not only to the need for providing adequate guidelines to authors for citing as many types of electronic works as they may choose to use in their scholarship, but also to the need to recognize that new publishing spaces may require new methods of determining credibility. As universities explore online publication of theses and dissertations, we need to be sure that these important works won't be overlooked by future scholars simply because they are published in bits and bytes rather than ink.

CITING ETDs

One step in authorizing ETDs is, of course, to provide guidelines for citing them in other works, including guidelines for citing them in work published online as well as in print. While most of the major documentation styles have attempted to deal with citation of electronic sources, these suggestions usually presume that they will be cited in print, or at least in print-based, publications. To date, even software such as Bibliocite and EndNote, designed to automate the formatting of bibliographic citations, also follow guidelines established for traditional print-based forms. Document style and citation formats are intimately connected, however, and any style guidelines proposed must consider the possibilities as well as the limitations of the publication medium. For example, Christina Haas notes that "Writers' representation of their texts' semantic content may . . . be tied to spatial structures, including page layout, paragraph shape, or size of manuscript. Spatial location does not remain constant on a computer screen (because of scrolling), and the computer text is two dimensional, not having the additional spatial cues of the print text's physical pages. " (10) What this means is that, unless the author has designated such spatial clues as page, section, or paragraph numbers, these elements of a traditional citation may be meaningless in online texts. While some style guidelines advocate counting the number of paragraphs, replacing the page number in the citation with the paragraph number, this could prove unwieldy for lengthy documents. Furthermore, it may be unnecessary since most electronic applications include search or find features that can easily locate key words or phrases within a document or file. COS thus recommends treating electronic sources similarly to nonpaginated printed sources, including only the author's last name (or the author's last name and the year of publication for scientific styles) in the in-text reference.

Other features of document style and citation also need to be reconsidered for electronically published works such as ETDs. The printing press and modern word processing technology have allowed for the use of different fonts, colors, and other textual features, or signs, that in turn impact the meanings of these signs. For instance, underlining in print texts is often used to indicate titles, foreign words, or terms—that is, text that should be italicized. However, MLA is now alone in continuing to provide examples in its published style manual and Web sites that use underlining rather than italics to format these elements (11). By so doing, it contributes to the confusion over the "proper" way to format print documents, and further confusion is possible when authors create work for electronic publication. Many newer word processors, as well as hypertexts published on the World Wide Web, use underlining to designate links between files or parts of files. Underlining such textual features as titles could, therefore, confuse the reader. COS avoids this problem by recommending that these features be italicized rather than underlined.

The use of angle brackets to surround email addresses and Uniform Resource Locators (URLs, or the address of a site on the WWW) in some citation formats is also seriously problematic. In some hypertexts, for instance, angle brackets are reserved characters, used to denote tags such as are specified in document-type definitions (DTDs) that define the appearance or elements of a document. Authors must therefore include specific codes (&lt and &gt) in the file in order for the browser to display the < and > characters. This adds to the already complex task of coding a hypertext document, while adding no functionality whatsoever. Additionally, many word processors now make the use of angle brackets to surround URLs difficult (if not impossible) even for printed manuscripts created using these programs. For example, in recent versions of Microsoft Word, URLs are automatically reformatted as hypertext links. The word processor changes the color (and sometimes the font size) of the text and underlines the URL. The quick-correct feature (the default setting for the software application) perceives the angle brackets as an error and deletes them. Authors may very well follow MLA's recommendations for formatting a citation including a URL, typing:

<http://www.cas.usf.edu>

only to find that, in their finished paper, the URL appears as blue underlined text and the angle brackets have somehow mysteriously disappeared. Again,

COS avoids this problem: since angle brackets add no functionality anyway, COS does not use them.

Even such features of print documents as double spacing and hanging indents used to format bibliographies in most styles can be difficult to simulate in electronically published files. Further, these features can actually be counterproductive. One reason for double spacing printed manuscripts is to make the text easier to read; in a hypertext, attempting to force double spacing or hanging indents can actually have the opposite effect by interfering with the browser's automatic word-wrap capability. Of course, these features can be easily retained in PDF files, and DTDs can define such structures if we so desire, but I would argue that we should seriously consider whether or not such typographical elements as underlining, double-spacing, hanging indents, and other features of traditional print-based styles can or should be preserved for electronic venues. Nonetheless, it is important for us to remember that the same tenets should hold true for electronic texts as apply to print-based ones: scholarly citations should provide sufficient information for the reader to be able to access the source as efficiently as possible.

In *The Columbia Guide to Online Style*, the authors present a format based on five principles of citation style—access, intellectual property, economy, standardization, and transparency—which, while continuing to recognize the logic of the major humanities and scientific styles, also recognizes the uniqueness of many electronic publications (11–15). The purpose of citations, as noted previously, is first and foremost to enable the reader to access the original sources consulted by an author. By translating the elements of a print citation in a way that makes sense for electronic sources, COS facilitates this access. For example, for sources published on the World Wide Web, a key element of citation is the URL, or Internet address. Since Internet sources are often missing such elements as the name of the author, a readily discernible title, or page designations, COS offers advice to locate or translate these elements. In place of an author's name, for instance, a source may be cited using the author's login name (if known) or, instead, the name of a Web master, compiler, or other person responsible for maintaining a site. In place of a designated title, it may be necessary to use a file name or information contained in the document source code, document information screen, or workflow record, if available. Previous publication information, including the date of publication, is included, if known, along with the electronic publication information (including the protocol, i.e., http://, ftp://, etc., and the electronic address; the name of the sponsoring site, if applicable; the date of electronic publication or last modification, if known; and any directories, links, keywords, or other commands necessary to access the source). COS also includes a designation of the date of access, enclosed in parentheses in recognition that this date is not part of the document, even though, often, it may be the only identification of the specific "edition" of an electronic source being cited. That is, since electronic sources may change or disappear without notice, the only assertion that the author can make about the bibliographic information is that it was correct as of the date the author last accessed the source.

In humanities-style papers, such as those following MLA guidelines, the basic COS format for a bibliographic entry is:

> Author's Last Name, First Name. "Title of Document." *Title of Complete Work* [if applicable]. Version or File Number [if applicable]. Document date or date of last revision [if different from access date]. Protocol and address along with the access path or directories (date of access).

In scientific styles such as APA, COS recommends the following basic format:

> Author's Last Name, Initial(s). (Date of document [if different from date accessed]). Title of document. *Title of complete work* [if applicable]. Version or File number [if applicable]. (Edition or revision [if applicable]). Protocol and address along with the access path or directories (date of access).

Various suggestions have been made to ensure the availability of the information necessary to cite ETDs. The Networked Digital Library of Theses and Dissertations (NDLTD), a group of member universities started by a project team at Virginia Tech, provides guidelines to students for formatting ETDs that include specifications to facilitate archiving and online publication. For example, author and submission information are contained in workflow records created as part of the ETD submission process and provide important cataloging and search information essential for adequate citation of these works in other scholarship. (12) MLA's Committee on Computers and Emerging Technologies has attempted to address this need as well by recommending that authors of hypertexts create an information page with the author's name, the title of the work, the date of publication and/or the date of last modification or revision, the document URL, the sponsor and purpose of the site, any software requirements, site configuration, and other information that might be useful to the reader. (13) And COS recommends that authors include necessary information in "meta-tags" in hypertext documents as well as stipulating publication information to be included in documents intended for print as well as electronic publication. Obviously, we need some standardization of these recommendations in order to avoid confusion about which guidelines authors should follow. At any rate, providing this type of information not only aids researchers in citing ETDs in other works, but also helps to certify the credibility of electronically published work (including ETDs) for future researchers.

EXPANDING THE (SCHOLARLY) WORLD

Many schools are debating whether or not to allow authors of ETDs to include links to external sources or sources not contained within the ETD itself. Since online sources may change or disappear without notice, including such links could adversely affect electronically published scholarship that depends on them. However, limiting students to only those sources that can be guaranteed to continue to be available could also limit the students' ability to explore new areas or to explore older areas in new ways. For purposes of inclusion in ETDs, therefore, committees may want to consider ways to ensure that necessary resources will be available to future researchers.

One suggestion is to require students to maintain digital or paper copies, as appropriate, of Web pages, synchronous or asynchronous communications, or other material used in the ETD. Capturing a copy of the screen, keeping copies of logs, photos of devices, or videos of processes may also be valuable in this regard, as one reviewer of this article pointed out. However, requiring students to maintain these files could complicate further the work of librarians or other agents responsible for archiving and cataloging this information, since student files may be difficult to access years later. Will librarians be required to track down the authors of 10-year-old theses and dissertations in order to locate these materials? Moreover, it would complicate the task of future researchers who need access to this material to support information or arguments in ETDs, thus effectively negating at least one important benefit of publishing theses and dissertations on the WWW in the first place—making access to them quicker and easier. Students could, of course, be required to obtain permission for publication (or republication) of these sources, but limiting students only to those sources for which such permissions are granted could also be restrictive, preventing authors from including important information for which permission is refused. Although the Fair Use doctrine allows for certain usages of copyrighted material for purposes of scholarship, criticism, or research, determination of fair use is predicated upon the amount and substantiality of the use. (14) Thus, without the express consent of their authors, inclusion of copies of source materials in ETDs, even as appendices, clearly constitutes a violation of copyright law. Of course, digital libraries also can be set up to control access such that an appendix to an ETD, for example, could have a data file that is only available through password access according to an arrangement with the copyright holder, enforced by the digital libraries, similar to interlibrary loan programs.

(15) However, yet again, we are faced with adding complexity to the library's task of archiving and ensuring appropriate access to this information.

Instead of limiting the types of sources that may be used in ETDs or imposing requirements that may be difficult—or even illegal—to fulfill, students could be required to include a description of information contained in any outside sources that are likely to become unavailable. Such annotations would supply information about the source and the author's intention in including it. For example,

> The link *Agrippa: A Book of the Dead* originally pointed to http://www.astro.utoronto.ca/~reid/htmldocs/agrippa.html, the text of a "book" by William Gibson and artist Dennis Ashbaugh that, although disguised as a mild-mannered traditional text, ceases to exist upon being read. This book, then, is an example of the ephemerality of all text, both traditional print and hypertext. (16)

While it would obviously be preferable to guarantee access to sources used in creation of scholarship, no such guarantees have ever been possible. Many classical works contain references to no longer extant sources, and the Internet has made it likely that, at least in the short term, we may find our sources subject to the same ephemerality. The Library of Congress, as well as other libraries, consortiums, and scholarly institutions, are, of course, attempting to address this and find ways to ensure the availability of Internet sources to future scholars. But until such time as a reliable means of archiving here-today, gone-tomorrow sites can be accomplished, providing an annotated bibliography of sources may be our best option.

Online publication of theses and dissertations that use student-based (or person-based) research, including research conducted online with human subjects and/or private, or semi-private, information in such sites as MOOs, chat rooms, or newsgroups, also may require more stringent review by Institutional Review Boards (IRBs) than their print counterparts. Even though print copies of theses and dissertations are available through interlibrary loan programs or services such as UMI, the time, costs, and difficulty involved often made it less likely that these works would be read by more than a handful of researchers. Electronic publication of theses and dissertations, however, makes these works easier to access and may therefore require the same conformance to copyright and IRB restrictions as required by print publishers.

NEW FORMS, NEW STANDARDS

The use of multimedia elements in ETDs also deserves further consideration. Currently, in most online applications, users must have the appropriate software to access or view many elements of electronic files. For example, reading PDF files requires that users locate, download, and install the Adobe Acrobat Reader; sound files and video files may also require appropriate applications such as Apple Quick Time or Real Audio. Many of these applications are available for free downloading on the WWW, or some applications can be embedded into the ETD file itself, thereby simplifying the process for readers. Nonetheless, the necessity to consider how a reader will access information in ETDs further complicates the already-complicated process of authoring these works of scholarship in any form—print or electronic. Of course, the goal of the NDLTD is, as Ed Fox has pointed out, is to "promote graduate education." That is, "students learn by doing. Enhanced access is an extra benefit." (17) Nonetheless, since access to this software can sometimes be difficult (not to mention costly) as authors use a wide variety of formats requiring a wide variety of software applications, and as some applications may require higher-end hardware in order to use them, the task of ensuring access to the necessary software to read ETDs may very well fall to libraries as well. While requiring that students use specific formats for multimedia would help to simplify what could otherwise be a daunting task, deciding which formats to require may be difficult in the short run as changes in technology and literacy practices in the academy continue to evolve. The inclusion of multimedia *not* submitted in digital form is also a concern for libraries as they question how to distribute this material in an electronic environment. Do libraries need to take on the responsibility for transforming VHS video into digital forms, for example? Most interlibrary loan programs do not currently allow users to borrow multimedia materials, which may run counter to the whole idea of increased distribution of dissertations, if indeed increased distribution is a goal. ETDs may very well represent a move to make the graduate thesis more than a mere scholarly exercise for students, to make it what it was originally intended to be—the first truly scholarly work by a new member of the profession. But it is also entirely possible that these works could quickly fall prey to the same obsolescence as last year's new software unless there is some agreement as to which formats will be supported.

CONCLUSION

Electronic publication of theses and dissertations, like electronic publication of other scholarly works, brings to light new questions that need to be answered. For instance, although the NDLTD offers options to students designed to ensure that electronic publication of theses and dissertations will not interfere with students' ability to publish their work in more traditional print venues, nonetheless, institutions must still consider how electronic publication will be viewed by hiring and tenure-and-promotion review committees.

According to a recent issue of *The Chronicle*, some academic publishers consider online publication to be "great advertising" (18); however, as electronic publications become more the norm for scholarly journals and academic publishers, it is likely that this optimistic vision may need to be reconsidered. As of September 2001, over 26% of authors at Virginia Tech had refused to grant permission to distribute their writings electronically beyond their campus, possibly concerned that publishers would refuse their related work since electronic distribution might be considered prior publication, thus negating one reason for ETDs. (19) Obviously, we may need to reconsider our definitions of "scholarly publishing" in the face of changes in the technologies of reading, writing, research, and publication.

At any rate, developing guidelines to help evaluate scholarship, whether it is published in traditional or nontraditional venues, can help as we try to find ways to bridge the gap between existing forms of literacy and new practices. While obviously it is not possible to concretize standards for emerging media, some guidelines as to which formats to use for authoring ETDs, for publishing them, for multimedia elements included in them, and for citing them in other works are nonetheless necessary to help students, graduate committees, hiring committees, and other evaluators deal with these changes in ways that do not stifle new developments but instead recognize that new forms of literacy (and scholarship) are not created anew from primordial matter but continue to exist side by side with existing forms. Ensuring that documentation styles adequately address the citation of ETDs in future scholarship as well as the sources used in the creation of these works is one mini-step toward ensuring that these works are more than mere curiosities.

REFERENCES

1. Young, J. R. (December 13, 2001). Requiring Theses in Digital Form: The First Year at Virginia Tech. *The Chronicle of Higher Education, February 13, 1998.* http://chronicle.com/che-data/articles.dir/art-44.dir/issue-23.dir/23a02901.htm
2. Virginia Tech's Scholarly Communications Project, "Some Facts About VT ETDs," (updated November 28, 2001), http://scholar.lib.vt.edu/theses/data/somefacts.html (December 13, 2001). The Virginia Tech site notes further that over 3500 ETDs have been submitted to and approved by the Graduate School as of September 7, 2001.
3. See note 1.
4. Walker, J. R., Taylor, T. (1998). *The Columbia Guide to Online Style.* New York: Columbia University Press, pp 4.
5. Olson, G. A., Drew, J. (September 1998). (Re) Reenvisioning the Dissertation in English Studies. *College English* 61(1):59.
6. Gibaldi, J. (1998). *MLA Style Manual and Guide to Scholarly Publishing.* 2nd ed. New York: Modern Language Association, pp 209.

7. *Publication Manual of the American Psychological Association.* (2001). 5th ed. Washington, DC: APA.

8. See note 6, 210.

9. The 15th edition of *The Chicago Manual of Style.* (2003). Just as other style manuals have done, it also offers more models for more types of electronic sources.

10. Haas, C. (1996). *Writing Technology: Studies on the Materiality of Literacy.* Mahwah, NJ: Lawrence Erlbaum, pp. 127.

11. The 5th edition of the APA *Publication Manual* now recommends that authors italicize book titles, suggesting that underlining be used only by authors composing with a typewriter to designate text that publishers should italicize, unless otherwise instructed by editors.

12. Kipp, N. (December 13, 2001). Schema for SGML ETD Workflow Record. *Networked Digital Library of Theses and Dissertations (NDLTD), November 7, 1997.* http://ndltd.org/workflow/workflow.htm

13. MLA Committee on Computers and Emerging Technologies in Teaching and Research (CCET). (December 13, 2001). *Draft Guidelines for Providing Web-Site Information, 19 July 1998.* http://www.mla.org/beta/reports/ccet/ccet_webguidelines.htm

14. United States Code, Title 17, Section 107. (December 13, 2001). *Legal Information Institute*, Cornell Law School. http://www4.law.cornell.edu/uscode/unframed/17/107.html

15. I am indebted to Ed Fox for noting this information on access controls in his review of this article.

16. Walker, Taylor. *Columbia Guide*, 187 (see note 4).

17. See note 15.

18. Winkler, K. J. (September 12, 1997). Academic Presses Look to the Internet to Save Scholarly Monographs. *The Chronicle of Higher Education*, A18.

19. See note 2.

24

Indexing and Accessing Electronic Theses and Dissertations: Some Concerns for Users

Ilene Frank and Walter C. Rowe
University of South Florida
Tampa, Florida

Once a dissertation or thesis is completed and the degree granted, how do others know it exists? Libraries have a long history of housing and cataloging the intellectual output of the graduate degree process. Catalogers have worked in online environments since the early 1970s, first sharing cataloging records, then placing them into online databases using standards for input such as the MARC (Machine Readable Cataloging) format, Dublin Core, and Text Encoding Initiative (TEI). The transition from drawers of printed catalog cards to online databases is part of an evolutionary process of information retrieval based upon existing library practices.

How then does the electronic format for theses and dissertations affect the effort to describe these items? This paper will focus on a general overview of issues involved in providing access through the cataloging process for electronic theses and dissertations (ETDs). We will discuss cataloging issues from the point of view of the user rather than the cataloger. This paper is based in part on discussions held at the University of South Florida (USF) during 1997 as the librarians developed a proposal for managing ETDs. We will use the term "dissertations" to include theses as well.

A key goal of the movement toward ETDs is to improve awareness of and increased distribution of student research. The Networked Digital Library of Theses and Dissertations (NDLTD), which has been under discussion since 1987, has provided a focus for these efforts. This project is international in scope. A "federated search system" has been developed that allows for searching for dissertations from diverse databases from a number of countries including Canada, the United States, and Germany. With the goal of increasing awareness of ETDs in mind, libraries are taking a number of approaches to improve points of access. One method is to integrate records for ETDs into the library catalog. As users search the catalog for books and documents, they will find dissertations as well. This approach is useful for researchers who want the whole range of material available on a given topic. It is not unusual for a search in a Web-based library catalog to include references to books, videos, other multimedia, and references that include clickable URLs. The records for ETDs will include clickable links to the material itself.

The other approach to dealing with documents like ETDs is to segregate them into a special database, perhaps as part of a "Virtual Library." This second approach is useful for more sophisticated researchers who view dissertations as a type of resource. They seek out ETDs as a special class of materials. This solution can be useful for public relations purposes. It becomes clear to users that there is an extra effort being made to highlight the intellectual efforts of the school's graduates.

Fortunately, it is reasonable to have both strategies coexist. For example, the University of South Florida will maintain records for ETDs in both the online catalog (currently WebLUIS/USF) and a second search tool with a second record for those researchers who would like to head directly to the ETD collection. The record for the dissertation used in the online catalog will serve as part of the record for the second search engine. Virginia Tech has used the same approach. Dissertations are included in the campus online catalog (supported with VTLS software and the Addison front-end). The material is also searchable as a discrete database via a search engine.

One might think that having multiple points of access would be a straightforward and a foregone conclusion. After all, when no electronic version is available, librarians have been including dissertations in their collections for more than a hundred years. Many libraries create cataloging records for their school's dissertations to add to their library catalogs. Subject, author, title, local notes, and, at times, table of contents have all been basic staples in the construction of a bibliographic record for a thesis or dissertation. Some include abstracts of dissertations as well. Local notes can include major professor, department for which the dissertation was completed, etc.

The proposal to set up a system to distribute theses and dissertations electronically gave the catalogers an opportunity to reexamine their practices. Should the records for ETDs be enhanced in any way? For example, should abstracts be added to the University of South Florida cataloging record? Librarians could use Optional Character Recognition software to provide access to the abstract and make the abstract full text searchable. What about subject headings? Subject headings take a lot of time to construct. With improved searching capabilities, would it be possible to save staff time by providing fewer access points since the material itself would be online and searchable? Adding subject headings has always proven to be a time-consuming task for dissertations dealing with very specialized topics. Will context-sensitive search capabilities improve? Would a traditional-style record describing the dissertations be necessary at all? Other questions have emerged.

It is important to review the ways in which the existence of dissertations is brought to the attention of users:

> The institution's library catalog. Now that so many library catalogs are accessible electronically, users can visit catalogs via Telnet or the Web to determine which dissertations might be available at a given institution. Users need to be alert to the differing search capabilities at each institution.
>
> OCLC's WorldCat. The database is available to users at many libraries as one of the FirstSearch databases. This source covers material in many libraries. Using keyword features available through First-Search, users can locate a wide array of theses and dissertations. A sampling study done by OCLC in 1998 suggests that there are several million such records.
>
> Indexing services provided by professional associations. The American Psychological Association lists dissertations in its versions of "Psychological Abstracts," including the electronic form PsycINFO. These services only cite dissertations in certain disciplines.
>
> UMI's "Dissertation Abstracts International" (DAI), which is available in many libraries, in either hardcopy, CD-ROM, or online formats. UMI is offering free guest accounts, which allow for searching authors, titles, and keywords for the last 2 years of dissertations through their "ProQuest Digital Dissertations" products (http://wwwlib.umi.com/dissertations/). (The complete database is accessible to institutional subscribers.) DAI has always been a prime source for locating doctoral dissertations since the indexing goes

back to 1861 and provides coverage of dissertations from the United States.

Notices in professional journals or via websites that compile dissertation listings that are discipline specific. The American Musicological Society provides a searchable database of dissertations in musicology called "Doctoral Dissertations in Musicology Online" (http://www.music.indiana.edu/ddm/index.html). This was formerly a feature of the print publications of the Society. This source includes works in progress as well as listings for completed dissertations.

The Networked Digital Library of Theses and Dissertations (NDLTD) has developed the ability to search across databases of collections of theses and dissertations via a system of federated searches (http://www.theses.org).

Each one of these access tools provides differing interfaces and differing searchable fields. As noted above, ProQuest Digital Dissertations provides guest users with the capabilities of searching for author, title, and keyword of dissertations. Since only 2 years of dissertations are accessible in this abbreviated guest version of the database, these fields will provide many users with enough capabilities to find recent dissertations. Other subscription-controlled versions of the DAI database allow for more sophisticated searching techniques. How many searchable fields are enough?

Virginia Tech's ETD database is powered by OpenText, and the initial search screen (http://scholar.lib.vt.edu/theses/etd-search.html) provides a simple keyword access to title pages and abstracts. This system accommodates the information queries mentioned above since the data elements are available on the title pages of dissertations. Major professor, department, and other pertinent information are searchable. In addition, Virginia Tech includes a cataloging record of each dissertation and thesis in its online catalog. This ensures that the dissertations can be found along with all of Virginia Tech's other books and periodical titles. The specialized, separate database devoted to ETDs serves as a means of showcasing the material. Users outside the institution are likely to seek out this specialized database.

As mentioned above, the plan for the University of South Florida ETD project is similar. USF started by using OCLC's SiteSearch software to provide searching capabilities for the database devoted to ETDs. (With SiteSearch no longer supported by OCLC as of 2001, USF began looking at other solutions.) Current plans allow for search capabilities much like Virginia Tech's. Users of the ETD database will be able to search the cataloging record for each dissertation and the abstract as well. USF will be adding searchable abstracts provided by the graduate student as part of the submission process.

This is the first time these abstracts will be included in the USF cataloging records. This approach should prove helpful to the average users of library systems. Abstracts provide a valuable, additional searchable field which expands the vocabulary found in the titles of dissertations.

Users are seeking information beyond author and title. Kay E. Lowell's article (1998) on added access points in theses cataloging points out many local needs, some of which are still poorly accommodated by national cataloging standards. Students at a given institution want to see what other graduates have produced. They want examples of other students' writing and research. They may be less interested in the specific research presented in the dissertation. For example, they may want a list of recent dissertations done for the department of psychology. They may want to know which professor chaired which dissertation committee. They may want similar information for other schools as well. What kinds of dissertations are being done for the Ph.D. program in art education at New York University? Since schools like Virginia Tech and the University of South Florida are providing searches run against the title pages of dissertations, names of major professors and other data can be retrieved.

In our Position Paper for Electronic Theses and Dissertations (University of South Florida, 1998), USF librarians address the issue of cataloging as follows: "Full level cataloging will be continued and records will continue to be added to OCLC. Records will be added for both physical and electronic versions of dissertations until the University mandates electronic submission for all students. Access points will include author, title, keyword, LCSH (Library of Congress Subject Headings) subject headings, level, Department, and Major Professor. It is anticipated that current levels of staffing will be maintained."

The decision to add full-blown subject headings is an important topic of discussion. The most time-consuming part of theses and dissertations cataloging is adding subject headings. This is the kind of work that necessitates a well-trained, professional cataloger. Why add subject headings to a cataloging record when keywords for the entire cataloging record and even full-text searching of entire documents are available? As noted above, one way that users discover dissertations is within the confines of the library's online catalog. Without the additional subject headings added to the cataloging record in Figure 1, a researcher using the library's online catalog is not likely to find this thesis on self-esteem. The title mentions "coping strategies," but neither the term "stress" nor the term "self-esteem" appears in the title of the thesis. The inclusion of the approved Library of Congress subject heading (labeled "Subjects, general" in Fig. 2) "self-esteem in children" ensures that users will find this item along with other books on the topic.

> Santa-Lucia, Raymond C.
> A situational investigation of hassles, uplifts, coping strategies, and adjustment in 3rd- through 5th-grade children/by Raymond C. Santa-Lucia.
> 1998.
> v, 35 leaves : ill.; 29 cm.
> Thesis (M.A.)–University of South Florida, 1998.
> Includes bibliographical references (leaves 33–35).
> (s =):
> Self-esteem in children.
> Stress (Psychology) in children.
> Adjustment (Psychology) in children.
> Dissertations, Academic–USF–Psychology–Masters.

FIGURE 1   Example of cataloging record.

Another reason to add subject headings is that English is a notoriously imprecise language. (Context excerpt indexing and searching would help in this regard.) The word "pitch" is a good example. The term means different things to musicians, reading teachers, vocal coaches, architects, engineers, etc. Is it the pitch of the roof or the pitch of the actor's voice? Figure 2 shows examples from the University of South Florida's WebLUIS/USF online catalog using the keyword search "pitch and dissertations."

The likelihood that these theses will reach interested readers depends in part on the addition of subject headings. "Subjects, general" is a designation for a field for approved Library of Congress subject headings.

In spite of the benefits, some libraries choose not to add subject headings due to staffing constraints—a very real concern in libraries faced with increasing workloads. The application of authoritative subject headings can be a daunting task.

However, without the addition of subject headings, users may find that they need to exercise some inventiveness in order to uncover everything a given institution has to offer. The addition of abstracts as searchable elements of the cataloging record is also necessary since abstracts include all the key concepts that describe the dissertation. Some institutions may decide that the addition of abstracts provides enough additional data for successful searching even though the use of the controlled vocabulary used to create subject headings is valuable to users.

This important access point of subject headings has consistently consumed the most discussion among librarians. One method for supplying sub-

Author, etc.: Goodwin, Mark A.
Title: The effectiveness of Pitch Master compared to traditional class-room methods in teaching sight singing to college music students/by Mark A. Goodwin.
Published: 1990.
Description: xi, 167 leaves: ill., music; 28 cm.
Notes: Thesis (Ph. D.)–University of South Florida, 1990.
Includes bibliographical references (leaves 135–141).
Subjects, general: Sight-singing–Instruction and study.
Music–Programmed instruction.
Dissertations, Academic–USF–Music education–Doctoral

Author, etc.: Shaw, Jill D. K.
Title: The relationships in the usage of oral contraceptives and their effects on vocal pitch and vocal quality: a short term study/by Jill D. K. Shaw.
Published: 1979.
Description: viii, 42 leaves; 29 cm.
Notes: Thesis (M.S.)–University of South Florida, 1979.
Bibliography: leaves 34–36.
Subjects, general: Oral contraceptives–Side effects.
Larynx.
Dissertations, Academic–USF–Speech-Language Pathology–Masters.

Author, etc.: Lutfi, Robert A.
Title: The effects of uncertain mask intensity and frequency on pitch judgments in the backward recognition masking paradigm/by Robert A. Lutfi.
Published: 1977.
Description: iv, 54 leaves; 29 cm.
Notes: Thesis (M.A.)–University of South Florida, 1977.
Bibliography: leaves 52–54.
Subjects, general: Psychology, Experimental.
Human information processing.
Dissertations, Academic–USF–Psychology–Masters.

FIGURE 2 Results of searches using the keywords "pitch and dissertations" in the University of South Florida online catalog, WebLUIS.

ject headings depends upon the input of the author as part of the submission process rather than the librarian's evaluation of the content of the material. This practice came about partially as a method to save librarians' time and thereby save costs. The theory seemed like an excellent strategy, but in practice problems arose. The cataloger learned that subjects submitted by the author were not consistent with standard subject headings. A student in the throes of submitting a dissertation is not a good candidate for a course of study on Library of Congress Subject Headings. (For a time, the University of South Florida catalogers tried setting up meeting times with authors. Even in the face-to-face interview, it was difficult for the students to contribute useful subject headings. Also, since meetings between authors and catalogers were deemed necessary, this approach was not a time-saver for the catalogers. Even though it is not a time-saver, it should be said that contact with the authors of dissertations can result in better bibliographic records.)

Since the rules for cataloging dissertations do not provide guidance, this may be one of the reasons that "local notes" have become a necessary addition for the expedient input of the bibliographic record for a thesis or dissertation. Catalogers have developed in-house standards for adding local information. The use of in-house standards means that searching across databases is problematic. The record becomes searchable, but users may need to learn local rules for search strategies in order to retrieve local notes. The standards for MARC records have been improved and should lessen the perceived need for local notes.

The student provides the abstract of the dissertation. As part of the ETD submission process, students are asked to input information, which is used as part of the cataloging record. The student submits the title of the dissertation, the name of the department, the committee members, abstract, and other pertinent information. Students are asked to assign keywords to their dissertation. These keywords enhance the verbiage used in the title and abstract of the dissertation. Since the students themselves have expert knowledge of the work in hand, they can best provide synonyms and/or alternate terms that describe the topic of their dissertation. Thoughtful keyword selection can ensure that the dissertation finds its reader. With improved standards for bibliographic records, librarians can transfer this information to the record destined for the online catalog.

In fact, much of the work of developing the cataloging record can be done automatically as part of the submission process. The ETD projects can provide catalogers with important information for descriptive, subject heading, and information notes. For example, at Virginia Tech, catalogers "copy and paste" the student's abstract into the cataloging record. Virginia Tech is also developing PERL script to map the submission information to a MARC record. Assistants can handle this kind of work University of Virginia Library, 1998. This would free up the librarian's time to handle other matters such as the application of subject headings. Other solutions might include the use of Access databases and some programming.

Since some libraries will continue to add cataloging records to their online catalog, we have already mentioned the MARC record as a standard tool for constructing bibliographic records. There are also other ways to construct a bibliographic record in an electronic environment. These are mentioned in other chapters of this book. One is Dublin Core, a metadata (data about data) element set intended to facilitate access of electronic resources. This is based upon many of the elements used in a MARC formatted record but constructed for use specifically in a web-based environment. Another is the Text Encoding Initiative (TEI), an international project to develop guidelines for the preparation and interchange of electronic texts for scholarly research. A TEI file is an example of the SGML (Standard Generalized Markup Language) approach to a bibliographic record. It contains many of the elements of MARC and the Dublin Core but was from its inception designed for electronic dissemination of information. As librarians seek to improve access to electronic material, some of these tools will supplement or eventually supplant the more traditional cataloging record.

To noncatalogers this attention to details, the discussion of national and international standards in terms of record elements, subject headings, etc. might appear to be overly complex. However, all this foundation-laying activity benefits the user. As we move toward constructing the "database of databases," articulation of record elements becomes vital.

One of the biggest questions for cataloging and identifying ETDs is likely to be the changing nature of a dissertation. As graduate schools decide to accept multimedia dissertations, librarians will have to develop a language for describing these formats. University of South Florida has already begun this process. Virginia Tech has already seen an influx of dissertations that include digital movies, audio files, and a variety of graphics files. Until access to all these formats is transparent to the user, catalogers will need to carefully describe these file types. Catalogers have taken this challenge head on. They have developed notes fields to indicate what software is needed to view all the parts of a particular thesis or dissertation. These notes are included in the bibliographic record for the ETD. OCLC has also accommodated these kinds of notes in standard records for electronic resources.

Files types are bound to change. It is inevitable that software and hardware will continue to evolve. Adobe Acrobat's PDF format seems to be a current favorite due to the capability to produce an electronic version that maintains the look and feel of a printed dissertation. If the nature of the dissertation changes, as seems likely, other solutions may emerge. If older materials are transferred to new media, cataloging records will have to change. Why change the record if the intellectual content has not changed? Cataloging records provide information about the media in which the material is presented. A long-playing record provides a different quality of sound than a CD recording, even though both items may be recordings of the same performance of Beethoven's Ninth Symphony. Also, the two formats need different devices in order to play back. One could argue that if both a paper copy of a dissertation and its electronic equivalent are available in the same library collection, these items need two cataloging records.

This seemingly sensible arrangement can be confusing for users. Combining the information about the two formats into one cataloging record allows the user to select the one most suitable at a given moment. The University of South Florida has gone one step further. If a paper and an electronic copy of a item exist, the item is given a single cataloging record. Both the paper and the electronic format are indicated. A separate, additional record for the electronic version is added to the catalog as well so that users can easily identify material available in electronic format. The ETDs will be among those items readily identifiable as part of the "electronic partition."

Cataloging records should indicate the file formats in which the material is stored. Users will need to know what software and hardware is needed in order to retrieve ETDs. Catalogers will need to develop routines to change cataloging records as ETDs migrate to new formats.

CONCLUSIONS

Strategies that integrate ETD cataloging records into a library's main online catalog aid the average user, who may overlook useful dissertations if only listed in a separate database.

Decisions about the level of cataloging provided should be user-driven. This may necessitate clever use of national cataloging standards to accommodate user needs. Also, as noted by many frustrated web searchers, full-text keyword searching can result in many hits, few of which are useful.

Adroit cataloging (which may be embedded in the electronic file itself) generally means fewer false hits.

Graduating students are advised to think carefully about writing abstracts and suggesting keywords, keeping retrieval in mind. Good keywords, can ensure that a dissertation finds its reader.

Subject headings are time-consuming to add, but help users to develop precise searches. Today librarians add subject headings taking care to use controlled vocabularies. Research may lead to automatic aids or means to add subject headings with less human intervention.

Librarians should be alert to emerging tools and strategies for describing electronic documents. This, too, will ensure that useful material falls into the hands of interested readers.

REFERENCES

Lowell, K. E. (1998). Added access points in thesis cataloging enhancing public service—without running athwart input standards. *Cataloging & Classification Quarterly* 26(2):57–71.

McMillan, G. (1996). Electronic theses and dissertations: merging perspectives. *Cataloging & Classification Quarterly* 22(3/4):105–125.

University of South Florida Libraries. Electronic Theses and Dissertations Team (1997). Draft electronic dissertations and theses position paper. (http://www.lib.usf.edu/ref/ifrank/edtposition.html).

University of Virginia Library. Cataloging Services Department. Ad Hoc Committee on Digital Access (1998). Final Report. June 15, 1998. (http://www.lib.virginia.edu/cataloging/policies/local/digital.html), November 21, 1998.

25

The Australian Digital Theses Program: A National Collaborative Distributed Model

Tony Cargnelutti
University of New South Wales
Sydney, Australia

PREAMBLE

Theses are underutilized information resources. This is due to limitations on information about their content and restrictions on access to them. Providing easy access to this information is a common problem around the world. Following are details on developments, from a pilot project to a sustainable distributed national program, with the potential to significantly enhance knowledge about, and access to, Australian theses via the Web. The Australian Digital Theses (ADT) Program used the prospicient work on ETD submission and dissemination, led by the team at Virginia Tech [see: http://etd.vt.edu/], as a starting point in developing its own distributed model. The ADT model creates a database of digitized theses, accessible via the Web by way of a simple self-submission and administration software, using a few critical but simple standard protocols. This Australian project, a collaborative effort originally involving seven universities, further extends the Virginia

Tech (VT) concept to develop a prototype nationally distributed database of theses from participating institutions.

THESES IN GENERAL AND THE ADT PROJECT

Approximately 4000 research degrees are awarded each year in Australia, representing a significant proportion of Australia's research activity. The question then arises as to how best to "unlock" the valuable information contained in theses and make it easily available to researchers everywhere. A relatively simple and timely solution is to create a searchable metadata repository and deliver the theses in digital format via the web. This has been the principal aim of the ADT Program.

This pilot project developed the model over 1998–1999. The collaborative effort involved seven Australian universities: The University of New South Wales (lead institution), Australian National University, Curtin University of Technology, Griffith University, University of Melbourne, University of Queensland, and University of Sydney, with start-up funding coming from an Australian Research Council grant.

The central aim of the ADT Program was to establish a distributed database of Web-delivered digitized theses initially from the seven original partner institutions, and when the model was sufficiently robust to then open membership to all Australian universities, and possibly to the region.

The ADT has four primary objectives:

To establish standards for electronic thesis creation, storage, and access
To create an electronic archive of frequently requested theses
To establish procedures for the submission of electronic theses by students as part of the conditions of the award of the degree
To ensure compatibility with other scholarly communications initiatives by using emerging communications, archival, and format protocols wherever possible

THE ADT MODEL

While the ADT pilot used as a starting point the concepts and software developed at VT, significant differences from the Australian proposal called for a considerable intellectual and creative effort from the development team. It meant a good deal of leading edge work, particularly in the development of a truly distributed national model using common tools and conventions.

The major issues that had to be dealt with in developing the ADT model were as follows:

As a collaborative project the Web form used for submission, and the software program behind it, had to be both generic and flexible

enough to be used by up to 40 institutions. The submission software
also had to allow for the full range of access options, including open
access, partial access, and restricted access

The model was also to be flexible enough to allow for the range of
options described in the original project proposal, e.g., ultimate self-
submission, parallel paper/electronic submission (as will be the case
for the foreseeable future), plus retrospective conversion and
submission of older theses (for ILL purposes, etc.).

The automatic generation of metadata from the submission form.

Creation of a distributed database initially across the seven institutions,
to be expanded to cover all Australian universities, and for this metadata to be gathered automatically.

Factor in the possibility of using e-commerce options for charging a fee
or royalties for access to the full text of theses.

Develop a range of protocols and conventions to facilitate all the
operational processes described above. Use of these standards would
also provide member institutions with the option of not having to use
the ADT software.

Develop standards and processes in keeping with current and emerging
international trends and practices.

Liaise with the National Library of Australia and work together on
resolving common issues as they emerge, e.g., metadata, Universal
Resource Name (URN) Resolver service.

Maintain transparency and simplicity of all processes and protocols.

ADT PROGRAM STANDARDS

During the software testing and modification phase, the ADT team proposed a set of draft standards. The initial standards were ratified, after further augmentation and amendment, at two workshops, a year apart,
involving all project partners. The standards and conventions have been
further refined as the ADT moved from pilot phase to full production and
program status.

The simple core standards are:

Definition of thesis. The ADT project will only process Ph.D. dissertations or master's theses (research only).

Simple Dublin Core metadata, automatically generated out of the ADT
Submission form. This metadata is automatically gathered and creates the metadata repository or ADT database across all member
institutions. The metadata gathered a1nd search engine used has been
developed in Australia by Distributed Systems Technology Centre
(DSTC) and is called HotMeta.

A unique URI addressing convention is used and is automatically generated from the submission software. The URI uses a combination of a unique National Union Code (NUC) for each institution with the year, month, day, and exact time of submission. This simple combination assures unique URIs across all member sites.

The standard document format will be Adobe Acrobat PDF with security set to allow read and print only.

Filename standard. There will be a minimum of two PDF files for each thesis. The first file will always be called 01front.pdf and will contain title/author information; abstract; acknowledgments; table of contents; introduction; preface and any other introductory text that is not part of the main body of the thesis. The front file is small and allows for a greater and quicker overview of the contents before downloading/printing the full thesis. The front file can also be used as the taster before any charge-per-view kicks in should members decide to charge for access.

Retrospective conversion. Although the software is best suited for self-submission, it can be used for retrospective conversion of theses as well. This will involve obtaining permission from the authors concerned and for a third party to do the submission, e.g., a staff member. The ADT Program sees retrospective conversion to ultimately service interlibrary requests for theses, as well as digitizing rare and/or fragile theses.

THE FUTURE

There are many issues and concerns specifically relating to digitizing theses and their subsequent archiving that will need further rigorous investigation in time. Archival standards have slowly emerged during the ADT's development, and this is no longer the issue it was at the beginning. The ADT Program has proven, and will further demonstrate as it continues to evolve, that a successful Australian collaborative and distributed model has been established. This model is flexible, scalable, and could become a prototype for a truly comprehensive national database of digital theses. As the program further evolves, with the possibility of including other interested institutions within the region, more work and research will need to be done on issues such as governance, strategic directions as well as production issues such as document integrity, copyright and IP, and the long-term archiving of digital media.

The ADT Program team is aware that not all theses can be fully converted into digital format, e.g., theses containing geological samples, unique artwork, or Websites. However, the team is confident that most theses can be digitized to some extent at the very least, and for those that cannot, alternatives will have to be explored in the short to medium term. One possibility the ADT Program will be looking at adopting for difficult theses is to use the deposit/submission form to create the metadata, which would be included in the distributed ADT database. This would at least provide some information about the thesis and its existence, as well as how to obtain a copy or a viewing if at all possible. To this end, the project team has always focused on what has been realistically achievable and, when necessary, sought creative and simple ways around difficulties. This philosophy will be maintained as the program continues to develop and evolve.

The ADT has also always endeavored to complement other scholarly communications initiatives as they emerged and will continue to maintain this objective. It will seek to further support and integrate with such scholarly communications initiatives at both the national and international levels.

The ADT Program supports the development of ETD programs worldwide and the implementation of access structures having the potential to enhance significantly the opportunity for all researchers, independent of geographic and economic constraints, to make their contribution to the global research effort.

All information about the program is maintained on the ADT homepage.

MORE INFORMATION

Cargnelutti, T., Piper F., Kealy K. (April 1999). "The Australian Digital Theses (ADT) Pilot Project: the trials, tribulations and (some) successes." EDUCAUSE in Australasia: People and Technology Doing IT Right. Sydney Hilton Hotel, Sydney, Australia.

URL: http://www.library.unsw.edu.au/~eirg/cause99.html

26

Dissertationen Online: The ETD Project
of the German Learned Societies

Peter Diepold
University of Berlin–Humboldt
Humboldt, Germany

THE INITIATIVE (1)

In 1996 four German learned societies - comprising the fields of chemistry, informatics (computer science) mathematics, and physics—signed a formal agreement to collaborate in developing and using digital information and communication technologies (ICT) for their members, scientific authors, and readers. The objectives of this collaboration were:

1. On a local level to bring together the activities of individual—and often isolated—university researchers and teachers in the various academic fields.
2. Nationwide to join forces in voicing the interests and needs of scientific authors and readers to the educational administration, granting agencies, research libraries, documenting agencies, publishing houses, and media enterprises.
3. Globally to use the widespread international contacts of the learned societies to exchange concepts, developments, and solutions and adapt them to the specific needs within particular fields.

The initiative soon attracted public attention, leading to the enlargement of the group. Since then, learned societies in the fields of education, sociology, psychology, biology, and electrical engineering have also committed themselves to the advancement of the goals of the IuK Initiative (2).

Funds were granted for 3 years by the Federal Ministry of Education and Research (BMBF) (3) to cover travel allowances for international experts and to make possible four international meetings (4) and a number of highly specialized workshops that reflect central activities of the growing group.

At present, the following work groups are active within the ICT Initiative:

> Metadata and classification: developing common standards, according to Dublin Core, for structuring, documenting and retrieving scientific documents from Web servers, be they texts or multimedia (5).
>
> Electronic journals: publishing peer-reviewed articles in digital journals on theWeb (6).
>
> Dissertations online: (7) establishing standards for metadata, retrieval, and workflow.
>
> Security and quality of scientific digital publications (8).

Plans for further activities include:

> Developing international contacts with digital library projects, to W3C, (9) to similar national ICT initiatives abroad, and to scientific organizations.
>
> Establishing a nationwide network of ICT experts to act as reviewers and representatives of the learned societies on national and international boards.
>
> Defining requirements of multimedia in the natural sciences, organizing and coordinating the interests of the scientific community towards the *Länder* (10) ministries, and international academic publishing houses.
>
> Introducing standards for the metadata of personal home pages of scientists, departments, and institutions.
>
> Formulating guidelines for authors with special emphasis on copyright questions, including recommendations for proposal contracts with publishers.
>
> Developing an interdisciplinary network of Web servers and setting up a networked pool of ICT experts within the German universities.

DISSERTATIONEN ONLINE

Funding by the German National Research Foundation

The activities of one of the work groups led to a proposal to the German Research Foundation (DFG) (11) to fund an interdisciplinary project to present dissertations online on the Internet involving five universities (Berlin, Duisburg, Erlangen, Karlsruhe, and Oldenburg) and five academic fields (chemistry, education, informatics, mathematics, and physics). Funding was initially restricted to one year. It started in the spring of 1998 and was terminated in March 1999 with a conference held in Jena, Germany, provoking much attention among librarians and academics. Though an infrastructure had been set up and a number of problems were solved, much remained to be done. Therefore, a subsequent proposal to DFG was drafted. DFG funds were awarded for a second year, this time with a heavy emphasis on collaboration with libraries and university computing centers. The project's research and development extended from May 1999 to May 2000. The overall total of both grants was approximately $700,000.

New participants in the second proposal were computing centers and the German National Library (DDB) (12). The project was directed by the author, a professor of computer use in education at Humboldt University, Berlin.

Rationale

By law, every graduate student in Germany is obliged to publish his or her dissertation, putting a heavy financial burden on young professionals. Unless the dissertation is published by a well-known publishing house, dissertations often are not easily accessible. Furthermore, retrieval by means of bibliographic sources are cumbersome, if not impossible. With the advent of digital production, a convincing alternative model is being developed, using the Internet as a means of dissemination as well as retrieval, thus making scientific research more productive.

The learned societies can establish guidelines regarding graduation procedures and the search aspects necessary for their respective fields of science and offer a fast and economic publication form to graduate students, enabling a quick worldwide dissemination of research findings. For libraries, a precise arrangement is necessary, defining the format of documents and metadata for different objectives: retrieval, reading, printing, and archiving. The inclusion of the German National Library (DDB) in the project is also necessary, since this library is obligated legally to collect dissertations of the Federal Republic (also in electronic form) and have them accessible in the future. Also, cooperation with publishing houses seems necessary.

The project evoked extensive communication between learned societies and libraries. The discussions, which have gone far beyond valuable but isolated single projects in the past, made the meaning and consequences of electronic documents lastingly clear: archiving and supply of research results laid down in dissertations do not represent a mere act of administration of the libraries. Rather, under the conditions of modern electronic publication possibilities, archiving and protection of scientific work in electronic form as well as retrieving scientific information via "metadata" from digital sources necessitates active participation and collaboration between learned societies, libraries, and graduate students.

At a time of rapid development in the electronic publication field, coordination between the parties involved—faculty, computing centers, libraries, publishers—is indispensable. Learned societies need to work out mutually acceptable solutions in order to produce synergies and to guarantee widespread acceptance.

DEVELOPMENT IN SUBGROUPS

Within an interdisciplinary approach, the project comprises several fields of science, computing centers, and libraries.

Metadata for Dissertations

This subgroup, headed by mathematician Prof. Törner of Duisburg University (13), has developed a tool to register bibliographic dissertation metadata in accordance with the German National Library, the MyMetaMakerfor-Theses (MMMfT) (14). It has also developed a broker for a metadata-based search for dissertations.

It is developing methods of registering or extracting:

Structural metadata, i.e., table of contents, headings of tables and graphs

References to important content wide terms (special index, name index, etc.)

References (links) to external sources (printed as well as Web sources) the bibliography

References within the work

Definitions

Mathematical/chemical formulas

The group is adapting the MMMfT to multimedia material (e.g., video sequences) in cooperation with the multimedia subgroup and the German national library, cooperating with the format subgroup with respect to digital dissertations in the natural sciences.

Retrieval and Legal Aspects

This subgroup is headed by physicist Prof. Hilf of Oldenburg University (15). It has a twofold objective.

Retrieval

Using Research Description Frameworks (RDF) and the Dublin Core (DC), this subgroup has been working on transferring metadata in retrieval procedures and a workflow, installing an upload tool for the electronic full text, and running a Harvest Broker to search for dissertations worldwide, including a map of online dissertations in Europe (16).

Legal Aspects

The group has interpreted German Copyright Law provisions with regard to dissertations and formulated recommendations for graduate students concerning legal aspects. It has collected university provisions concerning digital dissertations and formulated drafts for faculties and universities to enable publishing of dissertations on the Internet.

Formats for Retrieval, Reading, and Storing

Information technologist Dr. Schirmbacher, director of the Humboldt University computing center in Berlin (17), has joined the project and brought into its context the local Humboldt project DiDi (*Digitale Dissertationen*) (18) for a digital library of Humboldt dissertations, ultimately aiming at a secure and robust document server for all kinds of digital publications (storing, searching, archiving). His subgroup has been developing a document-type definition (DTD) for digital dissertations (DiML) in the natural sciences and in educational science, transferring metadata from text processing systems used by the graduate student into general formats such as HTML, XML, and SGML, implementing and testing conversion tools to create SGML/XML-based documents from texts produced by commonly used word processing systems (MS Word, LaTeX, Word Perfect), and conducting a usability study of new XML tools.

Multimedia and Dissertations

Prof. Gasteiger of the chemistry department of Erlangen University (19) has been assigned the task of integrating multimedia elements (i.e., chemical structures, specters, raw data, references, pictures, animations, audio, and video sequences) into multimedia dissertations in chemistry, medicine, mathematics, physics, and education, providing search tools specific to the different scientific disciplines, and creating an easy-to-use tool set for libraries.

Support of Authors, Faculties, and Libraries

The group at the department of educational science, headed by Prof. Diepold at Humboldt University, Berlin (20), has been developing guidelines for digital dissertations, testing a tutorial system for graduate students, evaluating the acceptance of guidelines with graduate students, and providing basic support information for faculties, libraries, universities, and learned societies on the diss_online Web server and on CD-ROM.

Libraries: Workflow and Archiving

The State and University Library of Göttingen (21), headed by Prof. Mittler, has been testing the products developed in the subgroups, defining procedures for a library workflow to be adopted by other university libraries.

The German national library (DDD) (22) in Frankfurt, headed by Dr. Niggemann, has developed an entry tool for digital dissertation metadata based on HTML 4, in close cooperation with subgroup Meta Data (23). There is complete documentation with the DDB and a well-structured table of dissertation specific and technical metadata (24). The DDB has defined a preliminary list of formats acceptable to the German National Library and is developing procedures for long-term deposit.

Coordination of the Subgroups

Responsible for the overall coordination is Prof. Diepold of Humboldt University, Berlin (25). This includes presenting the project in the Internet, acting as clearing house for national and international contacts, organizing meetings and workshops, informing the scientific community, including libraries, presenting the project on exhibitions, editing reports, and advising faculties, libraries, and learned societies.

RESULTS AS OF OCTOBER 1999

As of October 1999, the following materials were operable:

> An entry form for digital dissertation metadata that is being used in the participating projects, for bibliographic documents with the German National Library
>
> Complete documentation (26) available at the German National Library along with a well-structured table of dissertation specific and technical metadata at the DDB
>
> A Harvest gatherer at several universities with a central broker at Oldenburg University for digital dissertations (27)
>
> A Harvest network of online dissertations in physics (28)
>
> A document-type definition for digital dissertations (DiML) (29)
>
> Style sheets for Microsoft WinWord (30)
>
> Conversion procedures to transform WinWord and LaTeX documents into SGML

Approximately 50 documents in SGML format
A procedure for digitally signing documents
Training materials and guidelines for authors (31)

LINKING THE GERMAN ACTIVITIES TO INTERNATIONAL ETD PROJECTS

In March 1999, *Dissertationen Online* formally joined the Networked Digital Library of Theses and Dissertations (NDLTD), thus drawing on the broad international experience of colleagues from a dozen countries and bringing into this common enterprise its specific expertise. Some of the Web pages are being translated into English in order to facilitate contacts. At the recent workshop on ETDs, organized by UNESCO in September 1999 in Paris, a close cooperation with a number of ETD projects was agreed upon, with *Dissertationen Online* serving on a steering board, together with the ETD projects of Virginia Tech, Australian universities, Montreal and Lyon Universities, and the Organization of American States. The overall coordination will be by NDLTD.

Dissertationen Online has offered to UNESCO and NDLTD use of the facilities of the German Educational Server (32), namely, the relational database system for institutions, material, persons, and events, operational since 1997, to set up an ETD clearing house, structuring information on universities that offer their students ETD facilities or are interested in developing ETD programs; project descriptions, guidelines, training packets, etc.; experts in the field of ETD; international ETD conferences as well as regional workshops of general interest.

For further information, use WWW address http://www.dissonline.de.

NOTES

1. Information on the ICT Initiative is available at www.iuk-initiative.org
2. IuK stands for *Information und Kommunikation.*
3. BMBF stands for *Bundesministerium für Bildung und Forschung*(www. bmbf.de).
4. Berlin 1995: New Ways of Scientific Information and Communication; Munich 1996: New Media in Science; Wurzburg 1997: Multimedia in the Sciences; Hamburg 1998: Integrated Scientific Information Systems; Jena 1999: Dynamic Documents.
5. www.mathematik.uni-osnabrueck.de/ak-technik/
6. www.iuk-initiative.org/ej
7. www.dissonline.de/index_e.htm
8. www.physnet.uni-hamburg.de/secu/

9. The World Wide Web Consortium (www.w3c.org)
10. *Länder*: the 16 federal states of Germany.
11. DFG, *Deutsche Forschungsgemeinschaft* (www.dfg.de), is Germany's National Science Foundation.
12. DDB stands for *Die Deutsche Bibliothek* (www.ddb.de).
13. www.ub.uni-duisburg.dc/dissonline/eindex.html
14. http://elib.Uni-Osnabrueck.DE/MMMfT/
15. http://elfikom.physik.uni-oldenburg.de/dissonline/olengl.html
16. http://elfikom.physik.uni-oldenburg.de/dissonline/disEUROPE.html
17. http://dochost.rz.hu-berlin.de/epdiss/tp3-en.html
18. http://dochost.rz.hu-berlin.de/epdiss/projekt.html
19. http://www2.chemie.uni-erlangen.de/services/dissonline
20. www.educat.hu-berlin.de/diss_online/projekt5.htm
21. www.sub.uni-goettingen.de
22. www.ddb.de
23. http:// www.ub.uni-duisburg.de/cgi-mmmft/Edit-1.2.cgi
24. http://www.ub.uni-duisburg.de/dissonline/englmetatags.html
25. www.educat.hu-berlin.de/diss_online/projekt8.html
26. http://deposit.ddb.de/metadiss.htm
27. http://elfkikom.physik.uni-oldenburg.de/dissonline/PhysDis/dis_ europe. html
28. elfkikom.physik.uni-oldenburg.de/dissonline/PhysDis/dis_europe.html
29. dochost.rz.hu-berlin.de/epdiss/projekt.html
30. dochost.rz.hu-berlin.de/epdiss/vorlage.html
31. www.educat.hu-berlin.de/diss_online/autoricht/autor1.htm
32. DBS *Deutscher Bildungs-Server* (www.eduserver.de)

27

Deposit Collections of Digital Thesis and Dissertations

José Luis Borbinha
National Library of Portugal
Lisbon, Portugal

Nuno Freire
Engineering Institute for Systems and Computers
Coimbra, Portugal

INTRODUCTION

The Portuguese legal deposit law requests the deposit of theses and dissertations in the National Library. The actual law concerns only printed material, but the National Library has been defining a strategy to address the problem of the deposit of digital publications. These efforts are concentrated in three main areas: an overall analysis of the structure of the problem, the development of the concept of publication genre, and the development of the concept of deposit by scenarios.

In this context, the deposit of thesis and dissertations emerged as an ideal case study for a scenario concerned with a specific genre, which deserves to be addressed not only as a purpose in itself, but also as an experiment from which we expect to learn valuable lessons for the overall problem.

DEPOSIT COLLECTIONS

National libraries are generally mandated to maintain deposit collections of published documents, usually for the purpose of preservation of cultural heritage. Through this mission, those institutions are supposed to guarantee the long-term availability of those manifestations of intellectual works.

Depending on the country, or nation, the deposit framework is defined usually based on one or more of the following principles:

> Legal deposit: corresponds to a system legally enforced, whereby authors, publishers, or other agents must deliver one or more copies of every publication to the deposit institution (this is the case with the National Library of Portugal, for example).
>
> Voluntary deposit: corresponds to a system usually based on agreements between the deposit institution and the publishers or authors, under which those agents deliver one or more copies of each publication for preservation (this is the case with the Royal Library in the Netherlands, for example)
>
> Pro-active acquisitions: correspond to a system where the deposit institutions have to take the initiative to identify, select, and acquire the publications relevant for deposit, according to their defined mission and strategy. This principle is followed by almost all the libraries, especially for those publications relevant for their deposit policy but which are published abroad.

Independently of the deposit framework, usually each deposit institution also has an internal rule (sometimes defined by law) to specify the so-called "deposit policy." These policies try to make it clear what kind of manifestations of works have to be or must be deposited, and so they became fundamental in the definition of the practical organization and operation of those deposit institutions.

In some contexts, the official purpose for legal deposit is also the registration of the copyright of the deposited publications. In those cases, the deposit institutions are supposed to receive, register, and preserve those materials as a proof, to guarantee to the authors the recognition of their intellectual ownership (which is the case with the National Library of France and of the Library of the Congress in the United States, for example).

In the traditional print paradigm, the selection criteria specified by the deposit policies are based on the identification of common types of publications, produced by recognized sources (usually from registered publishers or publishing houses). In special cases, those criteria also include the selection of publications or documents of less common types, or produced by informal sources, but which have relevant contents according to the deposit policy.

In this paradigm, the main problems for the deposit institution are the identification and acquisition of the proper manifestations of works, assuring that the producers and the institution itself comply with the law. Yet in this scenario, most of the publications fit into standard genres, and they are produced by large publishers. For the libraries, the standards and rules for cataloguing are generally accepted, and there is an established market of computerized systems to help in the processes of managing those publications (acquisition, cataloguing, deposit, registration, storage, search, loan, etc.).

DIGITAL DEPOSIT COLLECTIONS

Digital publishing has been emerging as a new paradigm in the production and dissemination of publications. We have been registering an increased growth in the publication of digital documents, and their preservation is a mission for deposit institutions that cannot be ignored. This raises new challenges, requiring a thorough understanding of the new paradigm in order to deal with it in a proper way.

The type of publication is the main concept in the traditional deposit frameworks. However, in a digital paradigm other dimensions need to be identified and addressed since the very beginning, especially those imposing limitations on the deposit institution or deposit policy. Those limitations can be technical, if related for example to the ability to store, access, or preserve the publications, or formal, if related to copyright threats and economic models.

Functional Requirements

The problem of the deposit of digital publications was addressed by the project NEDLIB—Networked European Deposit Library (< http://www.konbib. nl/nedlib >). This 36-month project started in January 1998 with a grant from the TELEMATICS Program of the European Commission. A result of NEDLIB was a generic structure of the problem as represented in Table 1 (Borbinha, 1998).

The problem of acquisition is to determine what should be selected or accepted by a deposit institution to be integrated in its collections, and how that can or has to be done. That implies selection criteria, defined usually in the context of a deposit framework regulated by a national law for legal deposit. For countries or institutions with a legal deposit framework for printed publications, the tendency has been to extend such frameworks to include digital off-line publications. That has been done by adapting the law, or just by negotiating with the publishers. However, this approach cannot be

TABLE 1 Functional Requirements in the Management of Digital Collections

Acquisition	Delivery by the publisher	
	Capture by the library	
	Harvesting by the library	
Verification	Medium integrity	
	Content integrity	Logical integrity
		Authentication
Registration	Metadata	Bibliographic and content description
		Installation and deinstallation
		Preservation
		Access
Preservation	Physical preservation	Medium refreshing
		Medium migration
	Logical preservation	Format conversion
		Emulation
	Intellectual preservation	
Access	Conditions of use	Local access
		Remote access

directly adapted to on-line publications, where the traditional concepts of "document," "publication," "publisher," "author," etc. may have no direct relation to the printing or off-line paradigm. On the other hand, on-line publications are sometimes generated dynamically, or have embedded applications, making it quite impossible to define robust deposit policies based on harvesting strategies. Those cases recommend strategies based on voluntary and pro-active scenarios, involving agreements with the publishers and creators.

Verification is required to confirm the shape of the deposited works, assuring their technical and logical quality. For physical media it means to verify if all the bits can be read, for example. Checking of the logical structures assures the logical consistency of the publications, verifying if all the files are present, if they are in the correct formats, etc. Authentication can be assured implicitly for off-line publications, such as is done for printed material, but for on-line publications it remains an important technical issue, inherent in the infrastructure of the Internet (it requires future developments, such as more secure communication infrastructures—secure TCP/IP, HTTP, etc.—authentication services, etc.).

Registration of a publication in a deposit institution means the registration of metadata for content and bibliographic description. It comprises the traditional tasks of indexing and cataloguing, but it can include other new tasks now in the digital paradigm. Some tasks in the registration of digital publications can be automated, such as identifying and reusing embedded information provided with the publications, or even using special software applications for automatic analysis of the contents. However, it is necessary to address new requirements for new metadata structures. We will need, for example, to register metadata for the installation and removal (deinstallation) of some of the publications, especially for those requiring executable software. We will need also metadata for access (decryption keys, passwords, metadata to represent legal terms and conditions of use, etc.). And we will need to register, as much as possible, metadata for preservation (file formats, logical structures of hypermedia publications, etc.).

The problem of the preservation of digital publications represents a completely new set of new and unforeseen issues, which need to be addressed from three perspectives: physical preservation, logical preservation, and intellectual preservation.

The entire problem starts with physical preservation. Until recently, the off-line media for distribution was associated mainly with the diskette, while the designated media for storage was associated with the magnetic tape. Those magnetic media have been shown to be quite fragile, requiring constant refreshing. However, the constant congestion of the Internet and new reliable off-line storage technology, such as the DVD, with very high capacity, is bringing a new relevance to the off-line model. This will create a probable scenario favorable to strategies of physical preservation based on media migration, where materials previously "published" on-line will be most likely stored and preserved locally in off-line media using the most recent technology, or vice-versa. This can also be favorable for agreements with publishers to assure the deposit of on-line publications in off-line media.

The problem of logical preservation is associated with the need to assure format conversions when original formats become obsolete or too expensive to maintain. Besides its complexity, this carries other potential problems, namely the definition of the legal status of the new versions of the publications, a potential source of conflict with the rights owners. It also may have implications in the intellectual preservation of the contents of the initial work, since a format conversion can imply a change in the layout, presentation, or interaction with the publication, and thus a loss of its original intellectual content that can be declared unacceptable for the original author. For these cases emulation can be a solution, but an emulator is in reality an application for a specific environment (software and/or hardware), which will just delay the problem to the future, perhaps making it worse. In fact, after the building of an emulator (usually a very expensive thing to do), it will be necessary to preserve the publication in its original format as well.

Finally, the potential offered by the digital paradigm opens attractive perspectives for easier access and the development of new services. However, it creates potential threats to the copyright and economic interests of the publishers. The new problems for the deposit institutions are related mainly to the control of copying and remote access.

A Strategy

The reality of "digital publishing" has been characterized by great heterogeneity and dynamism of objects and models. To deal with that in a cost-effective way, deposit institutions will need to clearly identify each object and model in order to understand their specific requirements. This is much more complex now than in the printing paradigm, where classes are fewer and where they are usually already defined for a long time. Now, those institutions need to permanently update their knowledge of the reality and adapt their behavior to that reality just like any other technological player in the digital world.

A possible approach to this problem may be a strategy for action (implying dynamism) instead of a model or architecture (usually promoting the idea for static attitudes). This strategy can be supported by an approach with two levels: identification of publication genres, and addressing it in scenarios.

GENRES

A publication genre can be defined as a class of publications characterized by multiple common dimensions relevant for a specific stage in their management, handling, and access in deposit collections. The idea is to try to describe each digital publication as a point in multidimensional space, where each dimension represents an important property that has to be taken in account. In each context, the concept of genre must be applied independently to each stage of the process. This means that a group of genres identified by an institution in its acquisition stage does not need to be the same group found in the verification, registration, preservation, or access. A genre can be specific to just one of these stages, or it can cross more than one (a desirable scenario).

In this sense, a system to support digital collections will be based, in the worst case, in a structure of multiple specialized blocks, each one supporting a specific genre in a specific stage of the process. In the best case, merging genres across multiple stages will make it possible to develop common blocks to support them across those stages, so new genres entering a group later on will be processed using already defined blocks. A challenge for the deposit institutions will be identifying relevant genres and linking them to standard models for deposit.

The main dimensions relevant for the definition of a publication genre, from the point of view of a deposit institution, can be identified as technical factors or contextual factors. Technical factors are factors related to the technical characteristics of the publication, which can be typically:

Publication medium, referring to the media in which a publication is disseminated, which can be physical, defining an off-line pub lication (CD-ROM, DVD, etc.) or virtual, defining an on-line publication.

Publication formats, related to the logical and technical formats of a publication, such as the file formats and encoding, the hypertext structures. (ASCII, HTML, PDF, Postscript, GIF, JPEG, MPEG, etc.).

Contextual factors are factors related to the context of the publication, which we can group as:

Publication type, referring to classes of publications, independent or not of their media and formats, but related to specific contents, cultural or commercial practices and activities of organizations, institutions, communities, groups, etc. Traditional examples are newspapers, scholarly journals, theses and dissertations, financial reports, etc.

Publication characteristics, referring to factors of the publication related to the legal and/or temporal status of the contents relevant to its management and access. Examples of such characteristics are the copyright status of a publication, legal terms and conditions imposed on the publication by its author or publisher, and the dynamic or static nature of the publication.

Table 2 relates these factors and the main blocks of the structure of the problem (dependent = conditioning factors imposed on the institution by reasons out of its control; relevant = a nonconditioning factor whose impact depends on the strategy of the institution or its deposit framework).

TABLE 2 Dependencies Between Dimension Factors

Dimension factors	Acquisition	Verification	Registration	Preservation	Access
Medium	Relevant	Dependent	Relevant	Relevant	Dependent
Formats	Relevant	Dependent	Relevant	Relevant	Dependent
Type	Relevant	Relevant	Relevant	Relevant	Relevant
Characteristics	Dependent	Dependent	Relevant	Relevant	Dependent

SCENARIOS

Genres are important for the definition of selection criteria for deposit guidelines. Deposit institutions should define deposit criteria related to genres they can support. The application of selection criteria in a real case with which the deposit institution will be able to deal is called a scenario. The identification, implementation, and management of scenarios will be, therefore, a main practical concern of a deposit institution.

The actual Portuguese legal deposit law does not cover digital publications, but the issue was addressed in a new proposal that is under consideration. The new law will give to the National Library a framework to promote the voluntary and proactive scenarios for digital publications. Meanwhile, the library has identified a set of scenarios for testing, including a scenario for the deposit of scientific theses and dissertations.

PROJECT DiTeD—DIGITAL THESES AND DISSERTATIONS

Theses and dissertations are traditionally covered by the legal deposit law in Portugal. Nowadays, almost all theses and dissertations are created using word processors, confirming the fact that science and technology became one of the first areas to make use of digital publishing.

In this context, the deposit of thesis and dissertations emerged as an ideal case study for a scenario concerned with a specific genre, which deserves to be addressed not only as a purpose in itself, but also as an experiment from which we expect to learn valuable lessons for the overall problem. For that, the National Library promoted the project DiTeD—Digital Dissertations and Theses (< http://dited.bn.pt >), launched in cooperation with IST, the school of engineering of the Lisbon Technical University, and INESC, a research institution with an important background in computer science.

Requirements

A scenario for the deposit of theses and dissertations calls for special care with regard to acquisition and verification, requiring strong involvement of university libraries and authors. At this moment, the genre does not require special attention to preservation. Usually theses and dissertations are simple documents, with a clear structure defined by the university for printing purposes. However, one must expect important changes in the near future, with theses possibly including multimedia applications, simulators, etc. It is not clear how this will evolve formally in the Portuguese academic community, but we need to assure that DiTeD will be involved in the decision process.

Theses and dissertations carry special requirements for registration and access, since their contents are usually used to produce other genres, such as books and papers, or they can include sensitive material related to, for example, patents. This requires the management system to make it possible for authors to declare special requirements for access, which must be registered and respected.

Universities have a long tradition of independence in their organization, culture, and procedures. As a consequence, it was soon learned that it would be impossible to reach, in the short and medium term, any kind of overall agreement about common formats or standard procedures between the different administrative services (concerning the formats, for example, an initial survey had showed a preference of the authors for Microsoft Word, PDF, and Postscript as the formats for deposit and for public access to the documents). On the other side, Portuguese university libraries in the mid-1990s started a movement for cooperation, which resulted in 1998 in the network RUBI—*Rede das Bibliotecas Universitárias*. A political decision of the National Library was to try to work as closely as possible with this structure, instead of with the administrative services, which became a key requirement for DiTeD. Therefore, the main objective defined for DiTeD was the development of a framework that would connect the National Library to local university libraries and would make it possible to support a full digital circuit for the deposit of theses and dissertations.

It also was learned that number of local libraries would not have the necessary technical resources or skills to play an active role in the project (such as, for example, to maintain a server). It was decided that a way should be found to allow them to participate.

The technical framework would be designed as a distributed and asynchronous architecture, composed of local modules that would implement autonomous local digital libraries and a central module at the National Library for the formal deposit. Theses and dissertations would be uploaded in the local modules using the local networks and arrive at the National Library via the Internet after the successful execution of a specific workflow. This workflow would be implemented locally at the university libraries, centrally at the National Library, or possibly a combination. For local libraries that could not manage a local server, a virtual local server would be implemented at the National Library for them.

Architecture

A solution for this framework was found in the DIENST technology (< http://www.cs.cornell.edu/cdlrg/dienst/software/DienstSoftware.htm >), which provides a good set of core services. DIENST also has an open architecture that can be used with great flexibility, making it possible to extend its services and build new functionalities. The basic entities of this

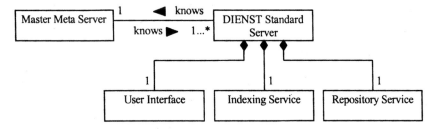

FIGURE 1   DIENST architecture.

architecture are shown in Figure 1, as a class diagram in UML—Unified
Modeling Language (< http://www.rational.com/uml >).

MASTER SERVER

The Master Meta Server provides the centralized services, including a directory of all the local servers members of the system. Only one of these
servers exists in each system. In DiTeD this server exists at the National Library. It was renamed Master Server and differs substantially from the original
versions developed for DIENST. The original server was designed to manage
only metadata, while now it is also necessary to manage the contents of the
thesis or dissertation and give support to the workflow for its submission and
deposit.

DIENST STANDARD SERVER

The DIENST Standard Server is the server installed at the university libraries.
This server was modified in DiTeD, and renamed Local Server. It consists of
the following core modules:

Repository Service: This is where the documents are stored. It manages
metadata structures and multiple content formats for the same document, functions that were substantially extended in DiTeD (to support a specific metadata format, to recognize a thesis or dissertation
as possibly composed of several files). It is also possible to define and
manage different collections in the same server.
Index Service: This service is responsible for indexing the metadata and
responding to queries. Small adjustments were made in DiTeD to
support diacritical marks in indexes and queries, a requirement in
Portuguese writing.

User Interface: This service is responsible for the interaction with the user. It was extended in DiTeD to support a flexible multilingual interface and a workflow for submissions using HTTP.

IDENTIFIERS

Two Local Servers are running at the National Library. One, named Deposit Server, is used to store locally the deposited theses and dissertations coming from all universities (the deposit will consist of a copy, so in the end each thesis or dissertation will exist in two places, the Local Server and the Deposit Server). A second Local Server is used as a virtual system for those university libraries that do not have the necessary technical resources or skills to maintain their own server.

Each thesis or dissertation deposited in DiTeD automatically receives a URN (Sollins and Masinter, 1994), which will be registered and managed by a namespace and resolution service. This service is maintained as part of the strategy of the National Library for the overall deposit of digital publications (Borbinha et al., 1998). This is in fact a simple implementation of the concept of PURL—Persistent URL (< http://purl.org >), with the particular property that it resolves any PURL by returning its real URL to the original Local Server, unless it is no longer available. In this case it resolves it by returning its URL to the Deposit Server. The entities of this final DiTeD architecture are shown in Figure 2.

Workflow

The workflow consists of two main steps: submission and deposit.

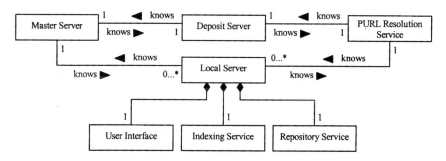

FIGURE 2 DiTeD architecture.

Submission

The submission process consists of the following steps:

1. Delivery: The process starts with the submission by the student of the thesis or dissertation to a local server. In this step the student fills in a metadata form, recording the bibliographic information and the access conditions. All of this information is held in a pending status until it is checked.
2. Verification: In a second step a librarian checks the quality of the submission (a login in the local server gives access to all the pending submissions). This task should be assured by a local librarian, but it can also be assured remotely, such as by a professional from the National Library (in a first phase of the project, the National Library will ensure uniformity of the criteria and test and tune the procedures).
3. Registration: If everything is correct (metadata and contents), the thesis or dissertation is stored in the local repository, and the student receives a confirmation. Otherwise, the student is contacted to solve any problem, and the submission remains in the pending status.

Deposit

The deposit consists of the copy of the thesis or dissertation, and of its metadata, moving from the Local Server to the Deposit Server. This is done in the following steps:

1. What's new: Periodically, the Master Server contacts the repository of a Local Server to check if there are new submissions. The Local Server replies, giving a list of the identifiers of the new submissions.
2. Delivery: For each new submission, the Master Server sends a request to the Local Server to deposit it in the Deposit Server. Because this Deposit Server is also a Local Server, this deposit works just like a normal local submission.
3. Verification: A librarian in the National Library checks the deposit. This double-checking is important, especially in the first phase of the project, to reassess the procedures and test the automatic transfer of files over the Internet—not always a reliable process.
4. Registration: If everything is correct, the thesis or dissertation is stored in the deposit repository, the final URN (a PURL) is assigned, and both the student and the local librarian receive a confirmation. The metadata is also reused to produce a standard

UNIMARC record for the national catalogue. If a problem is detected, the local librarian is contacted and the deposit remains in the pending status.

One can argue that if the Deposit Server is really also a Local Server, then the first step would be eliminated and the Local Server could perform the delivery automatically after a successful submission. This can be a future optimization, but for now the reason for this extra step is to preserve the requirement of an asynchronous system, making it possible for the Master Server, for example, to better control the moment of deposit (such as to give preference to night periods).

Metadata

DiTeD requires the metadata elements described in Table 3. This metadata is structured in blocks, each one containing one or more mandatory or optional elements. Some of the blocks are repeatable, while others are unique. The student generates the content of most of the elements during the submission, but some information is generated automatically by the system.

In general, a thesis or a dissertation can be submitted in Portugal in any language. Most are submitted in Portuguese, with an important number of exceptions in English. Submissions in other languages are rare, but possible. In any case, the fundamental elements are always required in Portuguese and English, and those were the requirements decided for DiTeD.

The bibliographic description comprises a set of mandatory and optional elements for the title and identification of the author. The type of document (masters thesis, doctoral dissertation, etc.), its language, and a list of free indexing keywords are mandatory. Optional is a list of controlled keywords, chosen from a list of indexing languages available from the user interface [such as, the CCS—Computing Classification System (< http://www.acm.org/class/1998 >) or the MSC—Mathematics Subject Classification (< http://www.ams.org/msc >)].

It is suggested that the author and the adviser also register their birth years to make it possible to build a standard authority entry according to the Portuguese Cataloguing Rules (e.g., "Silva, José, 1962," where 1962 represents the year of birth of the author José Silva"). The date of approval is not mandatory, since according to the Portuguese legal deposit law, a thesis or dissertation has a legal existence when it is submitted, and keeps it even if it is rejected.

As far as the structure and format of the thesis or dissertation, we suggest submission of the work in more than one file and format if possible. Having the full document in more than one format might be valuable in the long term for preservation purposes. It is also required in the short term if

TABLE 3   Metadata Elements in DiTeD

Blocks	Mandatory Elements	Optional Elements
Produced by the student/librarian		
Unique		
Title	Title in Portuguese	Subtitle in Portuguese
	Title in English	Subtitle in English
Author	Author's Name	Author's Birth Year
	Author's Institution	Author's Email
	Author's Department	Author's Postal Address
	Course or Area	Author's Telephone
Type	Type of the Manifestation	
Language	Language of the Manifestation	
Abstract	Abstract in Portuguese	
	Abstract in English .	
Adviser	Adviser's Name	Adviser's Birth Year
	Adviser's Affiliation	Adviser's Email
		Adviser's Postal Address
Approval		Date of Approval
Notes		Notes
Repeatable		
Indexing	Free keywords in Portuguese	Controlled keywords in Portuguese
	Free keywords in English	Controlled keywords in English
Jury		Jury's Name
		Jury's Affiliation
		Jury's Birth Year
File and Access	File Name	
	File Format	
	Conditions for Access	Conditions Revision Date
Aut		
Unit		
Publishing Library	Library's Name	Library's Email
		Library's Postal Address
Identifiers	Internal Identifier	
	URN	
Submission	Date of Submission	
Statement	Copyright Statement	

the author wants to specify different conditions of access for different parts of the work. In this case, it is possible to submit several files and specify different conditions of access for each one, as well as the dates when these conditions expire (3, 6, 12, 24, or 36 months).

FUTURE

In the future, the project will promote a national agreement for common national formats. The actual scenario is quite unclear, with the emerging of XML as a possible future format but with a large platform of tools and users familiar with Microsoft Word, PDF, Postscript, etc. Another important issue will be the full automatization of the workflow, from the submission to the deposit and registration in the national catalogue. This will be a complex task, since it requires a minimum level of technical quality in the local systems and processes, as well as agreements about the processes.

At the international level, DiTeD intends to work closely with the NDLTD—Networked Digital Library of Thesis and Dissertations initiative (< http://www.ndltd.org >), with a special focus on the definition of a common metadata format for interoperability and interoperable document-type definitions. The project plans to release the modified DIENST package as a "black box" (and maintain it), which can be especially suitable for other small countries.

The National Library of Portugal sees DiTeD as a project that will help it better understand the paradigm of the "digital library." This paradigm raises a completely new set of new issues, and it would be good if we could address them to benefit from our accumulated experience with the "traditional library." We expect help in answering these questions:

Preservation of digital information—What are the new challenges? How can a deposit library address them?

Document genres—In the printed paradigm we are familiar with newspapers, books, journals, etc. What are the new genres that the "digital paradigm" will bring to us? The understanding of new genres is very important for deposit institutions, since they are related to new technological challenges, new business models, new social realities, new classes of users, etc. What should be covered (and how) from the perspective of a legal deposit law?

Metadata—Libraries are used to bibliographic formats, such as the family of MARC formats (the National Library of Portugal uses UNIMARC), and reliable metadata contents (usually created by high skilled professionals). The new challenges involve dealing with heterogeneous metadata requirements, sources and schemas, being aware of XML, RDF, Dublin Core, etc. What is the new "metadata taxonomy" for the "digital library"?

Classification, indexing, and contents description—Metadata is not going to be created only by librarians (which would be too expensive and complex in the face of the explosion of genres and the quantity of information objects), but also (mainly?) by unknown people. In this scenario, what are the new concepts, definitions, requirements, tools, etc., for classification, indexing, and resource discovery? What will be the equivalent of the actual catalogue in a "digital library"?

REFERENCES

Borbinha, J. (1998). Digital libraries: a perspective from Portugal. *LIBER Quarterly* 8(1):81–85.

Borbinha, J., Campos, F., Cardoso, F. (December 1999). Deposit collections of digital publications: a pragmatic strategy for an analysis. In: Fletcher, P. D., Bertot, J. C., eds. *World Libraries on the Information Superhighway: Preparing for the Challenges of the Next Millenium*. Idea Group Press.

Sollins, K., Masinter, L. (1994). Functional requirements for uniform resource names. RFC 1737.

28

Training Teams for ETD Projects

Ana M. B. Pavani
Pontifical University of Rio de Janeiro
Rio de Janeiro, Brazil

INTRODUCTION

Information has been recorded since time immemorial. On the walls of caves (1,2) our early ancestors drew and scratched images of animals, human figures, stars, the moon, the sun, and geometric symbols.

We have come a long way in a few thousand years. All along this road, which has recently led to digital libraries, our ancestors have used stones, clay, papyri, parchment, charcoal, ink, brushes, feathers, easels, hammers, etc. (see Fig. 1). We have invented ideograms, alphabets, numbering systems, libraries, archives, catalogs, the printing press, authority files, bits and bytes, records interchange, OPACs, etc. (3–11).

All of the above are technologies and methodologies for recording intellectual, commercial, administrative, artistic, and/or legal contents within the information process. However, we must not forget the third party of this equation—the creators of the contents. Thus, we can identify three types of players in the process of recording information: those who create information, those who define the methods of dealing with it, and the ones who provide the means to record, store, and distribute it. We can call these parties authors, information professionals, and technologists.

FIGURE 1   A modern electronic realization inspired by the creation of our early ancestors. (Courtesy B. Hedler and T. Peres.)

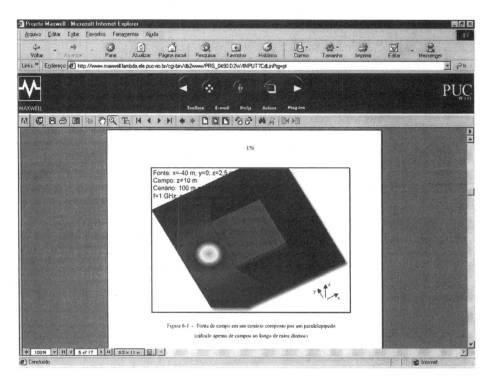

FIGURE 2   Page of an electronic dissertation.

Let us consider an example: a medieval Arabic medical manuscript written and illustrated on parchment with ink, feather, and brush and cataloged on a paper manuscript in some seventeenth-century library. In this case the author was a medieval physician, the information professional was a seventeenth-century librarian, and the technologists were people who manufactured the parchment, the brushes, and the inks.

The evolution in creation, methodology, and technology enabled the development of electronic theses and dissertations (ETDs) (12,13) and *The Guide to Electronic Theses and Dissertations* (14). (A page of an electronic dissertation is shown in Fig. 2.)

This chapter addresses some important aspects of training the teams who will engage in ETD projects. The following section presents some considerations on how digital libraries and ETDs are affecting access to information. The idea of a team to implement an ETD project is explored. A discussion ensues on the training program for a set of courses taught in the last several years and the importance of training graduate students.

DIGITAL LIBRARIES AND ETDs

The expression theses and dissertations (T&D) defines the creation of contents that are the result of graduate studies and whose authors are graduate students. Contributing to these contents are the students' supervisors, who are faculty members. Since T&D are quite traditional, they have been contained in university and/or national libraries for a long time, where they have been cataloged, searched, retrieved, stored, and preserved. Librarians have been the information professionals who have taken care of T&D after these have been separated from their authors, that is, after they have been deposited.

Before personal computers became available, the technology used for T&D was paper and typewriters. In general, authors did not get involved with the "technology"—typists did the work.

The first use of personal computers was to emulate typewriters and paper; word processors were used, but paper was kept as the medium. Authors then started getting involved with "technology"—many students could and can use word processors and indeed do it.

The fast development of information and communication technology (ICT) in the last decade allowed the creation of digital libraries and, as a consequence, of ETDs. This has been a real revolution in terms of our concept of accessing information. Let's examine some points:

Authors have become involved in the process of recording their ideas—almost all university students can use word processors, spreadsheets, image software, etc.

Digital files have become the usual way of exchanging information—students and their professors feel comfortable attaching files to e-mails.

Paper copies have lost importance in the process of creating documents—electronic files are used up to the last minute before the final version is printed, if ever.

Remote access to contents has become a matter of having an Internet connection and knowing the URLs of digital libraries with ETDs.

With Open Archives (15) servers, remote access will be made progressively easier since the knowledge of only one URL will be necessary.

We have stopped thinking of our library as the only source of information—the Internet connected us to the world.

We have changed our minds about the time to find the references we look for—we can do it in minutes.

English has become a necessary language to move about in the networked world.

As it stands now, the contents we create must be identified in English to be located on the Internet.

At the same time, ETDs have changed the way universities deal with T&D. From the creation to the distribution on the Internet, the processes in the universities have been affected. This is true for all the universities that have ETD projects, even the ones with projects at very early stages.

One very interesting aspect of an ETD project is that it requires discussion of habits that used to be taken for granted. This can be noted in each ETD workshop, as will be discussed later on in this chapter.

Creation has been affected because students are now able to use templates and submit the electronic files using the system and the network. In some situations they can suggest the metadata elements for the cataloging. Storage and preservation have been changed because electronic files must be received, stored and preserved—the system and the network are the tools for these activities. The characteristics of the electronic files must be recorded in addition to the traditional cataloging fields; metadata elements have been added. Servers to hold and provide access to ETDs have become parts of the infrastructure, as have the network connections that enable their use.

ETDs integrate, in a new way, the library and the graduate programs. ICT is the thread that sews the parts.

TEAMS FOR ETDs? WHY?

The previous section suggested that ETDs are connecting the library and the graduate programs through ICT. Therefore, it is clear that to start an ETD project it is necessary to coordinate three groups in the university. They make up the ETD team: the graduate programs, the library, and the ICT staff. They are the players of the game.

The more integrated and cooperative is their work, the better for the project and for the university. The training program for the staffs of the three groups is a good start in the building up of "team behavior." Each group needs to learn the requirements, the potentials, and the limitations of the others.

The training program is a good forum to discuss the tasks to be performed from the different perspectives of each group.

BASIC ASPECTS OF THE TRAINING PROGRAM

In general, when someone enrolls in a ETD workshop or training program, they do so with the approval of their higher administration. However, it is also true that normally it is not the higher administration that originally finds out about the training program. The requirement for training comes from one or more of the three players. This is important in terms of training because it influences the final part of the program, as will be discussed in the following sections.

Since a team needs to be trained and each group in the team has different skills and needs, the training program must address all the aspects of the project and show where each group fits in. It must also show where the higher administration of the university must step in.

UNESCO, through the Regional Office of Science and Technology for Latin America and the Caribbean (16), started a training program for managers of ETD projects. Some of the comments presented in this work are based on my experience as an instructor in this program—the course has been taught four times in South America and has had more than 80 students from libraries, graduate programs, and ICT staff from universities in more than seven countries.

The program is divided in eight parts:

1. Introduction to an ETD project
2. Basic concepts of ICT and of digital information
3. Basic concepts of digital collections
4. Standards for information and systems
5. Metadata
6. Intellectual property
7. ETDs
8. ETD preproject

Each part has an objective and a set of content items that may vary with the audience; this is very common with part 2. Experience has shown that the items must vary with time too, since the digital culture is becoming more popular and people are becoming more skilled in the use of technology. The following section discusses each part.

THE CONTENTS OF THE TRAINING PROGRAM

Introduction to an ETD Project

The objective of this part is to define the context of an ETD project. It focuses on four items:

Motivation—this aims at identifying the different motivations that have taken the members of the group to the training program or to start an ETD project.

Objective—this aims at clarifying the participants' expectations and needs in terms of the project type.

Benefits—this aims at teasing out the benefits that will be brought to different groups (students, universities, countries, regions, etc.) in the implementation of the project.

Requirements—this aims at determining the ways the institutions must be committed to the ETD project. The introduction also serves the purpose of raising ideas that will be used to write the first part of the preproject.

Basic Concepts of ICT and of Digital Information

This part introduces the basic concepts and tools of ICT. It also discusses digital information—its nature, formats, and how it can be generated from traditional collections. The concepts of digital object and of a born digital object are presented. The processes to deal with digital information are addressed, and special issues (like preservation) are discussed.

This part may vary in different courses according to the audience since the level of digital culture varies too. This happens due to the mix of students (many from ICT staff) and also due to the types of universities they come from (in more developed regions the ICT infrastructure allows people to be more proficient in the use of technology).

Currently, in some courses it is necessary to present some fundamental concepts and functions of the Internet. As time goes by, it is expected that the gap in technology knowledge will decrease and the topic will focus on the specific items that are important for the ETD project.

Basic Concepts of Digital Collections

This part introduces the basic concepts of digital collections in general and digital libraries in particular. It presents the main parts of the collection and compares them with their traditional counterparts. The functions that are available to end-users and to the professional staff are discussed; they are related to the processes used to deal with digital information presented in the previous topic. The definitions to be used during the implementation of a digital collection are covered. Specific problems related to developing countries are mentioned.

This topic is, in general, new to most of the students, even those familiar with automated library systems.

Standards for Information and Systems

The objective of this part is to introduce standards for information identification, system functionality, and technology. It emphasizes the importance of standards and draws a parallel with similar situations in Web-based education and E-business. It presents the standards associated with traditional collections and libraries.

The main organizations devoted to discussion and maintenance of standards are presented.

Metadata

This part discusses the identification of digital objects. It presents the concept of metadata elements and the most important metadata element sets. The Dublin Core Metadata Element Set (17,18) is analyzed to introduce not a standard but a consensus for digital information identification. Other metadata element sets are mentioned: Library of Congress Digital Repository Development Metadata—Core Metadata Elements (19), Instructional Management System Project (20), IEEE Learning Technology Standards Committee Learning Objects Metadata (21), and ETD-ms: an Interoperability Metadata Standard for Electronic Theses and Dissertations (22).

The relationship with traditional cataloging schemes is commented upon. The metadata elements that must be added to identify T&D are discussed, as well as the ones required for national and international harvesting to create Open Archives servers (23,24).

Intellectual Property

This part addresses the issues of intellectual property concerning e-publishing of T&D: legislation in different countries, internal procedures in the universities, and technology solutions to protect the contents.

ETDs

The objective of this part is to explore:

> The different ways of generating electronic documents. It focuses on T&D in digital format generated either from the capture of original paper versions or from electronic editing.
>
> The important points to be considered when starting an ETD project—library systems and cataloging practices, ICT infrastructure, procedures to deal with intellectual property rights, etc.
>
> The basic definitions of an ETD project in terms of the institutional commitment to the project—funding, allowing modification of processes, addressing intellectual property issues, etc.
>
> The basic definitions of an ETD project in terms of new T&D—review of formats, definition of metadata, definition of workflow, preservation, etc.
>
> The basic definitions of an ETD project in terms of old T&D—analysis of necessity, definition of workflow, etc.
>
> The need for training students and staff on how to submit ETDs.

Considerations as to workflow, equipment, cataloging, etc. are also raised. The international and national initiatives and support are presented, e.g., UNESCO (13,14,16), NDLTD (12), ISTEC (25), and BDB (24).

ETD Preproject to Take Back

As mentioned above, the attendees of the courses have the approval of their managers. Nevertheless, many institutions misunderstand the nature of the course.

Some institutions don't seem to be aware that this training is to prepare for the establishment of an ETD project. Therefore, when the attendees return to the institutions, they have yet to "sell" the idea of an ETD project.

An ETD project means that:

> Old ways of doing things will be questioned and, perhaps, changed.
>
> Unsolved problems will have to be addressed (e.g., intellectual property rights).
>
> Training will be necessary.
>
> A budget for hardware, software, training, etc. will be necessary to start the project.
>
> A budget for hardware, software, training, etc. will be necessary to keep the project going.
>
> The different groups in the university will have to start working as a team.

The last part of the program is devoted to writing a preproject. The preproject states the ETDs project's motivation, objectives, benefits, methodology, steps, etc. Each section of the preproject is discussed and the main topics are noted after consensus is reached among the members of the group. When attendees return to their institutions, the preproject is customized according to the context of each university. This customization is necessary because institutions vary in their structures and processes.

When the preproject is finished, the students have an organized draft to start an ETD project. The preproject addresses all the topics discussed during the training program.

THE IMPORTANCE OF TRAINING STUDENTS

Students are key players in the process of creating ETDs. They must receive special attention so that their participation is simple and runs smoothly in the university workflow.

An example of the facilities for students, the authors of T&D, can be seen in the area "For ETD Authors" on the site "Digital Libraries and Archives" of Virginia Tech (26). The authors are offered introductory workshops, the guidelines of the Graduate School, information on copyright, and examples of ETDs.

A second example to be cited is that of Cybertesis of Universidad de Chile (27). There is a complete manual for the students with the instructions on how to present the dissertation both in paper and in digital format.

The more the students participate in the process of generating the electronic files, in submitting them to the library, and in suggesting the metadata elements, the more important the training of students becomes.

IMPLEMENTATION OF THE TRAINING PROGRAM

An example of implementation is the set of courses that UNESCO-UY has sponsored since August 2000. They have been held in Colombia (2000), Uruguay (2000, 2001) and Brazil (2001). In all four sessions, there were students from different countries in Latin America, from Mexico to the southern cone (Argentina and Chile). It is obvious that in each one there was a concentration of students from the host country; nevertheless, travel expenses were still high.

The courses were taught in the traditional way-lectures, discussions, slides, Internet access to visit digital libraries, and the development of the preproject. There is an alternative way to hold this program—using a self-learning distance learning implementation. Each method has positive characteristics and some limitations.

TRADITIONAL FACE-TO-FACE SITUATION

As a first approach, the traditional face-to-face course may be best. It can be implemented more quickly since, as long as there is an instructor, the development of suitable courseware is easier and faster. Remember that, in this case, courseware is only a supplement.

The traditional way can also be adapted with less effort, since the instructor can adjust to the background of the trainees. On the other hand, it can be more expensive when travel is required for the attendees. Unless there are sessions in different locations allowing people to attend where they live.

At the same time, the fact that there were people from different areas enriched the course. There was a lot of discussion and sharing. Not only were issues related to ETD projects discussed, the generalities of graduate education, the role of libraries, the ICT infrastructure, etc., were discussed during meals or breaks.

Another interesting aspect of two of the sessions (Colombia and Uruguay, 2001) was that they were held simultaneously with other events in ICT, digital libraries, and distance learning. This allowed outside speakers to lecture on topics related to the program. There were plenary sessions that integrated all participants. These activities much enriched the participants' experience.

SELF-LEARNING DISTANCE LEARNING

The self-learning distance learning alternative seems very reasonable in terms of cutting costs. Travel costs will not exist. This will happen after good courseware is developed. This task is made easier if there is experience with teaching in the traditional way. The interaction among trainees can be accomplished through the use of discussion forums on the Internet. This situation implies a fixed cost to get things started—courseware and a distance learning system.

This manner of implementing a training program can be used with the graduate students who write the dissertations. Digital courseware, FAQ's, guides, etc. can be used within the universities to help the students become proficient in presenting their T&D as ETDs. If the students are skilled in the use of the ETDs tools, the universities will benefit.

COMMENTS

The training program is a very enriching experience for the instructor. It is a unique opportunity to get to know groups from different institutions and to discuss common problems.

Another interesting aspect for all is the fact that the three groups are together and problems and solutions are discussed from three different points of view. The training program becomes a forum for an integration that facilitates team work.

The discussion among different institutions shows that many characteristics are common to all—the need to review the T&D formats, modeling of new workflows, a new look at intellectual property rights, the concern with preservation of digital formats, etc. The evolution of the digital culture will yield a permanent update on the contents of the course up to a point when it will not be needed at all. Digital libraries will be commonplace, and ETDs will be the usual way of recording the results of graduate programs.

ACKNOWLEDGMENTS

The author thanks UNESCO's Oficina Regional de Ciencia y Tecnología para América Latina y el Caribe for the opportunity to be the instructor in the four sessions of the Curso de Formación de Directores de Proyectos ETD-Net. B. Hedler and T. Peres are also thanked for their creative electronic version of cave wall art.

REFERENCES

1. Furna do Estrago. http://www.unicap.br/furna
2. The Cave of Chauvet-Pont-D'Arc. http://www.culture.gouv.fr/culture/arcnat/chauvet/en/index.html
3. Book Information Website. http://www.xs4all.nl/~knops/index2.html
4. Computed Tomography and Archaeology. http://www.hum.huji.ac.il/Archaeology/ct/index.htm
5. Digital Scriptorium. http://sunsite.berkeley.edu/Scriptorium
6. Incan Quipu. http://www.humanities.ccny.cuny.edu/history/reader/quipus.html
7. Paper, Leather, Clay and Stone: The Written Word Materialized. http://rmc.library.cornell.edu/Paper-exhibit/default.html
8. Quipus: The Sacred Text of Tahwantansuyo. http://www.spanish.sbc.edu/MMLatAm/Tahwantansuyo.html
9. The Quipucamayu. http://www.spanish.sbc.edu/MMLatAm/Quipus.html
10. Manguel, A. (1997). *Uma história da leitura*. 1st ed. Brazil: Companhia das Letras.

11. Gomes, S. M. V. (2001). Um espetáculo para os olhos ou a ilustração como teoria. *Master's thesis*, PUC-Rio, Brazil.

12. Networked Digital Library of Theses and Dissertations. http://www.ndltd.org

13. UNESCO. http://www.unesco.org/webworld/report.html

14. UNESCO ETD Guide. http://etdguide.org

15. Open Archives Initiative. http://www.openarchives.org

16. UNESCO-Oficina Regional de Ciencia y Tecnología para América Latina y el Caribe. http://www.unesco.org.uy

17. Dublin Core Metadata Element Set. http://purl.org/dc/documents/rec-dces-19990702.htm

18. Dublin Core Metadata Initiative. http://www.purl.oclc.org/metadata/.dublin_core/

19. Library of Congress Digital Repository Development Metadata—Core Metadata Elements. http://lcweb.loc.gov/standards/metadata.html

20. Instructional Management System Project. http://www.imsproject.org/

21. IEEE Learning Technology Standards Committee Learning Object Metadata. http://ltsc.ieee.org/doc/wg12/LOM_WD4.htm/

22. ETD-ms: an Interoperability Metadata Standard for Electronic Theses and Dissertations. http://www.ndltd.org/standards/metadata/current.html

23. Suleman H., Fox, E. (December 2001). A framework for building open digital libraries. *D-Lib Magazine*. Vol. 7. No. 12.

24. BDB—Biblioteca Digital Brasileira—Consórcio Brasileiro de Teses Eletrônicas. http://www.ibict.br/dbd/inicio.htm/

25. IberoAmerican Science and Technology Education Consortium. http://www.istec.org

26. Digital Libraries and Archives—Virginia Tech. http://scholar.lib.vt.edu/theses/

27. Universidad de Chile Cybertesis. http://www.cybertesis.cl/

Glossary

Active migration Migration (q.v.) of digital objects accompanied by their conversion from a data formats that custodians believe might succumb to technology obsolescence, e.g., because the purveyors of essential interpreting software cannot be counted on to maintain that software sufficiently reliably for old data formats. Although some technologists recommend active migration as part of digital preservation strategies, we believe it to be a troublesome and expensive measure compared to emulation methods using UVCs (q.v.).

Bit stream Sequence of binary characters; a synonym for file or dataset used to emphasize that it denotes an information representation readily transmitted via a serial channel or stored on a disk or tape.

Blob Binary large object (or binary little object), used to describe information formatted as a sequence of contiguous bits when we wish to avoid implying anything at all about its interpretation.

Boolean Based on the algebra developed by George Boole, which involves two values, often 0 vs. 1, or T vs. F, and has primary operations AND, OR, and NOT as well as less used operations such as XOR. Some IR systems accept Boolean queries, wherein words, phrases, or descriptors are required to occur in retrieved documents in a way that satisfies (makes true) the Boolean expression supplied.

Bush Vannevar Bush was science advisor to President Roosevelt, onetime president of MIT, and founder of the National Science Foundation. His influential article "As We May Think" appeared in 1945 in *Atlantic Monthly* and *Life* and influenced subsequent work on hypertext and information retrieval.

CD-DA Compact Disc Digital Audio, the standard 120 mm CD developed by Philips and Sony in the early 1980s, which is commonly used to distribute music and other audio works. Approximately 60–74 minutes of high-quality stereo recording is supported, sampled 44,100 times per second using 16 bits per sample.

CD-ROM Compact Disc Read-Only Memory, the type of CD developed in the mid-1980s to store digital data, usually around 600 megabytes (552,960,000 bytes for 60 minutes, 681,984,000 bytes for 74 minutes). The original playback rate was about the speed of a T1 communication link, also the target for MPEG-1 digital video: 1,228,800 bps. Newer drives support 24 × the original rate of spin, but the access time still is measured in 100s of milliseconds.

Cluster Group of items, often formed because the similarity among them is high relative to the similarity of them with other items in different clusters, sometimes characterized by a cluster centroid (representative, either a member or a constructed item, often the group average).

CODER COmposite Document Expert/extended/effective Retrieval—a system developed in the 1980s at Virginia Tech to explore distributed expert-based information systems technology. Early work involved Fox, France, Weaver (Smith), Barnhart, and others.

Collision Circumstance in which independently chosen strings that ideally would differ accidentally get the same value.

Content In a body of information, the core of what originators intend to communicate to readers; alternatively, any information that is to be conveyed.

Controlled vocabulary Set of words, phrases, or other descriptors that is limited in number, sometimes by an editorial group, and used by indexers and searchers for indexing and searching, so that consistency is encouraged and so that descriptions can proceed at the conceptual level. Examples include MeSH for medicine, Library of Congress Subject Headings for cataloging, and ERIC for the educational literature.

Data object Digital representation of any kind of information; often used as a synonym for document (q.v.), file, dataset, video signal, drawing, image, etc.

Digital library Combination of a collection of digital objects (repository); descriptions of those objects (metadata); a set of users (patrons or target audience or users); and systems that offer a variety of services such as capture, indexing, cataloging, search, browsing, retrieval, delivery, archiving, and preservation.

Document Item of information, such as an article, book, story, report, thesis, letter, memo, patent, legal decision, or other unit that might be the target of retrieval.

ETD Electronic thesis or dissertation.

ENVISION Digital library project and system that began in 1991 with funding by NSF of the Virginia Tech proposal. A user-centered database from the Computer Science Literature. The project director was Fox, co-PIs were Heath and Hix, and many were involved including staff member France; graduate students Brueni, Nowell, and Wake; as well as undergraduates including Labow. For more information see pointers from the homepage of the follow-on project, EI.

Essence (noun); In the context of a digital document, the core content or original matter provided by originators, in contrast to metadata, q.v.

Eye catcher Bit string or character string used as a search target in order to locate other information whose content and format cannot be predicted. Typically, the eye catcher immediately precedes the information of interest.

Facet Aspect or characteristic that can have various values. A collection of facets and values can serve as the basis for a faceted classification system.

Flat file String of bytes stored as a file in computer storage that can be viewed as lacking structure, just a sequence or list of characters.

Filtering Given a set of newly arriving documents (e.g., from a news service, or from a newly available publication), selecting just those that are most appropriate to send to a given user, usually based upon a previously stored profile that describes that user's interests.

Guide Early hypertext system developed for PCs.

HTML *see* HyperText Markup Language.

HTTP Protocol used in the WWW by servers and clients (browsers) so that documents can be obtained, links can be followed, CGI scripts can be launched, and other related operations carried out.

Hyperbase Large collection of (linked) hypertext or hyperbase objects.

HyperCard Product developed by Apple, originally in 1987, to make it easy to prepare hypertexts and hypertext applications, which build upon the concepts of buttons, fields, cards, and stacks. The HyperTalk scripting language follows object-oriented programming principles.

Hypermedia Hypertext whose documents include not only text but also other media forms, such as graphics, images, audio, video, and virtual reality constructs. When a node is presented, the multimedia object is rendered as appropriate for that media type, and if an anchor is involved (which might designate a part of an image, an object in a video sequence, or a musical interlude), that part is selected.

Hypertext Collection of items (nodes) that are connected by arcs (links) which have source and target either from a node or to a location in a node (anchor). When one selects an anchor, the corresponding link is traversed and the target node is presented (positioned to show the target anchor if there is one). Hypertexts usually involve text documents.

HyperText Markup Language Language used for documents on WWW. This is described by a document-type definition according to the SGML standard, and so HTML is an application of SGML.

Hypertext on Hypertext ACM product delivered in three forms (using Guide, HyperCard, and KMS) as a hypertext representation of the 1988 CACM special issue which had important papers from the first ACM Hypertext Conference, fall 1987, held at University.of North Carolina at Chapel Hill.

HyTime Standard for hypertext and hypermedia interchange, extending SGML to handle temporal and spatial event scheduling as well as synchronization, ISO/IEC 10744.

ID Abbreviation for "identifier."

Identifier Blob for referencing a set of blobs and/or physical objects and chosen so that the probability of collision with any other identifier instance is tiny.

Indexing Describing the content of information objects (e.g., documents) in some condensed way that facilities subsequent retrieval. Manual indexing is done by humans (indexers). Automatic indexing is done by computers, as part of the processing by information retrieval systems.

Indexing language Language (set of words following natural or artificial rules) used when indexing, often a controlled vocabulary, or a full natural language (in so-called full-text systems).

Inverted file Data structure or collection of supporting data structures used in many information retrieval system to speed up processing. Each term (word or stem or root or phrase or descriptor or concept) has an entry (often found by hashing, through a trie, or with a B-tree) which points to all the occurrences of that term in the collection. Sometimes the entry points to a short record that contains the number of occurrences and a pointer to where the list of occurrences begins, in another data structure. Often the occurrences indicate documents, though they may identify every match inside any document.

JPEG   Name of the Joint Photographic Experts Group and the standard they developed (for ISO/CCITT) to compress images in one of several modes. Most often the lossy mode is used, which makes use of the Discrete Cosine Transform to achieve variable degrees of compression, depending on user selection of desired quality. Very good quality images are often available even with 10:1 compression.

KMS   Knowledge Management System, a sophisticated hypertext system now in its 11th version, marketed by Knowledge Systems, Inc. and generally made available free of charge to universities. The ACM Hypertext Compendium is available through KMS and covers the early work in that field.

Link   Connection between a location within a data object with some other location within a data object, which might be the same object or another object. Often "link" is a synonym for "reference" and "pointer."

MARC   MAchine Readable Catalog, the standard used for catalog records in most libraries. The US Library of Congress coordinates standards efforts, especially for USMARC. There are other versions as well, such as UNIMARC, and conversions (crosswalks) between. Cataloging with MARC usually follows AACR2 rules.

MARIAN   Retrieval system developed at Virginia Tech in the Computing Center and Department of Computer Science, with partial support from NSF and the National Library of Medicine (for the Java version). This MARIAN system is used to run a production catalog search service that parallels the campus VTLS service. MARIAN also has been for research in digital libraries, including in the Envision and EI projects.

Metadata   Information describing a document with text elements and other information needed for using or managing the document and usually not contained in the document itself. The distinction between metadata and content is opportunistic and fuzzy. Often metadata is created and attached to a document by someone other than the document originator, e.g., a library cataloguer might create metadata for a book, doing so because she does not want to alter the book as delivered to her by its author.

Migration   Copying digital objects from media or systems that are becoming obsolete to their successors—a process that every digital object is expected to need every 5–10 years. If the objects are stored as ordinary files, this will be accomplished within the regular backup and recovery procedures of any properly managed data storage service, i.e., without any special attention or work by users or libraries, apart from prudent choice of their storage service vendors. (Cf. active migration, q.v.)

MIME Multi-purpose Internet Mail Extensions, a specification (i.e., RFC1521 and RFC1522) that offers a way to interchange text in languages with different character sets, and multimedia e-mail among many different computer systems that use Internet mail standards. MIME is used for transferring multimedia information in the WWW.

MJPEG Motion JPEG, a way to represent streams of video as a sequence of JPEG images, usually compressed separately at the rate of 30 per second.

Mosaic The first popular browser for the WWW, developed by NCSA at the University of Illinois, Urbana-Champaign. The team developing Mosaic founded Netscape.

MPEG Moving Picture Expert Group—digital video standard.

Namespace Collection of assigned and potential identifiers with a common portion (conventionally the prefix).

Netlib An early service that can be viewed, as it has evolved, as a digital library of algorithms, of particular interest to numerical analysts.

NII National Information Infrastructure, a name for the U.S. efforts to extend networking and computing, such as Internet, WWW, and digital libraries, to be widely used especially in education, business, and government.

OAIS Open Archival Information System.

Originator Person or organization that creates a document intended to be communicated to others, either directly and soon, or by way of intermediaries such as archives and research libraries that hold the document for long and unpredictable periods.

Paperless society World or culture in which there is little need for paper, since data and information would flow through over data networks, and since systems supporting hypertext and information retrieval would encourage the shift from paper to digital communication. This is sometimes given as a target or goal, even in partial form, aiming to reduce the consumption of resources (paper) and to improve productivity through automation of activies involving information, in processing, storage, retrieval, and use.

Payload Set or sequence of one or more payload elements (q.v.).

Payload element   Document or data object prepared at one place for use somewhere else, optionally accompanied by zero or more metadata objects, and part of a whole ready for transmitting or carrying.

Query   A formal expression given according to the requirements of a retrieval system, aimed to characterize a particular information need.

RDF   Resource Description Framework.

Ranking   Ordering items based on some value, so that the first item has rank one and the largest value.

Reader   Human being or digital machine that usefully interprets documents it obtains or receives independently of the kind of information, e.g., if the information is a musical performance, reader is a synonym for listener.

Recall   A measure of the extent to which all items corresponding to a user's information need are retrieved, usually expressed as a percentage or a fraction (earlier, recall ratio).

Relevance judgment   Determination by a human, often a user with an information need, or an expert informed about that information need, of whether a particular document is relevant to that information need. Judgments may be binary (yes/no) or on some categorical (not, partially, definitely) or real (in range between zero and one) scale.

Relevance ranking   Listing retrieved items in an order based on the system's computation of how closely documents correspond to the user's information need. Thus, the first item is that which the system determines corresponds most closely.

Resolver   A network service that accepts the name or identifier of a digital object and, either alone or by cooperation with other resolvers, returns the network addresses of storage servers that can deliver objects with the name provided.

Schema   A pattern or set of rules by which a class of information objects is to be represented.

Search   Process of identifying those items (most) appropriate to retrieve from a collection, given a particular information need.

Search engine   Computer system that manages a collection of items (usually documents) and supports locating those that are (most) related to a stated information need (query).

SGML   Standard Generalized Markup Language, an international standard for describing any type of document, ISO 8879.

Signature Condensed characterization of an information object, usually a (fixed-length) string of bits used to represent a list of words, often determined by taking an initially zero string and turning on bits that correspond to the hashed position in the string, for each word in the list.

Signature file File of signatures that supports rapid search. Usually documents are summarized with a signature that is stored in the file. Later, a query is hashed to produce a signature, and any entry in the file is retrieved that has all bits on for 1-bits in the query signature. Though this requires a linear traversal of the signature file, it is much smaller than the document file, and rapid processing for conjunctive queries is afforded. This method was originally used for HyperCard text search.

Similarity Measure of how closely two items correspond, often on a scale of zero to 1. Typically this reflects closeness of query to a document (for retrieval), or a document to another document (for clustering). Similarity can be computed using a similarity measure (e.g., the cosine correlation) or an an inverse function of distance.

Specificity Measure of how precisely or specifically the detailed concepts that occur in a document can be described by a given indexing language.

Stop word Word that should be ignored when indexing a document. Stop words usually are function words, often chosen from a list of up to several hundred word forms (e.g., "a," "of," "the," "with") that carry little content. Sometimes collection-specific words are included, because they occur too often to be useful, like the word "computer" in a collection of computer science works.

Term An element or token used to characterize information objects, often a stem, word, phrase, descriptor, or concept.

Thesaurus An organization of terms that groups them based on meaning. *Roget's Thesaurus* was the first human-developed work. Many controlled vocabularies are organized according to a thesaurus. There may be loose grouping of related terms, as from clustering, or a complete hierarchical organization, from high-level concepts, down a taxonomic chain, ultimately to words. Various relationships may be represented, including broader, narrower, see also, subordinate, superordinate, and synonym.

Truncation Method employed by users of retrieval systems to broaden words by removing the final part from consideration during the matching process. Users, for example, might enter "retriev" to find occurrences of "retrieve," "retrieved," "retrieval," and "retrieving."

Trustworthy Describing information deserving people's confidence that it can prudently be used for its announced purposes. Specifically implied is that a user is able to test that information purported to come from announced authors has not been tampered with by third parties and that it surely originates with the purported author(s).

Trustworthy Digital Object (TDO)   Kind of digital object prepared for long-term digital preservation.

Trustworthy institution   Institution or enterprise that can be trusted to certify faithfully the authenticity of documents and other critical information, such as the association of a public key with an individual or another institution. For instance, for scholarly documents this might be a national library such as the U.S. Library of Congress. Depending on the application area, it might otherwise be a bank such as Barclay's Bank, a government agency such as the U.S. National Archives and Records Administration, a private enterprise such as IBM, or any other kind of institution that some community trusts sufficiently for its certifying role in protecting some class of digital documents.

TULIP   The University Licensing Program run by Elsevier along with nine universities in the United States, involving 40 bitmap journals on materials. This was an early digital library project, with a number of different retrieval systems used by the universities. Elsevier provided table of contents and other metadata along with the bitmap pages.

URI, URN   Uniform Resource Identifier and Uniform Resource Name.

UUID   Universal unique identifier, used to denote a string whose referents, if it has more than one, are all equal, i.e., all referents are bit-by-bit identical to each other.

UVC   Universal Virtual Computer, a Turing-compatible computing machine.

WAIS   Wide Area Information Service, developed by Brewster Kahle and others especially at Thinking Machines prior to the advent of the WWW, a client-server method for searching a distributed network of information servers. Based on an early version of the Z39.50 protocol and descriptions of the various available information sources, a user would first search for a suitable source and then submit queries to the various sources. WAIS supported relevance feedback in the form of using retrieved relevant documents as part of later queries.

WWW   World Wide Web, a hypertext service that has spread to many regions of the world. It is coordinated (in terms of standards) by W3C, the World Wide Web Consortium, based at MIT, led by Tim Berners-Lee, founder of WWW. It is a collection of servers (with documents written according to the HTML standard.

Z39.50   National standard that has become an international standard. It is a protocol for client-server communication with retrieval systems, allowing a single client to interact with one or more systems or retrieval systems (or gateways) to communicate with other retrieval systems. It supports connection-oriented sessions, having a system EXPLAIN itself, submission of queries, obtaining information about the query results, obtaining results lists, and obtaining retrieved documents. (See also the Library of Congress WWW page for Z39.50.)

Index